METHODS FOR EDUCATING THE HANDICAPPED

an individualized education program approach

STEPHEN C. LARSEN

MARY S. POPLIN

Allyn and Bacon, Inc.
Boston, London, Sydney, Toronto

Patricia Larsen
A consistent friend and supporter
SCL

and

George and Inez Poplin
Parents who know the true meaning of the word
MSP

Printing number and year (last digits):
10 9 8 7 6 5 4 3 2   85 84 83 82 81 80

Library of Congress Cataloging in Publication Data

Larsen, Stephen C   1943–
   Methods for educating the handicapped.

   Includes index.
   1. Handicapped children—Education. 2. Individualized instruction.
I. Poplin, Mary S., 1951–   II. Title.
LC4015.L37   371.9   79–13924
ISBN 0–205–06678–X (paperbound)
ISBN 0–205–06679–8 (hardbound)

Printed in the United States of America.

Contents

Preface

Educational practices in the 1970s have been beset by many changes. These changes have taken the form of innovative theoretical positions regarding how best children may be aided in the learning process, the development of technology that directly relates to the presentation of instructional concepts, and an increased demonstration of advocacy on the part of both parents and educators concerning the manner in which children are taught in the nation's school systems. Perhaps no more profound change has occurred in America's educational system than can be witnessed in the educational opportunities afforded the handicapped. For years relegated to residential schools, special day schools, and self-contained classrooms, increasing numbers of disabled youngsters are now being moved to less restrictive environments as a prelude to providing them a truly free and appropriate education. While segregated placements within our educational system will always be viable for some children, it is now abundantly clear that growing numbers of handicapped students will be integrated with regular pupils and programs to the maximum extent feasible. This change in orientation, as it pertains to the handicapped, exemplifies the proposition that disabled persons are citizens with the same rights and safeguards as all other citizens.

As with other changes that have come about in our society, the move to provide handicapped children with an appropriate education was not initiated on a volunteer basis. It was not until the passage of Public Law 93–380 and its amendment, Public Law 94–142 (passed in 1975), that educators began seriously to consider the inequalities of educational opportunities that were being afforded disabled youngsters. In effect, these two pieces of federal legislation have dictated that *all* handicapped children, regardless of the degree or type of disabling condition, must be provided with a free and appropriate education. The *Rules and Regulations* governing the implementation of P.L. 94–142 were published in 1977 and clearly delineated the responsibilities of school systems and other public agencies as to the specific elements that *must* be addressed when planning for and actually instructing handicapped children and youth. The passage of these public laws and the subsequent *Rules and Regulations* have done much to stimulate the thoughts and actions of educators at all levels in terms of how these new federal mandates may be attained and how appropriately designed instruction may be directed at handicapped students in whatever settings they find themselves.

As would be expected of such far-reaching and all-encompassing legislation as Public Laws 93–380 and 94–142, many school districts have been primarily concerned with what some have termed "staying clean." That is, many school administrators have devoted much of their time and energy to meeting the "letter of the law," and have ignored its basic *intent*. This is an understandable phenomenon in that policies, structures, and guidelines must be established in order for exemplary educational services to be provided all handicapped children. However, it is untenable to think that administrative arrangements, in and of themselves, will be adequate to insure that handicapped youngsters are educated to a level that is commensurate with their ability. To meet the *intent* of the federal law, it is necessary for educators to redesign and reorient their current views regarding (1) the definition of education for the handicapped, (2) how disabled children are to be evaluated, planned for, and afforded an appropriate education, and (3) how the effectiveness of the instruction given the youngster will be assessed.

The purpose of this book is to provide educators with a method that, if followed, will result in a well-grounded and defensible approach when planning for or actually teaching disabled children. The concept of the Individualized Education Program (IEP), mandated in federal law, is used as a focal point for discussion since it must be provided for all handicapped children in today's schools as well as being a reasonable structure through which a viable instructional plan may be developed. The reader will quickly note that, in some instances, the components of the IEP discussed in this text exceed the minimum requirements stipulated by law. The reason for this is that in actual school practice, the pragmatic necessities of instructional programming demand the need for more specificity than was written into the law itself. Consequently, the authors recommend that, at certain points in the development of the IEP, school staff insert intervening steps to avoid omitting crucial elements of the instructional process.

Perhaps the most important feature in any attempt to plan for handicapped children is that teachers *define for themselves* those educational areas that will constitute the child's curriculum throughout his/her time spent in special education. It has been the authors' experience and belief that the areas of self-help/basic living, social/behavioral patterns, career/vocation, and academics represent the domains of behavior in which most handicapped children experience deficiencies. To plan efficiently in these areas, educators must be knowledgeable in the constructs that comprise these areas and the specific breakdown of skills that, if mastered, will result in efficient performance. Extensive discussions of these educational areas are provided in the chapters that pertain to the development of goals and objectives for a given youngster (Chapters IV, V, VI). It is hoped that educators will utilize these discussions and subsequent delineations of goals and objectives as the primary vehicle through which the IEP is developed. Other chapters introduce the reader to education of the handicapped and federal legislation (Chapter I), the legal constraints of the IEP (Chapter II), the referral, screening, and evaluation of the handicapped child (Chapter III), evaluation of the instructional program (Chapter VII), educational services and the concept of least restrictive environment (Chapter VIII), and features necessary to consider when conducting the IEP meeting (Chapter IX). It was the authors' intent to provide as broad a spectrum as possible from which to address both the legal requirements of serving disabled children and the optimal manner in which these children may be afforded an appropriate education.

A final note of caution is offered to all readers. The method of curricular planning and instruction delineated in this book is primarily the product of the authors' invention and has proven to be a profitable approach for them. Undoubtedly, it will be necessary for teachers to adapt the techniques discussed here to make them feasible for use in their own situations. Throughout the book the authors have continually urged instructional staff to *formulate for themselves* the procedures that seem to hold the most potential for benefiting the youngsters put in their charge. The concept that teachers need to understand curricula prior to planning and initiating actual instruction is central to effective teaching. In other words, effective teaching of the handicapped will likely not occur if curriculum is not adequately understood and implemented. If instructional staff have somewhat differing attitudes regarding teaching methodology, they are encouraged to use them. There can be little doubt, however, that the generation of viable IEP's and efficient teaching of disabled youngsters rests entirely upon the knowledge and expertise of the teacher. If he/she is not equal to the task, many disabled children will be denied their legal right to appropriate educational opportunities. This, of course, is unthinkable to the mind of any professional educator and must be avoided if education is to continue as a bona fide endeavor where the foremost concern is the welfare of each child.

S. C. L.
M. S. P.

Acknowledgments

We would like to express our appreciation to those who provided invaluable assistance throughout the completion of this book. Particular thanks are given to Richard Gray, Anne Poplin, Jim Saski, and Jan Writer who gave freely of their time, energy, resources, and moral support in instances when it was greatly needed. Fred West was also generous in supplying time and materials that served to direct attention to the practical aspects of the development of individualized education programs. Ann Shaughness was virtually indispensable in helping to prepare the manuscript through its various states of preparation. Diane Silver provided great insight in the development of the case studies. Finally, a special note of thanks must be directed to our students who suffered through early attempts to formulate the concepts and ideas that are presented in this book. The patience exhibited by them was exemplary and their feedback essential.

1

Education
of the Handicapped

One of the primary goals in American education during the past 100 years has been developing individualized instructional programs. Early interest in individualized instruction was spurred by the inflexible, age-graded, lock-step system in which all pupils, regardless of differential abilities, were made to study the same materials in the same way for the same length of time (Harris, 1960). While the main current of education has continued resolutely in the practices common to a graded system set in its course by the textbook or basal series and frequent examinations, some programs that make schooling more adaptable to differences among children have been proposed and developed. Many individualized programs currently employed in the schools have long historical precedence and have been found suitable for some children in specific scholastic environments. Other approaches are, by virtue of their technology, relatively recent and their ultimate utility still remains to be determined.

The concept of *self-paced unit plans,* for example, dates back to 1888 when the Pueblo Plan suggested permitting a youngster to pace his/her own coverage of academic material rather than await the tedium of daily recitation (Search, 1894). *Programmed and computer instruction* have been devised as an attempt to obtain the type of behavioral control shown possible in the laboratory. Each segment of this type of instruction is divided into small steps successful mastery of which is assumed rewarding (Holland, 1960; Skinner, 1961). *Independent study programs* and other administrative plans which became fashionable in the mid 60s emphasized that some portion of the school day should be set aside to attain some freedom from the constraint of supervision (Bishop, 1967). The relative freedom provided students was to permit such activities as

1

independent study, seminars, and "questtype" programs for the development of special interests and aptitudes. *Grouping for individualization,* long a staple in most schools, is intended to minimize differences among children as a prelude to effective instruction. While a common practice for purposes of academic and affective teaching, grouping students seldom reduces variability among the grouped children by more than 20 percent (Westby-Gibson, 1966).

A host of additional miscellaneous individualized programs have been formulated to aid in the instructional effort. It is important to note that all the administrative arrangements just listed were designed for the diversity of "normal" pupils comprising the majority of most school populations. That is, programs of individualized instruction have been designed primarily for students with normal or near normal intellectual abilities who are capable of achievement and behavior that approximates grade-level or above performance. Little attention has been directed at designing individualized instruction for those students who are *handicapped* and require extensive intervention to perform at levels commensurate with their ability. The following section delineates some of the major elements associated with individualizing instruction for handicapped children and youth.

INDIVIDUALIZED INSTRUCTION AND THE HANDICAPPED

Through the years, efforts to individualize instruction for the handicapped have displayed a highly variable and widely discrepant range of trends. According to Hewett and Forness (1977), historical determiners of treatment of the handicapped can be grouped under the headings survival, superstition, science, and service. Survival and superstition describe early reactions to the handicapped including infanticide, eugenics, harsh treatment, demonology, exorcism, and worship. Science refers to a more developed attitude in which the handicapped were recognized and studied objectively to gain information regarding the parameters of their disabilities. Finally, in the nineteenth and twentieth centuries the attitude became one of service with increased understanding of the handicapped which resulted in humane treatment, custodial care, educational opportunities, and social acceptance.

Within the United States, educating the handicapped was attempted initially in the home through the ministrations of parents, siblings, and paid tutors. In 1817 the first residential school for the handicapped was established in the United States. Founded by Thomas Hopkins Gallaudet to service deaf persons, this school was followed quickly by the advent

2

of similar schools designed for other handicapping conditions. Consequently, early attempts to provide educational opportunities to the handicapped were largely home based and, later, were comprised almost totally of isolated residential schools where children were placed as a result of their disability. There can be little doubt that children so placed exhibited relatively severe manifestations of mental retardation, deafness, blindness, emotional disturbance, and so on. In addition, although residential schools were geared to educating and treating various handicapped persons, they tended to be poorly funded and staffed and, for the most part, merely provided custodial care.

By the early 1900s, public school classes for the retarded (and some other conditions) had been established across the country. By 1922, a total of 23,000 children were enrolled in special classes in over 100 cities. Much of the increased attention given to the handicapped was derived directly from the work of such pioneers as Seguin, Binet, and Terman. These physicians and educators espoused the belief that individual differences are definable and that appropriate instructional opportunities may ameliorate manifestations of the disability. However, the early programs devised to educate the obviously handicapped in an individualized fashion were frequently somewhat less than satisfactory. Hewett and Forness (1977) report an example of these early efforts that occurred in the Cleveland, Ohio public schools in 1918:

> About 14 of the most serious cases of imbecility in the most congested quarters of the city were gathered together and a superior, conscientious teacher placed in charge. The good folk responsible for this inauguration were united in their belief that the pupils would soon become normal children, once they were properly taught. The teacher heroically attacked the problem, but before the close of the school year, all were aware their experiment was doomed to failure at the close of the term, the class was disbanded—the imbeciles returned to their homes, probably not much the worse for their "schooling," but the poor teacher suffered a mental collapse which necessitated a sojourn at our capital State Hospital. (pp. 51–52)

The unrealistic expectations and lack of experience among pioneer advocates of educating the handicapped undoubtedly resulted in many situations similar to the one described above.

As efforts continued to educate handicapped youngsters, it became increasingly apparent that some method of individualization must be designed and implemented. At the conclusion of World War II, educating the handicapped was approached with renewed vigor. The primary method of individualized instruction revolved around two main factors: (1) training teachers to instruct specific types of handicapped youngsters and (2) segregating children thought to possess disabilities severe

3

enough that their diverse needs could not be met in the regular classroom. If handicapped youngsters were severely impaired (for example, profoundly retarded or seriously emotionally disturbed), usually they were sent to a state institution where the major emphasis was on custodial care and developing self-help skills. Where the handicapped children were of normal intelligence, as with blind and deaf persons, educational concerns typically focused on language training, mobility skills, vocational training, and academic instruction.

Children who exhibited handicapping conditions that were not severe enough to warrant institutionalization typically were placed in special day schools or in self-contained classrooms located in the regular school. In these situations, the teaching staff were trained specially to work with the handicapped. Instruction in these environments was meant to facilitate establishing basic concepts related to academic performance, language, and vocational skills. In most settings, the curricula employed were modifications of those used in the regular classroom. Children placed in special day schools or self-contained classes were seldom integrated with "normal" children and programming, probably because they were commonly thought to be "deviant," "disordered," "idiots," or in some way dangerous to themselves or others. It was assumed that, by virtue of being grouped homogeneously and placed with a specially trained teacher, the handicapped youngsters' educational needs were being met to the maximum extent possible. In fact, little was done to ensure that handicapped youngsters were receiving an individualized instruction geared to their many and varied needs.

The late 1960s witnessed alterations in traditional concepts of instructing the handicapped. Beginning with an article by Dunn (1968), educators were besieged consistently by reports that handicapped youngsters (particularly the mild to moderately involved) placed in self-contained classrooms were not learning at a rate that would be expected given their demonstrated abilities. Seemingly, the prevalent trend of removing mild to moderately disabled children from the *presumed* pressures generated from an unrealistic and inappropriate program of studies was working to the disadvantage of many handicapped youngsters. Efficacy studies regarding special classes, particularly for the mentally retarded, indicated that pupils make as much or more progress in the regular grades as they do in special education. When coupled with the negative connotations associated with labels (such as emotionally disturbed or mentally retarded) designating a handicapping condition, this information seriously questioned the manner in which special education was being administered. The overriding themes of the time were: (1) true individualized instruction for the handicapped was largely illusory, (2) innovative educational strategies must be developed to educate

4

these children effectively, and (3) some method of *ensuring* or being accountable for the educational opportunities being provided the handicapped must be devised and implemented.

As an outgrowth of this controversy, school systems across the country attempted to establish new curricular approaches and service delivery options for handicapped children. While residential and special schools continued to be used for severely and profoundly handicapped individuals, resource rooms and itinerant teachers were instituted to supplement and/or supplant self-contained classrooms. This arrangement is exemplified by the child receiving individualized or small-group instruction while spending large amounts of time in the regular classroom. Regrettably, this trend to circumvent past mistakes by "mainstreaming" handicapped children led to many unrealistic placements of children who did not possess the academic and/or social competency to be matriculated into regular school curricula or activities. The special instruction afforded through the activities in the resource room or itinerant teacher were variable from location to location and were not always sufficient to meet the unique needs of handicapped youngsters. Obviously, school systems would need to develop a continuum of placement alternatives permitting implementation of specially designed education if individualized instruction for the handicapped were to become a reality.

In the early 1970s congressional action resulting in the passage of Public Law (PL) 93–380 (1974) and its more elaborate counterpart PL 94–142 (1975) caused major shifts in the manner in which educational opportunities were to be provided handicapped students. These laws specify standards that must be followed in identifying, evaluating, placing, and educating handicapped youngsters. The specifications of PL 94–142 are comprised of the standards laid down by the courts, legislatures, and other legal bodies throughout the United States. Not only does this law hold promise to establish minimal standards in educating the handicapped, it also mandates certain accountability features that must be carried out to validate that handicapped youngsters are indeed receiving individualized instruction geared to their specific needs.

PUBLIC LAW 94–142

The purposes of PL 94–142 are far reaching. The first and most important purpose is to require all handicapped children be given access to a free and appropriate public education. While this requirement may seem obvious and, consequently, unnecessary, it should be kept in mind that in the 1970s:

1. Over 1.75 million children with handicaps in the United States were being excluded entirely from receiving a public education solely on the basis of their handicaps.
2. Over half of the estimated 8 million handicapped children in this country were not receiving the appropriate educational service they needed or were entitled to.
3. Many other children with handicaps were still being placed in inappropriate educational settings because their handicaps were undetected or because of a violation of their individual rights. (Abeson and Zettel, 1977)

In essence, PL 94-142 stipulates that school systems and other public agencies are no longer able to exclude handicapped children simply on the basis that they exhibit problems too severe to be handled in the school setting, do not have appropriate programs, or are judged to be uneducable. On the contrary, this legislation unquestionably dictates that *all* children can learn if education is viewed as a process that includes instruction in self-help, career/vocational, basic living, as well as academic areas. Handicapped youngsters must be eligible for all programs and activities provided in the schools for children who are not disabled including all extracurricular activities such as clubs, art, music, and debate. School systems must also assume all costs for educating children who are handicapped. In those instances where an appropriate education entails enrollment in residential or other tuition-based programs, the child's local school system must assume the financial burden associated with transportation, tuition, and room and board. Of course, this occurs only when the school system does not possess the educational placements necessary to provide for the youngster.

Not only must the handicapped child be provided a free and appropriate education, he/she also has the right to a nondiscriminatory evaluation of educational needs. That is, whatever tests and evaluation materials are administered must not be culturally discriminatory and must be given in the youngster's native language (the predominant language spoken in the home) or mode of communication. The evaluation must be conducted by a team of parents and professionals and must utilize more than one procedure or test as the criterion for designing and implementing the educational program for the child. The latter consideration is intended to serve as a mechanism by which the problems identified are assessed accurately by a variety of techniques that delineate viable areas of concern in planning the child's specific individualized education program (IEP).

If a child or his/her parents are dissatisfied with any facet of the identification, evaluation, and placement decisions made by the school system, they have access to procedural due process. The purpose of due process as stated in PL 94–142 is to ensure that the rights granted handicapped children are, in fact, being provided by the schools. Inversely, school systems also have rights and responsibilities safeguarded by due process. The particular elements of due process included in PL 94–142 are as follows:

1. Written notification before evaluation. In addition, the right to an interpreter/translator if the family's native language is not English (unless it is clearly not feasible to do so).
2. Written notification when initiating or refusing to initiate a change in educational placement.
3. Periodic review of educational placements.
4. Opportunity for an impartial hearing including the right to:
   Receive timely and specific notice of such hearing;
   Review all records;
   Obtain an independent evaluation;
   Be represented by counsel;
   Cross examine;
   Bring witness;
   Present evidence;
   Receive a complete record of proceedings;
   Appeal decisions.
5. Assignment of a surrogate parent for children when:
   The parent or guardian is not known;
   The child's parents are unavailable;
   The child is a ward of the state. (Abeson, Bolick, and Hass, 1975)

Handicapped youngsters must be placed in the educational environment that, while permitting the provision of specially designed individualized instruction, also allows the maximum interaction with regular children and programming feasible.

The potential of PL 94–142 to alter drastically the educational fate of handicapped individuals is great. However, it is important to note that, unless the mandates of this law are followed, many disabled youngsters will continue to be denied their educational rights as granted by the Congress of the United States. Additionally, while crucial to the protection of legal rights, due process is largely moot if the handicapped child does not have an individually written and implemented educational plan that is designed to attenuate his/her observed problem. To this end, PL 94–142 stipulates that each handicapped youngster undergo an evaluation process terminating in the development of an *individual-*

ized education program (IEP) which should comprise all the components necessary to provide individualized instruction.

THE INDIVIDUALIZED EDUCATION PROGRAM

Developing the IEP is the central feature in effective and efficient education of the handicapped. The IEP is also the major building block to understanding and complying with PL 94–142. A progression of actions is necessary in order to devise an IEP for a given handicapped child. Initially, a youngster must be judged to be suffering from a handicapping condition to the extent that he/she requires special education and/or related services in order to profit from instructional opportunities. Handicapped children are defined in PL 94–142 as children who are "mentally retarded, hard of hearing, deaf, orthopedically impaired, other health impaired, speech impaired, visually handicapped, seriously emotionally disturbed, or children with specific learning disabilities who by reason thereof require special education and related services" (Sec. 4,a,1).

Special education is defined as specially designed instruction intended to meet the unique needs of a handicapped child. This includes classroom instruction, instruction in physical education, home instruction, and instruction in hospitals and institutions. Related services, an important concept in PL 94–142, refers to any services provided in the school necessary for a child to benefit from special education. Related services that meet these criteria are physical and occupational therapy, counseling, speech pathology and audiology, medical and psychological services, social work, recreation, and early identification and assessment of handicapping conditions (Sec. 4,a,17). Public agencies must also assist handicapped youngsters by providing transportation for them between and within buildings and home.

Once the child has been evaluated and found to be handicapped and in need of special education and related services, a team comprised of parents and professionals devises an individualized education program. The term "individualized" implies that the IEP must be geared to the needs of a particular child. "Education" refers to the elements of the child's education that are specific to his/her needs for special education and related services. The word "program" is used to denote the instruction that will *actually* be provided the child. The components of the IEP as delimited within PL 94–142 are:

> A written statement for each handicapped child developed in any meeting by a representative of the local education agency or an intermediate

educational unit who shall be qualified to provide or supervise the provision of specially designed instruction to meet the unique needs of handicapped children, the teacher, the parents or guardians of such children, which statement will include (A) a statement of present levels of educational performance of such children, (B) a statement of annual goals, including short term instructional objectives, (C) a statement of the specific educational services to be provided such children, and the extent to which such children will be able to participate in regular educational programs, (D) the projected date for initiation and anticipated duration of such services, and appropriate objective criteria and evaluation procedures and schedules for determining, on at least an annual basis, whether instructional objectives are being achieved. (PL 94–142, 1975, Sec. 4,a,19)

Many of the remaining chapters in this book are devoted to discussing and expanding upon the basic requirements of the IEP. However, the total value of PL 94–142 rests on the extent to which the IEP is actually implemented in schools and by other public agencies responsible for educating handicapped children. Indeed, unless the IEP is followed to its fullest extent in educational practice, the instruction provided handicapped youngsters will continue to be ill-conceived and poorly administered and the concept of realistically employed individualized instruction for the handicapped will have no basis in fact. How to implement the IEP specifically and PL 94–142 in general is still open to question. Only one thing is certain: as of October 1978 all public agencies must provide *appropriate* education to all handicapped children or be in violation of the law.

References

Abeson, A.; Bolick, N.; and Hass, J. A primer on due process: Education decisions for handicapped children. *Exceptional Children,* 1975, *42:* 68–74.

———, and Zettle, J. The end of the quiet revelation: The education for all handicapped children act of 1975. *Exceptional Children,* 1977, *44*:114–128.

Bishop, L. K. Independent study. *The Clearinghouse,* 1967, *42*:9–14.

Harris, C. W. *Encyclopedia of educational research.* New York: Macmillan, 1960.

Hewett, F. M., and Forness, S. R. *Education of exceptional learners* (2nd ed.). Boston: Allyn & Bacon, 1977.

Holland, J. G. Teaching machines: An application of principles from the laboratory. *Journal of Experimental Analysis of Behavior,* 1960, 3:275–287.

Search, P. The pueblo plan of individual teaching. *Educational Review,* 1894, 8:84–85.

Skinner, B. F. Teaching machines. *Scientific American,* 1961, 205:90–102.

Westby-Gibson, D. *Grouping students for improved instruction.* Englewood Cliffs, N.J.: Prentice-Hall, 1966.

2

Introduction to Individualized Education Programs

Historically, the major function of special education has been to provide handicapped students with individualized instruction tailored to meet their unique educational needs. As discussed in Chapter 1, varying models of instruction have been proposed through the years to facilitate the educational opportunities for both normal and handicapped students. In addition, a myriad of methods and materials have been developed that are purported to maximize the opportunity for individual instruction. In many instances, special educators have utilized such methods and materials as programmed texts, applied behavioral analysis, behavioral objectives, task analysis, directive teaching, computer-assisted instruction, and various behavior modification systems as a means to educate the handicapped. Each of these methods has been shown to be effective to some degree with a wide variety of handicapped students. However, it is important to note that none of these activities, in and of themselves, have proven adequately comprehensive to effect appropriate individualized instruction for all students receiving the services of special education. This fact is undoubtedly due to the diverse nature of students exhibiting various degrees and combinations of handicapping conditions.

In an attempt to coordinate instructional efforts, Public Law 94–142 proposes a comprehensive structure to use in developing and delivering individualized instruction to handicapped children and youth regardless of the particular model or method to be used. This systematic structure or format has been established in law by mandating that *individualized education programs* (IEPs) be written for *each* student who receives special education services. The individual education program is defined as a document written by a team of professionals and parents that

11

specifically delineates the content and procedures by which to provide the handicapped student an appropriate instructional intervention. As with any new federal legislation, an agency of the U.S. government is assigned the task of developing guidelines or *regulations* that specifically define the intent of that particular law. The Bureau of Education for the Handicapped (BEH), through the U.S. Office of Education of the Department of Health, Education and Welfare, is the agency responsible for implementing PL 94–142 and has "operationalized" the law in a series of federal regulations. The regulations that specifically address individualized educational programs include the specification of *procedures* and *content* required in developing, implementing, and maintaining each program. The *mandated general procedures* established by BEH include state agency responsibilities, effective dates, descriptions of IEP meetings, participants of the meetings, and provisions for parent participation.

One of the most important sections of both the law and regulations governing the development of individual educational programs specifies the content to be included in each student's program. The *mandated content or components* of IEPs include (1) statements indicating the student's present levels of educational performance, (2) statements of annual goals, (3) short-term instructional objectives, (4) specific educational services to be provided to the student, (5) the extent to which the student will participate in the regular educational program, (6) the dates for initiation and projected duration of services, and (7) objective criteria, procedures, and schedules for evaluating the extent to which short-term instructional objectives are being met. At first glance, the scope and specificity of these guidelines may appear overwhelming; however, after considering the purposes for which the individual educational programs are comprised, these regulations are more easily seen in their proper perspective. One must keep in mind that, as far as educating an individual handicapped child is concerned, the ultimate appropriateness of his/her educational program is essential to appropriate instructional intervention. Consequently, effective IEP development must be given the utmost professional care and consideration. The purpose of this chapter is to present the reader the purposes for developing individual educational programs and the procedures and components mandated as necessary for their successful use in educating handicapped students.

PURPOSES OF INDIVIDUALIZED EDUCATION PROGRAMS

The basic rationale underlying the development of any individual educational program is the implicit need to derive a comprehensive plan for systematically providing a handicapped student with an education appropriate to his/her unique needs. In order to ensure that this basic rationale becomes fact, adequate provision must be made in every program for three essential purposes: to provide for (1) direct educational planning and programming, (2) some degree of accountability, and (3) adequate communication among all persons within the school and between home and school concerning the particular student. In order to fulfill the first purpose, the educational plan and program must be written into the IEP as a means to delineate general directions, goals, objectives, and educational services necessary to educate the student properly. In all cases, a team of educators, parents, and other support personnel initiates the process with information gleaned from the diagnosis that has documented the presence of a handicapping condition and the subsequent need for special services. As mentioned earlier, this diagnostic assessment, in and of itself, does not provide instructionally relevant data. Frequently, the personnel conducting the diagnosis have had little opportunity to interact with the student in an educational environment. The diagnostic data and background information available for the student usually provide adequate information concerning the student's potential and performance for purposes of establishing general directions and goals.

Once general directions and goals have been determined through *educational planning* activities, it is then essential for the IEP team to establish the specific *program* necessary to reach the goals. That is, the student's individual program is developed following a further assessment of the student for instructional purposes. This assessment is conducted to determine which objectives underlying particular goals should become the focus of instructional intervention activities. In addition, the program must specify the special education and related services necessary to implement the proposed educational program. Specifying these services along with the short-term instructional objectives comprises the educational programming aspect of the IEP. Once the development of the IEP has fulfilled the purpose of providing direction for the best educational planning and programming, school personnel possess a guide by which it is possible to determine the daily activities necessary to provide any handicapped student with appropriate instructional opportunities.

If the only purpose of the IEP were to provide a "guide" for instruction, constructing the IEP would be greatly simplified. However, the individualized education program must also establish methods to monitor and assure the effectiveness of the program. Therefore, the second purpose to be accomplished by developing and implementing individual educational programs is to provide some degree of accountability for the success of the individual's program. Obviously, merely developing an educational program for a particular student in no way assures its

13

success. However, educators are aware of ways to increase the chances that a specific program will be effective through continual interactions with students. Continual modification of existing program activities can be accomplished through procedures designed to promote some degree of accountability regarding attainment of goals and objectives and delivery of services. An adequate system of accountability should (1) indicate which qualified personnel are assigned the responsibility of implementing the program, (2) specify a system for monitoring pupil progress so that the appropriateness of plan, program, and personnel can be continuously evaluated, and (3) establish a system of investigation in the event that progress is insufficient so that the program may be revised as necessary. Therefore, one of the major purposes of an individual educational program is delineating a system designed to ensure educational accountability.

The third purpose involved in making a student's individual program comprehensive, continuous, and appropriate is to establish a system of communication among all persons concerned with the child or youth's education. At best the IEP should increase communication among persons involved in the student's education automatically since the IEP is developed by an interdisciplinary team. In addition to the added communication among school personnel involved directly in the student's education, provisions must be made for parent and, in some cases, even student participation. The degree to which parents become involved in the IEP development, implementation, and maintenance undoubtedly is related to its effectiveness. Increased effectiveness results from additional information, assistance, and feedback that can only be provided from the home. Parents should also be provided the information from which they can develop more realistic expectations of their children's abilities and needs.

A well-developed and carefully constructed individual educational program sets the stage for appropriate instructional intervention by establishing systematic structures or procedures to fulfill the purposes of providing for direct educational planning and programming, accountability, and communication between home and school. While the brief discussion just given introduces basic concepts regarding these purposes, it is not sufficient to acquaint the reader fully with these very crucial points. The remainder of this section focuses on an in-depth discussion of the basic purposes of the IEP.

Direct Educational Planning and Programming

The primary purpose for developing individual educational programs is to provide a format for direct educational planning and programming

14

to guide instructional personnel in individualizing instruction for a particular student. Attaining this goal is necessary before accountability and home/school communication can be realized. Abeson and Weintraub (1977) differentiate between the terms "plan" and "program" by stating that a *plan* provides the guidelines from which to develop a *program.* For purposes of this discussion the authors utilize the same basic differentiation. It must be remembered that, although we refer to individual educational programs, the IEP contains elements of both a plan as well as a program. Following this particular section, the terms plan, program, individual plan, and individual program are used synonymously to refer to the entire IEP document. The authors do feel, however, that distinguishing between the terms plan and program at this point may be relevant to many readers. The distinction may be more clearly understood if one equates *educational planning* with formulating general directions and establishing goals that parents and professionals have agreed are appropriate for the student's education. From these general directions and goals, specific objectives and needed educational services are defined to guide personnel in their instructional efforts. These objectives and services technically comprise the student's *educational program* and should lead directly to attaining established goals. Figure 2–1 graphically represents the entire process of developing plan and program components of an individualized education program from examining a school's philosophy to stating short-term instructional objectives and assigning methods and materials.

For further clarification of the practical differences between aspects of planning and programming, consider the following example. Lee is an eight-year-old student who has few measurable reading skills. He was recently diagnosed as learning disabled and has exhibited average scores on an individual test of intelligence. Parents and professionals agreed that it would be appropriate to provide Lee with academically oriented educational experiences as opposed to vocational training, self-help skills, or some other general direction. In effect, this decision determined the general direction that parents and professionals followed in establishing educational goals for Lee. The primary goal set forth in the IEP stated that Lee should acquire certain word-attack skills involved in early reading acquisition. This goal and other goals such as spelling, handwriting, and written expression together with the statement of general direction comprised the *educational planning* aspect of Lee's IEP. Further, Lee's IEP contained a sequential listing of those word-attack skills not yet acquired by Lee. These skills were further broken down into short-term instructional objectives and directly related to specified methods and materials. For example, one of the word-attack skills mentioned in the IEP was the ability to read aloud consonant-vowel-consonant words. Several of the short-term instructional objectives included were: (1) produces the sound of consonant when shown

15

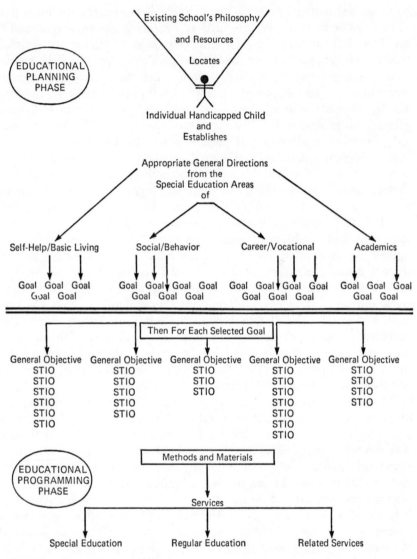

STIO=Short Term Instructional Objectives

FIGURE 2–1   Process of Educational Planning and Programming

the letter symbol; (2) produces the short vowel sound when presented
the letter /a/; and (3) blends orally three letter symbols using short
vowel /a/ into proper word. A phonetic-linguistic method and a familiar
linguistic-based reading program were suggested to be utilized in the
instruction of these objectives. In addition to delineating instructional
objectives, Lee was assigned to receive one hour of reading instruction
in a special education resource class each day. Obviously, the instruc-

16

tional objectives, techniques, and services to be provided form the *educational programming* components of the IEP. It must also be noted that these specifically defined objectives, services, methods, and materials would have been extremely difficult to formulate had the educational plan component containing the general directions and goals not been previously established.

The educational planning and programming provisions of the individual educational programs are basic to the remainder of the IEP; therefore, these portions of the program must be developed in order to fulfill the other purposes, that is, accountability and communication among all persons concerned. The plan together with the program establishes general directions, goals, objectives, services, methods, and materials to be utilized in providing the student with individualized instructional intervention. Because of the crucial nature of appropriate planning and programming, it is necessary to examine more closely the development of both educational plans and programs. Since educational plans are established prior to programs, the authors begin with a discussion regarding fulfilling the purpose of establishing educational plans—general directions and goals.

Educational planning—general directions and goals. In order to establish appropriate general directions and goals during the educational planning stage of IEP development, educators and parents must first examine the local educational community's philosophies and goals toward the education of all students. It is not unusual to find the school philosophy and goals, while appropriate for most children and youth, inappropriate for a handicapped student. This does not mean, however, that the school will not accept its responsibility and amend its philosophy and goals for this individual, but it will be necessary to establish an individual philosophy for this student's education to follow. From this general direction, alternative goals must be determined. Establishing a general direction and goals to be followed in educating an individual student constitutes the process of educational planning. Let us examine how to determine these general directions and goals.

Following the diagnostic assessment of a particular student, persons concerned with developing the individualized educational program possess the necessary background and assessment information to determine, generally, the student's present level of functioning and predict, to some degree, his/her potential for achievement in various areas. With this information the school can determine an appropriate *general direction* on which to plan the student's future educational experiences. Although often not articulated as such, there are four basic directions generally selected for special education students: (1) self-help and basic living skills, (2) academic skills, (3) vocational and career skills, and

17

(4) sociobehavioral skills. For example, a student who has been repeatedly diagnosed as severely mentally retarded probably requires educational services designed to prepare him/her to become as self-sufficient as is possible, that is, to acquire self-help and basic living skills. This student may also require partial assistance in preparing for and seeking employment as well as other general living activities at the end of his/her school career. Therefore, the general direction for educational services for severely mentally retarded youngsters probably should emphasize self-help and basic living skills. However, a student diagnosed as learning disabled, who is determined to be highly intelligent but a nonreader, would need educational experiences directed toward helping develop either the reading skills necessary to better reach his/her potential and/or a highly successful coping system that would allow him/her to secure information without functional written language skills. In any event, the general educational direction for Lee, the student in our example on p. 15, to take would be primarily an academic one. Each of the cases we have discussed illustrates how the diagnosis along with some general background information can lead to establishing an appropriate educational direction or individual philosophy upon which to direct a handicapped student's education. This is the first step in devising an educational plan to provide a student with appropriate instructional intervention.

Assuming that the diagnosis and background information have led to forming realistic and appropriate general directions, school personnel and parents must now proceed to the second step of educational planning by establishing viable *educational goals*. Whereas general directions constitute what may be considered long-term or ultimate goals to have accomplished by the time a student completes a public school education, educational goals are established on an annual basis, thus concentrating on a shorter time span. An example of the interrelationship between general directions and annual goals may be seen in the following. Jim, age 16, and Tom, age 7, have both been diagnosed repeatedly as severely mentally retarded. The general direction established by both students' IEPs was acquiring self-help and basic living skills. For Tom, annual goals included such things as toilet training and self-feeding. Inversely, for Jim, who was already capable of performing such self-help skills, such goals as being able to locate and utilize public transportation systems and locate and obtain emergency assistance were listed. It is important to note here that, although the goals for Jim and Tom were quite different, the ultimate goal or general direction was identical (self-sufficiency through the acquisition of self-help/basic living skills). Realizing the annual goals described above would place both Jim and Tom one step closer to the ultimate goal of self-sufficiency.

It is apparent that, while the elements mentioned above are imperative to successful instructional programming, there are other factors to consider when developing the educational plan for a particular student. A sampling of these includes parent and student expectations, the flexibility and availability of both special and regular educational services, and previous educational experiences. It must be remembered that, while general directions and goals form a plan for future educational services and are based on sound diagnostic and background data, they should at no time be considered unalterable or permanent. Because of the number of factors to consider in constructing the plan and the variable characteristics of handicapped children, it may well be that goals and directions should be equally as variable. With these factors taken into account, one can readily see that one of the major purposes for developing individual educational programs is to provide a plan containing goals and directions for the school to follow in educating a particular student. Obviously, without this major step the school could not determine the services, specific objectives, methods, or materials necessary to assure appropriate individualized instruction. Defining these objectives, services, methods, and materials that are derived from these goals is essential in providing instructional personnel the necessary guidance for programming the student's educational activities. Developing this programming component of the pupil's IEP is discussed next.

Educational programming—services and objectives. Probably the most significant component in any individual educational program is determining those educational services, objectives, methods, and materials that will guide instructional personnel in establishing appropriate and effective activities for instruction. The IEP provision that defines the aspects used in planning daily activities comprises the educational programming component of the individual educational program. The purpose of the programming component is to provide school personnel with specific guidelines that, if followed, should lead to attaining established goals. These guidelines take two forms: (1) identifying general and specific *objectives* that should lead to accomplishing each goal, and (2) determining what educational *services* the school offers to meet the goals.

The first component of educational programming for the purpose of guiding instructional personnel is establishing specific *short-term instructional objectives*. Because of the specificity of short-term instructional objectives, this component is probably the most difficult to develop. More than any other component of planning programming, the short-term objectives outlined in the individual educational program determine the day-to-day instruction to be provided the student. Because of the tremendous utility of instructional objectives in developing daily lessons, it is essential that members of the IEP team take great care in ensuring that the objectives are clearly stated and, in fact, are within

19

the student's level of competency. In addition, it is equally important for these objectives to be comprehensive, orderly, and appropriate for the individual student so that, when accomplished, these objectives lead directly to goal attainment. In order to develop such short-term instructional objectives, several points must be kept in mind:

1. Short-term instructional objectives *cannot* be derived directly from educational goals and diagnostic data.
2. Short-term instructional objectives must be based upon a thorough understanding of all the specific skills involved in any educational goal, such as math calculation, reading comprehension, occupational readiness, and, when appropriate, these skills must be delineated in a sequential manner.
3. Short-term instructional objectives for a particular student are determined only after the student has been assessed by instructional personnel on those general skills necessary for goal attainment.
4. Short-term instructional objectives must specify the overt behaviors and criteria for performing these behaviors that are necessary for a student to demonstrate competence in a specific skill.
5. Short-term instructional objectives should lead to the selection of appropriate methods and materials for use in instructing the student in that particular skill.

Each of these points is discussed briefly below and thoroughly explained in Chapter 6.

Although the federal regulations governing the IEP document mandate developing annual goals and short-term instructional objectives, the two activities are *not* consecutive. Any experienced teacher is aware that it would be extremely difficult, if not impossible, to select a particular goal such as "Increase word-attack skills" or "Develop self-help skills" and write all the short-term instructional objectives necessary to accomplish that goal without obtaining further information regarding both the goal and the student. The established goals obtained from the diagnostic information provide merely the starting point from which instructional personnel and other members of the team can begin to determine the general objectives upon which to base the short-term instructional objectives.

It is essential for persons developing an individualized educational program to have or obtain thorough knowledge of all the specific skills involved in accomplishing a particular goal. The skills comprising a curricular area usually are referred to as general objectives. These general objectives must be organized in a comprehensive and orderly manner so as to be of maximum benefit to persons developing individual education programs. In order to organize these skills within curriculum areas, it is essential for educators to construct *curricular maps.* Curricular maps contain all the general objectives necessary for goal attainment. For example, there are obviously a number of complex skills necessary for proficiency in the area of written expression. As when developing a curricular map for any curriculum area or goal, one must determine the constructs that define the act of written expression: what in fact does written expression involve? For instance, one way in which the area has been conceptualized is by designating the mechanical skill components and the compositional skill components. Within the mechanical skills one can identify penmanship or typing, spelling, capitalization, and punctuation. Compositional components can be identified as vocabulary, word usage, grammar, sentence construction, paragraph construction, and thesis construction. Once the constructs of a particular curriculum area are determined, one can develop general objectives within each area. Thus far, a curricular map for written expression would appear as in Figure 2–2.

The skills involved in each of the nine areas of written expression must now be determined. They are written as general objectives. Samples of general objectives or skills of capitalization as defined by Hammill and Poplin (1978) are shown in Figure 2–3. There are four important points to recognize concerning the delineation of general objectives within curricular maps: (1) they must be comprehensive, (2) they do not specify behaviors or criteria, (3) they must be sequenced, and (4) series of objectives must be clustered into levels. First of all, it is quite important for the list of skills involved in a particular goal to be compre-

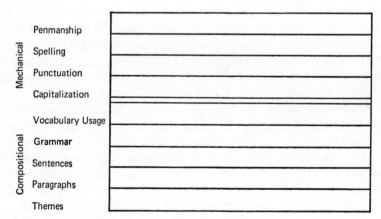

FIGURE 2–2   Outline of Curricular Map Constructs

21

	I	II	III	IV	V
Capitalization	First word of sentence First and last name Name of teacher, school, town Word "I" *ı*	The date Titles of compositions Names of titles: Mr., Mrs., Ms. Proper names used in children's writings	First word in a line or verse Period after abbreviations Period after an initial Comma in a list	Local geographical names Names of organizations "Mother", Father "Father" when used in place of name	Names of streets Capitalization used in listing Titles when used with names Commercial trade names

FIGURE 2–3   Sample General Objectives within Curricular Map

hensive, that is, for the list to contain all the possible skills necessary to achieve the goal. In the same case, it is equally important not to include irrelevant skills or objectives for this would result in wasting valuable instructional time. Both including relevant objectives and excluding inconsequential skills increases the chances of accomplishing a particular goal.

Second, general objectives do not specify the behavior or criteria for mastery of the skill. The skill itself usually can be broken into a series of steps that require different behaviors leading to mastery. These steps constitute instructional objectives (discussed later) and each contains criteria for success. General objectives merely define the skills involved in a curricular area in a rather broad manner.

Third, general objectives written into curricular maps are sequenced from simplest to most complex. Sequencing general objectives is most important when attaining a specific skill depends on acquiring a previous skill. Also, it is often obvious that one skill requires less effort and is less complex than another. There are instances, however, where the order of particular skills is relatively unimportant. In these instances placement is done in a rather arbitrary manner.

A fourth point is that, for convenience, several general objectives are clustered or grouped together on the curricular map. These clusters, generally referred to as levels, may or may not approximate actual grade or age levels. Once the sequential and comprehensive set of general objectives within each area of the curriculum or for each goal is organized within a curricular map, student assessment may be accomplished and short-term instructional objectives may be easily defined for different students individually.

Assuming that the IEP team has obtained the necessary information regarding the skills or objectives comprising the particular goals set for the student and that a comprehensive and orderly list of those objectives has been developed, the team must now begin activities to determine which of those objectives are appropriate to the individual student. In order to determine which of these objectives are appropriate, instructional personnel must assess the extent to which the student possesses the necessary skills or general objectives contained in each goal. This procedure is referred to as *assessment for instruction,* differentiating it from assessment for diagnosis that led to establishing goals. Basically, the procedure involves constructing and administering informal assessment devices or direct observation designed directly from the general objectives listed in the curricular maps. The results of this assessment provide instructional personnel with two important pieces of information: (1) the general level or point within the sequence of skills at which the student is currently functioning, and (2) the specific skills the student has and has not mastered. For instance, it may be discovered that a student is functioning at a second grade level in word-attack skills but that he/she has not mastered several skills listed for grade one. The assessment of general objectives provides direct attention to deficit areas and prevents wasting instructional time on previously mastered skills. The needed general objectives or skills that the student has not mastered can now be delineated.

Once a series of general objectives or skills the student has not mastered has been determined within each goal, the IEP team must translate these into specific short-term instructional objectives. Technically, to make this transition one must add to the general objective (1) the series of instructional steps leading to mastery of the general objective, (2) the overt behavior required of the student to demonstrate competency in each step, and (3) the criteria to be used to determine whether or not the student has actually mastered the particular objective. Other components of instructional objectives are also desirable and are discussed later; however, the specific behavior and criteria of performance are minimum requirements of short-term instructional objectives. The instructional objectives therefore direct the teacher's attention to certain behaviors he/she should expect following instruction in a particular objective. It is important to point out that there are usually several short-term instructional objectives leading to mastery of one general objective or skill. Let us utilize the following goal and general objective as an example:

Special Education Area: Academic
Goal: To increase written expression ability.
Performance Area: Capitalization
    General Objective: Capitalize the first word in a sentence.
    Short-Term Instructional Objectives:

        The student can identify capital letters used to indicate the first word of a sentence.

        The student can identify errors in capitalization involving the first word of a sentence.

        The student capitalizes the first words of dictated sentences.

23

The student capitalizes the first words in self-constructed original sentences.

Obviously, adding the overt behaviors required provides instructional personnel with added guidance in daily planning. One of the essential components of instructional objectives must still be added to the above short-term objectives in order to make them truly instructional objectives—the criteria considered necessary for mastery of the instructional objectives. These criteria might be represented as the number of times a task is completed without failure, percentage of tasks completed correctly, or specific number of consecutive days in which the task is correctly achieved. Establishing these criteria focuses the teacher's attention on obtaining a certain quantitative and/or qualitative level of performance in the particular behavior. Constructing short-term instructional objectives from lists of skills or general objectives can be, of course, a far more complex task than the illustration. For this reason an entire chapter of this book is devoted to developing curricular maps and general objectives, as well as short-term instructional objectives.

The last point to remember when constructing short-term instructional objectives is that an instructional objective should be written in such a way as to allow instructional personnel to determine methods and materials appropriate to attaining the specific objectives easily. A properly constructed short-term objective should lead instructional persons to use appropriate methods because the overt behavior required of the student is specified. For example, the short-term instructional objective "The student will orally sound blend 20 consonant-vowel-consonant (c-v-c) words utilizing the short vowel /a/ on five consecutive days" involves using a structured phonetic method of reading instruction and calls for the teacher to keep a record of correct and incorrect responses. In addition to specifying behaviors and criteria, it is helpful to delineate any relevant conditions under which the behavior is to be performed. For instance, in the short-term objective discussed above, it would be even more helpful to know whether the c-v-c words were contained in a word list or within some reading material. If this were provided, instructional personnel would be given further direction in determining the *materials* that could be utilized. Therefore, the more specific the short-term instructional objective, the easier for instructional personnel to select appropriate methods and materials. Obviously, some personnel feel more comfortable with specifics while others feel them unnecessary. The individual IEP team should remain sensitive to these variations and adjust provisions throughout the programming phase of delineating services and objectives to accommodate these differences.

Once the goals and objectives for a particular student have been determined, it should not be difficult to ascertain what types of regular, special, and related educational *services* the school has to offer that would assist the pupil in achieving these goals and objectives. However, it is not uncommon to discover that the school does not offer a particular service necessary for appropriate individualized education. In this instance, the school may choose to either supply these services directly or contract for them to be provided through a private or other public agency. In the past, it has been assumed that schools were responsible for only those services directly related to instruction. With the advent of special education and Public Law 94–142, schools are *legally* responsible for providing both instructional and related services. Related services are defined in law as "transportation and such developmental, corrective and other supportive services . . . as are required to assist a handicapped child to benefit from special education, and includes the early identification and assessment of handicapped conditions in children" (Public Law 94–142, 1975). Examples of supportive services a school may need to offer a student include social work, speech pathology and audiology, psychological and psychiatric services, physical therapy, occupational therapy, recreation, medical services for diagnostic or evaluation purposes, and parent and student counseling. Most related services that would assist a handicapped child to benefit from special education become apparent immediately following the establishment of educational goals and objectives. These services comprise one part of the programming aspect of the individual educational program.

It is easy to see the tremendous utility and importance of the educational programming provisions in providing personnel with the appropriate guidance in establishing specific objectives and services to follow in daily planning. The quality of instructional services improves when the guidance provided to the instructional staff is appropriate and comprehensive. Ultimately, the success of any educational program depends on the quality of these day-to-day instructional activities provided the student.

Summary. There are three purposes to be accomplished in developing, implementing, and maintaining individualized education programs: (1) to provide for direct educational planning and programming that will guide the instructional personnel in delivering special education and related services; (2) to provide for some degree of educational accountability to ensure the success of an individual's educational program; (3) to increase communication between home and school. In order to provide truly effective instructional intervention, each of these purposes must be fulfilled by the development and implementation of the IEP.

As previously discussed, once general directions, goals, objectives, and services have been delineated in the student's individualized education program, the first purpose of the IEP (that is, providing for direct

25

educational planning and programming) has been accomplished. Unfortunately, merely providing guidelines, regardless of how well written and appropriate, does not ensure the effectiveness of the student's program. No provision has yet been made to (1) ensure the activities written in the individual program will be carried out, or (2) monitor the effectiveness of these activities toward the accomplishment of goals and objectives once performed. However, these written guidelines established through educational planning and programming provide the basic structure upon which educators can begin to become accountable for the success or failure of the student's educational program.

Accountability

In recent years, the term accountability has been used extensively in the field of education. A casual survey of the titles of education journal articles over the past five years provides evidence of its popularity. A more thorough investigation of the topic reveals that, although educational accountability is often discussed, it is rarely defined. According to the *American Heritage Dictionary* (1973), the term "accountable" means "answerable, capable of being accounted for"; further, the phrase "account for" is defined as "to make or render a reckoning . . . , to be the explanation or cause of, to be answerable for." These terms imply that there is (1) an ongoing act observable by two or more persons, (2) criteria by which to judge that act appropriate or successful, and (3) persons responsible for performing that act. Applying each of these elements to the educational process simplifies the development of procedures to facilitate being accountable for student progress. In education the act consists of those instructional activities provided to the student. The criteria are interpreted as the mechanisms established to measure the extent to which the student achieved individual goals and objectives. The persons responsible for performing the act are various members of the particular education community. These three elements are essential in any discussion regarding the process by which an education system becomes accountable for the services it renders.

From an educational standpoint, accountability is the mechanism or procedures established by persons in the education community so that they may become accountable for the success or failure of education programs. In other words, the *process* of accountability is realized through those established procedures by which an individual or group of individuals becomes answerable for the success or failure of education programs, in this instance, individualized education programs for handicapped students. With regard to procedures designed to promote the effectiveness of a student's IEP, it is recommended that a system be developed based upon the three essential elements of being account-able—the act, the criteria, and the personnel. To some extent, the act and criteria are provided by the IEP in which the goals or criteria for success and instructional objectives or activities to be performed are defined. Therefore, procedures to establish a system of accountability include (1) the IEP, itself, as a document containing measurable goals, objectives, and activities; (2) assigning specific responsibilities to appropriate members of the educational staff; (3) continuously monitoring pupil progress toward established goals and objectives; and (4) investigating signs of ineffective programming for the purpose of program revision.

The IEP document. The entire accountability system is developed around those general directions, goals, objectives, and services delineated thus far in the student's individualized education program. Therefore, the IEP is not only a mechanism for developing a system of accountability, but is an essential ingredient in the system itself. The federal regulations governing individualized education programs comment that, although the document is written, it is not to be considered a binding contract. In addition, the regulations also provide that if projected goals and objectives are not met the education agency personnel are not to be held accountable. However, it is specified that education agencies "must provide special education and related services to a handicapped child in accordance with the individualized education program" (PL 94–142, 1975). Therefore, any significant discrepancy between the stated services and those services actually rendered without notification and agreement by each member of the original team, including the parent, would be a violation of law. Abeson and Weintraub (1977) state that such alteration probably would constitute a "breach of agreement" and could be interpreted as meaning the pupil was no longer receiving a free, appropriate public education as mandated by law.

Assigning responsibilities. With the increased emphasis upon placing and serving handicapped students in the regular classroom and with the various types of special and related services and arrangements becoming available through the schools, it is essential to assign the particular services needed and objectives set for the student to appropriate members of the school staff. This allows for the coordination of services and prevents duplication of efforts by school personnel. The individual educational program should provide that this division of responsibilities is written and signed by all persons to be concerned with the child's education, including the child's parents. Personnel directly responsible for particular special and related services such as speech therapy, physical therapy, and adaptive physical education (PE) are easily assigned responsibilities dealing with their areas of expertise. However, when one or more instructional personnel is involved, it becomes necessary for the IEP team to divide and assign specific instructional objectives to members of the school staff. To illustrate, a student may be in need of intensive oral language instruction in order to benefit most from his/her educational opportunities. In certain instances, particular oral language objectives may be best taught by the speech therapist, particularly if the child is experiencing difficulty in speech sound production. Other objectives such as the child's ability to construct and utilize complete sentences may be assigned to the learning disability specialist or other special education teacher trained to deal with these types of language problems. Skills such as initiating oral communication with one's peers may best be accomplished by the child's regular education teacher. Therefore, although the goal may be to increase the child's oral language skills, specific objectives and skills inherent within that goal may be assigned to various school personnel in order to provide the most effective instruction. When set forth in the written individual educational program this division of responsibility provides some degree of accountability by assuring that each objective set in the IEP is assigned to a member of the educational team. This method of accountability may also inadvertently aid in the discontinuation of the often negative practice of assigning responsibilities based on personnel titles and positions rather than on actual competencies involved in teaching specific objectives. In any event, assigning specific responsibilities to staff does much toward assuring effective individualized instruction based on the needs of handicapped students and certainly provides an added degree of accountability.

Monitoring pupil progress. An additional safeguard to ensure accountability of individual educational programs involves establishing a system to monitor students' progress toward attaining established goals and objectives. This system is designed to determine those appropriate and effective portions of the student's IEP so that they may be continued and/or expanded while indicating those areas that have been ineffective. Obviously, the portions of the IEP that have proven ineffective must be revised, deleted, and/or completely reconstructed.

The process of monitoring pupil progress for the purpose of determining the success of the individualized education program can only be accomplished by establishing a system of continuous assessments of a student's achievement. These assessments of pupil achievement determine the degree to which goals and objectives contained in the IEP are being accomplished. Therefore, the selected or teacher-constructed assessment instruments must be designed to determine progress made toward the specific goals and objectives established in the IEP. There are essentially two types of assessment instruments that must be incorporated in any pupil evaluation system: one measures the extent to which goals have been attained and the other measures the extent to which a student has mastered specific instructional objectives.

Assessing the degree to which *goals* are being accomplished is an important part of any system that attempts to evaluate the appropriateness of a student's individual educational program. Ultimately, it is the only factor that can determine the success or failure of a particular program. It is important to remember two basic characteristics of educational goals when establishing an assessment system to evaluate the actual progress toward attaining stated goals—that they are long term and broad based. As a result of the long-term nature of educational goals, goal assessments are most profitable when conducted annually. Furthermore, annual evaluations and revisions are now mandated by law. The broad-based nature of educational goals is because of the number of specific skills and objectives that comprise a single educational goal. This makes it necessary to select assessment instruments designed to measure achievement in the particular curricular area for which the goal is written.

In order to determine the progress a student has made toward a particular goal, one must first have some idea of the student's level of achievement within that curricular area prior to implementing the individualized education program. This measure of achievement provides the evaluation team a point of reference from which they can determine the success of a particular student's program. When selecting a device to assess progress toward achieving a goal, it is helpful to review the process by which the goal was established. It is important to remember that educational goals are based on the data obtained during diagnosis of the handicapping condition(s). These data consisted of a student's scores on (1) standardized measures of current performance or achievement levels and (2) standardized measures of intelligence, aptitude, or other measures of potential for performance. Each of these is administered to the particular student being considered for special education services and is available on every student for whom an educational program is being written. Current performance is generally diagnosed through the administration of standardized achievement tests. These tests report measurements in the form of norms or comparisons with performance made by a similar group of persons presumed to represent the general population. The scores on standardized tests of performance derived at the time of the diagnosis can provide the point of reference from which the evaluation team can determine whether or not progress has been made. In order to make this determination, diagnostic personnel must either administer the same instruments or similar instruments that are also standardized and purport to measure the same content or curricular area. Once the test is administered, after approximately a year of receiving the instructional intervention provided in the student's IEP, a comparison of pre- and post-test scores can be made to determine whether or not the student is making progress toward achieving established goals. Assessing the degree to which goals are attained is crucial; without detectable progress toward goals, serious questions must be asked regarding the appropriateness of not only goals, but also objectives, services, and instruction as well. This annual assessment comprises the portion of the educational accountability system that monitors pupil progress toward desired levels of achievement. In addition to annual assessments, the accountability system also must include provisions for *continuous* monitoring of pupil progress.

Although educational goals established in the student's individual educational plan are a crucial element of the IEP, the broad-based nature of these goals makes continuous monitoring or assessment impossible. The most efficient way in which to monitor progress continuously is by assessing the extent to which *short-term instructional objectives* contained in the IEP are being achieved.

Assessing the degree to which *short-term instructional objectives* are met can be continuous and is best conducted by personnel involved in *actually instructing* the student. Remember, the specific objectives contained in the IEP were determined following delineation of general objectives taken from a curricular map and a period of instructional assessments during the educational programming phase. Similar evaluation methods are appropriate to determine the extent to which objectives have been met. There are four types of measures appropriate for assessing progress toward objectives: (1) standardized tests, (2) commercially produced nonstandardized measures, (3) teacher-constructed informal tests based on the objectives stated in the IEP, and (4) subjective measures. Standardized measures and commercially produced informal devices applicable to evaluating specific objectives usually have a criterion-referenced format. That is, these instruments typically are accompanied by a listing of specific objectives that each test item is purported to measure. Most often, however, each objective specified is measured by only one test item; therefore, in most cases the task required is not sufficient evidence to establish either the presence or absence of such skills. Readers interested in investigating both standardized and informal measures of various subject/content areas are referred to Wallace and Larsen (1978) for complete review and description of currently available instrumentation.

By far the most accurate and efficient devices for measuring progress toward specific instructional objectives are those constructed and administered by the instructional personnel themselves. These teacher-constructed devices allow for assessment of the exact objectives considered important and eliminate sampling of irrelevant objectives.

30

A detailed procedure for constructing such devices is provided in Chapter 6. The only disadvantage in using teacher-constructed devices to measure pupil progress toward objectives exclusively is that they are often constructed much like an instructional activity; therefore, the activity itself may be being assessed rather than the objectives per se. In any event, the degree to which a student has mastered a specific skill or objective must be monitored continuously through assessments conducted by instructional personnel.

Additional measurement devices that can be purchased or teacher-constructed are *subjective measures* that can evaluate to some extent goals and objectives that are not easily definable, such as self-concepts, attitudes, and interests of students. These devices generally take the form of checklists, rating scales, sentence-completion tasks, Q sorts, and interest inventories. It is necessary for a school to conduct each of the three types of assessments—goal assessments, short term instructional objective assessments, and subjective measures—to assure thorough and continuous monitoring of pupil progress toward established goals and objectives.

Investigating ineffective programs. Thus far, the accountability system discussed has provided for a complete educational program, designated the responsibility for services and instruction to appropriate personnel, and developed mechanisms for evaluating the long- and short-term effectiveness of the program. Ideally, the system has been designed to ensure that appropriate problems are detected immediately so that appropriate revision of the student's progress can be developed and implemented. The third major part of the accountability system is utilized only in the event that insufficient progress is noted in the student's achievement toward stated goals and objectives. In that case, several questions must be answered through whatever evaluative efforts are employed. Probably the evaluations will be subjective in nature and may be conducted through informal observation and investigation or through a more systematic method developed by an individual school. Some of the questions to be answered by this investigative system are as follows.

- Are goals realistic and in line with student potential?
- Do objectives delineated clearly lead to accomplishing set goals?
- Are the objectives clearly defined and written into instructionally relevant language?
- Are objectives sequenced appropriately?
- Are services provided adequate?
- Are responsibilities properly assigned to school personnel?

31

- Do school personnel have the necessary competencies?
- Are there other factors not previously considered involved?

Such questions as these are difficult to answer and often quite threatening to educators. Of course, they imply that either the program or the school personnel has failed. It is for this reason that the term "accountability" itself has in the past projected negative connotations to educators. Effective systems of accountability have been slow to develop because of educators' reluctance to accept the responsibility for the results of their activities especially with regard to educating handicapped children and youth. Inherent in any education system that has accepted the responsibility of being accountable is an unstated confidence that the system can offer all students effective instruction. *An accountable education community views failure as a natural part of the continuous process of developing effective educational programs and utilizes this failure as a signal for changing or revising the student's individual program.*

Once the school has developed an effective system for determining accountability by establishing a program, assigning responsibilities for this program to appropriate personnel, establishing a mechanism for monitoring pupil progress, and developing a process to investigate ineffective programs, the second purpose of the IEP—establishing a system for accountability—is accomplished.

Communication between Home and School

In addition to the increase in communication among school personnel brought about by developing and implementing individual educational programs and coordinating various services, the IEP also fulfills the purpose of establishing an effective communication network between home and school. This third purpose is accomplished (1) by providing for parent and, in some instances, child participation and (2) by providing information to families of handicapped children upon which they can build realistic expectations. As is discussed later, one of the guidelines set forth in the new public law mandates that parents and, when appropriate, the children themselves are to be members of the team that develops the handicapped child's educational program. This provision alone leads to an increase in communication between home and school. Providing parents with knowledge of the education community's goals and objectives for their children is long overdue in the education of exceptional children. Although this provision is not directly provided to parents of regular classroom students, some knowledge of regular school curriculum goals and objectives is available so that parents can form general assumptions regarding the education of their children. Not only do parents have the right to participate in setting expectations, goals, and objectives, but this participation undoubtedly eases frequently negative relations between home and school. What is sometimes viewed by educators as apathy by parents of handicapped children is often merely the acceptance of years of exclusion felt by parents—*exclusion from information regarding their child's potential and progress.*

Historically, excluding parents from information regarding their handicapped child by the education community is probably a result of one or more of the following reasons: (1) the school's uncertainty about what can be accomplished for handicapped children, (2) the fact that often goals and objectives have not been established, (3) the fear that parents will be unable to accept realistic expectations about their child's education, and/or (4) a reaction to the parents' initial unacceptance or grief at having a handicapped child. Therefore, in efforts to protect either itself and/or parents, the school has often compounded the problem for families of handicapped children by not being completely honest and sharing this information with them. Parent participation increases the sharing of information between both the home and school and, therefore, offers a more complete picture of the student to both parties. This leads to better coordination and cooperation among services offered by the school and expectations and demands placed on the student at home. This could well become one of the most important purposes the development of individualized education programs will serve.

Direct educational planning and programming, educational accountability, and communication between home and school are all purposes of the individualized education program. Developing, implementing, and maintaining the IEP provides a structure for fulfilling these purposes while providing handicapped children and youth with appropriate instructional intervention. Many of the mandated procedures and components of IEPs contribute to the accomplishment of these three purposes. Let us examine the procedures or guidelines to be followed in developing, implementing, and maintaining an individual's educational program.

MANDATED PROCEDURES AND GUIDELINES

The Bureau of Education for the Handicapped (BEH) under the Office of Education, the agency charged with interpreting and implementing Public Law 94–142, has developed regulations designed to maximize the likelihood that the actual intent of the law is met. Compliance with the law and regulations qualifies state and local education agencies to receive federal dollars to supplement their special education and related service programs. Noncompliance constitutes a violation of the law making such agencies liable for suit and risking the withholding of not only special education monies, but any federal monies received for education.

With regard to individualized education programs, the BEH has established certain procedures and guidelines in addition to those in the law itself. It is hoped that these will lead to the actualization of the three purposes for IEPs discussed earlier—direct educational planning and programming, accountability, and improved communication between home and school. As the mandated procedures are discussed it should be evident that each one serves in some way to promote one or more of these purposes. Within these regulating guidelines, the BEH specifically assigns the state education agencies the authority and responsibility of ensuring that local education agencies within their state comply with these regulations. State agencies are also given authority to establish any additional requirements over and above those federal guidelines regarding the IEP development and implementation. The persons within the *local* education agencies, however, are the ones ultimately responsible for carrying out these requirements for each handicapped student in their particular school district. The mandated federal guidelines and procedures can best be discussed by first examining the characteristics of IEPs outlined in the legal definition of an individualized education program.

The definition of the IEP, which is included in federal law, forms the basic structure from which the more specific federal regulations are developed. Initially, it is vital to note that, while the entire intent of Public Law 94–142 was that every handicapped child be provided free and appropriate public education, the definition of what constitutes "appropriate education" for any student is defined as that which is written into his/her individualized education program. Ultimately, the intent and impact of this law rests within the content of each student's IEP. Specifically, there are several characteristics that, by definition, must be a part of every IEP. Public Law 94–142 states that the IEP is (1) a *written statement* (2) for each *handicapped student* (3) that is to be developed in a *meeting* (4) by a *team* including a representative of the local education agency, the student's teacher(s), the student's parents, and, when appropriate, the student him/herself; and that the statement must be (5) *reviewed and revised* at least annually. A second part of the definition delineates specific components of the program and is discussed later. Understanding that these five elements are basic to developing any IEP, we will examine those regulations developed by BEH as they further define these five *elements* or characteristics of the IEP.

A Written Statement

The first, and most basic, characteristic of an individualized education program is that it must be in the form of a written document. This written statement is necessary to determine eligibility for being officially counted as among those receiving special education services. This count is necessary in order to determine amounts of federal dollars to which a state is entitled; therefore, the state education agency must assure that the student counted has on record a written individualized education program. This program must be developed within 30 days of determining that the student has a handicapping condition and is in need of, and consequently, eligible for special services and must also be on file prior to the student's receiving any special education and related services. Were the student to receive these services prior to or entirely without the written individualized educational program, he/she would not be eligible to be counted as a special education student for the purposes of obtaining federal funds and, in addition, would constitute a violation of federal law.

The advantage in mandating that the program be written is that it provides a more direct and accessible guide for all instructional personnel. This guide should also assist those parents requesting a copy of the document in setting their expectations of both child and school. Any questions regarding the school's intent in providing the student with particular services are immediately answerable. Therefore, each of the three purposes for developing IEPs is promoted by placing the student's program in writing. Contents of the written programs are described and discussed later, but let us next examine more closely who is "each handicapped student" for whom this written statement must exist and who is responsible for the student's IEP.

Each Handicapped Student

Federal law requires that any student diagnosed as handicapped automatically becomes eligible to receive a free and appropriate public education and defines which agency is responsible for his/her IEP. The ultimate responsibility for developing and implementing an IEP for each of these handicapped students rests with the local education agency or intermediate educational unit serving that student. The phrase "intermediate educational unit" is defined as "any public authority, other than a local education agency, which is established by State law for the purposes of providing free public education on a regional basis, and which provides special education and related services to handicapped children within that State" (PL 94–142, 1975). Therefore, if the student is provided services through an intermediate educational unit such as a regional service structure, it is the responsibility of that intermediate unit to develop and implement the eligible student's individualized education program, while it remains the responsibility of the local education agency to develop and implement programs for students served by the local school districts.

In addition to these two classes of special education students, there may be handicapped students in need of special education and related services for whom the local district does not have the expertise or resources to provide. It should be noted that the local school district is required to secure these needed services. In order to secure the proper services, local education agencies may contract for services through another public agency, an institution, or a private facility. Although the local education agency may delegate the student's IEP or portions of the IEP to be developed and implemented by these contracted facilities, by law the ultimate responsibility for development and implementation rests with the contracting local education agency. In other words, the local education agency is responsible for developing and implementing an IEP for every handicapped child to whom they provide services either directly or indirectly. The method by which the agency develops and maintains this program for each handicapped child is also set forth in federal regulations.

IEP Meetings

Once members of a local or intermediate education agency have diagnosed a student as handicapped and in need of special education and related services, developing the student's individualized education program must be undertaken at a meeting of school and home personnel conducted within 30 calendar days following the diagnosis. In addition, no student may receive special education or related services prior to this meeting and subsequent development of the IEP. For students currently receiving special education and related services, no changes can be made in their programs prior to an IEP meeting. From October 1, 1977 on, the annual IEP meeting for review and revision must be conducted by the anniversary date of the last IEP meeting until the student is no longer receiving special education services. It is important to note that no IEP can be developed or revised by any individual without conducting or reconvening the IEP meeting or notifying parents and other persons of the proposed change(s). Regulations designating the selection of particular persons who *must* participate in these meetings are also provided.

IEP Team

Federal regulations designate three different groups of persons who must be represented on the team that meets to develop or revise the student's individualized education program: general participants, evaluation personnel, and, when appropriate, private school personnel. Persons representing each of these categories are further defined in the guidelines and are discussed below.

General participants. General participants mandated to be involved on the IEP team include (1) a representative of the public agency, other than the student's teacher, who is qualified to provide or supervise special education services, (2) the student's teacher or teachers, (3) one or both parents, (4) the student him/herself, when appropriate, and (5) other individuals at the discretion of the parent(s) or education agency. It is obvious from this listing that the mandatory general participants, alone, constitute a minimum of a three-person team. This assumes that there must be at least one teacher, one parent, and one other member of the school staff present. The member of the school staff who is not the student's teacher must be a person *qualified to provide or supervise special education services.* Persons qualified to "provide" special education services include anyone certified, licensed, or approved by the state education agency in an area of special education. This may include any special education teacher as long as this person is not the particular student's teacher. Persons qualified to "supervise" special education services could be interpreted to include a building principal, special education director, supervisor, or any other member of the special education support staff. This person may or may not be delegated as chairperson of the team and may well be an excellent person to make the actual arrangements for the meeting among all the team members.

Probably the most important member(s) of the IEP team is the *student's teacher or teachers.* In most instances, the student either already has or soon will have more than one teacher, generally a regular classroom teacher and at least one special education teacher. The authors recommend the composition of the team from its onset include (1) all the special education and regular education teachers presently serving the student, (2) any and all special education or regular teachers who are being considered possibly to serve the student, and (3) any possible related service personnel. A team composed of these individuals should assure that all personnel having any involvement with the student are allowed to give input to decisions being made, as well as to understand clearly what the responsibilities of each concerning the education of this student will be.

The mandate of *parent participation* on a school team is most exciting and long overdue in the education of exceptional learners. Prior to PL 94–142, very few education agencies actually required that parents attend meetings concerning their children. As a result of the novelty involved in such a mandate, the regulations governing this provision are quite specific. The public education agency providing the student's education is required to initiate and document steps taken to ensure that one or both parents of a handicapped student are present at each IEP meeting or are afforded at least the opportunity to participate. These steps must include scheduling the team meeting at a mutually agreed upon time and place. If neither parent can attend, the agency must use other methods to ensure parent participation in the IEP development including individual or conference telephone calls. In the event that the IEP meeting is held without a parent in attendance, that is, if the agency is unable to convince parents that they should attend, the agency must have documentable records of its attempts to arrange a mutually agreed upon time and place. These records may include (1) detailed records of telephone calls made or attempted and the results of those calls, (2) copies of correspondence sent to the parents and any responses received, and (3) detailed records of visits made to the parents' home or place of employment and results of those visits. In addition, the agency must make every effort to assure that parents understand the proceedings at the IEP meeting including providing for an interpreter for deaf parents and parents whose native language is not English. Recommendations are given in Chapter 9 for building an effective parent communication network that takes into account these mandates as well as incorporating appropriate and viable procedures within education agency structures.

Although federal regulations provide no specific criteria for when it may be appropriate to include the *student* him/herself, regulations do include the student as a possible general participant. It is recommended by the authors that individual education agencies develop policies regarding student participation. It will probably be to the school's advantage to include the student whenever the student is capable of understanding and participating in any of the discussion that will be conducted. Obviously, at the request of the parents, the student must be included because of the parents' right to select other individuals to attend such meetings.

In addition to representatives of the education agency, teachers, and parents, *other individuals* may also be included as members of the

IEP team. These additional persons may be at the discretion of the agency and/or at the will of the parent. Other persons the agency should include are such persons as may provide related services to the student, additional supervisory persons, student or parent counselors, school nurses or doctors, and visiting teachers. Parents may well want to include family physicians, other members of the family such as older siblings, friends, or advocates who are familiar with the process of IEP development; or private agency persons familiar with the child and family. In addition, the parents may include legal representation if they deem it necessary. One of the advantages of the provision allowing parents to invite other persons to the meeting is that it allows parents to include their child, him/herself, or another parent who is familiar with the system and the concept and procedures of the IEP meetings. Therefore, general participants composing the IEP team include a representative of the public agency other than the child's teacher; the child's teacher or teachers; the student's parent(s); the student, where appropriate; and other individuals requested by the agency or parents. These persons, however, do not always complete the IEP team for, by regulation, the team must in some instances also include evaluation personnel.

Evaluation personnel. The IEP team *must* involve a member of the agency's evaluation personnel if the child has been evaluated for the first time and *may* include evaluation personnel on the team for meetings regarding students currently served. Evaluation personnel include persons in the agency qualified, certified, or licensed by the state education agency to conduct individual evaluations of students. These persons include school psychologists, educational diagnosticians, counselors, and associate psychologists. It is recommended that the person representing evaluation personnel be the same individual who conducted that particular student evaluation. It is also recommended that for students currently served in special education, a member of the evaluation personnel participate in the meeting when there is a question regarding the student's original evaluation or when the original diagnosis is *three years old*. Any diagnostic workup that is over three years old makes it necessary to completely reevaluate the student. In the event that a member of the evaluation personnel in the school cannot attend for initially placed or currently served students, it is possible to conduct the meeting if the representative of the public agency is knowledgeable about the evaluation procedures used with the student and is familiar with the results of the evaluation. Following evaluation, if the student is determined to be in need of services to be provided through a contractual agreement between the public school agency and a private agency, the IEP team must also include a representative of the private agency.

Private school representative. If the state or local education agency places or refers a student to a private school or facility, the agency is responsible for assuring that a representative of the private school participates in each IEP meeting. If, for some reason, the private school representative cannot attend the IEP meeting, the agency must assure participation by the private school or facility by other methods such as individual or conference telephone calls. As with parent participation, the agency should endeavor to document attempts to secure meetings and participation with private school persons.

While the above individuals are mentioned in the federal regulations governing memberships on the IEP team, it is important for education agencies to make every attempt to include any individual who may contribute to providing background information regarding the student in question. Guidelines for reviewing and revising the student's IEP, one of the duties of the IEP team, are also set forth in federal regulations and are examined in the following section.

Review and Revision

All individualized education programs must be reviewed and revised at least once a year. The process for review is the same as that for initial development in that it must be undertaken in a meeting of the IEP team as defined earlier. The meeting must be held by no later than the anniversary date of the last IEP meeting and should be reviewed and revised prior to each new school year so that revisions in the program can be effected immediately upon the student's return to school. The purpose of the review is to determine the effectiveness of the established program and either *expand* its contents to include the following school year, *revise* those sections that are now inappropriate or have proven ineffective, or completely *rewrite* programs that have led to insufficient progress or progress reversals. This regulation serves to establish one basis around which to build a more thorough accountability system.

Summary of Procedures and Guidelines

Many federal regulations governing the procedures and guidelines to be used in developing, implementing, and maintaining a student's individualized education program serve to promote the purposes of the IEP. Procedures mandating parental involvement serve to increase home and school communication. Procedures for reviewing and revising the IEP add structure to the accountability system. Guidelines for selecting the various members of the team that is to write the IEP document lead to more comprehensive educational planning and programming to guide instructional personnel. Although these regulations represent only minimum requirements for IEPs, they do facilitate appropriate individualized instruction to a large degree. Later chapters of this book provide recommended methods for the step-by-step development, implementation, and maintenance of the IEP encompassing not only these minimal requirements but aids to putting these regulations into effect and further desired procedures to ensure appropriate education to each handicapped student.

Thus far we have discussed a great deal regarding the procedures to follow in developing individualized education programs. However, there are additional federal regulations that govern the minimum contents of each individual education program. These, too, are established in law and can be categorized and examined by first looking at another part of the legal definition of individualized education programs expressed in PL 94–142.

MANDATED COMPONENTS

By definition, an individualized education program for any student

> shall include (A) a statement of the present levels of educational performance of such child, (B) a statement of annual goals, including short term instructional objectives, (C) a statement of the specific educational services to be provided to such child, and the extent to which such child will be able to participate in regular educational programs, (D) the projected date for initiation and anticipated duration of such services, (E) appropriate objective criteria and evaluation procedures and schedules for determining, on at least an annual basis whether instructional objectives are being achieved. (PL 94–142)

The five elements defined here are the five components mandated for inclusion in each student's individualized education program. These can be thought of as the minimal contents of any IEP. Unlike the federal regulations governing procedures and guidelines, regulations governing these components are not further defined. In other words, where mandated components were concerned, the Bureau of Education for the Handicapped did not see fit to expand upon the components set forth in the law when establishing federal regulations.

Each of the five legally mandated components serves to fulfill the purpose of providing instructional personnel with specific guidelines in individualizing the student's instruction. In addition to instructional guidance, some of these components directly aid in realizing a comprehensive accountability system. When examining each component individually, it is more readily seen how each facilitates the overall purposes of the IEP—educational planning and programming, accountability, and increased communication systems. These components are examined in detail in Chapters 4, 5, 6, 7, and 8.

Present Levels of Educational Performance

The first component that must be present in each individualized education program is a statement or statements regarding the student's present level of educational performance. Depending on the individual student's handicapping condition and severity of that condition, these performance levels cover a variety of subject/content areas in education. For the younger and/or severely handicapped students, subject/content areas may include self-help, language skills, and so on. For older and/or less severely impaired students, subject/content areas to be evaluated may include academic and vocational skills. Once the subject/content area appropriate to the student's condition is determined, evaluation personnel can determine the general levels of student performance. Standardized instruments available in each of the subject/content areas of concern are generally administered by evaluation personnel to acquire a broad idea of the level within this area at which the student is functioning. Normative data provide this information in age and grade norms, percentiles, and so on. Obviously, these kinds of determinations generally are made and documented while diagnosing a handicapping condition. Therefore, establishing a student's present level of educational performance generally is accomplished during or immediately following diagnosis and must make two important determinations: (1) what subject/content areas are appropriate to this student and (2) what his/her general level of performance within each of these areas is. Once these present levels of functioning have been determined, there is sufficient information for the team to use in establishing annual educational goals for the student.

Annual Goals and Short-Term Instructional Objectives

The second component that must be present in all individualized education programs can be broken into several components. Annual goals would be the first of these and could be established immediately following determination of the student's present level of functioning. These goals demonstrate the general direction the school intends to follow in educating the student, such as self-help/basic living skills or academics. Once goals are established, the team is provided with an education plan upon which to build the student's specific educational program. These goals are also suitable for annual evaluations of student progress that assist the IEP team in determining the extent to which the program has been successful. However, as required by law, annual evaluations must be made regarding accomplishment of short-term instructional objectives. Nevertheless, annual evaluations of goals are also essential. In addition, the goals are helpful in determining those portions of the IEP that need to be retained, expanded, revised, or rewritten.

A second step in completing this component is determining what general objectives comprise this particular educational goal or curricular map. Although not specifically required by law, general objectives must be established and assessed prior to developing short-term instructional objectives. This step prevents including unnecessary short-term objectives and omitting relevant objectives necessary for goal accomplishment.

The third step involved in this component is developing short-term instructional objectives that constitute specific guidelines for instructional personnel to follow in programming daily activities for the students. These short-term instructional objectives can only be determined following the establishment and assessment of the extent to which the student has mastered general objectives. Short-term instructional objectives also form the basis upon which evaluation of student progress is mandated.

Educational Services

The third component of any student's individualized education program specifically delineates three types of educational services that may be provided the student: (1) special education, (2) related services, and (3) regular education programs. In other words, under this component an agency must describe those services within each category with which the student will be provided. Of course, any student for whom an IEP is being written is receiving special education services. However, the specific special education services demanded must also be established. These may include the type of special arrangements or class in which to serve the student such as self-contained, resource, homebound, hospital. The specific subject/content areas involved in special education instruction and amount of time spent per day or week in special education should also be determined.

For students in need of related services (defined previously as speech therapy, physical therapy, counseling, special transportation, and so on), the specific related service to be provided must be described in the IEP as well. It is also recommended to define the approximate type and amount of related services to be provided weekly in this section of the IEP. In addition, the way in which the service is to be rendered, such as the type of instructional arrangement and any additional conditions, should also be documented.

In addition to special education and related services, the extent to which a student is to participate in regular education programs is also required to be documented in each IEP. This requirement is consistent with a basic premise in the law; that is, the assumption that handicapped students are most appropriately educated with nonhandicapped students to the maximum extent possible. Therefore, all educational services should be rendered in the "least restrictive environment." Although the concept of "least restrictive environment" is generally thought of as the regular classroom alone, it is important to note that, for severely involved students, the least restrictive environment probably is not the regular classroom. Rather, for a student of this severity level, a self-contained setting, integrated or resource class may be the most appropriate and least restrictive. This assumption implies that, where the student is able to function in a more normal environment, it is to his/her benefit to be allowed to do so. The required documentation of the extent to which a student receives regular education services focuses attention on this important concept each time an IEP is developed for a particular student. Once all the educational services, special, related, and regular, to be provided the student are delineated, the third component of the IEP is completed and the team must now turn its attention to projecting important dates for these services.

Projected Dates

The fourth component mandated for inclusion in each student's IEP calls for the team to project initiation dates for each service and anticipate the duration of such services. This component may be interpreted as only referring to special education and related services since regular education services are obviously ongoing. However, if the student's time spent in regular classroom instruction is expected to increase or decrease within the year, the dates of these expected modifications should also be determined. As with specifying all services, this component demands that educators focus their attention on possible termination of the special education services, making full educational support through regular education an ultimate goal. Without question, it also provides a date on which to initiate special services for the student, focusing educators' attention on a timely securing of certain services. These dates are not considered binding, but merely projections forcing educators to consider important factors. Obviously, duration of special services depends on the student's progress toward meeting educational goals and objectives and the extent to which these goals prepare a student for regular education instruction. Evaluating progress toward goals and objectives is the issue to which the fifth, and last, mandated component is directed.

Evaluation Criteria and Procedures

Next to determining goals and objectives, establishing evaluation criteria and procedures is the most complex of the five components. In fact, determining appropriate evaluative criteria and procedures depends to a great extent on the goals and objectives outlined in the student's program. Although the law specifically mandates evaluating the extent to which short-term instructional objectives are being met, the authors warn that, without evaluating the extent to which goals are accomplished, there can never be any assurance that the objectives are, in fact, goal appropriate. Therefore, there must be two types of assessment conducted representing (1) pupil progress in goals and (2) pupil progress toward short-term objectives. Prior to determining what procedures to use in evaluating goals and objectives, the team must first establish objective criteria for evaluating achievement and/or adjustment to established goals and objectives.

To define appropriate objective criteria for goals or objectives, one must first determine what behavior constitutes or serves as evidence that the student has mastered the goal or objective. This behavior becomes the criterion by which the student is evaluated to determine whether or not mastery of the goal or objective has been met. Ultimately this criterion determines the degree of success the student's program has afforded and can be the only criterion for evaluating any IEP.

Procedures for evaluating these criteria include any instrumentation or observations needed and schedules for the evaluation to take place. The criterion set for mastery of each objective dictates the types of instrumentation used to evaluate the student's mastery or the type of observations that must be made to document mastery. We recommend employing standardized instruments in appropriate subject/content areas to measure goal achievement annually. Teacher-constructed devices or recording pertinent behaviors during observation may best be employed, more or less continuously, to evaluate progress toward attaining short-term instructional objectives. Scheduling evaluations should be done with certain characteristics of goals and short-term objectives kept in mind. For example, scheduling goal evaluations more frequently than every six months is probably useless because the broad-based nature of goals is such that achievement toward them is not evident before the student has mastered many of the objectives underlying these goals. In most instances, the nine-month school year is best for goal assessments. Schedules for evaluating short-term instructional objectives could range anywhere from daily checklists of skills to one- to two-month intervals. Short-term instructional objectives are stated in such a manner that long-range evaluations are unnecessary and inappropriate. Establishing these schedules, procedures, and criteria for evaluation is the most important component of the IEP for fulfilling the purpose of accountability.

Each of these components—establishing levels of performance, goals and objectives, services, dates, and evaluations—in each student's IEP can do much to fulfill two of the three purposes of the IEP. The two purposes most affected by the mandated components are providing direct educational planning and programming to assist school personnel and establishing a system of accountability for program success. Along with the mandated procedures discussed previously, these activities constitute the development, implementation, and maintenance of the IEP as required by law.

SUMMARY

Public Law 94–142, federal legislation passed in November 1975 and effective October 1, 1977, mandates that all handicapped students in the United States are entitled to and must be provided with a free and appropriate public education. At the very core of this law is the stipulation that every handicapped student must be provided with an *individualized education program* based upon his/her unique educational needs. This program should be written in such a fashion that, if followed, provides the student with appropriate educational services in the form of individualized instruction.

In order to provide appropriate individualized instruction, each individualized education program must fulfill three purposes. The program must provide for *direct educational planning and programming* designed to guide instructional personnel in designing daily instructional intervention activities. In addition, the student's program must establish in writing a system by which the education agency can monitor and increase the chances for program success. This system of checks and balances can be referred to as a mechanism for *accountability*. The third purpose for developing, implementing, and maintaining an IEP on a particular student is to *increase communication* within the school and between home and school regarding the particular child or youth.

In order to promote fulfillment of these purposes, federal regulations developed by the Bureau of Education for the Handicapped define and to some degree assure that the actual intent of the law is met. These regulations include procedures and guidelines that must be followed in developing, implementing, and maintaining individualized education programs, as well as those specific components mandated to be addressed in each IEP. Procedures and guidelines set forth in the federal regulations cover the actual writing of the program, students for whom an IEP must be written, responsibilities for writing the IEP, composition of the team or committee that develops or revises the program, and procedures for revisions. Components specified by law include present level of educational performance, annual goals and short-term instructional objectives, educational services to be provided, dates for such services, and evaluation criteria and procedures. Each guideline, procedure, and component required by law is related directly to fulfilling the three purposes of the IEP.

As Public Law 94–142 emerged on the education scene in 1975 and as the proposed regulations were released in 1977, it was interesting to note the various responses of individuals and organizations, especially regarding the specificity of both law and regulations. The deputy commissioner of the Bureau of Education for the Handicapped, voiced his reservations by stating that he felt the federal government was out of place in requiring specific teaching strategies stated in federal law. He also warned that monitoring 94–142 was going to be no simple task and would involve quite a complex evaluation model. The National Advisory Committee for the Handicapped (advisers to the Department of Health, Education and Welfare) voiced concern that the technical features of the IEP were replete with educational jargon and would prevent some effective parent participation. This same body of professionals and parents was also concerned that the IEP regulations not be so general as to make student evaluation impossible. Other administratively oriented groups and several state education agencies also protested portions of the IEP purporting that they were far too specific, unrealistic, and not implementable.

It has been equally as interesting to note the kinds of comments and opinions held by the more advocacy-oriented groups. For instance, the National Center for Law and the Handicapped formally commented that regulations were insufficient, too general, thus leading to administrative manipulation and abuse particularly regarding developing and implementing individualized education programs. Several parent organizations have praised the specificity in the law formally and, in particular, the emphasis placed on parent participation and due process. Obviously, the authors would contend that IEPs as defined are implementable and sufficiently detailed to provide meaningful interpretation and evaluation. We laud the efforts of the federal government to mandate such a comprehensive system for providing handicapped students with individualized instruction. The remainder of this book is developed to serve as a guide for school personnel and parents in the most efficient and effective step-by-step procedures for developing and implementing effective individualized instruction while assuring that federal mandates regarding the IEPs are met.

References

Abeson, A., and Weintraub, F. Understanding the individualized education program. In S. Torres (ed.), *A primer on individualized education programs for handicapped children.* Reston, Virginia: The Foundation for Exceptional Children, 1977.

Davies, Peter (ed.) *The American heritage dictionary.* New York: Dell Publishing Company, 1976.

Hammill, D., and Poplin, M. Problems in writing. In Hammill, D., and Bartel, N. *Teaching children with learning and behavior problems.* Boston: Allyn & Bacon, 1978.

Wallace, G., and Larsen, S. C. *Educational assessment of learning problems: Testing for teaching.* Boston: Allyn & Bacon, 1978.

3

Referral, Screening, and Evaluation

The first step in evaluating handicapped students comes at the time of *referral*. While not mentioned in the regulations for PL 94–142, the referral process is an important and frequently overlooked phase in the efficient program planning for handicapped persons. The reason for the importance of the referral phase is that it permits professionals to (1) distinguish between those students likely to meet the criteria for inclusion in a handicapping condition and those effectively managed through other, already existing, non-special education programs; (2) plan the best strategies (that is, assessment procedures) to be utilized during the evaluation phase; (3) contact parents for the purpose of informing them that their child is exhibiting difficulties in the educational environment and may undergo an educational or medical evaluation; (4) begin a general screening procedure to yield data regarding potential problem areas in the student's environment that may be causing or maintaining the educational disability (such as classroom interactional patterns or peer relationships); and (5) conduct an initial *screening* meeting on the referral that includes appropriate professionals and the parents to determine whether formal evaluation is desirable and/or needed.

If care is taken at the referral level to ensure that pertinent general information is obtained and that the pupil is an obvious candidate for receiving special education services, much time, effort, and monies may be saved the individual professional as well as the school system. Indeed, enacting a well-planned and coordinated referral process makes the formal evaluation of the child and/or adolescent a much more viable and efficient proposition. The remainder of this chapter discusses aspects of referral and evaluation that are particularly germane to developing the individualized educational program. The reader is encouraged to

49

consult the appendix to this book for several case studies that serve to illustrate various handicapping conditions. In this chapter, the basic referral and evaluation data pertinent to these cases will be presented and discussed.

REFERRAL AND SCREENING OF
HANDICAPPED CHILDREN

The initial referral of handicapped children can come from many and diverse sources. As is discussed in depth under the section on evaluation, handicapped children may be classified as mentally retarded, hard of hearing, deaf, learning disabled, speech impaired, visually handicapped, seriously emotionally disturbed, orthopedically impaired, other health impaired, deaf-blind, or multihandicapped. In addition, as a result of their impairments handicapped children must be in need of special education and related services in order to correct or circumvent their handicapping conditions. Depending on the age of the child and the type and severity of the disability, the referral to special education may come from a variety of sources. In the case where the problem is relatively severe *and* apparent, the parent or physician is likely to make the first contact with the local school system. In many instances, this type of referral is made for a child who has not yet reached school age. Obviously, a child who is born with an apparent and severe visual disability or who exhibits persistent clinical symptoms of cerebral palsy will be referred for special or related services during his/her first year of life. Preschool children may also come to the attention of their parents or physicians if they demonstrate more than usual difficulties in developing language, relating to family or peers, or mastering such essential motor tasks as toileting, walking, dressing, or manipulating objects. When the alert and perceptive parent and/or physician determines that the observed problem is at a severity level that possibly requires special intervention for its successful amelioration, a referral to the appropriate officials in the local system will undoubtedly be forthcoming.

While some referrals to special education are made by noneducational personnel, the majority of referred pupils come from the regular classroom. That is, the largest numbers of handicapped students pass through their preschool years with few if any symptoms that would suggest the need for special or related services. It is only after they have matriculated into the school environment that their handicapping conditions are manifested in an inability to master the social and curricular tasks demanded within the regular classroom. For school-aged students, the most typical referral symptoms include that he/she does not attend to task, is disruptive, cannot learn to read, write, spell, or perform mathematical calculations, is difficult to understand, does not appear to be able to see or hear adequately, daydreams frequently, exhibits a great deal of "excess movement," and is exceedingly clumsy and generally inept in most school-related activities.

Regardless of the sources and symptomology that generates a referral, professional educators must be prepared to *screen* all potential candidates to ascertain whether special education and/or related services are necessary as a result of the perceived disability. It comes as little surprise to experienced educators that many children referred by parents, physicians, and teachers ultimately are not found to be suffering from a handicapping condition. Factors such as poor motivation, inadequate instruction, dull-normal intelligence, and nonstimulating home environments are common reasons for referral but, in most cases, are not qualifications for special education or related services. Children experiencing problems in the home and/or school due to the factors mentioned above are most certainly in need of assistance to overcome their academic and/or social difficulties; however, this assistance must come from the many already existing programs in the schools designed for the nonhandicapped but underachieving and acting out students (such as right-to-read and bilingual programs, remedial math classes, and reality therapy). An appropriately devised screening program, conducted *as an integral part of the referral process*, can do much to identify those pupils whose disabilities are such that they are likely to meet the criteria for possessing a handicapping condition as specified in PL 94–142. Undoubtedly, an initial screening of all referred children is time and cost efficient in selecting only those youngsters who are most probably truly handicapped, as well as beginning alternative non-special education programs for those who can be best helped via this avenue of educational intervention.

For those children exhibiting disorders severe enough to warrant an intensive evaluation, screening activities can be of great benefit. This phase of the referral process can result in the first contact with parents, probing the environments that seem to be particularly deleterious to the child's development, meeting professionals and parents to discuss the variables specific to the individual child, estimating the primary handicapping condition, and developing the structure of the formal evaluation. These factors naturally occurring as a result of the referral procedures are discussed below.

Contact with Parents

As mentioned in Chapter 2, one of the primary features of PL 94–142 is that parents of handicapped children have the legal right to be informed of and included in any educational decisions affecting their off-spring. While logical from all points of view, parent involvement in the educational process is a new and threatening proposition for many of today's school systems. Given the fact that the parents or their surrogates *must be* included in planning their handicapped youngsters' education, it is only reasonable that they be utilized to the fullest potential possible. The utilization of parents can best be obtained from the first moment their children are referred for special services. Usable information such as family relationships, problems that seem to "run in the family," serious health problems, insights into personal habits, routines, and apparent reinforcement systems are frequently only available from the parent and can shed much light on an existing problem. In addition, the first few contacts with the parents should establish a pattern for how they will respond to the school throughout the remainder of the time their child is associated with special education. For this reason, much care must be exercised to ensure that incipient problems do not come to a head by exhibiting a sincere concern for the needs of the child as well as the feelings of the parents. Effort taken with parents in the beginning stages of their child's referral attenuates many ill feelings and confusion that can accompany a youngster's school, social, or medical difficulties. It is recommended that educators wishing information on conducting parent conferences consult Losen and Diament (1978) and Kroth (1977) for detailed discussions of this topic.

In many instances, educationally pertinent information is derived from parents through a questionnaire format. The information obtained through this device may be taken through a personal interaction or simply by sending the form home via the mails. When the questionnaire is sent home, educators are well advised to visit the home or school personally to elaborate on any questions asked and to provide parents with a personal contact in the local school system. Parents should always be encouraged to call their contact person whenever a question arises regarding their child and his/her educational status at any given point in time. Table 3–1 provides a sample parent questionnaire currently used in a local school system. Interested readers are encouraged to study and adapt this form for use in other situations where contact needs to be made with parents of handicapped children.

In a few isolated cases, it is impossible to locate the parents or legal guardians for the child. It may also be that the youngster is a ward of the state under the laws of that state. In these events, the public agency must assign an individual to act as a surrogate for the parents. This selection must be in accordance with existing state law. The person assuming the role of surrogate parent must have no interest that conflicts with the child he/she represents and possess knowledge and skills that ensure adequate representation of the child. The individual assigned as a surro-

TABLE 3–1   Sample Parent Questionnaire

Dear _____,

In an effort to provide _____ with a truly appropriate education, we are beginning to collect any information that might help us in determining his/her specific needs. If you so desire, please complete this short questionnaire and feel free to add any comments you feel would help us in this endeavor. Thank you so much for your continuous assistance.

1. How does your child feel about school?

2. Has he/she ever been in special classes or retained?

3. Have there been any specific problems in school?

4. What about homework and study habits?

5. Does he/she have close friends at school or in the neighborhood?

6. Describe your child's play. (Who does he/she usually play with? What does he/she usually play with? Where does he/she prefer to play?

7. Does he/she belong to any outside organized group?

8. Does he/she have certain duties or chores that he/she is responsible for at home? How does he/she feel about these?

9. How would you describe your child's eating and sleeping habits?

10. What do you consider your child's main problems to be? Is he/she able to talk to you about these problems?

11. How would you say this child gets along with the other members of the family?
    Father
    Mother
    Siblings

12. Who in the family is usually with this child when he/she is at home? Is he/she ever allowed to stay alone?

TABLE 3–1 (*cont.*)

13. Who in your family most often disciplines this child?

14. What kind of punishment generally is used? *For what offenses?* Are certain kinds of punishment more effective than others? How does he/she generally react to punishment?

15. What kinds of rewards are generally used? Which ones seem most effective?

gate may *not* be an employee of a public agency involved in the education or care of the child. The responsibilities of the surrogate parent are to represent the child in all matters related to the identification, evaluation, and educational placement of the child and to ensure that a free and appropriate public education is provided for him/her.

Probing the Environment

In general, there are two reasons for exploring the environment(s) of the child during the referral and screening process: (1) helping determine if the child is truly handicapped or is suffering from environmental factors that are depressing his/her academic and/or social performance, and (2) identifying those environmental settings that may be inhibiting development regardless of whether a handicapping condition exists or not. To illustrate these points, it is a common occurrence to find referred youngsters who are experiencing problems in only one environmental setting (such as science class, PE, or nursery school) and are essentially normal in all other settings. This relatively isolated deficit may or may not be indicative of a handicapping condition; however, most handicapped children typically manifest their disabilities in *every setting* in which they find themselves. A deaf child is not just deaf in school and normally hearing in the home. On the contrary, the handicap of deafness (as well as orthopedically impaired, visually handicapped, and so on) is pervasive throughout the child's total life space. Equally apparent is the fact that special education and related services are needed to assist the child in overcoming the observed disability.

Other handicapping conditions, frequently exhibited as mild to moderate disorders, are not as readily observable or debilitating as severe medical and/or sensory deficits. For example, learning disabilities and educable mental retardation seem to be most pronounced in the academic environment and may or may not be accompanied by emotional overlap. For children with these conditions, environment exploration is particularly important since subtle pressures and interactional patterns are sufficient to exacerbate the existing problem significantly.

Regardless of the type or severity of the referral symptoms, the well-conceived and conducted screening procedure serves to identify those environmental factors that may be contributing to observed problems. Effective environmental analyses necessitate skills in systematic observation as well as knowledge in methodology concerning parent-child and teacher-child interactional systems and sociometric techniques. Using these procedures should permit efficient exploration of a child's divergent environmental settings and their role in facilitating a real or presumed disability.

Often the first step in isolating elements of a child's environment for more in-depth study is using a process called *ecological mapping* (Laten and Katz, 1975). While perhaps most effectively employed with school-aged youngsters, this procedure permits estimating how children "fit" into the various environmental components in which they find themselves. For example, Don, an eighth-grade student, has been referred to special education because his English teacher suspects he is exhibiting behavior patterns indicative of emotional disturbance. In order to determine if this pupil is indeed "seriously emotionally disturbed" to the extent that special education or related services are required, the screening staff have decided to construct an ecological map to determine the extent of the problem. Currently, Don is enrolled in art, shop, PE, history, and social studies in addition to the troublesome English class. As in most junior high schools, Don has different teachers for each class; each teacher has the option to refer students for special services. This student also plays on a baseball team and holds down a part-time job at a local hardware store. Don and his two younger brothers live with their parents in a lower-middle-class neighborhood.

In the process of devising an ecological map, the screening staff contacted each of Don's teachers and his parents to ascertain whether they had noted or had become concerned with his academic performance or social behavior in the last year. With the exception of those who taught art and shop, Don's teachers reported that he was doing slightly below grade-level work and presented little if any behavior problems in their classes. The shop teacher reported that Don was doing the class work expected of him; however, he seemed distraught and anxious when he came to class. It was also noted that the shop class was scheduled immediately following English in the school day. The art teacher indicated that Don's performance remained superior to that of his classmates and that he frequently remained after class to complete assignments. The parents stated that Don was a "good boy" but lately had complained of increased pressures at school. He particularly stressed that his English class was difficult this year. They also commented that Don was enjoying baseball and had not missed a day's work at the hardware store.

With this information, the screening staff was able to make an initial ecological map that depicted Don's current "fits" into his primary environmental settings. The resultant map is provided in Figure 3–1. Perusal of this map indicates that Don's major problems seem to stem from his English and shop classes. Not surprisingly, continued discussions with Don's English teacher indicated that she stressed developing exemplary speech skills and that all students were expected to deliver five extemporaneous speeches of 10 minutes duration during the course of a semester. On Don's first attempt he was very nervous, forgot the major points of his presentation, and refused to go on after presenting for only 90 seconds. She also stated that, while some of the other students in class laughed during and after Don's presentation, she felt he had to overcome his fear by repeating his first presentation and completing the remaining four required for her class. Don's continual outbursts at the prospect of being made to present orally again had led to his referral to special education.

Armed with this information, it became apparent to the screening staff that Don's school-related problems were caused primarily by his interaction in one class and were not exhibited in other classes, the home, or in community-related areas. In all likelihood, Don was not emotionally disturbed and relatively simple modifications of his course schedule, if done in time, would attenuate the perceived problem. Subsequently,

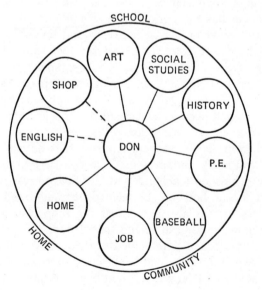

FIGURE 3–1

Don was moved into another English class where public speaking was not required, and his behavior in that class was acceptable to the teacher. In addition, the nervousness and anxiety evident in shop also disappeared when Don was transferred to another English class. This approach to the initial referral and the resultant ecological mapping and screening procedures saved Don, his parents, and the school system much time, effort, and money that would have been expended if Don had been subjected immediately to a formal evaluation. Don's transitory acting out problem was recognized, assessed, and managed without recourse to more intensive, and in this case, irrelevant special education intervention.

The concept of ecological mapping also may be applied to young children whose environmental settings are not as extensive or complex as those of a junior high-aged pupil. In many instances, a structured ecological map may need not even be drawn and the process can be conducted by one professional. An illustration of this is Nick, a four-year-old child, who has just entered nursery school. The teacher immediately noted that the youngster's receptive and expressive language is delayed significantly and that it is impossible for either him to communicate effectively with the other children in the class or they with him. For children of this age and situation, the primary environmental settings include only the school and the home. Upon conferring with the parents, the teacher learned that Nick's language disability certainly has been noted by them and that neighbors and relatives frequently have commented on Nick's problem. In fact, Nick's enrollment in the nursery school was explicitly for the purpose of "helping his speech." Not being qualified to deal with language problems of this magnitude, the teacher suggested that the parents take Nick to the local school system in order to have a complete language evaluation conducted. She felt sure that special education or related services would be necessary for Nick to be able to participate successfully in a regular nursery school program. By determining that Nick's disability was demonstrated in environments other than the school, his teacher confirmed her suspicions that the problem probably was a true handicap and was able to refer the parents to appropriate special education services so as to permit full evaluation of the extent of Nick's communication disorder.

While the process leading to an ecological map is very useful in the referral and screening process, it is sometimes necessary to explore *specific* aspects of environmental settings in order to delimit their influence in causing or maintaining a perceived problem. The more common elements analyzed include parent-child and teacher-child interactional patterns and peer relationships.

Parent-child and teacher-child interactional patterns. As mentioned previously in this section, the educational tool with greatest utility in probing environmental settings is systematic observation. In its more formal form, systematic observation usually is discussed in terms of duration recording, interval recording, continuous recording, and time sampling (Hall, 1970). These techniques have specific criteria for their effective use and yield highly reliable records of an individual's behavior. Many instances, however, do not permit recording of data in a systematized format. For example, visits to the home for conferences with parents may be inappropriate for rigorous coding of information. Many parents would consider such activities unwarranted intrusions and invasions of privacy. In these cases, the professional should endeavor to observe, informally, those events of particular interest. Using the parent questionnaire presented earlier in this chapter can do much to alert the professional to potential problem areas that may require additional study. Most commonly, through a series of interactions with parents, the professional is able to determine whether or not the home environment (interactions between the parent and child) is a contributing factor to the severity of the possible handicapping condition. At the conclusion of the screening process as it pertains to the home environment, it should be possible to (1) gain a perspective of the early stages of the disorders, (2) determine any interaction patterns that are not conducive to normal development, (3) ascertain the manifestation (if any) of the handicap in the home setting, and (4) gain clues as to how best to evaluate and remediate the existing condition.

Exploring teacher-child interactional patterns as they relate to a potentially handicapping condition can be instrumental in determining whether effective learning is taking place within the classroom setting. Differing from parent-child patterns of interaction that must be probed through informal observational strategies, student-teacher interactions are more amenable to structured techniques. Usually, once the referral has been made, the first phase of analyzing this aspect of the classroom environment is to require the teacher to complete a *teacher referral form.* If designed with care, this form can yield data regarding current levels of functioning, behavioral descriptions of the child in question, results of tests that have been administered previously, attendance records, previous sensory screening findings, occupation of the parents, birth dates, and suggested strategies to attenuate the perceived problem. A sample teacher referral form is provided in Table 3–2. As with the parent questionnaire, professionals are encouraged to adapt this device for use in particular school systems. It is important to note that it is not sufficient merely to require a teacher to complete a form when referring a student for special or related services. It is always advisable to follow up with a personal visit with the teacher to clarify elements of his/her responses and to explain the purpose for obtaining any further screening data desired.

TABLE 3–2   Sample Teacher Referral Form

REFERRAL FOR INDIVIDUAL STUDY

To Be Completed by Classroom Teacher   Date Referred _____

Name _____ Date of Birth _____ Age _____

Address _____ Parent _____ Phone _____

School _____ Grade _____ Sex _____ Teacher _____

Father's Occupation _____ Phone _____

Mother's Occupation _____ Phone _____

Referral Approved by Parent: Yes _____   No _____

Reason for Referral:

Academic Progress _____   Suspected Mental Retardation _____

Behavior _____   Vision _____

Emotional _____   Hearing _____

Reading _____   Suspected Language Disability _____

Speech _____

What grade(s) has this child repeated? _____

Has he/she ever attended summer school? _____ Dates _____

List other schools attended, beginning with kindergarten:

School	*City and State*	*Grade Level*
_____	_____	_____
_____	_____	_____
_____	_____	_____
_____	_____	_____
_____	_____	_____

Does the student have a history of excessive absences? _____

If yes, why? _____

TABLE 3-2   (cont.)

Describe student's academic program. Check as many as are applicable.

1. _____ Regular (self-contained)
2. _____ Nongraded
3. _____ Departmentalized
4. _____ Remedial Reading
5. _____ School Counselor
6. _____ Speech Therapy
7. _____ Resource Room
8. _____ Self-Contained Special Education.   Explain _____
9. _____ Integrated Special Education.   Explain _____
10. _____ Pre-vocational
11. _____ Vocational
12. _____ Other.   Explain _____

Describe student's academic weaknesses as you see them _____

_____

_____

_____

_____

Describe student's emotional or behavioral difficulties _____

_____

_____

_____

_____

Describe student's strong points or assets _____

_____

_____

_____

_____

Can this student express his/her thoughts in writing satisfactorily? _____ Yes

._____ No   If no, explain his/her deficiencies _____

_____

_____

TABLE 3-2   (*cont.*)

Can he/she express his/her thoughts orally? _____ Yes _____ No   If answer

is no, explain his/her difficulties _____

_____

In the past, grades have been: Below average _____; Average _____;

Above average _____; Inconsistent _____; Additional Comments _____

_____

_____

List any recent group achievement tests that have been given the student and his/her scores.

_____   _____
Date   Signature of Teacher

Once the completed teacher referral form has been analyzed, it is sometimes necessary to probe the classroom environment in order to determine the communication patterns that exist between the teacher and the child. The reason for this analysis is that recent research has demonstrated that teacher perceptions and expectations can influence academic achievement and general classroom behavior of their students significantly. Such student characteristics as membership in racial and ethnic minority groups, underachievement, sex, and obvious handicapping conditions all have been demonstrated to be strong determinants of teacher behavior (Larsen, 1975; Good and Brophy, 1973; Hoehn, 1954; deGroat and Thompson, 1949; Morrison and McIntyre, 1969; and Good, 1973). It is axiomatic that considering teacher-child interactional patterns can help determine if a student is truly handicapped or is merely an unfortunate pawn of his/her environment. In addition, if a child is judged to be suffering from a handicapping condition, interaction patterns present in the classroom can assist in determining if the specific class is facilitating the youngster's social and/or academic development.

Basically there are two methods available to measure classroom interaction patterns. These include using formal devices that frequently provide data related to reliability and validity. A second method entails using informal techniques that are easily designed and constructed by school personnel. Regardless of whether formal or informal strategies are chosen, they are all predicated upon several fundamental premises:

1. The classroom is an open system, where a myriad of complex interactions are taking place continually.
2. The interaction patterns that do occur are overt.
3. The interaction patterns that are observed can be categorized to permit efficient analyses.

Examples of formal teacher-child interaction systems that are quite popular in the schools include the *Observation Schedule and Record* (OScAR 5) (Medley, Schluck, and Ames, 1968), *Teacher-Child Dyadic Interaction* (Brophy and Good, 1969), and *Flanders' System of Interaction Analysis* (Flanders, 1970). Each of these systems possesses the capacity to yield a significant amount of classroom interaction data from the standpoint of both quality and quantity. Interestingly, the majority of formal observational systems are somewhat complex, require training prior to their effective use, and, consequently, may be beyond the needs and scope of screening procedures in most schools. For those professionals interested in exploring formal systems in more depth, Table 3–3 gives a listing of sample teacher-child interaction systems that span age ranges from nursery to senior high school.

Often the initial probing of teacher-child interaction patterns can be accomplished by using informal techniques. One informal device with great utility has been developed by Bradfield and Criner (1937). In essence, this system permits the observer to indicate variations in a teacher's positive and negative attention to certain students and to record the frequency of those students' nontask behaviors (that is, any behavior that interferes with completing an assignment). The code used to indicate the direction of teacher attention and the frequency of nontask behavior is as follows:

P: Teacher's attention to *positive* behavior ("You're doing fine" or "Very good response").

N: Teacher's attention to *negative* behavior ("Stop doing that!" or "You should be ashamed!").

I: Teacher's instruction (academic or social) to a certain child.

√: Child's nontask behavior.

TABLE 3-3   Teacher Interaction Systems

1. *Reichenberg-Hackett Teacher Behavior Observation System*	Focuses upon nursery school teachers and pupils. Teacher-Behavior is coded according to five major categories.
2. *Teachers Practices Observation Record*	Consists of 62 items grouped into seven categories. Requires little training of observers and possesses high reliability and validity.
3. *Connors-Eisenberg Observation System*	Is appropriate for use in nursery school and elementary grades. Yields three sets of scores that relate to "episodes," "activities," and "overall judgements."
4. *The Purdue Teacher Evaluation Scale*	Is designed to provide junior or senior high school teachers with an evaluation of their performance as seen through the eyes of students.
5. *Classroom Observational Scales*	Bases observations in 12 variables from "pupil attention" to "enthusiasm." Easily learned and administered.
6. *Flanders' System of Interaction Analysis* (Flanders, 1970)	Is intended to gather data on teacher behaviors that restrict or increase student freedom of action. Focuses upon categories of behavior.
7. *Nonverbal Interaction Analysis*	Provides a method of recording nonverbal behavior in classrooms. Designed to parallel the categories of verbal behavior in *Flanders' System of Interaction Analysis.*
8. *Fuller Affective Interactions Records 33* (Fuller, 1969)	Assesses interpersonal behaviors of preservice teachers and their students. Utilizes five interpersonal dimensions.
9. *Teacher-Child Dyadic Interaction* (Brophy & Good, 1969)	Categorizes each teacher-student verbal interaction. Requires 20 hours of training to be used effectively. An excellent research tool.

SOURCE: Wallace, G., and Larsen, S. *Educational assessment of learning problems: Testing for teaching.* Boston: Allyn & Bacon, 1978.

Administering this system is quite simple. To begin, the observer draws five rectangles, four of which represent students of interest and one of which indicates all other students in the class. An illustration of the basic format of this device is given in Figure 3-2. The observation period should last for approximately 10 minutes. The observer should sit with a clear field of vision of the entire class and attempt to indicate the direction of the teacher's attention and the frequency of the student's nontask behaviors.

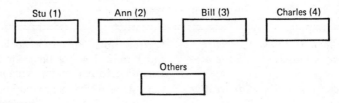

FIGURE 3–2

An example of a complete 10-minute observation period is provided in Figure 3–3. Inspection of this figure indicates that Child 1 did not engage in nontask behavior and received direct instruction once and a negative comment once. Child 2 was given positive attention three times, direct instruction once, and did not demonstrate nontask behavior. Child 3 exhibited nontask behavior four times and was given four negative comments by the teacher during the 10-minute period. Child 4 obtained no direct attention and engaged in nontask behavior only once. Other children in the class received three positive comments from the teacher and did not attend to task on six separate occasions. By tabulating the total number of times the teacher gave positive and negative comments and dividing by 10, it is possible to determine the rate per minute of each type of teacher attention. In addition, the rate of nontask behavior is also possible to ascertain by counting the total number of times it occurred and dividing by 10. Anecdotal records also may be kept by the observer in order to clarify and, in general, flesh out the coding system. These records are quite helpful in analyzing and interpreting the results of the observational process.

The informal approach to coding teacher-child interactions is somewhat subjective when compared to formal procedures. Equally apparent is the fact that this type of observation system provides much information regarding how a given pupil is being attended to within the context of the classroom. Such data are extremely useful in determining if the

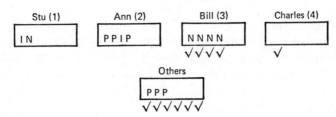

FIGURE 3–3

perceived problem is of a type and severity level that indicates the need for more intensive evaluation to determine the presence of a handicapping condition. Many derivations of the informal procedure discussed above are easily devised by school personnel. Interested readers are encouraged to consult Wallace and Larsen (1978) and Gordon (1966) for examples and discussions of informal techniques useful in analyzing teacher-child interactional patterns.

Peer relationships. An additional aspect of the environment that is frequently deserving of attention during the referral and screening process is peer relationships. Undoubtedly, youngsters who feel at ease and comfortable with peers are far more likely to utilize their various skills and abilities more completely than those who do not. Students referred as a result of a perceived handicap probably are experiencing extraneous problems in relation to their peer culture. It is the responsibility of the screening staff to determine the role of this variable in facilitating successful academic and social development as a prelude to assessing the presence and nature of the reported disability.

One common means of analyzing peer relationships is through behavioral rating scales. A sample listing of selected devices that measure such variables as group problem-solving skills, seating preferences, social status and acceptance, and personal-social needs of students is provided in Table 3–4. In general, these instruments are administered easily and can provide usable information as to how students perceive and react to each other. Some of the data already generated from the teacher referral form can also supply some insight into the peer relationships taking place within a given classroom.

In those instances where commercially produced sociometric techniques are not available or are unsuitable to the particular situation, it is a simple proposition to construct devices that measure social relations in many differing environments. By using these techniques it is possible to delineate children who are definitely liked or disliked as well as the extent of social power and ability to influence others. Fox, Luszki, and Schmuck (1966) have devised a technique based on the "Guess Who" procedure first described by Tyron (1943). "The People in My Class" device presented in Table 3–5 can be employed to analyze a child's perceptions of others in the class, both from the standpoint of popularity and the ability to influence peers. For the potential special education student, this information is invaluable with regard to whether he/she is perceived as a "significant force" by his/her classmates or who he/she particularly emulates and wishes to be like if possible. Screening staff should not hesitate to compose additional questions to tap areas germane to individual children and settings.

TABLE 3–4   Sample Listing of Instruments to Assess Peer Relationships

Instrument	Grade Level	Brief Description
1. Russell Sage Social Relations Test	3–6	Provides information regarding the problem-solving skills of various classroom groups.
2. Syracuse Scales of Social Relations	5–6 6–9; 10–12	Pupil rate types of need relationships with classmates and others.
3. A Class Play	3–7	Peer rating instrument designed to indicate negative, neutral, and positive influences of others.
4. The Class Picture	K–3	Given individually, this scale estimates how students are perceived by their peers.
5. Ohio Social Acceptance Scale	3–6	Consists of six headings: 1. My very, very best friends 2. My other friends 3. Not friends, but okay 4. Don't know them 5. Don't care for them 6. Dislike them Each student is asked to place each of his or her classmates in one of these categories.
6. Minnesota Sociometric Status Test	Preschool and early primary grades	Measures social status or acceptance of students by peers. Testing materials on a board with photographs of every child in the peer group. Each student is interviewed and questioned about the photographs.

SOURCE: Wallace, G., and Larsen, S. *Educational assessment of learning problems: Testing for teaching.* Boston: Allyn & Bacon, 1978.

A very simple procedure to determine leaders, followers, and isolates in a given environment may be obtained by ascertaining participation in classroom or home settings. Observing small group sessions should provide a reliable estimate of those children who are making relevant contributions to an activity. An example of a "participation chart" designed to yield such data is presented in Figure 3–4. As is readily seen, the basic organizational format is simply to list the child's name, record the length of the observational period. and mark the number of times

TABLE 3–5 People in My Class

It is a job of teachers to find ways to make school life more interesting and worthwhile for all the students in the class. This form is your chance to give the teacher confidential information that will help him to help each pupil. *There are no right or wrong answers.* The way you see things is what counts.

1. Which three persons in this class are most often able to get other pupils to do things? Using your class list, write the numbers of the pupils you select.

     Pupil's number

   The three who are most often able to get others to do things are: _____
     _____
     _____

2. Which three persons in the class do the girls most often do things for?

     Pupil's number

   They are: _____
     _____
     _____

3. Which three persons in the class do the boys most often do things for?

     Pupil's number

   They are: _____
     _____
     _____

4. Which three persons in this class are most cooperative with the teacher and like to do what the teacher wants the class to do?

     Pupil's number

   The three most cooperative pupils are: _____
     _____
     _____

5. Which three persons in this class most often go against the teacher and what he would like the class to do?

     Pupil's number

   The three pupils who most often go against the teacher are: _____
     _____
     _____

6. Which three persons in this class do you think could make the biggest improvement in their schoolwork if they wanted to?

     Pupil's number

   The three who could improve most are: _____
     _____
     _____

7. Which three persons in this class do you think show the most ability to learn new things that are taught in school?

SOURCE: Fox, R. S., Luszki, M. B., and Schmuck, R. *Diagnosing classroom learning environments.* Chicago: Science Research Associates, 1966. Used with permission of publisher.

Activity : Language Stimulation

Observer : Ms. McCuller

Length of Session : 15 minutes

Name	Contributions
1. Becky E.	0 0 0 0 0 0
2. Rich G.	X X Δ X X Δ
3. Lee P.	Δ Δ 0 0
4. Howard S.	Δ

Key

0 = relevant contribution made by child
X = irrelevant contribution made by child
Δ = neutral contribution made by child

FIGURE 3–4

a contribution was noted. If desired, annotations also can be recorded to document the quality of the child's statements.

Analysis of the participation chart indicates that Children 1 and 2 are providing the majority of contributions, Child 1 all relevant, and Child 2 mostly irrelevant and neutral. While giving two relevant contributions, Child 3 also exhibited an equal number of neutral statements that may or may not be germane to the topic at hand. Child 4 makes only minimal verbalizations during the activity and may feel uncomfortable in the group or does not possess the basic information needed to be an active participant in the session. The type of data provided by this and other forms permits the screening staff to make determinations regarding a child's relative "placement" within a group and to estimate the amount of learning and productivity taking place on a day-to-day or week-by-week basis.

For school-aged children, the popular sociometric technique commonly referred to as the *sociogram* can also be used effectively (Gronlund, 1976; Wallace and Larsen, 1978; Wiederholt, Brown, and Hammill, 1978; and Cartwright and Cartwright, 1974). When employed, the sociogram yields a map of the classroom that indicates the youngsters with whom a particular child would prefer to study, plan an activity, play, and so on. Using this procedure, it is possible to generate a graphic picture of the social relations currently existing in a given group.

When used as an initial screening technique, the results of a sociometric analysis can identify children who seem to be isolated, socially immature, or seemingly unhappy. When considered with data derived from parents and teachers, this information can aid significantly in determining the extent and manifestations of a possibly existing handicapping condition.

In any event, this information should be considered in the screening meeting that recommends whether a given child is to be subjected to intensive evaluation by appropriately qualified specialists. For those youngsters whose educational problem is obviously the result of negative environment and influences and not due to a handicapping condition, modifications of the environment can be enacted immediately to attenuate the existing learning and/or social disability.

Screening Meeting

At the termination of the referral and screening process (which usually takes no more than three weeks), a meeting should be held to summarize the findings that have been generated regarding a particular child. Participants in the meeting should include the individual who made the initial referral, parents, classroom teacher if available, a school administrator, and the personnel who have participated in collecting and summarizing the screening data. The purpose of the screening meeting is to (1) inform all participants of the results of the screening activities; (2) make a determination whether or not a handicapping condition is likely to exist; (3) if appropriate, obtain necessary parent consent to conduct formal evaluation procedures; (4) formulate plans for the best fashion in which to conduct the formal evaluation; and (5) plan viable educational strategies for those children judged not to be in need of special and/or related services. Accomplishing these purposes will go far to enable a smooth transition into the evaluation process and to ensure that all interested parties are adequately informed as to the educational and/or medical status of a specific child at any given point in time.

It is important to note that the screening meeting is not a legally mandated aspect of PL 94–142 and that there can be no hard and fast rules as to how to conduct the meeting. In addition, determining whether a bona fide handicapping condition is present in the child in question can only be *estimated* at this point. The formal evaluation is required in order to garner, through the use of standardized testing devices, conclusive evidence that a youngster is mentally retarded, learning disabled, hard of hearing, deaf, speech impaired, visually handicapped, seriously emotionally disturbed, deaf-blind, orthopedically impaired, other health impaired, or multihandicapped. One rule of thumb in *estimating* the presence of a handicap is to use the screening data collected on the child to ascertain whether the educational and/or medical disability is severe enough to indicate that special education and/or related services are necessary to ameliorate the condition. If other services offered in the school seem adequate to manage the observed problem, formal evaluation for special education would be inappropriate. If these traditional services prove not to be adequate for the youngster in question, he/she may be referred again at a later date. In the case where other services are not available or the disability is an obvious handicapping condition, formal evaluation procedures should be begun at the earliest possible time.

Once the decision has been made to pursue the formal evaluation, an additional function of the screening meeting is to obtain *parental consent*. It is crucial to note that, according to the regulations governing PL 94–142 (published in the Federal Register on August 23, 1977), parental consent must be obtained prior to conducting a preplacement evaluation of a child. That is to say, *written notice must be provided the parents*, in their native language or mode of communication, as to the precise nature of the evaluation and the records that will be released and to whom. The parent must also be informed that granting consent is voluntary and may be revoked at any time. In addition, parents must be informed that, if the evaluation conducted by the public agency is not acceptable to them, they have the right to obtain an independent educational evaluation at no cost to the parents. The procedures that must be followed if the parent is not in agreement with the evaluation results obtained by the public agency are discussed in Chapter 9. A sample of a form that explains the parents' legal rights and includes a place for them to give their written consent is provided in Table 3–6.

Of course, parents have the right to review records with respect to identifying and evaluating the child at any time. Once the parents are fully informed *and* understand the procedures to be used with their child, they must state *in writing* that the evaluation has their consent. If, by some chance, parents refuse to permit the evaluation of their youngster, procedures are available to circumvent the need for consent for the best interests of the child. If available, state procedures govern the public agency in overriding a parent's refusal to consent. If no state law is available regarding this matter, additional procedures are available. These procedures stipulate that the public agency must initiate an "impartial due process hearing" that is chaired by an impartial hearing officer (that is, someone who is *not* employed by the public agency and has no professional or personal interest that conflicts with his or her objectivity in the hearing). The parents and public agency in the due process hearing have rights to (1) legal counsel and other professional assistance; (2) present evidence and confront, cross examine, and compel the attendance of a witness; (3) prohibit the introduction of any evidence at the hearing that has not been disclosed at least five days before the hearing; (4) obtain a written or electronic verbatim record of the hearing; and (5) obtain written findings of fact and decisions. The hearing may be open to the public and the youngster who is the

TABLE 3–6   Sample Form Explaining Parents' Rights during Evaluation

Dear _____,

It has come to our attention that your child may not be receiving the full benefit of our public education system since all children are eligible for an appropriate education including certain special services. In order to determine
whether or not your child qualifies for these services, it is necessary to test
_____, individually. The procedures and tests recom-
mended include: a behavioral observation in school, individual intelligence
test, math, reading and language arts assessments, and speech and hearing
assessment. The results of the testing will be used by the school team to
develop an individual educational program for _____
so that we can better serve him/her. The tests are offered at no cost to you,
and you will be invited to review and discuss the results with us as soon as
the assessment is completed.

We also want to assure you that no change in _____'s classes
will be made until discussing _____'s needs and our school
district's services with you. Below you will find a list of all your rights regarding this testing and we urge you to call us if you have any questions before
signing this permission form. Your rights include:

1. The right to look at all the school records about your child.
2. The right to have all results of the testing clearly explained.
3. The right to take part in any meeting held by the individual education
   program team and evaluation team.
4. The right to get independent testing of your child.
5. The right not to give permission for any suggested individual testing.
6. The right to make a complaint and appeal to either school team about anything having to do with the assessment, placement, or plans for special
   services for your child.
7. The right to a due process hearing held by an impartial hearing officer.

Thank you so much for your continued cooperation in helping us plan an
appropriate education program for _____. Once again, don't
hesitate to call our office at _____ and ask for _____.

I do understand my rights as parent regarding the educational testing of my
child and would like at this time to formally request that the school proceed
to test _____ in an effort to provide him/her with an appropriate education.

_____   _____
Date   Signature

subject of the hearing may also be present if desired. If the impartial hearing officer upholds the agency, the agency may evaluate or initially provide special education and related services to the child *without* the parents' consent. Appeals regarding the hearing decision are possible for both the parents and public agency. The child's status during the hearing procedures and subsequent appeals (if any) is that he/she must remain in the present educational placement. The specific regulations governing the rights of the parents and public agency are delineated in depth in the Education of Handicapped Children: Implementation of Part B of the Education of the Handicapped Act (document FR 77–24033). Interested readers are encouraged to consult this document since it contains all the regulations dictating the procedures for evaluating and developing the individualized educational program of handicapped children. The sections of this document that particularly pertain to the evaluation process include subpart E, sections 121a.500–505 and 121a.530–534.

Assuming that the screening meeting results in the parents granting their consent to the evaluation, a final step is to formulate a plan that suggests how best to conduct the formal evaluation. In fact, a description of each evaluation procedure, test, record, or report must be agreed upon in writing by the public agency and the parents prior to their being administered or composed. Ideally, the screening meeting should culminate in some indication of the areas of educational or medical conditions that are most in need of exploration. Specific tests to probe these areas may be delimited and, if possible and appropriate, the child should be consulted to determine his/her wishes and desires in the matter. A time schedule should be established as to when it is reasonable to expect the evaluation to be completed and the individual educational program written. All parties should be encouraged to keep in contact during the evaluation period so as to circumvent any problems that might arise or to answer questions regarding procedures being employed. There can be little doubt that, if properly conducted, the screening meeting can do much to ease the fears and anxieties of the parents and child as well as adding structure to the evaluation process. The specific components of the educational evaluation are discussed in the following sections of this chapter.

EVALUATING HANDICAPPED STUDENTS

Upon completing the referral and screening process and obtaining written parental consent, an evaluation of the perceived handicapping condition is initiated. In this instance, *evaluation* refers to procedures used to determine

> whether a child is handicapped and the nature and extent of the special education and related services the child needs. The term means procedures used selectively with an individual child and does not include basic tests administered to or procedures used with all children in a school, grade, or class. (Implementation of Part B of Education of the Handicapped Act, 1977, p. 42494)

The primary purpose of the evaluation is to document by means of individual testing that a given child or adolescent does or does not meet the criteria for inclusion in one of the 11 categorical areas of handicapping conditions stipulated under existing law. This "evaluation for placement" is primarily administrative in orientation and is not necessarily intended to yield instructionally relevant data. Deriving instructionally usable information comes during a later phase in developing the individualized educational program.

The first step in becoming knowledgeable regarding the evaluation process is to define explicitly as possible what actually constitutes a handicapping condition. When coupled with available screening data, information as to the particular elements of each disability area is very helpful in selecting appropriate evaluative techniques. It is obvious that tests appropriate to adaptive behavior, while indispensable to the evaluation of the mentally retarded, may or may not be needed in assessing the visually handicapped. This and similar decisions as to using specific evaluation techniques can only be made after becoming thoroughly familiar with the "definition" of *each* handicapping condition. The various disability areas mentioned in the implementation of part B of the Education of the Handicapped Act are discussed in the following section.

Handicapping Conditions

It is a rare professional or lay person who does not have some preconceived notion as to what entails a handicapping condition. Many states and local school systems have formulated their own disparate and idiosyncratic definitions of given disability areas. Let there be no doubt, however, that all public agencies must, in order to be in compliance with federal law, utilize the terms mentioned both in PL 94–142 and its subsequent rules and regulations. These categorical areas include mentally retarded, hard of hearing, deaf, specific learning disabilities, speech impaired, seriously emotionally disturbed, visually handicapped, deaf-blind, orthopedically impaired, other health impaired, and multihandi-capped. The "definitions" of these terms, taken from the implementation of part B of the Education of the Handicapped Act are provided below.

Mentally retarded means significantly subaverage general intellectual functioning existing concurrently with deficits in adaptive behavior and manifested during the developmental period that adversely affects a child's educational performance.

Hard of hearing means a hearing impairment, whether permanent or fluctuating, that adversely affects a child's educational performance but which is not included under the definition of deaf.

Deaf means a hearing impairment so severe that the child is impaired in processing linguistic information through hearing, with or without amplification, that adversely affects educational performance.

Specific learning disabilities means a disorder in one or more of the basic psychological processes involved in understanding or in using language, spoken or written, that may manifest itself in an imperfect ability to listen, think, speak, read, write, spell, or to do mathematical calculations. The term includes such conditions as perceptual handicaps, brain injury, minimal brain dysfunction, dyslexia, and developmental aphasia. The term does not include children who have learning problems that are primarily the result of visual, hearing, or motor handicaps, of mental retardation, or of environmental, cultural, or economic disadvantage.

Speech impaired means a communication disorder, such as stuttering, impaired articulations, language impairment, or voice impairment, that adversely affects a child's educational performance.

Seriously emotionally disturbed is defined as follows:

A. The term means a condition exhibiting one or more of the following characteristics over a long period of time and to a marked degree that adversely affects educational performance:
   1. An inability to learn that cannot be explained by intellectual, sensory, or health factors
   2. An inability to build or maintain satisfactory interpersonal relationships with peers and teachers
   3. Inappropriate types of behavior or feeling under normal circumstances
   4. A general and pervasive mood of unhappiness or depression
   5. A tendency to develop physical symptoms or fears associated with personal or school problems
B. The term includes children who are schizophrenic or autistic. The term does not include children who are socially maladjusted, unless it is determined that they are seriously emotionally disturbed.

Visually handicapped means a visual impairment that, even with correction, adversely affects a child's educational performance. The term includes both partially seeing and blind children.

Deaf-blind means concomitant hearing and visual impairments, the combination of which causes such severe communication and other developmental and educational problems that they cannot be accommodated in special education programs solely for deaf or blind children.

Orthopedically impaired means a severe orthopedic impairment that adversely affects a child's educational performance. The term includes impairments caused by congenital anomaly (such as clubfoot or absence of some member), impairments caused by disease (such as poliomyelitis or bone tuberculosis), and impairments from other causes (such as cerebral palsy, amputations, and fractures or burns that cause contractures).

Other health impaired means limited strength, vitality, or alertness due to chronic or acute health problems such as heart condition, tuberculosis, rheumatic fever, nephritis, asthma, sickle-cell anemia, hemophilia, epilepsy, lead poisoning, leukemia, or diabetes that adversely affects a child's educational performance.

Multihandicapped means concomitant impairments (such as mentally retarded-blind or mentally retarded-orthopedically impaired), the combination of which causes such severe educational problems that they cannot be accommodated in special education programs solely for one of the impairments. The term does not include deaf-blind children.

Perusing these "definitions" of the various handicapping conditions reveals several interesting considerations. Importantly, they tend to be quite general in scope. The reason for the lack of specificity is undoubtedly to permit public agencies some flexibility in interpreting the parameters of the conditions. The particular levels of severity that must be demonstrated in order to qualify for one of the disability areas varies from state to state and school system to school system. Each public agency needs to establish its own guidelines and criteria by which to admit children in their purview into special education.

While the definitions of handicapping conditions permit public agencies the opportunity to develop their own criteria for inclusion, they do indicate broad areas that need to be addressed in the evaluation process. For example, if the referred child gives indications of suffering from mental retardation, it is apparent that IQ and adaptive behavior are relevant considerations for the individual(s) conducting the evaluation. Deaf, hard of hearing, and visually handicapped children probably should be seen by a physician to determine the physical condition causing the disorder, whether it is progressive, can be corrected, or is of a permanent nature. In addition, evaluative efforts should include acuity testing and determination of which (if any) amplification devices may be used to attenuate the manifestations of the condition. This information leads to an understanding of the nature of the handicapping condition and the extent of the special education and related services required by the child.

Prior to identifying and evaluating specific children, it is essential for professionals to be thoroughly familiar with the procedures and safeguards provided in the rules and regulations of PL 94–142. Knowledge of these procedures is necessary to ensure that the child is in receipt of his/her rights as granted under the law and that public agencies are protected against possible legal action that may be taken by the child, parents, or their surrogates. The following section discusses evaluation procedures that must be considered in each evaluation conducted on handicapped children in the United States.

Evaluation Procedures and Safeguards

The evaluation procedures utilized with handicapped youngsters are of great importance in that *prior to any action being taken with respect to initial placement of a handicapped child in a special education program,* a full and individual evaluation of the child's educational needs must be conducted. As a result of this stipulation, it is crucial to conduct the evaluation with all due speed to minimize the time before an individualized educational program is written and the youngster begins to receive services. The speed with which the evaluation is conducted must not, however, result in violation of the child's rights as specified in the rules and regulations of PL 94–142.

The safeguards built into the evaluation of handicapped children are straightforward and serve to ensure that the best interests of the child are being served. To illustrate, testing and evaluation materials and procedures used for the purposes of evaluation and placement of handicapped children must be selected and administered so as not to be racially or culturally discriminatory. State and local education agencies must ensure, at a minimum, that tests and other evaluation materials:

1. are provided and administered in the child's native language or other mode of communication, unless it is clearly not feasible to do so;
2. have been validated for the specific purpose for which they are used;
3. are administered by trained personnel in conformance with the instructions provided by their producer;

4. tests and other evaluation materials include those tailored to assess specific areas of educational need and not merely those which are designed to provide a single general intelligence quotient;

5. tests are selected and administered so as best to ensure that when a test is administered to a child with impaired sensory, manual, or speaking skills, the test results accurately reflect the child's aptitude or achievement level or whatever other factors the test purports to measure, rather than reflecting the child's impaired sensory, manual, or speaking skills (except where those skills are the factors which the test purports to measure);

6. no single procedure is used as the sole criterion for determining an appropriate educational program for a child;

7. the evaluation is made by a multidisciplinary team or group of persons, including at least one teacher or other specialist with knowledge in the area of sensory disability;

8. the child is assessed in all areas related to the suspected disability, including, where appropriate, health, vision, hearing, social and emotional status, general intelligence, academic performance, communicative status, and motor abilities (Implementation of Part B of the Education of the Handicapped Act, 1977, pp. 42496–42497).

The evaluation procedures just mentioned apply to all handicapping conditions. That is, children suspected of being mentally retarded, multihandicapped, deaf, or visually handicapped must be evaluated in compliance with these stipulations. Additional procedures have also been developed specific to the category of *specific learning disabilities*. Published in the Federal Register on December 29, 1977, these procedures were intended to *supplement* (not supplant) the existing regulations governing the evaluation process. The major components addressed in the additional procedures for evaluating specific learning disabilities include team members, criteria for determining the existence of a specific learning disability, observation, and the written report.

Additional team members. In evaluating a child suspected of possessing a specific learning disability, each public agency must include on the multidisciplinary team: (1) the child's regular teacher or, if the child does not have a regular teacher, a regular classroom teacher qualified to teach a child of his or her age; (2) for a child of less than school age, an individual qualified by the state educational agency to teach a

77

child of his or her age; and (3) at least one person qualified to conduct individual diagnostic examination of children.

Criteria for determining the existence of a specific learning disability. A team may determine that a child has a specific learning disability if the child does not achieve commensurate with his or her age and ability levels when provided with learning experiences appropriate for the child's age and ability levels (that is, exhibits a "severe discrepancy"). The areas in which to conduct the evaluation include (1) oral expression, (2) listening comprehension, (3) written expression, (4) basic reading skill, (5) reading comprehension, (6) mathematical calculation, or (7) mathematical reasoning. The team may not identify a child as having a learning disability if the severe discrepancy between ability and achievement is primarily the result of a visual, hearing, or motor handicap, mental retardation, emotional disturbance, or environmental, cultural, or economic disadvantage.

Observation. At least one team member other than the child's regular teacher must observe the child's academic performance in the regular classroom setting. With a child of less than school age or out of school, a team member shall observe the child in an environment appropriate for a child of that age.

Written report. At the conclusion of the evaluation, the team must prepare a written report that includes statements of (1) whether the child has a specific learning disability, (2) basis for making the determination, (3) relevant behavior noted during observation of the child, (4) relationship of the behavior to the child's academic functioning, and (5) the educationally relevant medical findings, if any. The report must also delineate the severe discrepancy that exists between achievement and ability that is not correctable without special education and related services. The written report must also show that the specific learning disability is not because of the effects of environmental, cultural, or economic disadvantage. If a team member disagrees with any of the conclusions reached by the total team, he/she must submit a separate statement presenting his/her conclusions.

The results of evaluating learning disabled as well as all other categories of handicapping conditions are to be used in making the placement decisions regarding the best educational environment for a given youngster. To accomplish this, interpretation of evaluation must:

1. Draw upon information from a variety of sources, including aptitude and achievement tests, teacher recommenda-

tions, physical condition, social or cultural background, and adaptive behavior;

2. Insure that information obtained from all of these sources is documented and carefully considered;

3. Insure that the placement decision is made by a group of persons, including persons knowledgeable about the child, the meaning of the evaluation data, and the placement options. (Implementation of Part B of the Education of the Handicapped Act, 1977, p. 42497)

From the regulations regarding placement procedures, it is evident that the accuracy of the evaluation is essential in terms of determining whether a handicapping condition is, in fact, present and, by its presence, is severe enough to warrant the services of special education. The evaluation should also serve to define those broad areas of disability that are of definite concern to those who will be effecting the individualized educational program.

As with the definitions of handicapping conditions, the evaluation procedures are somewhat general. In other words, they *do not specify particular tests* that must be used to evaluate areas of educational need. This is done to permit qualified examiners the opportunity to use their own judgment as to which assessment tools would be most appropriate for a given situation. Selecting tests must be done with care since the primary component of the evaluation is to gear it to the specific and unique needs of the child suspected of having a handicapping condition.

Since the evaluation is intended to document the presence of a handicap, the majority of tests and other evaluation materials employed are standardized in format. This is because standardized tests (that is, tests with known reliability and validity that provide normative data to compare a child's score with those of a group) yield numerical scores that can be easily interpreted. It is also possible to determine the adequacy of standardized tests at least as they relate to such technical features as item analysis, content validity, standard error of measurement, and so forth. Consequently, defending scores generated from appropriately chosen and administered tests and testing materials becomes a realistic proposition. Only rarely do school systems use procedures that have not been standardized (at least in some fashion) for purposes of the evaluation. When nonstandardized devices are employed, it is usually because no standardized test is available to tap the behavior of concern or the norms of existing tests have been based upon populations with whom the potentially handicapped child has little in common. For example, using spoken language tests that have been standardized on white, middle-class children clearly would be inappropriate for a black or Mexican-American youngster who resides in a low-income neighborhood where a subdialect of English is spoken in the home. Such a test would not yield valid information regarding the child's suspected disability and would, in all probability, violate his/her rights granted under the law. In some states, school systems have been successfully sued by parents whose children have been placed inappropriately in special education because the tests used in the evaluation were either racially or culturally discriminatory to them. In situations where no appropriate standardized test is available to assess the suspected area of disability, using informal, nonstandardized techniques is necessitated. Where this occurs, the evaluation team should be well advised to *state in writing* why such devices were used and how they were interpreted to determine the presence or absence of a handicapping condition. The rationale should be well grounded and logical enough to stand up in a court of law if necessary.

The evaluation conducted with children suspected of having a handicapping condition must address all areas potentially related to the disability. As mentioned previously, the rules and regulations of PL 94–142 include the areas of health, vision, hearing, social and emotional status, general intelligence, academic performance, communicative status, and motor abilities. Undoubtedly, most children would not require evaluation in each area; however, some, by nature of their handicap(s), would need such broad-based assessment. In addition, other areas of behavior also should be given consideration in some instances (such as adaptive behavior). Which areas to evaluate and which tests and other evaluation materials to use is decided by the multidisciplinary team. The most common areas related to suspected areas of disabilities and tests and materials designed to evaluate those areas are discussed in the following section.

Evaluating Suspected Handicapping Conditions

The evaluation of children suspected of having a handicapping condition is made by a multidisciplinary team of persons including at least one teacher or other specialist with knowledge in the area of supposed disability. Ideally the team should include the parents or their surrogates, a person qualified to administer tests that require special training (such as the *Wechsler Intelligence Scale for Children*), the child's regular classroom teacher, if available, and, as needed, other professionals who may possess knowledge helpful in isolating specific parameters of the disorder. Representatives from the local school system's administrative staff should also be on the team as regularly attending members. The composition of the evaluation team *must* be fluid. Care must be exercised so the most appropriately qualified specialists, given the suspected handicapping condition under question, are invariably included. It is inconceivable, for example, that the exact same team members would serve to evaluate a child who may possibly suffer from a visual handicap and a child who is evidencing symptoms of severe emotional disturbance. Two such children require decidedly different evaluation strategies and techniques to assess their educational problems. Consequently, membership on the evaluation team should be based solely on knowledge of the child, skills in assessing the suspected disability, and information regarding services available for children with varying handicapping conditions.

Predicated upon the referral and screening data gathered prior to the evaluation, the team decides (1) the most likely handicapping condition(s) present in the child based upon behavioral manifestations, and (2) the tests and evaluation materials necessary to document the suspected disability(ies). This phase of the evaluation is crucial in that cogent judgments of the child's educational and medical status result in time and energy efficiency for both the team and the child. To illustrate, if a child were referred for primary academic underachievement (with no evidence of sensory deficits or emotional problems), the probable first thought of the team would be that the youngster is either mentally retarded or learning disabled. The primary feature differing in these two conditions is intelligence or potential to do grade-level schoolwork. The team may decide to administer a standardized intelligence test to determine if "significantly subaverage intellectual functioning" is exacerbating the problem. "Subaverage intellectual functioning" is defined by individual state education agencies. In many states, this phrase is defined as scoring two standard deviations below the mean on a standardized intelligence test. If the child is found to have normal or near normal intelligence, the category of mental retardation will be excluded as a potentially handicapped condition and the behaviors and criteria associated with the category of specific learning disabilities should be probed in more depth. Consequently, there would be no mandated need to probe the child's "adaptive behavior" since this is a criterion most commonly associated with mental retardation.

It is self-evident that, as a prelude to efficient evaluation, the team must be thoroughly familiar with the definitions of the various handicapping conditions discussed earlier in this chapter. These definitions, as well as those supplied at the state level, structure the observations as well as the tests and evaluation materials employed in the evaluation. When coupled with the peculiarities of the individual child as reported during the referral and screening process, this information should point up areas in need of more intensive study. When evaluated, each area serves to delimit the handicapping conditions in which the child most logically "fits." The evaluation team should never lose sight of the fact that the termination of the evaluation must result in either (1) a *specification* as to which handicapping area the child is judged to possess, or (2) the determination that the child is, in actuality, not handicapped. The areas in which to conduct the evaluation are discussed below. As stated previously, the *specific* levels of deficit that need to be documented in order to classify a child as handicapped are determined by individual state education agencies and not the federal government. The tests and other evaluation materials mentioned under each area are *not intended to be inclusive.* Rather, they are for purposes of illustration only.

Intelligence. The concept of intelligence has long been considered in education. During most evaluations conducted by public agencies, a child's intelligence is routinely assessed. This is done to determine if the child is mentally retarded and to gain some estimate of how rapidly the youngster can progress in mastery of concepts (that is, the prognosis) regardless of the handicapping condition he/she is judged to have. Intelligence testing frequently has been said to measure primarily what the child has learned related to adequate performance in school rather than "intelligence" in general. While this fact is undoubtedly true in some instances, the fact remains that the IQ score is an adequate predictor of later school performance. It is important to realize that the intelligence test has been criticized roundly as it applies to the culturally or economically different child. When intelligence tests are used with such children, it is imperative to scrutinize the tests to determine if they are appropriate with the youngster under question. In some cases, adaptations of intelligence tests must be made to ensure that they are administered in the native language of the child (that is, language spoken by the parents) or assess elements that the child has had experience with. When used in this way, intelligence tests must be normed on the population with which they will be used.

   In essence, intelligence tests are designed to *sample* behaviors indicative of "intelligent" behavior. The domains hypothesized to underlie intelligence in most tests include discrimination, sequencing, memory, vocabulary, motor skill, analysis, abstract reasoning, pattern completion, and general information. It is axiomatic that as with all other devices, intelligence tests are influenced by a child's idiosyncratic characteristics, abilities, and deficits. It is necessary to exercise extreme care when interpreting the results of intelligence tests and to realize that they only *superficially* estimate a youngster's true intellectual skills. If used appropriately and in light of their specific weaknesses, intelligence tests can provide invaluable assistance in documenting the presence of a handicapping condition.

Most tests of intelligence used in the evaluation are given individ-ually. The most commonly employed individual tests of intelligence in-clude the *Stanford-Binet Intelligence Scale* (Sattler, 1974), *Wechsler Scales* (Wechsler, 1949, 1967, 1974), *Slosson Intelligence Test* (Slosson, 1971), and the *Peabody Picture Vocabulary Test* (Dunn, 1965). In addi-tion to these tests, which are designed for use with "normal" children and adults, other scales have been built for special populations. These scales have been devised primarily to accommodate various handicapped populations. For example, the *Nebraska Test of Learning Aptitude* (Hiskey, 1966) is designed to assess the learning potential of deaf and hard of hearing children between the ages of 3 and 16; the *Blind Learn-ing Aptitude Test* (Newland, 1969) assesses learning aptitude of pre-school and primary-aged blind children; *Arthur Adaptation of the Leiter International Performance Scale* (Arthur, 1950) was developed for chil-dren who may experience verbal problems—the deaf, hard of hearing, articulatorily impaired, bilingual, nonstandard speakers of English; and the *Pictorial Test of Intelligence* (French, 1964) requires no verbal re-sponse from the child and may be used with normal as well as handi-capped youngsters.

Selecting an individual test of intelligence is, of course, entirely within the purview of each evaluation committee. Criteria for selection should center around such variables as the adequacy of norms, reliability, and validity. Each test should be carefully surveyed to ascertain the type of items used, response mode required, and the scores yielded at the conclusion of the test. Readers who wish to study intelligence testing in more depth should consult Salvia and Ysseldyke (1978), Anastasi (1976), and Gronlund (1976). Each of these texts provides excellent reviews, discussions, and critiques of commonly used intelligence tests.

Sensory. Assessing visual and auditory acuity is an integral part of many evaluations. In instances where a child is suspected of being hard of hearing, deaf, deaf-blind, or visually handicapped, acuity testing is the cornerstone of the evaluation effort. Results of such assessment docu-ment that a child does, indeed, have sensory deficits that adversely affect his/her communication ability and/or educational performance. In all probability, acuity testing should also be conducted with any child re-ferred for special education or related services. Difficulties in receiving environmental stimuli certainly would impair *any* handicapped child's ability to perform at the level he/she is capable. For this reason, acuity assessment should be routine in most, if not all, evaluations of children suspected of having a handicapping condition.

Evaluating visual acuity usually involves measuring far- and near-point vision. While most persons are familiar with the *Snellen E Test* (to indicate the direction the letter E is facing at the distance of 20 feet with the stimulus becoming continually smaller), it only evaluates acuity at a far point. Comprehensive tests of visual skills, commonly used in today's schools and clinics, assess both near- and far-point vision. The specific skills measured include fusion, vertical and lateral eye posture, depth perception, and usable vision of the eyes separately and together. The tests most frequently employed to evaluate near- and far-point vision include the *Keystone Telebinocular, Bausch and Lomb Orthorater,* and the *Titmus Vision Tester.* The range of these techniques is from preschool to adulthood. Unfortunately, the comprehensive devices are somewhat expensive; however, they do tend to be diagnostically accurate. That is, they do indicate those children who do indeed have visual handicaps.

Evaluating auditory skills is usually accomplished with an audiometer. The audiometers employed in the schools assess acuity by presenting *pure tones* to the student through earphones and asking for a response when the sound is heard. The test results indicate a child's hearing proficiency at differing levels of loudness and frequency. More advanced forms of auditory testing go beyond mere acuity assessment and can yield data regarding auditory discrimination, speech-reception threshold, adequacy of the middle and inner ear, and degree of "central deafness."

The levels of sensory deficit qualifying as handicapping conditions in relation to hard of hearing, deaf, deaf-blind, and visually handicapped are determined by state education agencies. Evaluation of auditory and visual acuity may be conducted by a variety of personnel. Since the evaluation of potentially handicapped persons must be more than what is routinely done for all children in a school or clinic, this evaluation should be done by someone specifically trained in this aspect of evaluation. For example, the audiologist that can be typically located in university clinics and larger school systems is the most logical person to consult in the case of suspected hearing loss. He/she has access to the necessary equipment and expertise to do a reliable and valid evaluation of possibly significant auditory deficits. Vision specialists are also knowledgeable in acuity testing and should be utilized when appropriate. In any event, the evaluation of sensory acuity should be undertaken only by those professionals who, through training and qualification, are competent to conduct the type of assessment necessary to identify deficits that unquestionably impair a child's ability to process sensory information and achieve in school. Readers desiring additional information in sensory evaluation are encouraged to read the bulletins of the National Society for the Prevention of Blindness (1961) and United States Public Health Service (1971), Barraga (1976), Newland (1971), Berg and

Fletcher (1970), and O'Neill and Oyer (1966). These references supply discussions of tests and techniques necessary to assess a child's possible defects in sensory acuity.

Academic performance. The evaluation of academic performance is usually done in two phases. The first phase entails administering *individualized* tests of achievement for the purpose of probing for *general* areas of difficulty. The second phase, when undertaken, involves a more detailed analysis of a child's ability in specific curricular areas (that is, reading, math, and written expression). The academic performance of any child who exhibits academic problems in relation to the suspected handicapping condition should be assessed. Of course, the category of specific learning disabilities is predicated upon documenting a "severe discrepancy between achievement and intellectual ability." In part, verifying the existence of a learning disability must entail evaluating academic abilities (or the lack of them). For children of preschool age, it is sometimes valuable to measure the child's readiness for school. These tests are useful in *predicting* a child's chances of adequately mastering various curricular areas.

In order to document the existence of academic problems of a severe nature, the screening committee may choose to administer an individual achievement test. At present, there are essentially only two norm-referenced tests designed to be given individually. The *Peabody Individual Achievement Test* (Dunn and Markwardt, 1970) samples five areas: mathematics, reading recognition, reading comprehension, spelling, and general information. While there is some difficulty with some of the subtest reliabilities, this instrument does serve to identify general areas of deficit worthy of further evaluation in grades kindergarten through 12.

The *Wide Range Achievement Test* (WRAT) (Jastak and Jastak, 1965) measures performance in reading, spelling, and arithmetic. The test spans two levels: level 1 for youngsters less than 12 years of age and level 2 for those older than 12. The WRAT may be used to gain some idea of a child's achievement level; however, it suffers from extreme weakness in the fashion in which it was normed and the actual items that are employed to sample the curricular areas of concern. Of the two individualized achievement tests, the *Peabody Individual Achievement Test* is superior and should be used when possible.

Once the general areas of academic deficit have been determined through individually administered achievement tests, teacher referral, or other means, it may be desirable to document significant problems in specific areas of the curriculum. The areas of the curriculum that are most often assessed include reading, mathematics, and written expression. Examples of evaluation tools of a normative nature in the area of reading are the *Gray Oral Reading Test* (Gray and Robinson, 1967), *Gilmore Oral Reading Test* (Gilmore and Gilmore, 1968), *Gates-McKillop Reading Diagnostic Tests* (Gates and McKillop, 1962), *Stanford Diagnostic Reading Test* (Karlsen, Madden, and Gardner, 1976), and the *Silent Reading Diagnostic Tests* (Bond, Balow, and Hoyt, 1970). The domains of reading sampled by these and most reading tests include word-attack skills, word-recognition skills, rate of reading, and other related reading behaviors. The evaluation team must peruse the technical features of whatever test is chosen for use carefully. Many devices available in this and other curricular areas have remarkably low reliabilities and validities and questionable norms. They can be used for purposes of evaluation, however, when supplemented with other, more school-related data pertaining to the child's actual performance in academic areas addressed in the classroom.

The curricular area of mathematics is not as replete with normative instruments as is the area of reading. The primary tests available include the *Key Math Diagnostic Arithmetic Test* (Connolly, Nachtman, and Pritchett, 1971), and the *Stanford Diagnostic Mathematics Test* (Beatty, Madden, Gardner, and Karlsen, 1976). These devices sample knowledge in number systems, computation, counting, geometry, fractions, reasoning, problem solving, money, applications, and other associated knowledge bases. Both tests report reliability, validity, and normative data. In addition, they are easily administered and can be employed in a criterion-related fashion. As with reading assessment, it is always wise to supplement test results with other documentation to verify the existence of a severe and pervasive mathematical disability.

Written expression has been much neglected as it relates to handicapping conditions. The domains of concern in written expression encompass the mechanics or conventions (handwriting, punctuation, capitalization, spelling) and the more symbolic aspects such as word usage, syntax, and creativity. At present, there are only two available individualized norm-referenced tests: the *Test of Written Language* (Hammill and Larsen, 1978) and the *Picture Story Language Test* (Myklebust, 1965). Each of these instruments asks a child to look at a set of pictures and to write a story that tells "what the pictures are about." From the story, different scores are obtained as to the particulars of the child's writing ability. The *Test of Written Language* includes subtests for the domains of word usage, spelling, capitalization, and punctuation. These scores may then be corroborated with the youngster's actual written output as provided in the story written. One individual, diagnostic, and norm-referenced test of spelling is also available. The *Test of Written Spelling* (Larsen and Hammill, 1976) is adequate to assess this particular component of written expression.

Predicting academic performance of preschool-aged youngsters may be a concern to the evaluation team. This information is particularly necessary in cases where the child is suspected of being mentally retarded or having a specific learning disability. In addition, in any situation where the child is likely to enter the regular school environment, readiness tests may provide insight into the amount of special education and related services needed to make the youngster's matriculation into the regular school as smooth as possible. Illustrations of school readiness tests with reliability, validity, and normative data include the *Test of Basic Experiences* (Moss, 1972), *Lee-Clark Reading Readiness Test* (Lee and Clark, 1962), *Boehm Test of Basic Concepts* (Boehm, 1971), *Denver Development Screening Test* (Frankenberg, Dodds, and Fondal, 1970), *Basic School Skills Inventory* (Goodman and Hammill, 1975), and the *Metropolitan Readiness Test* (Nurss and McGauvran, 1976). Most of these devices permit individual analysis of a given student for purposes of estimating the youngster's orientation to curricular skills and knowledge prerequisite to beginning instruction. Whatever test is chosen for use, it should be concluded that the items utilized do, in fact, tap skills that are *essential to the curriculum* in which the child will be placed. It is highly wasteful to assess areas that will not be of relevance in making educational decisions.

There are many excellent reference sources for professionals interested in evaluating academic performance. Of particular help are Wallace and Larsen (1978), Salvia and Ysseldyke (1978), Hammill and Bartel (1978), and Otto, McMenemy, and Smith (1973).

Sociobehavioral status and adaptive behavior. Sociobehavioral status and adaptive behavior are of particular concern to the categories of mental retardation and the seriously emotionally disturbed. Documenting deficits in these areas is essential for assignment to one of these two handicapping conditions. It is easily conceivable that these areas may also be of educational concern in determining the severity and extent of other disabilities. It is common knowledge that any handicap can frequently cause a child to suffer from problems that affect the way in which he/she interacts with the environment in general and his/her parents, siblings, peers, and teachers in particular. In cases such as this, the evaluation team undoubtedly should choose to assess sociobehavioral status. Where the handicap is severe, adaptive behavior tests can shed some light on the general competency of the child when dealing with various tasks that are demanded in daily living.

The evaluation of sociobehavioral status of a youngster may be conducted in a variety of ways. In today's schools and clinics behavioral rating scales are most commonly employed. Regrettably, many such instruments do not supply reliability, validity, or norms upon which educational decisions may be based. Importantly, unless supplemented with numerous behavioral statements from teachers and parents, rating scales are difficult to defend in and of themselves. In all likelihood, effective evaluation of sociobehavioral status requires a combination of norm-referenced tests *and* individualized ratings of the child's behavior in situations where he/she is experiencing particular problems.

In general, there are five basic categories of evaluating sociobehavioral measures: general personality, emotional development, interests, behavioral traits, and self-concept (Walker, 1973). These categories may be assessed by using observational techniques, self-report scales, projective procedures, and rating scales. Examples of measures in general personality and emotional development include the *Holtzman Inkblot Technique* (Holtzman, 1966), *California Test of Personality* (Thorpe, Clark, and Tiegs, 1953), *Family Relations Test* (Bene and Anthony, 1957), and the popular *Thematic Apperception Test* (Murray, 1943). Interests are commonly tapped by *A Book About Me* (Jay, 1955), and *Kuder Personal Preference Record* (Kuder, 1954). Behavioral traits are measured by the *Basic School Skills Inventory* (Goodman and Hammill, 1975), *Walker Problem Behavior Identification Check List* (Walker, 1970), and the *Peterson-Quay Problem Behavior Checklist* (Quay and Peterson, 1967). Measures of self-concept are the *Piers-Harris Children's Self-Concept Scale* (Piers and Harris, 1969) and the *Tennessee Self Concept Scale* (Fitts, 1965). Once again, readers are cautioned to be very selective in choosing measures of sociobehavioral status. By necessity, the instruments available in this area are somewhat vague with frequently poor reliabilities and validities. In every case, formal tests in this area should be augmented by documentation from persons in the child's immediate environment that a deficit in sociobehavioral status is evident to some degree. This will serve to validate or invalidate whatever instrument is used to assess this area.

Evaluation of adaptive behavior is most often undertaken to determine if a child is minimally competent in the skills necessary to live effectively in today's society. Most adaptive behavior scales assess such domains as self-help, social skills, communication, self-direction, and evidence of antisocial behaviors like inappropriate interpersonal manners, sexually aberrant behavior, or odd mannerisms. While suffering from problems with reliability, validity, and norms, the commonly used scales of adaptive behavior do yield valuable data regarding a child's social competence. The most frequently used instruments in this area are the *Vineland Social Maturity Scale* (Doll, 1953), *Cain-Levine Social Competency Scale* (Cain, Levine, and Elzey, 1963), *AAMD Adaptive Behavior Scale* (Nihira, Foster, Shellhaas, and Leland, 1969), and *AAMD Adaptive Behavior Scale Public School Version* (Lambert, Windmiller, Cole, and Figueroa, 1975). As with measures of sociobehavioral competence, adaptive behavior scales should be considered carefully and supplemented by the observations of teachers, parents, and school administrators who come in frequent contact with the youngster in question.

Since the evaluation of these two important areas of development is sometimes unfamiliar to evaluation teams, additional reading is necessary to become familiar with the constructs and tests underlying assessment. Interested readers may wish to consult Anastasi (1976), Gronlund (1976), Wallace and Larsen (1978), Cronbach (1970), and Walker (1973). These readings provide detailed discussions of the concepts necessary to evaluate sociobehavioral status and adaptive behavior.

Communicative status. As it relates to children suspected of having a handicapping condition, communicative status refers to the degree of proficiency evidenced in speech and language. *Language* is conveniently defined as a system of verbal symbols (words) used by human beings to communicate on an abstract level (Carroll, 1964). Obviously, this definition of language incorporates all aspects of communication: speech, writing, reading, sign, gestural, and so on. *Speech,* on the other hand, is simply the oral or spoken utterances of humans used to convey meaning. Since speech is the primary means utilized in day-to-day communication, its adequacy is very important to success in all phases of development and scholastic performance. For this reason, when a child, regardless of the suspected handicapping condition, exhibits potential problems in either speech or language, he/she should be assessed to determine how this disorder may influence his/her educational performance. In assessing speech problems, most evaluation teams should secure the services of a qualified speech therapist. When the speech therapist is involved in the evaluation, he/she also should be part of the evaluation team. The assessment of speech usually focuses on defects related to (1) articulation, (2) stuttering, (3) voice, (4) cleft-palate speech, (5) cerebral palsy speech, and (6) deficits due to impaired hearing. For convenience, these speech defects can be grouped under the headings articulation, voice, and stuttering. Evaluating voice and stuttering is largely subjective as to how they affect educational development. Tests of articulation are available and can be used to document the absence or presence of such a disorder. Illustrations of articulation tests include *The Templin-Darley Tests of Articulation* (Templin and Darley, 1960) and the *Goldman-Fristoe Test of Articulation* (Goldman and Fristoe, 1969). The purpose of each of these instruments is to ascertain how children produce vowels, diphthongs, single consonants, and consonant blends in a variety of combinations and situations. When deficits in speech are suspected, and tests and other evaluation materials are used to determine the extent of the deficit, it is important to validate the findings by observing the child's everyday speech. It should be carefully documented that a speech

89

defect, when present, does significantly interfere with the child's progress in the school and clinic.

Measurement of language centers on the areas of morphology (the smallest meaningful units of speech), semantics (knowledge of the meaning of words), and syntax (word order). There is one comprehensive test of language that is helpful in assessing general linguistic skill from four to eight years of age. The *Test of Language Development* (Newcomer and Hammill, 1977) measures aspects of morphology, semantics, and syntax. The reliability, validity, and norms provided in the *Test of Language Development* are well done and, if administered properly, yield valuable data regarding a child's overall language usage. Tests of linguistic structure (that is, morphology and syntax) can be employed in the evaluation efforts. These normative devices include the *Carrow Elicited Language Inventory* (Carrow, 1974), *Developmental Sentence Analyses* (Lee, 1974), *Northwestern Syntax Screening Test* (Lee, 1969), and *Test of Auditory Comprehension of Language* (Carrow, 1973). Tests of semantics that measure, to some extent, the comprehension and use of words are the *Peabody Picture Vocabulary Test* (Dunn, 1965) and the *Ammons Full-Range Picture Vocabulary Test* (Ammons and Ammons, 1958).

Assessing language is a difficult and arduous undertaking. To accomplish this task, the combined efforts of the entire team, particularly those of the regular classroom teacher (if available) and the parents, are essential to realistically determine the linguistic adequacy exhibited by a given child. The certified learning disabilities specialist, with his/her training in language development, assessment, and remediation, should probably take the lead in administering and interpreting the results of the language evaluation.

Health and motor abilities. Health and motor abilities of youngsters who may possess a handicapping condition are potentially momentous concerns of the evaluation team. In many instances, the orthopedically impaired or other health impaired child exhibits problems with both health and motor skills. Where there is a question of a child's health status, he/she should be referred to a physician immediately. The physician's examination should yield information as to the youngster's physical condition, necessary medication, need of orthopedic appliances, and so on. The physician often refers the child to additional medical specialists when the need is apparent (such as a neurologist, otolaryngologist, cardiologist, or urologist). Every effort should be made to include the physician on the evaluation team in order to fully utilize his/her expertise in determining the presence of a handicapping condition.

When severe, motor problems usually are evaluated by the physician and assessed for their physiological characteristics. In cases where the youngster is known to have motor deficits and has not been examined by a physician, he/she should be referred as soon as possible. When the motor problem is less severe with no apparent progressive physical etiology, motor proficiency can be assessed by specialists in the school. Unfortunately, relatively few tests of motor ability are available for use in the school or clinic. Standardized tests that have been developed for this purpose include the *Oseretzky Tests* (Sloan, 1954; and Bruininks, 1977), *Cratty Perceptual-Motor Battery* (Cratty, 1970), and the *Fleishman Motor Ability and Fitness Scales* (Fleishman, 1964). These tests are relatively easy to administer and assess elements such as running speed, balance, response speed, visual-motor control, gross agility, throwing, catching, and general muscular strength.

The evaluation of motor skills is undertaken, of course, for the purpose of detecting whether a problem in this area is negatively affecting educational ability. Improving motor skills is attempted to increase the youngster's acceptability to his/her peers and to foster feelings of self-worth. Obviously, training in these areas does not result in improvement in academic or language performance. While this correlation was hypothesized some years ago, it has consistently been shown to be without substance. When considering the relationships among motor skills and academic and language development, one is well advised to consider the astute observation made by Rosner (1975):

> General motor skills have been associated with learning problems for some time. In fact, when professionals first became aware of the child with learning disability, the major treatment methods emphasized general motor training activities that helped the child become better coordinated. As time passed, it became clear that good motor skills, in themselves, were not the answer. We all know too many beautifully coordinated illiterates and too many clumsy geniuses to support that position. (p. 80)

RESULTS OF THE EVALUATION PROCESS

At the conclusion of the evaluation process, it should be possible to reach conclusions regarding whether the child in question meets the criteria necessary to be considered handicapped. As stated previously, the criteria for determining the presence of a handicapping condition must follow directly from the rules and regulations pertaining to PL 94–142 and the more precise specifications that are issued from state education agencies. In the event that the child is found *not* to be handicapped, he/she should be placed in non-special education settings as a means of circumventing the perceived problem. On the other hand, if, at the termination of the evaluation process, the child is judged to be handicapped, it is also necessary to determine generally the extent and nature of the special education and related services required to ameliorate the disability.

Where a handicapping condition is present, the public agency is immediately faced with certain mandated deadlines as to actual implementation of services to be provided the disabled youngster. More specifically, the implementation of part B of the Education of the Handicapped Act states that the meeting to finalize the individualized education program "must be held within thirty calendar days of a determination that the child needs special education and related services" (p. 42490). It is self-evident that the school system or other public agency that conducts the evaluation must be prepared to move quickly in order to plan and implement appropriate educational services needed by the handicapped youngster. The speed required of public agencies to afford special education and related services to handicapped children necessitates establishing some systematized procedure that will culminate in developing a viable individualized education program. The minimum steps that should be taken to prepare adequately for the IEP meeting include: (1) notifying the parents regarding the results of the evaluation and, where a handicapping condition has been judged to exist, specifying a time for the IEP meeting to occur; (2) as needed, informal assessment of the child's potential needs in the broad curricular areas of sociobehavioral, basic living/self-help, vocational/career, and academic achievement; (3) a *tentative* pre-plan regarding the content of the IEP; and (4) estimating the best placement for the child given his/her diagnosed disability.

Notifying parents regarding the outcome of the evaluation is essential regardless of whether a handicap is judged to exist or not. Since the parents were contacted prior to the evaluation and gave written consent for it to occur, it is only professional to communicate the results to them. Certainly, if the child is found to be nonhandicapped, the parents will experience relief but still may be concerned regarding the problem for which the child was referred. However, the public agency should reassure the parents of nonhandicapped children that appropriate services will be initiated in order to manage the referred problem. Contact with parents of handicapped youngsters takes on important overtones in that, if they are in disagreement with the outcome of the evaluation, placement of their child, or the individualized education program, they may exercise their option of *due process*. That is, they may protest through a series of hearings the educational treatment that has been provided their child. For example, if parents are in disagreement regarding the evaluation conducted by the public agency, they have the right to an independent evaluation at the public expense. If the parents have played an integral part in the evaluation process, there is much less chance of misconceptions and disagreements between the parents and public agency. In any event, the parents must be informed that their youngster has been found to be handicapped through the evaluation conducted by the public agency. The parents must be informed (in their native language) of the need for an IEP meeting. The public agency and the parents must agree upon the terms and place for the meeting. The various aspects of importance in the IEP meeting are considered in more depth in Chapter 9.

More informal assessment in the curricular areas of sociobehavioral, basic living/self-help, vocational/career, and academic achievement may be necessary to enable the formulation of a tentative IEP and estimation of appropriate placement (that is, least restrictive environment) for the handicapped child. As is discussed in Chapters 4, 5, and 6, it is the authors' contention that virtually all the educational needs exhibited by handicapped children can be placed under these four categories. Present levels of performance, annual goals, and short-term instructional objectives, all necessary components of the IEP, can be derived from these curricular areas. Developing tentative (1) present levels of performance, (2) annual goals, (3) short-term instructional objectives, (4) statements of needed special education and related services and the extent to which the child will be able to participate in regular education programs, (5) projected dates for initiation and duration of services, and (6) appropriate criteria to evaluate attainment of objectives should be completed prior to convening the IEP meeting. This is so that the tentative and preliminary IEP can give the parents, school personnel, and other interested parties a point from which to start deliberations. It is unrealistic to think that without such preplanning and forethought a viable IEP can be derived from *scratch*. Of course it is vital that the individuals preplanning and generating possible present levels of performance, annual goals, and so on do not lose sight of the fact that the preliminary work is truly tentative and may be altered throughout the discussions occurring during the IEP meeting. To try to defend unilateral positions, even when presented with contrary evidence, works to the disservice of both the school system and the child.

Effective use of the results of the evaluation process can be of great importance in planning and conducting the IEP meeting. Determining that a handicapping condition is affecting the performance of a child can serve to set into motion a host of activities that culminate in providing appropriate educational opportunities to children in need. The parents of handicapped children can be helped to understand the parameters of their youngster's problem and to be active partners in planning and implementing the IEP. The evaluation-based "lead-in" to the IEP meeting is crucial to the primary goal for all handicapped children: providing appropriate educational opportunities.

SUMMARY OF THE REFERRAL, SCREENING, AND EVALUATION OF HANDICAPPED CHILDREN

Prior to determining if a given child is handicapped, a public agency should initiate an educational process that is necessary to generate information regarding a child suspected of having a significant disability. The first step in this process is the actual referral of a child who has been judged by someone as being deviant to a severity level that he/she may be handicapped. The referral may come from parents, physicians, neighbors, teachers, or counselors who have had some contact with the youngster in question. Whoever refers the child completes a referral form that delineates perceptions as to the suspected handicapping condition. In addition, persons with information regarding the youngster are asked to supply their own unique insights into the child's problem and various factors that may or may not be of concern in effectively planning educational programs.

Some referred children exhibit problems of such severity levels that their handicaps are manifestly apparent and in need of immediate intervention. In other cases, the perceived condition may not be as obvious and may require a screening procedure to determine if a handicapping condition is likely and, if so, the best strategies necessary to document it through a formal evaluation. Contact with parents is made at this point. Whenever possible, the child's environment is screened to identify those features that may be contributing to the observed problem. The youngster's parent-child, teacher-child interaction patterns and peer relationships are observed to determine if the problem is primarily based in the child in the form of some indigenous disorder, or in the environment that can be correctable by manipulation.

Once the screening data has been collected, a screening meeting is convened to summarize and interpret the results. At this time it is necessary to determine if it is likely that a handicapping condition exists. If this is the case, parental consent must be obtained before pursuing the formal evaluation. In addition, the structure for the formal evaluation can be discussed and tests and evaluation materials selected as they pertain to the referred and screened child.

The evaluation of the youngster is conducted to *document* that a handicapping condition is present. As a result of this, the techniques used center around standardized, norm-referenced tests designed to designate the child's present level of functioning and *not* to necessarily specify instructionally relevant data. The categories of handicapping conditions in which the child may be eventually placed include mental retardation, hard of hearing, deaf, deaf-blind, seriously emotionally disturbed, speech impaired, orthopedically impaired, other health impaired, multihandicapped, visually handicapped, and specific learning disabilities. The evaluation must address all areas related to the suspected disability such as sensory acuity, health, sociobehavioral status, adaptive behavior, communicative status, intelligence, academic performance, and motor abilities. The evaluation of handicapped children must be accomplished by a team of persons responsible for determining and documenting the presence of one of the handicapping conditions. When it is decided that a handicap is paramount and the child is in need of special education and related services, a meeting to finalize the individualized educational program must be scheduled.

The results of the evaluation process should be used to expedite developing the IEP. Initially, the parents must be contacted to inform them of the disposition of their child's evaluation. At this time, the time and place of the meeting to formalize the IEP can be mutually agreed upon by both the parents and the public agency. The 30 calendar days that can elapse between determination of the existence of the handicapping condition and convening the IEP meeting can serve to provide time to prepare *tentative* statements regarding the contents of the IEP. This preplanning effort provides positions to which the parents and public agency may react. If parents disagree with the results of the evaluation, placement, or IEP, they may institute due process hearings to contest them. Ideally, however, the careful and considered treatment of the evaluation results permits the successful completion and implementation of the best educational services to handicapped children. The components of the individualized education program and strategies for conducting the IEP meeting are discussed in the following chapters.

References

Ammons, R., and Ammons, H. *Full-range picture vocabulary test*. Missoula, Mont.: Psychological Test Specialists, 1958.

Anastasi, A. *Psychological testing*. New York: Macmillan, 1976.

Arthur, G. *The Arthur adaptation of the Leiter international performance scale*. Chicago, Ill.: C. H. Stoelting, 1950.

Barraga, N. *Visual handicaps and learning: A developmental approach*. Belmont, Calif.: Wadsworth, 1976.

Beatty, L. S.; Madden, R.; and Gardner, E. F. *Stanford diagnostic arithmetic test.* New York: Harcourt Brace Jovanovich, 1966.

Bene, E., and Anthony, J. *Family relations test.* Windsor, Berks, England: NFER Publishing, 1957.

Berg, F. S., and Fletcher, S. G. *The hard of hearing child.* New York: Grune and Stratton, 1970.

Boehm, A. E. *Boehm test of basic concepts.* New York: Psychological Corporation, 1971.

Bond, G. L.; Balow, B. T.; and Hoyt, C. J. *Silent reading diagnostic tests.* Chicago: Lyons and Carnahan, 1955.

Bradfield, R. H., and Criner, J. *Classroom interaction analyses.* San Rafael, Calif.: Academic Therapy Publications, 1973.

Brophy, J. E., and Good, T. *Teacher-child dyadtic interaction: A manual for coding classroom behavior.* Austin, Tex.: Research and Development Center for Teacher Education, University of Texas at Austin, 1969.

Bruininks, R. H. *Bruininks-Oseretzky test of motor proficiency.* Circle Pines, Minn.: American Guidance Service, 1977.

Cain, L.; Levine, S.; and Elzey, F. *Manual for the Cain-Levine social competency scale.* Palo Alto, Calif.: Consulting Psychologists Press, 1963.

Carroll, J. B. *Language and thought.* Englewood Cliffs, N.J.: Prentice-Hall, 1964.

Carrow, E. *Test of auditory comprehension of language.* Austin, Tex.: Learning Concepts, 1973.

—— *Carrow elicited language inventory.* Austin, Tex.: Learning Concepts, 1974.

Cartwright, C. A., and Cartwright, G. P. *Developing observational skills.* New York: McGraw-Hill, 1974.

Connolly, A. J.; Nachtman, W.; and Pritchett, E. M. *Key math diagnostic arithmetic test.* Circle Pines, Minn.: American Guidance Service, 1971.

Cratty, B. J. *Perceptual and motor development in infants and children.* New York: Macmillan, 1970.

Cronbach, L. *Essentials of psychological testing.* New York: Harper & Row, 1960.

deGrant, A., and Thompson, G. A study of the distribution of teacher approval and disapproval among first grade pupils. *Journal of Experimental Education,* 1949, *18*:57–75.

Doll, E. *Vineland social maturity scale.* Circle Pines, Minn.: American Guidance Service, 1965.

Dunn, L. M. *Peabody picture vocabulary test.* Circle Pines, Minn.: American Guidance Service, 1965.

——, and Markwardt, F. C. *Peabody Individual Achievement Test.* Circle Pines, Minn.: American Guidance Service, 1970.

Fitts, W. *Tennessee self concept inventory*. Nashville: Counselor Recordings and Tests, 1965.

Flanders, N. A. *Flanders' system of interaction analysis*. Reading, Mass.: Addison-Wesley, 1970.

Fleishman, E. A. *The structure and measurement of physical fitness*. Englewood Cliffs, N.J.: Prentice-Hall, 1964.

Fox, R. S.; Luszki, M. B.; and Schmuck, R. *Diagnosing classroom learning environments*. Chicago: Science Research Associates, 1966.

Frankenberg, W. K.; Dodds, J. B.; and Fondal, A. W. *Denver developmental screening test*. Denver: Ladoca Project and Publishing Foundation, 1970.

French, J. L. *Pictorial test of intelligence*. Boston: Houghton Mifflin, 1964.

Gilmore, J. V., and Gilmore, E. C. *Gilmore oral reading test*. New York: Harcourt Brace Jovanovich, 1968.

Goldman, R., and Fristoe, M. *Goldman-Fristoe test of articulation*. Circle Pines, Minn.: American Guidance Service, 1969.

Good, T. Which pupils do teachers call on? *Elementary School Journal*, 1973, 70:190–198.

———, and Brophy, J. *Looking in classrooms*. New York: Harper & Row, 1973.

Goodman, L., and Hammill, D. D. *Basic school skills inventory*. New York: Follett, 1975.

Gordon, I. J. *Studying the child in school*. New York: John Wiley, 1966.

Gray, W. S., and Robinson, H. M. (eds.) *Gray oral reading test*. Indianapolis: Bobbs-Merrill, 1967.

Gronlund, N. E. *Measurement and evaluation in teaching*. New York: Macmillan, 1976.

Hammill, D. D., and Bartel, N. *Teaching children with learning and behavior problems*. Boston: Allyn & Bacon, 1978.

———, and Larsen, S. C. *Test of written language*. Austin, Tex.: PRO/Ed, 1978.

Hiskey, M. *Hiskey-Nebraska test of learning aptitude*. Lincoln, Neb.: Union College Press, 1966.

Hoehn, A. A study of social status differentiation in the classroom behavior of 19 third-grade teachers. *Journal of Social Psychology*, 1954, 39:261–292.

Holtzman, W. *Holtzman inkblot test*. New York: Psychological Corporation, 1966.

Jastak, F. J., and Jastak, S. R. *Wide range achievement test*. Wilmington, Del.: Guidance Associates, 1965.

Jay, E. *A book about me*. Chicago: Science Research Associates, 1955.

Karlsen, B.; Madden, R.; and Gardner, E. F. *Stanford diagnostic reading tests*. New York: Harcourt Brace Jovanovich, 1966.

Kroth, R. L. *Communicating with parents of exceptional children.* Denver: Love Publishing Company, 1975.

Kuder, R. *Kuder personal preference record.* Chicago: Science Research Associates, 1954.

Lambert, N.; Windmiller, M.; Cole, L.; and Figueroa, R. *Manual for AAMD adaptive behavior scale* (1974 revision). Washington, D.C.: The Association, 1975.

Larsen, S. C. The influence of teacher expectations on the school performance of handicapped children. *Focus on Exceptional Children,* 1975, 6:1–14.

――, and Hammill, D. D. *Test of written spelling.* Austin, Tex.: PRO/Ed, 1976.

Laten, S., and Katz, G. A. *A theoretical model for assessment of adolescents: The ecological/behavioral approach.* Madison, Wisc.: Madison Public Schools, 1975.

Lee, J., and Clark, W. *Manual for the Lee-Clark reading readiness test.* Monterey, Calif.: CTB/McGraw-Hill, 1962.

Lee, L. *Northwestern syntax screening test.* Evanston, Ill.: Northwestern University Press, 1969.

―― *Developmental sentence analysis.* Evanston, Ill.: Northwestern University Press, 1974.

Losen, S., and Diament, B. *Parent conferences in the schools: Procedures for developing effective partnership.* Boston: Allyn & Bacon, 1978.

Medley, D.; Schluck, C.; and Ames, N. *Assessing the learning environment in the classroom: A manual for users of OScAR 5.* Princeton, N.J.: Educational Testing Service, 1968.

Morrison, A., and McIntyre, D. *Teachers and teaching.* Baltimore: Penguin Books, 1969.

Moss, M. H. *Test of basic expression.* Monterey, Calif.: CTB/McGraw-Hill, 1972.

Murray, A. *Thematic apperception test.* Cambridge, Mass.: Harvard University Press, 1943.

Myklebust, H. *Development and disorders of written language.* New York: Grune & Stratton, 1965.

National Society for the Prevention of Blindness. *Vision screening in schools.* Publication 257. New York: The Society, 1961.

Newcomer, P., and Hammill, D. D. *Test of language development.* Austin, Tex.: Empiric, 1977.

Newland, T. E. *Manual for the blind learning aptitude test.* Urbana, Ill.: T. Ernest Newland, 1969.

―― Psychological assessment of exceptional children and youth. In W. Cruickshank (ed.), *Psychology of exceptional children and youth.* Englewood Cliffs, N.J.: Prentice-Hall, 1971.

Nihira, K.; Foster, R.; Shellhaas, M.; and Leland, H. *Adaptive behavior scales.* Washington, D.C.: American Association on Mental Deficiency, 1969.

Nurss, J. R., and McGauvran, M. E. *Metropolitan readiness test, teacher's manual, Part II.* New York: Harcourt Brace Jovanovich, 1976.

O'Neill, J. J., and Oyer, H. J. *Visual communication for the hard of hearing.* Englewood Cliffs, N.J.: Prentice-Hall, 1966.

Otto, W.; McMenemy, R. A.; and Smith, R. J. *Corrective and remedial teaching* (2nd ed.). Boston: Houghton Mifflin, 1973.

Piers, E., and Harris, D. *The Piers-Harris children's self concept scale.* Nashville: Counselor Recordings and Tests, 1969.

Quay, H. C., and Peterson, D. R. *Manual for the behavior problem checklist.* Unpublished manuscript, University of Illinois, 1967.

Rosner, J. *Helping children overcome learning difficulties.* New York: Walker, 1975.

Salvia, J., and Ysseldyke, J. E. *Assessment in special and remedial education.* Boston: Houghton Mifflin, 1978.

Sattler, J. *Assessment of children's intelligence.* Philadelphia: W. B. Saunders, 1974.

Sloan, B. *The Lincoln-Oseretsky motor development scale.* Genetic Psychology Monographs, 1955, *51*:183–252.

Slosson, R. L. *Slosson intelligence test for children and youth.* East Aurora, N.Y.: Slosson Educational Publications, 1971.

Templin, M. C., and Darley, F. L. *The Templin-Darley tests of articulation.* Iowa City: Bureau of Educational Research and Service, University of Iowa, 1960.

Thorpe, L.; Clark, W.; and Tiegs, E. *California test of personality.* Monterey, Calif.: California Test Bureau, 1953.

Tyron, C. Evaluations of adolescent personality by adolescents. In R. Baker, J. Kouner, and W. Wright (eds.), *Child behavior and development.* New York: McGraw-Hill, 1943.

Walker, D. K. *Socioemotional measures for preschool and kindergarten children.* San Francisco: Jossey-Bass, 1973.

Walker, H. *Walker problem behavior identification checklist.* Los Angeles: Western Psychological Services, 1970.

Wallace, G., and Larsen, S. C. *Educational assessment of learning problems: Testing for teaching.* Boston: Allyn & Bacon, 1978.

Wechsler, D. *Manual for the Wechsler intelligence scale.* New York: Psychological Corporation, 1955.

—— *Manual for the Wechsler preschool and primary scale of intelligence.* New York: Psychological Corporation, 1967.

—— *Manual for the Wechsler intelligence scale for children* (Revised). New York: Psychological Corporation, 1974.

Wiederholt, J. L.; Brown, V.; and Hammill, D. D. *The resource teacher.* Boston: Allyn & Bacon, 1978.

Present Levels of Educational Performance

The second step in preparing successful educational programs for children with special needs entails delineating present levels of educational performance. This component serves to orient the general direction of a handicapped student's education and, if done properly, simplifies subsequent instructional programming. Documenting the child's present level of functioning is necessary in those areas in which she/he is experiencing particular difficulty and those educational areas most in need of immediate intervention. This documentation requires educators to utilize the pertinent information regarding the individual student that was collected during the referral, screening, and evaluation stages discussed in Chapter 3. However, although helpful in establishing general directions for the child's education (and administratively—a necessity), evaluation data alone are not always adequate for establishing performance levels. That is, the evaluation of handicapped children as specified in PL 94–142 is designed primarily for placement and not to provide instructionally usable information.

In order to establish appropriate levels of functioning (and other subsequent program decisions such as goals and objectives), it is necessary for educators to rechannel their attention *from evaluation for placement to evaluation for educational planning.* In other words, additional evaluation is usually required in order to define appropriate areas of educational performance for a particular student and to determine the present level of performance within each educational area. From the present levels of performance documented within each area of concern, educators have some idea of the child's *educational* abilities and disabilities. This provides educators a point from which to begin to establish annual goals, objectives, and services.

100

To be effective, it is important for persons assessing any student's present level of educational performance to have a clear understanding of the constructs encompassed in the various areas of education for the handicapped, that is, self-help/basic living, academic, career/vocational, and sociobehavioral. Gray (1978) noted that the concepts and prejudices an educator held regarding what constituted "education" significantly affected the types of evaluations conducted. Therefore, when determining a child's present levels of educational performance, educators and parents must possess a futuristic orientation toward assessing or evaluating the general educational direction for the child's program to take. Although this attitudinal change away from evaluating for placement and toward specifying areas to ameliorate the problem appears slight, nonetheless it is a crucial one as individuals begin to plan and program the child's education. The following discussions exemplify how educators and parents can begin to focus their attention upon viable educational programming through a series of steps designed to establish present levels of performance.

As the first component of each individualized education program, PL 94–142 and subsequent regulations have defined "a statement of the child's present levels of educational performance." This clause implies that there are at least four major issues for the IEP team to consider during this phase of educational program development. First, one must be cognizant of the definition of education as it applies to handicapped children and youth. Next, educational planners must *conceptualize* the various aspects or specifics involved in each area of educational performance. Third, from the myriad of educational options available, the team must determine those areas that are appropriate to the particular student. This determination constitutes the general direction in which the child's education and educational planning is to follow. Last, once pertinent educational areas have been identified, additional assessment of the student may be necessary to further document present performance levels within each area that has been determined as relevant to the handicapped youngster. Results of this assessment constitute a "statement of the child's present levels of educational performance." Each of these four steps is elaborated upon in the following sections.

DEFINING EDUCATION

Until relatively recently, public school education has been primarily concerned with training "normal" students within a rather limited range of academic areas. The definition of education upon which most public schools have operated, and still do to a great extent, has been extremely limited. Ostensibly, the primary and overall goal of education has been to prepare students to enter even more formalized educational environments, that is, colleges and universities. This narrow concept of what constitutes education has been roundly criticized in that it tended to focus upon the needs of relatively few pupils. Not surprisingly, in the last few years, public schools have been besieged by a number of innovative concepts aimed at expanding the range of educational areas, including vocational education, values clarification, and other diverse curriculum expansions. Even these innovations in education, however, have been directed largely at the "normal" school population. Few, if any, of these educational expansions have affected the definition of all education as does the concept of special education, that is, education for handicapped students.

With the advent of special education for the handicapped, schools have seen drastic deviations from the traditional academic curricula. Beginning in the late 1970s with the legal mandate to provide appropriate education to *all* handicapped students, one finds the traditional definition of education no longer applicable to the scope of instructional activities now conducted within the school environment. Historically, handicapped children have been dichotomized into two distinct categories: those students who were considered "educable" and those considered "ineducable." This concept of handicapped children was used largely for purposes of excluding supposedly "ineducable" children from receiving educational opportunities. In several major court cases in the late 60s and early 70s, this categorization for the purpose of exclusion was ruled by U.S. federal courts as a violation of the civil rights of handicapped persons.* In essence, court rulings and recent legislation indicate that, indeed, no child is ineducable. These court cases represent major landmarks in the field of special education and hold great implications for all education in general. Together these judicial decisions and the passage of PL 94–142 in 1975 unquestionably call for a broad-based reconceptualization of education in order to include the handicapped. What does constitute education? What are the areas of education in which one might instruct a handicapped child? In addition, what are the areas of education in which one needs to assess performance?

Education is defined as the process of growth or development that results from instruction. In the context of the schools, instruction is provided to students within various instructional environments. Therefore, it may be said that public school education, today, is the act of training a particular child in *any* of the various aspects that relate to an individual's development, from feeding and toileting skills to com-

---

* *PARC* v. *Penn.* (1971). Civil Action No. 17-4L, 3 Judge Court, Ed. Penn., 1971. *Wyatt* v. *Stickney* (1971). Alabama Civil Action No. 3195-N, 1971. *Mills* v. *Board of Education* (1971). District of Columbia, Civil Action No. 1939-71, District of Columbia, 1971.

plex academic tasks in a number of instructional settings. Ultimately, the goal of education is to allow the individual to develop his/her full potential in *all* areas of life—personal, social, career.

Examining the areas of growth and development that relate to training or instructing handicapped children, it is possible to categorize the major components of special education into four broad areas: (1) self-help and basic living education, (2) career and vocational education, (3) academic education, and (4) sociobehavioral education. The authors have found this division convenient as well as comprehensive; therefore we use these four areas to discuss educational planning and programming for children with special needs throughout the remainder of this text. Each of these four areas is discussed utilizing various models and listings of skills to demonstrate their applicability to education for the handicapped.

DEFINING AREAS OF SPECIAL EDUCATION

In conceptualizing the performance areas of self-help/basic living skills, academic skills, career/vocational skills, and sociobehavioral skills, it is important to note that these areas of educational performance are not categorized according to handicapping conditions. Shifting from focusing on a specific disability to the actual educational needs of disabled children is crucial to efficient instructional planning. Remember, with regard to evaluation procedures for determining the existence of a handicapping condition, instrumentation was selected on the basis of a particular set of criteria necessary for documenting handicapping conditions. The criteria established for each condition must be met prior to placement in special education services for the handicapped. Further, these criteria stipulate for each handicapping condition those areas in which the student must exhibit inadequate performance in order to qualify as being handicapped. While these assessments do serve to provide educators many valuable insights, they are often not sufficient to permit in-depth educational planning. Most of the criteria documented during evaluation are not, in fact, amenable to amelioration. For instance, although measures of inadequate adaptive behavior and subnormal intellectual performance comprise the evaluation criteria for mental retardation, an appropriate education plan would not be developed to specifically increase the child's intelligence. Similarly, for a visually handicapped student it would be equally inappropriate for instructional efforts to concentrate upon increasing visual acuity. Instead of attending to deficits, educational planning must concentrate upon developing *needed skills* for successful living, such as personal skills, orientation and mobility, utilizing any residual vision. and advanced academic skills. Evaluating these types of student abilities allows documentation of educational performance levels to be more *functionally* oriented. Defining these levels in a functional manner greatly simplifies the educational planning of goals, objectives, and services and makes them more meaningful for educators and parents alike. In this way, professionals and parents can direct attention and energies away from "deficit diagnosis" and toward establishing viable educational goals, objectives, services, and evaluation criteria within the various areas of education.

Prior to any further educational evaluation or planning, it is imperative that professionals define more clearly the areas of educational performance of importance to handicapped children. In defining these areas, it becomes manifestly apparent that the scope of possible goals involved in special education is extensive. Once educators fully define these areas for themselves they will likely become more cognizant and sensitive to the possible needs of any handicapped student. One way to develop an overview of educational goals appropriate to handicapped students is to peruse the ways in which specific areas of education have been addressed in school practice. The following sections are provided as an accumulation of sources one might consult in defining concepts of the four areas of education necessary for handicapped youngsters. This section is by no means meant to be definitive; rather, it is included to stimulate the reader's own concepts of educational performance in various curricular areas. This knowledge base is essential as a prelude to establishing annual goals. In addition, a procedure discussed in Chapters 5 and 6 that simplifies educational programming depends on educators having formulated their own concepts regarding basic skill areas pertinent to special education.

Self-Help and Basic Living Skills

Self-help and basic living skills are those daily living and survival activities that allow a person to function as independently as possible in the home or residential environment. These skills begin in infancy and continue to adulthood with the ultimate goal of total self-sufficiency. Although these skills may not apply directly to a career or vocation, they are often important prerequisites and are necessary for a person to exercise vocational skills.

For the most part, special educators have associated self-help and living skills with the more *severely* handicapped students. Effective educational planning always must consider the severity of a handicap-

104

ping condition within the context of functional abilities. For purposes of this book, severely handicapped students are *not* necessarily those who at the present time have little or no independent skills. Instead, severely handicapped students are defined as those for whom the *prognosis* of independence is poor; that is, those students for whom some type of residential support (such as group homes, his/her own home, hospital, or special school) may be needed throughout life. With this concept in mind, one can see that, for instance, blind children (invariably and mistakenly classified as severely handicapped) often require initial instruction in basic living skills such as mobility training just to learn to move about in their environment. In addition, the same students often need instruction in basic living skills such as cooking and shopping which most take for granted and many handicapped persons do not simply acquire through experience. Because prognosis for independent living is excellent, many blind children would not be classified as severe using a functional orientation; however, appropriate educational performance areas would, to a certain extent, center around self-help and basic living skills. As Barraga (1976) points out, "permitting visually handicapped students to 'graduate' from educational programs without ever having been given the experience of shopping for food . . . makes a mockery of education." On the other hand, self-help and basic living skills for severely handicapped pupils (that is, where prognosis of independent living is poor) include such basic tasks as toilet training, feeding, and dressing. Whatever the severity level in a handicapped student, the goals involved in training for self-help and basic living skills should lead to a gradual increase in the individual's ability to function independently in daily life. Of course, the goal of independence for a three-year-old handicapped student is quite different from that for an adult, so the concept of self-help and basic living skills is also age dependent. Consequently, an overview of what entails skills in this area is essential to effective educational planning.

In examining various conceptualizations of self-help and basic living skills presented in this section, the reader will find: (1) a total curricular model emphasizing many daily living skills, (2) a suggested outline of skills needed by sensorially handicapped pupils of normal or above intelligence, (3) an overview of motor skills necessary for successful daily living, and (4) a brief discussion of other skills often considered within the realm of self-help and basic living skills education. These models will provide the reader with a variety of conceptualizations of self-help and basic living skills that will be useful in developing one's own concept of this area of special education.

Meyen (1972) designed an organizational model of curricula for mentally retarded youngsters (see Table 4-1). However, these skills may be applied to any handicapped child needing special education.

TABLE 4–1 Total Curricula for Handicapped Pupils Emphasizing Self-Help and Basic Living Skills

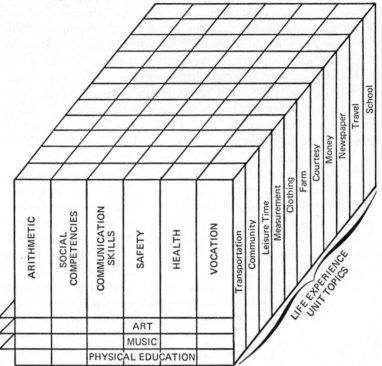

SOURCE: Meyen, E. *Developing units of instruction.* Dubuque, Iowa: William C. Brown, 1976. Used with permission of publisher.

The model subdivides each division or construct into life experience units, a familiar method of instruction involving concentrated blocks of time devoted to a particular instructional topic. For instance, a unit on transportation might involve aspects of vocation, health, safety, and communication skills. In further elaborating on the constructs or core areas, Meyen graphically represents possible units by core area or construct appropriate for intermediate level students. For instance, a unit on communication skills would involve skill in using the post office, telephone, telegram, and so on (see Table 4–2). Although Meyen's conceptualization was conceived originally for the purpose of devising certain instructional units, it is also helpful in determining pertinent self-help and basic living goals often required by handicapped students.

As mentioned earlier, in her discussions regarding educating visually handicapped children Barraga (1976) stresses the importance for schools to consider more than merely academic curricula. She refers to other important curricular areas under the broad heading of career

TABLE 4-2 Delineation of Constructs under Various Educational Areas

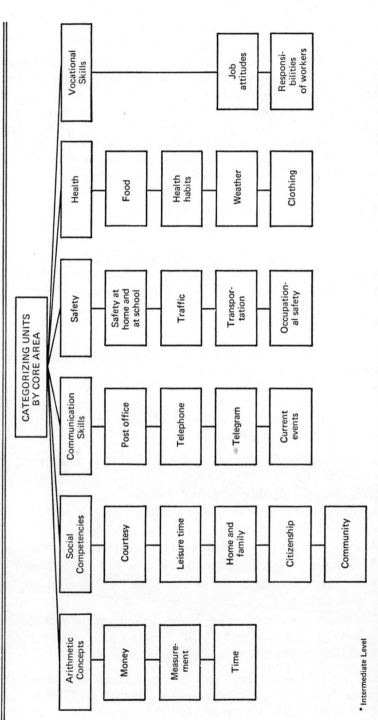

SOURCE: Meyen, E. *Developing units of instruction.* Dubuque, Iowa: William C. Brown, 1976. Used with permission of publisher.

* Intermediate Level

education. These components of an educational program for the visually handicapped are reproduced in Table 4–3 because they contain many elements of self-help and basic living curricula. The major constructs or divisions of these curricula are: (1) personal, social, and everyday living skills, (2) communication and business skills, (3) concept development and mobility skills, and (4) career and vocational skills. Home management, special equipment use, orientation and mobility skills are but a few of the unique components that are necessary to operationalize the four basic constructs. This listing of skills provides a good contrast to the previous example, in that it was developed for students with average or above intelligence who exhibit a sensorial disability.

Major components in self-help and basic living skill education are motor and mobility skills. Motor curricula entail evaluating and training both gross and fine motor tasks. Mobility skills, as demonstrated in Table 4–3, are necessary for many visually handicapped persons. In addition, mobility training is essential in self-help and daily living activities for the orthopedically handicapped. To various degrees, other handicapped children may also be in need of motor training. These skills include such tasks as using prosthetic devices and manipulating wheelchairs and braces.

Frostig (1970) provides a chart (Table 4–4) that consolidates various conceptualizations of the areas of fine and gross motor. The constructs of movement (a component of self-help and basic living skills) according to Frostig are:

1. coordination—the simultaneous use of several muscles or muscle groups
2. rhythm—the flowing, measured, balanced movement
3. flexibility—the ability to move parts of the body easily in relation to each other
4. speed—the tempo achieved during a movement sequence
5. agility—the capacity for fast reaction in body movement
6. balance—the maintenance of a position with minimal surface contact
7. strength—force exerted by the whole body or parts of the body
8. endurance—the ability to persist in activity

Barsch (1965) also defined motor skills with respect to a curriculum termed "movigenics." These concepts differ slightly from Frostig's which emphasize gross motor movement. Barsch's curriculum constructs of spatial awareness, body awareness, visual and auditory dynamics, kinesthesia, tactual dynamics, and bilaterality offer some additional considerations:

1. Muscular strength is the capacity of the organism to maintain an adequate state of muscle tonus, power, and stamina to meet the daily demands appropriate to his body size and chronological age.
2. Dynamic balance is the capacity of the organism to activate antigravity muscles in proper relationship to one another against the force of gravitational pull, to maintain alignment, sustain his transport pattern, and to aid in recovery.
3. Spatial awareness is the capacity of the organism to identify his own position in space relative to his surroundings with constant orientation to surface, elevation, periphery, back, and front.
4. Body awareness is the capacity of the organism to achieve a conscious appreciation of the relationship of all body segments to movement, to be able to label body parts, and to appreciate the functional properties of various body parts.
5. Visual dynamics is the capacity of the organism to fixate accurately on a target at near, mid, and far points in space, to scan a surround for meaning in the vertical and horizontal planes, to converge and accommodate, to equalize the use of both visual circuits in a binocular pattern to achieve fusion, and to steer the body in proper alignment for movements through space.
6. Auditory dynamics is the capacity of the organism to process information on a receiving and a sending basis for the world of sound and to attach appropriate relationships to the world of sound.
7. Kinesthesia is the capacity of the organism to maintain an awareness of position in space and to recall patterns of movement from previous experience for utility in resolving continuing demands.
8. Tactual dynamics encompasses the capacity of the organism to gain information from the cutaneous contact of active or passive touching.
9. Bilaterality is the capacity of the organism to reciprocally interweave two sides in a balanced relationship of thrusting and counterthrusting patterns around the three coordinates of vertical, horizontal, and depth in proper alignment from initiation to completion of the task.
10. Rhythm is the capacity of the organism to synchronize patterns of movement according to situational demands, thus achieving harmony, grace, and use of movement.
11. Flexibility is the capacity of the organism to modify or shift patterns of movement appropriate to the situational demands.
12. Motor planning is the capacity of the organism to plan a movement pattern prior to execution in order to meet the demands of a task. (1965, pp. 15–29)

Other areas often considered under the broad heading basic living skills include additional skills for sensorially handicapped youngsters such as low vision utilization training and residual hearing training. In addition, although language is classified here under the educational

TABLE 4–3 Outline of Curriculum Developed for Sensorially Handicapped Students

I. Personal, social, and everyday living skills to provide confidence, ease, and comfort in functioning, and independence in living arrangements.
  A. Knowledge and understanding of self as a person.
    1. Interests, capabilities, limitations.
    2. Attitudes about self and others.
    3. Personality characteristics and self-concept.
    4. Sexual identity, needs, and behaviors.
  B. Personal care and management.
    1. Eating, dressing, grooming.
    2. Selecting, purchasing, and caring for appropriate clothing.
    3. Skills in hair arrangement, tying ties, use of self-care tools.
  C. Social skills.
    1. Good manners and appropriate behaviors.
    2. Games and leisure-time activities.
    3. Interaction with others, especially sighted persons and those of the opposite sex.
  D. Home management.
    1. Selecting, purchasing, and preparing simple foods and meals.
    2. Use and manipulation of simple materials, utensils, and equipment.
    3. Simple mechanical repairs.
    4. Managing personal finances and budgets.
II. Realistic communication and business skills.
  A. Information gathering for study or for vocational preparation.
    1. Sources of available materials in all media.
    2. Selection and appropriate use of reading devices and equipment such as optical aids, listening equipment, Optacon, and others.
  B. Written communication.
    1. Braille labelling and organization of materials for efficiency.
    2. Typing skills for personal, vocational, and professional purposes.
    3. Formats for tax forms, bookkeeping, and so on.
  C. Computational and measurement skills.
    1. Selection and use of appropriate devices for home and occupational purposes.
    2. Inventory and recording accuracy.
III. Concept development, precane skills, and independent mobility.
  A. Orientation of self to objects and space.
    1. Functional understanding of vocabulary related to movement and spatial alignment.

TABLE 4–3   (*cont.*)

      2. Knowledge and skill in movement of body.

      3. Spatial orientation to work area of in-reach space.

  B. Organization of work areas and equipment.

      1. Arrangement of tools, materials, and/or devices for efficient use in a variety of job stations.

      2. Skill in spatial location of needed objects and return to designated positions after use.

      3. Maintenance of orderly work area in numerous work stations.

  C. Exploration and movement in familiar and unfamiliar environments.

      1. Skill in exploration of work space, classrooms, and other indoor settings.

      2. Efficient movement between work settings and/or classrooms and building.

  D. Independent travel.

      1. Cane travel or use of guide dogs in school and neighborhood areas.

      2. Use of public transportation to and from school and/or job setting.

      3. Travel in suburban and city areas without assistance.

IV. Career, vocational, and/or technical occupations.

  A. Exploration of, and exposure to, appropriate careers, vocations, or technical occupations.

      1. Simulation of work experiences.

      2. Group discussions with successful visually handicapped persons working in various roles.

      3. Workshop, office, business, or professional work experience in community.

  B. Training in general work skills.

      1. Attitudes toward self and others in work settings.

      2. General work habits and skills common to many vocations.

      3. General safety and manipulative skills related to various settings, such as laboratory, business, workshop, and/or professional careers.

  C. Training in skills for specific vocations, occupations, or professional careers.

      1. Selection according to interest, predicted potential for success, personal and family considerations.

      2. Skill development in work stations, contract work, or in-school work experiences.

      3. Placement in on-the-job training sites with full responsibility in community.

SOURCE: Barraga, N. *Visual handicaps and learning.* Belmont, Calif.: Wadsworth, 1976. Used with permission of publisher.

TABLE 4-4 Major Constructs Involved in Motoric Education

Attributes of Movement	Guilford[1]	Nicks and Fleishman[2] (Summary of 78 Studies)	Mosston[3]	Kephart[4]	Frostig and Maslow
Coordination and Rhythm	*Coordination* Gross body Hand dexterity Finger dexterity	*Coordination* Gross body Multiple limb		*Coordination* Gross motor Eye-hand Integration of both sides of body	*Coordination* Across body axis of different muscle groups simultaneously *Rhythm* Jerky vs. smooth movements Synchrony prerequisite (see Doll[5])
Speed and Agility	*Impulsion* General reaction time Tapping Articulation speed *Motor Speed* Arm-Hand-Finger	*Speed* Limb movement Running *Agility* Change of direction during movement	*Agility* Take-off Change of posture during movement	*Receipt and Propulsion* *Contact:* Reaching, grasping, releasing Manipulation to obtain information	*Speed* Continuous movement in space Running *Agility* Initiation of movement Change of direction
Flexibility	*Flexibility* Trunk Leg	*Flexibility–Speed*	*Flexibility* Spine and pelvis Shoulder girdle Bending forward and sideways	(Kephart uses the term flexibility for what is here defined as agility.)	*Flexibility* Maximum extension in trunk and limbs Rotation of joints

Strength	*Strength* General Trunk Limbs	*Strength* Explosive Dynamic Static	*Strength* Shoulder girdle and arms Upper back Abdomen Legs	*Strength* General, specific muscle groups
Endurance		*Endurance*	*Endurance*	*Endurance* Sustained movement over time (see Cureton [6])
Balance	*Static Precision* Static balance Arm steadiness *Dynamic Precision* Dynamic balance Arm aiming Hand aiming	*Balance* Static Dynamic Object	*Balance* Movements on ground Movements on apparatus Movements while supported by another person	*Balance* Maintenance Dynamic relationship to gravity	*Balance* Static Dynamic Object

SOURCE: Frostig, M. *Movement education: Theory and practice*. Chicago: Follet Educational Corporation, 1970. Used with permission of publisher.

1. Guilford, J. P. A system of psychomotor abilities. *American Journal of Psychology*, 1958, 71, 164–174.
2. Nicks, D. C., and Fleishman, E. A. What do physical tests measure—A review of factor analytic studies. Technical Report I, prepared for the Office of Naval Research by Yale University Departments of Industrial Administration and Psychology. New Haven: Yale Univ. Press, 1960.
3. Mosston, M. *Developmental Movement*. Columbus, Ohio: Charles E. Merrill, 1965.
4. Kephart, N. C. *The Slow Learner in the Classroom*. Columbus, Ohio: Charles E. Merrill, 1960. Also Godfrey, B. B., and Kephart, N. C. *Movement Patterns and Motor Education*. New York: Appleton-Century-Crofts, 1969.
5. Doll, E. Neurophrenia. *American Journal of Psychiatry*, 1951, 108, 50.
6. Cureton, T. K. 18-item motor fitness test. *Physical Fitness Workbook*. Champaign, Ill.: Univ. of Illinois Press, 1952.

performance area of academics, many persons consider lip reading and sign language to be self-help skills for the deaf and hard of hearing in the same way that orientation and mobility are for the blind or low vision student.

These few examples of self-help and basic living skills indicate the myriad of skills involved in this area of education. Especially crucial is the fact that self-help and basic living skills apply to *all* handicaps and all degrees of severity. These skills, each in a different way, assist the student in becoming a more self-sufficient individual. Another related area of special education urgently needed by handicapped youngsters is career/vocational. This educational performance area is discussed below.

Career/Vocational Education

The educational performance area of career and vocational skills includes the prerequisite and requisite skills necessary for a handicapped student to select, obtain, and maintain appropriate employment. Appropriate employment can be defined as holding a job for which one has or can obtain the necessary skills and for which one is sufficiently reinforced, that is, job match and job satisfaction. Those skills necessary to examine and select an appropriate job are generally considered within the framework of career-education while skills necessary on the job are generally emphasized in traditional vocational education programs Career/vocational education, like each area of educational performance, is applicable to all handicapped youngsters with varying degrees of severity. Like the self-help/basic living skills area, the ultimate goal in career/vocational education is to reach maximum self-sufficiency. This independence can only truly be achieved through appropriate and meaningful employment. Once again, the goal of self-sufficiency depends on the age and severity of the handicap of the particular student. There are students in special education who need training to work in an institutional or sheltered workshop setting, and there are handicapped students who become competent professionals within various occupational circles.

In examining the ways in which educators and other professionals have conceptualized the areas of career/vocational skills, one becomes acquainted with three major literature sources. One area of literature deals with the occupational clusters that describe specific occupations available. Another area of literature delineates curriculum development sources for career and vocational education; these emphasize skills in self-awareness, job exploration, and job acquisition. A third area to which much less attention has been directed is that of career and vocational education specifically designed for the handicapped. The following section provides the reader with (1) a popular job classification system, (2) two different curricular models for regular career and vocational education, and (3) two models proposed for the handicapped.

Roe (1956) developed a two-dimensional array of job possibilities to aid in occupational classification (see Table 4–5). The constructs involved in the job classifications in Table 4–5 are indicative of common characteristics of jobs such as service, business, outdoor, arts, and so on. For example, all the job possibilities listed under "outdoor" entail some degree of involvement in such areas as agriculture and wild life. Levels 1–6 correspond to gradations of professionalism from level 6, unskilled or paraprofessionals, to level 1, highly skilled persons who are leaders within particular professions. It is suggested that readers examine such classifications and clusters regularly to be able to arrange for appropriate student exploration of the various fields, as well as direct career and vocational training. An additional source is the most recent Dictionary of Occupational Titles (DOT). The U.S. Office of Education also regularly publishes a list of job classifications similar to the one below:

- Business and office occupations
- Marketing and distribution occupations
- Communication and media occupations
- Construction occupations
- Manufacturing occupations
- Transportation occupations
- Agri-business and natural resource occupations
- Marine science occupations
- Environmental central occupations
- Public services occupations
- Hospitality and recreation occupations
- Personal services occupations
- Fine arts and humanities occupations
- Consumer and homemaking occupations

With regard to the various curriculum models developed for regular career education, Bailey and Stadt (1973) defined a two-dimensional model (see Table 4–6). The constructs or domains of career education and their goals according to Bailey and Stadt are:

1. Concepts of self—developing accurate and comprehensive self-concepts

115

TABLE 4-5   Classification System for Occupational Clusters

Level	I. Service	II. Business Contact	III. Organization	Group IV. Technology	V. Outdoor	VI. Science	VII. General Culture	VIII. Arts and Entertainment
1	Personal therapists Social work supervisors Counselors	Promoters	United States President and Cabinet officers Industrial tycoons International banker°	Inventive geniuses Consulting or chief engineers Ships' commanders	Consulting specialists	Research scientists University, college faculties Medical specialists Museum curators	Supreme Court Justices University, college faculties Prophets Scholars	Creative artists Performers, great teachers, university equivalent Museum curators
2	Social workers Occupational therapists Probation, truant officers (with training)	Promoters Public relations counselors	Certified public accountants Business and government executives Union officials Brokers, average	Applied scientists Factory managers Ships' officers Engineers	Applied scientists Landowners and operators, large Landscape architects	Scientists, semi-independent Nurses Pharmacists Veterinarians	Editors Teachers, high school and elementary	Athletes Art critics Designers Music arrangers
3	YMCA officials Detectives, police sergeants Welfare workers City inspectors	Salesmen: auto, bond, insurance, etc. Dealers, retail and wholesale Confidence men	Accountants, average Employment managers Owners, catering, dry-cleaning, etc.	Aviators Contractors Foremen (DOT I) Radio operators	County agents Farm owners Forest rangers Fish, game wardens	Technicians, medical, X-ray, museum Weather observers Chiropractors	Justices of the Peace Radio announcers Reporters Librarians	Ad writers Designers Interior decorators Showmen

	Service	Business Contact	Organization	Technology	Outdoor	Science	General Cultural	Arts and Entertainment
4	Barbers Chefs Practical nurses Policemen	Auctioneers Buyers (DOT I) House canvassers Interviewers, poll	Cashiers Clerks, credit, express, etc. Foreman, warehouse Salesclerks	Blacksmiths Electricians Foremen (DOT II) Mechanics, average	Laboratory testers, dairy products, etc. Miners Oil well drillers	Technical assistants	Law clerks	Advertising artists Decorators window, etc. Photographers Racing car drivers
5	Taxi drivers General house-workers Waiters City firemen	Peddlers	Clerks, file, stock, etc. Notaries Runners Typists	Bulldozer operators Deliverymen Smelter workers Truck drivers	Gardeners Farm tenants Teamsters, cow-punchers Miner's helpers	Veterinary hospital attendants		Illustrators, greeting cards Showcard writers Stagehands
6	Chambermaids Hospital attendants Elevator operators Watchmen		Messenger boys	Helpers Laborers Wrappers Yardmen	Dairy hands Farm laborers Lumberjacks	Nontechnical helpers in scientific organization		

SOURCE: Roe, Anne. *The psychology of occupation.* New York: John Wiley & Sons, 1956. Reprinted with permission of publisher.

2. Occupational, educational, and economic concepts and skills—the ability to execute plans to qualify for a career
3. Sense of agency—a commitment to a career plan, the responsibility and initiative felt by an individual as she/he develops an occupation
4. Information-processing skills—the application of problem-solving and decision-making skills in executing a career plan
5. Interpersonal relations—understanding an individual's behavior as it contributes to or detracts from the group
6. Work attitudes and values—acquiring work discipline, that is, completing tasks and being satisfied with the product

An important concept in the Bailey and Stadt model is the progression toward each of these six goals through four levels. The first level is referred to as the stage of "awareness." In this stage students are *exposed* to various concrete aspects of each domain and given experience in categorizing and generalizing these exposures by being encouraged to make judgments as to how they appear to him/her. The second stage, "accommodation," requires the child to formulate solutions and explanations as opposed to mere judgments. The next stage, "orientation," involves the students' readying themselves for decision making, as well as applying problem-solving techniques to their own situations. The last stage, "exploration and preparation," involves an occupational decision, active student research regarding necessary prerequisites and student initiation of the efforts needed. This model is quite extensive with accompanying goals and objectives for each construct within each level.

An additional curriculum model for career/vocational education has been developed by Keller (1972). This model recommends six principal components to ensure an integrated career development curriculum (see Table 4–7):

1. Society and work—knowledge about the institutions and dynamics in society that generate, define, and lend meaning to jobs (interfaces with social studies).
2. Occupational information—information on broad occupational groups, related jobs, and individual jobs (interfaces with vocational counseling).
3. Self-knowledge—information needed to make accurate and relevant self-assessments in relation to career choice (interfaces with all student evaluation).
4. Career planning—utilizing information on world of work and self-knowledge in decision making (interfaces with all education).

TABLE 4–6   A Developmental Curriculum Model for Career Education

Domains of Career Development Behaviors	A. Awareness K–3	B. Accommodation 4–6	C. Orientation 7–8	D. Exploration and Preparation 9–12
1. Concepts of self	A1	B1	C1	D1
2. Occupational, educational and economic concepts and skills	A2	B2	C2	D2
3. Sense of agency	A3	B3	C3	D3
4. Information processing skills	A4	B4	C4	D4
5. Interpersonal relationships	A5	B5	C5	D5
6. Work attitudes and values	A6	B6	C6	D6

SOURCE: Bailey, L. J., and Stadt, R. W. *Career education: New approaches to human development*, p. 50. Bloomington, Ill.: McKnight Publishing Co., 1973. Used with permission of the publisher.

TABLE 4–7   Components for Career Development Curriculum

Society and Work

1. Components of a Working Society

Financial institutions	Trade unions
The public	Workers
Government as a third party	Managers
Government as an employer	Owners
Technical and professional societies	Commerce and business
Labor unions	Industry
	Agriculture

2. The Economics of Work

Cost of Living	Risk
Prices	Investment
Wages	Increasing wealth
Costs	Wealth and its changing meaning
Profit and loss	

3. How Work Rules and Values Are Defined

The relationship of social status to occupations
The impact of labor policies
Labor negotiations and disputes

(*continued*)

119

TABLE 4-7 (*cont.*)

Relationship of jobs to functions performed
Relationship of jobs to products produced
Education and occupational opportunity
Work and leisure

4. Change in the Working World

The interpretation of occupational trend data
Sources of occupational change information
Methods of measuring and predicting occupational change
The impact of industrialization, automation, and technological change on
   occupations
The nature of technological change

Occupational Information

1. Job Areas (opportunities and requirements)

Professional workers (physicians, lawyers, teachers, engineers, scientists,
   etc.)
Officials and managers (corporation executives, public officials, plant supervisors, store managers, etc.)
Technicians (electronic technician, X-ray technologist, computer program-
   mer, laboratory technician, etc.)
Craftsmen (carpenters, auto mechanics, electricians, air conditioning me-
   chanics, plumbers, welders, etc.)
Clerical workers (stenographers, typists, file clerks, secretaries, bookkeepers,
   etc.)
Distributive occupations (salesmen, buyers, stock clerks, wrappers, etc.)
Operatives (assemblers, inspectors, machine operators, drivers, deliverymen,
   etc.)
Service workers (policemen, firemen, waiters or waitresses, barbers, beauty
   operators, etc.)
Laborers

2. Job Opportunities and Hierarchies within Different Industrial Areas

Apparel
Agriculture
Communication
Construction
Education
Electric light and power
Entertainment and sports
Equipment manufacturing
Financing, insurance, real estate
Food and lodging
Government
Health and welfare
Maintenance and repair
Materials manufacturing
Merchandising and retail trade
Metal production
Personal and protective services
Research and engineering
Transportation

TABLE 4–7   (*cont.*)

3. Information Concerning Specific Jobs (available selectively to students)
   Specially prepared job descriptions
      The nature of social contribution
      Nature of tasks performed
      Success and failure criteria
      Causes for demotion or termination
      Skill and knowledge requirements
      Advancement prospects
      Training opportunities
      Employment opportunities
      Remuneration
      Work schedule
      Work environment
      Personal, family and social demands
      Travel required
      Status connected with the occupation
      Education, training, and other entry requirements
      Relationship to other occupations
      Probable change due to technological or social change

Self-Knowledge

1. Capacities
   Assessing one's bargaining position with respect to a job
   Evaluation of demonstrated proficiency with reference to occupational requirements
   Evaluation of age, sex, physical characteristics, and handicaps in relation to occupational requirements
   Financial status and training costs
   Scholastic aptitudes and educational achievement as indications of probable future educational success
   The aptitude profile and occupational requirements
   The sources of useful self-evaluation information

2. Motivational factors
   Assessing one's values with respect to job demands
   Assessing one's economic, social status, and individual dominance needs with respect to occupational opportunities
   Evaluation of interests and aspirations as these relate to occupational choice
   Sensitivity to the following as sources of satisfaction, motivation, and dissatisfaction
      Opportunity for creative effort
      Responsibility
      Recognition
      Accomplishment
      Amount and type of interaction with others
      Repetitiveness of tasks
      Status
      Wages
      The physical environment
      Working hours
      Failure and criticism

(*continued*)

TABLE 4-7 *(cont.)*

Full use of capabilities as a source of satisfaction
The development of capabilities as a source of satisfaction

Career Planning

1. Combining Occupational and Self-Knowledge

   Allowing for occupational change
   Avoiding under- and over-employment
   Choosing among employment opportunities
   Evaluating a potential position
   Matching individual characteristics to occupational profiles

2. Educational Planning

   Post-employment training as a route to advancement
   Part-time and cooperative school-industry employment opportunities
   Sources of financial aid for education and training
   Costs of training and time required
   The relationship of education to occupational achievement
   Alternative routes to career objectives
   How to develop a reasonable career plan
   The sequence of career-relevant choices
   Strategies of learning for flexible occupational proficiency
   Matching educational and training programs to occupations
   Sources for post-high school training

3. Securing a Job

   Making the initial impressions on the job
   The employment interview: behavior and appearance
   Resumes and application forms
   Placement services and sources of job availability information
   Common employment and personnel practices

Basic Technology

1. General work habits
2. Machines and mechanical principles
3. Electrical principles
4. Structures
5. Chemical and biological principles
6. Numerical operations
7. Verbal communications
8. Human relations

Specific Occupational Training

If we have a truly career development curriculum we will provide all students with entry skills/knowledges, attitudes. However, some students will want more specific training. This component of our curriculum will be initiated only when the student has made a relatively firm occupational choice, or is approaching sufficiently close to his planned education terminal point that further delay in specific training will be likely to preclude an opportunity to obtain employment which will fully use his capabilities. Specific occupational course content must be based on the results of job and task analysis.

Source: Keller, L. J. Career development—An integrated curriculum approach, K–12. In K. Goldhammer and R. Taylor, *Career education perspective and promise.* Columbus: Charles E. Merrill, 1972. Used with permission of publisher.

5. Basic technology—school reorganizes curricula around basic skills useful in occupations (interfaces with all education).
6. Specific occupational training—direct training for entry level skills and attitudes (integrates with specific occupational courses).

These components should be viewed as sequential levels in that one appears, in most cases, to depend upon acquiring the previous. Though drawn from the regular education literature, this hierarchy may also be helpful in planning career/vocational education for the handicapped. The only caution here is that for some handicapped pupils there will be limits imposed on the degree of attainment and the age of appropriateness.

Considering the importance that career and vocational education holds for handicapped youngsters, a large majority of whom never return to school for further education or training, it is surprising to see so little special education and career/vocational training literature meshing. Interested readers may frequently find it necessary to develop innovative models for educating handicapped students in the process of occupational development.

Stark (1969) developed a curriculum outline to use with moderately retarded individuals (see Table 4–8). This model may be particularly pertinent for students in self-contained special classes, for use in a unit approach to occupational training, and for residential or group home students.

In a similar view, Brolin (1976) has provided an extensive outline of 22 major competencies for the retarded adult when considering training in career/vocational programs. These competencies are divided into three major constructs: daily living skills, personal/social skills, and occupational guidance and preparation skills:

Daily Living Skills

1. Managing family finances.
2. Caring for and repairing home furnishings and equipment.
3. Taking care of personal needs.
4. Raising children and family living.
5. Buying, planning, and preparing food.
6. Selecting, buying, and making clothing.
7. Engaging in civic activities.
8. Utilizing recreation and leisure time.
9. Mobility (getting around the community).

TABLE 4–8   A Suggested Vocational Education Curriculum for Handicapped Youth

---

What Types of Jobs Exist (e.g., auto, construction, hospital service)

Knowing Job Requirements (how difficult, special skills needed, union regulations and dues, etc.)

Ways to Get a Job
A. References (friends, relatives, teachers)
B. Answering want ads (distance from your home, hours, salary, social climate, security)
C. Parents
D. Agencies (employment, federal, public, private, special)

Things to Consider in Getting a Job
A. Appearance (voice, manner, dress, poise)
B. Punctuality
C. Salary
D. Working conditions
E. Hours

Holding a Job
A. Skills (handling tools, punctuality, good attendance, conscientiousness)
B. Character traits (friendly, polite, self-control, honesty, ready to learn, ability to take criticism, desire to improve, etc.)

Forms and Blanks
A. Applications (telephone, letter, in-person interview, social security)
B. Work permits
C. Banking (checking, savings, deposits, withdrawals, interest, writing checks to pay bills)
D. Postal (change of address, money order, parcel post, etc.)

Jobs Needing Special Training
A. Barber and beautician
B. Carpenter's helper (plumber, electrician, mason, etc.)
C. Civil service jobs (hospital, sanitation, postal, highway maintenance)

What We Budget For (food, rent, clothing, recreation, health, etc.)

Ways of Buying (cash, installment, loan, etc.)

Getting Along With Others (manners, being honest, reliable, respecting rights of others, recognizing importance of parental advice, etc.)

Taxes (income, residence, sales, property, school, etc.)

Voting Requirements (age, residence, registration, etc.)

Civic Responsibility (obey law, defend country, respect rights of others, etc.)

Social Values (how to behave in a democracy, celebration of national holidays, etc.)

SOURCE: Stark, E. S. *Special Education: A curriculum guide.* Springfield, Ill.: Charles C Thomas, 1969. Used with permission of publisher.

Personal-Social Skills

10. Attaining a sufficient understanding of oneself (self-awareness and appraisal).
11. Obtaining a positive self-confidence, self-concept.
12. Desiring and achieving socially responsive behavior.
13. Choosing, developing, and maintaining appropriate interpersonal relationships.
14. Achieving independent functioning.
15. Making good decisions, problem-solving.
16. Communicating appropriately with others.

Occupational Guidance and Preparation

17. Knowing about and exploring job possibilities.
18. Selecting and planning the most appropriate occupational choice(s).
19. Exhibiting the work habits required in the competitive labor market.
20. Developing the manual skills and physical tolerances required in the competitive labor market.
21 Obtaining a specific and saleable entry-level occupational skill.
22. Seeking, securing, and maintaining jobs appropriate to level of abilities, interests, and needs.

Brolin's competencies are somewhat more flexible than others and could be adapted easily to fit most special education curricula that dealt with career/vocational training.

Prior to planning education for handicapped youngsters, it is important that educators define for themselves a comprehensive program of career and vocational education. In order to accomplish this goal, the reader is encouraged to consult other occupational dictionaries and categorizations, regular classroom career and vocational curricular models, and models developed specifically for special education. The competencies and strategies outlined by Saski (1977) and Humphrey, McEntire, and Saski (1978) would also be helpful.

Career and vocational education outcomes often depend largely on the behavioral and social aspects of a particular child's interactions within the environment. These interactions influence the ability to both obtain and perform jobs. The following section is designed to present the reader with various models relevant to the social and behavioral aspects of education.

Sociobehavioral Education

Sociobehavioral education can be defined as instruction designed to develop student self-esteem and confidence through the acquisition of appropriate social behaviors. The ultimate goal of sociobehavioral education is to allow the handicapped student the freedom and independence afforded other individuals within society. This freedom is only allowed individuals who behave and respond in a way that is generally acceptable to others. Sociobehavioral education involves two basic purposes: acquiring appropriate, productive behaviors and eliminating unacceptable, destructive behaviors. In order to gain some notion of the scope of sociobehavioral education in dealing with handicapped pupils, we present (1) a classification system for common behavior problems in the classroom, (2) a developmental sequence of educational goals as they relate to acquiring acceptable behaviors, (3) a social curriculum developed for use specifically with handicapped youngsters, (4) a discussion of the concept of normalization of handicapped persons in society, and (5) a discussion of values education.

In their work in training teachers to recognize and manage social and behavioral problems in the classroom, Gropper, Kress, Hughes, and Pekich (1975) have developed a model for classifying problem behaviors. In attempting to classify behaviors, these authors first defined 13 principal classroom problem areas:

1. Attention to classroom activities (inattention, daydreaming, withdrawal)
2. Physical activity (restlessness, noisemaking, hyperactivity)
3. Reaction to tension (emotional upsets)
4. Appropriateness of behavior (telling tales, collecting objects)
5. Meeting work requirements (self-criticism, giving up, not doing work)
6. Interest in work (playing, doodling, drawing)
7. Getting along with others (name calling, fighting, passivity)
8. Consideration for group needs (impatient with others, interrupting others, talking out loud)
9. Response to teacher requirements or instructions (arguments, rudeness, disobedience)
10. Degree of independence (seeking praise, attention, support; currying favor)
11. Regard for school rules and conventions (swearing, passing pictures, rule breaking)
12. Regard for general rules and conventions (truancy, tardiness, disallowed objects, destroying property)
13. Integrity (cheating, tattling, stealing) (1975, p. 87)

Additionally, in order to distinguish between typical behavior problems exhibited by all children and those encountered with children needing specialized assistance, 14 criteria for classifying severity of behaviors were developed (see Table 4–9). These criteria represent such factors as duration (how long does a particular behavior generally last?), frequency (how often?), and accessibility of circumstances (how easy is it to determine the circumstances that led to the behavior?). Levels of severity are ranked normal, problem, or referable. Normal refers to behaviors frequently exhibited by all children while problem levels describe a child who may be maladjusted and needs some intervention. Referable levels of behavior are indicative of students who need extensive specialized assistance. This classification system is quite useful in determining the severity of problems that are likely to be considered "deviant."

Hewett (1968) organized a behavior framework into a developmental sequence of educational goals. This sequence serves to add further direction to the educator in developing a plan of intervention for particular students. The sequence, represented below, moves from simplest to most complex.

1. Attention . . . children must notice and attend if they are to learn. This ability is fundamental to all learning.
2. Response . . . children must do something (make a response) in order to learn. Active participation in learning is vitally necessary.
3. Order . . . the child must develop order in attending and responding for increased learning efficiency.
4. Exploratory . . . multisensory exploration provides the child with the raw material, the basic facts which he needs in learning.
5. Social . . . at this level the child attempts to gain the social approval of individuals in his environment. Social relationships are important for the child.
6. Mastery . . . the mastering of basic intellectual and adaptive skills and the acquisition of a fund of information about the environment is the focus of this level.
7. Achievement . . . this highest level of the sequence is the enrichment level where self-motivation in learning is developed and where learning is extended in depth. (1968, pp. 48–55)

While these are broad categories, Hewett elaborates on each of the goals listed above and provides specific behaviors within each category; for example, paying attention is divided into visual, auditory, and tactual task orientation while also considering acuity, perception, and retention. Interested readers are urged to explore the original text for more in-depth analysis of specific behaviors classified under these constructs.

127

TABLE 4–9 Fourteen Criteria for Classifying the Severity of Problem Behavior

Description of Criteria	Normal	Problem	Referable
A. Intensity How disruptive of the child's other activities is the problem behavior?	NON-DISRUPTIVE Behavior does *not* interfere with the child's other activities	DISRUPTIVE Behavior interferes with the child's other activities	EXTREMELY DISRUPTIVE Behavior completely disrupts child's other activities
B. Appropriateness Is the behavior a reasonable response to the situation?	REASONABLE Response is acceptable or expected for the situation	INAPPROPRIATE Response is undesirable for the situation	EXCESSIVE Response is out of proportion to the situation
C. Duration How long does the behavior episode last?	SHORT-LIVED Episode lasts only a short time (short time within a class period)	MODERATELY LONG Episode extends over a longer period (some carryover from one class to the next)	LONG-LASTING Episodes are long-lasting (greater part of a day)
D. Frequency How often does the behavior occur?	INFREQUENT Behavior usually is not repeated (rarely repeated in a day; rarely repeated on other days)	FREQUENT Behavior is repeated (may be repeated several times a day; may be repeated on several days)	HABITUAL Behavior happens all the time (repeated often during day; repeated on many days)
E. Specificity/ Generality In how many types of situations does the behavior occur?	OCCURS IN SPECIFIC SITUATION Behavior occurs in specific type of situation	OCCURS IN SEVERAL SITUATIONS Behavior occurs in more than one type of situation	OCCURS IN MANY SITUATIONS Behavior occurs in many types of situations
F. Manageability How easily does the behavior respond to management efforts?	EASILY MANAGED Responds readily to management efforts	DIFFICULT TO MANAGE Inconsistent or slow response to management efforts	CANNOT BE MANAGED Does not respond to management efforts
G. Assessibility of Circumstances How easily can the circumstances that produced the behavior be identified?	EASILY ASSESSED Easy to identify situation or condition producing behavior	DIFFICULT TO ASSESS Situation or condition producing behavior difficult to identify	CANNOT BE ASSESSED Cannot identify situation or condition producing behavior
H. Comparison with Maturity Level of Class How close to the norm of the class is the problem behavior?	NO DEVIATION FROM LEVEL OF CLASS Behavior is par for the group	BELOW LEVEL OF CLASS Behavior is below the group level	CONSIDERABLY BELOW LEVEL OF CLASS Behavior is considerably below the group level

TABLE 4–9 *(cont.)*

Description of Criteria	Normal	Problem	Referable
I. Number of Problem Behaviors Exhibited	Rarely more than one	Usually more than one	Usually many and varied
J. Acceptance by Peers Does the child have difficulty being accepted by peers?	ACCEPTED Is accepted by peers	HAS DIFFICULTY GETTING ALONG May have difficulty with particular individuals	NOT ACCEPTED Unaccepted by group
K. Recovery Time How quickly is the situation leading to the episode forgotten?	RAPID Gets over episode quickly	SLOW Gets over episode more slowly	DELAYED Does not get over episode
L. Contagion 1. Does the behavior disrupt the activities of others? 2. Do others copy the problem behavior?	LITTLE OR NO EFFECT ON OTHERS Behavior does not disturb or does not serve as a model for others	CONSIDERABLE EFFECT ON OTHERS Behavior disturbs immediate neighbors or neighbors copy behavior	EXCESSIVE EFFECT ON OTHERS Behavior disturbs whole class or whole class copies behavior
M. Degree of Contact with Reality *Does the behavior represent a loss of contact with reality?*	NO CONFUSION BETWEEN REAL/UNREAL	SOME CONFUSION BETWEEN REAL/UNREAL	CONFUSES REAL/UNREAL
N. Response to Learning Opportunities How readily does the child respond when learning opportunities are provided?	RESPONDS POSITIVELY TO ENRICHMENT/ REMEDIAL WORK	RESPONDS SLOWLY OR WEAKLY TO ENRICHMENT/ REMEDIAL WORK	DOES NOT RESPOND TO ENRICHMENT/ REMEDIAL WORK

SOURCE: Gropper, G. L.; Kress, G. C.; Hughes, R.; and Pekich, J. Training teachers to recognize and manage social and emotional problems in the classroom. In A. Dupont (ed.) *Educating emotionally disturbed children.* (2nd ed.) New York: Holt, Rinehart and Winston, 1975. Used with permission of publisher.

Other competencies have been developed for instructing primarily social skills. Generally these goals are used in instructing the mentally retarded student. One such model for use with mentally retarded youngsters at the preschool, primary, intermediate, prevocational, and vocational levels has been proposed by Kolestoe (1975). Table 4–10 (pp. 134–138) presents his curriculum model which is divided into three constructs:

1. Self—social skills designed to protect or enhance the child's self-image to be incorporated within other curriculum areas or units.
2. School—social skills to be taught and reinforced directly in the school.
3. Home, neighborhood, and community—social skills that must be transferred through vocational training, etc., prior to the child's exit from school.

This curriculum model illustrates drastic differences from models presented previously and serves to acquaint educators with the wide range of concerns that must be addressed in order to meet the needs of various handicapped students. Many of the skills mentioned in relation to sociobehavioral education are also necessary to successfully develop self-help and basic living skills.

An interesting concept in the socialization of the mentally retarded that can apply to other handicapping conditions is that of normalization (Wolfensberger, 1972). Wolfensberger defines the principle of normalization as "Utilization of means which are as culturally normative as possible, in order to establish and/or maintain personal behaviors and characteristics which are as culturally normative as possible" (Wolfensberger, 1972, p. 28). While much of the Wolfensberger text is devoted to discussions regarding making institutional settings and group home settings as normal an environment as possible, he also emphasizes certain principles in establishing appropriate social skills so that a person may be acceptable within the mainstream of society. These concepts are particularly applicable for consideration when developing special education programs within special residential schools, self-contained classes and special schools, institutions, and group homes. Wolfensberger outlines the normalization principle in two dimensions as illustrated in Table 4–11 (p. 139). These two dimensions represent the structure involving the handicapped individual himself (the dimension of interaction) and the structure that involves the way in which that person is represented in the minds of others (the dimension of interpretation). There are three levels within each of these which correspond to the level of society that interacts with and interprets the handicapped individual. First, there is the person(al) level involving, for our purpose, the special educator. The second level is concerned with interactions within the student's daily environment, for instance, the school or residential staff and peers, the neighborhood, and so on. The third level corresponds to broad societal structures that influence the student but often not through direct contact, such as government. Several examples will clarify the concept of normalization.

Within the dimension of person/interaction a teacher develops goals and instructs a student in the acquisition of normal habits, such as walking with an appropriate gait or dressing in the latest styles and trends. In the dimension person/interpretation the teacher's goal is to lessen in any way possible the deviantness of the school or class environment so that the student is seen less as deviant (very similar to the concept of placing students in the least restrictive environment). In the level of primary societal systems, goals would be directed toward the system rather than the student. Examples of special intervention in the interaction/primary societal dimension would be parent counseling and teacher in-service. The concept of normalization holds particular implications for more severely handicapped students as special education attempts to integrate them into society through sociobehavioral education.

An additional current concept in sociobehavioral education, not specifically developed for the handicapped, is values education. The goal of values education is to help students clarify for themselves their *own* values. This concept is based on the assumption that values (rights and wrongs) are relative, personal, and situational (Harmin and Simon, 1973). Harmin and Simon suggest there are two major considerations in values teaching: (1) how one can help students develop their own values, and (2) how to manage student behavior while values are being formed. They suggest the latter is generally accomplished by establishing classroom rules not defined as values but as devices for protecting individuals and groups of individuals from pressures of the others. According to Kirschenbaum (1973), values education should be implemented through a process rather than by simply imposing or defining values for students or by defining criteria for values. Kirschenbaum suggests that the constructs of values clarification include feeling, thinking, communicating, choosing, and acting. These constructs are outlined below.

The Valuing Process

I. Feeling
  1. Being open to one's inner experience.
    a. awareness of one's inner experience
    b. acceptance of one's inner experience

II. Thinking
  1. Thinking on all seven levels.
    a. memory

131

b. translation
c. application
d. interpretation
e. analysis
f. synthesis
g. evaluation
2. Critical thinking.
  a. distinguishing fact from opinion
  b. distinguishing supported from unsupported arguments
  c. analyzing propaganda, stereotypes, etc.
3. Logical thinking (logic).
4. Creative thinking.
5. Fundamental cognitive skills.
  a. language use
  b. mathematical skills
  c. research skills

III. Communicating—Verbally and Nonverbally
1. Sending clear messages.
2. Empathetic listening.
3. Drawing out.
4. Asking clarifying questions.
5. Giving and receiving feedback.
6. Conflict resolution.

IV. Choosing
1. Generating and considering alternatives.
2. Thoughtfully considering consequences, pros and cons.
3. Choosing strategically.
  a. goal setting
  b. data gathering
  c. problem solving
  d. planning
4. Choosing freely.

V. Acting
1. Acting with repetition.
2. Acting with a pattern and consistency.
3. Acting skillfully, competently. (1973, pp. 105–106)

Knapp (1973) offers still another conceptualization of values education, which provides us with examples of the process in education using the situation of teaching the concept of pollution.

Seven Valuing Processes

Choosing

1. Valuing involves choosing freely, not as the result of peer or authority pressure. What beliefs and personal behaviors have you developed concerning the environment that are truly your own, not the result of external pressures?

2. Valuing involves considering alternatives before a choice is made. What alternatives did you consider before determining how you would help improve the environment?
3. Valuing involves carefully examining the consequences of each alternative. Did you consider the consequences of the various ways to combat environmental pollution?

Prizing

4. Valuing involves being proud of your choice (not boastful pride, but feeling-good-about pride). Are you proud of the ways you selected to ease the pollution problem?
5. Valuing involves sharing your convictions with others. Have you publicly affirmed your belief in what you chose to do to protect the environment?

Acting

6. Valuing involves acting according to your choice and not just having good intentions. What have you actually done within the past week to reduce pollution?
7. Valuing involves acting repeatedly and incorporating the behavior into your life pattern. Did you incorporate these antipollution behaviors in your life on a regular basis? (1973, pp. 162–163)

It is interesting to note the relation between sociobehavioral education and other curricular areas shown explicitly in the above examples. Sociobehavioral education is much more than the acquisition of specific skills or concepts; it is the integration of oneself into the curricula. For many handicapped youngsters, of course, a first step in socioemotional education is modifying disruptive behaviors or establishing appropriate social skills. All of the behaviors focused upon foster self-sufficiency through the constructive integration and internalization of emotional states.

To a large degree concern regarding specific behaviors centers on improving the handicapped student's ability to function adequately in various educational environments. In order to function successfully in the school, as well as society, the student must be able to perform certain academic tasks, primarily those of language, reading, math, and writing.

Academic Education

For purposes of special education instruction, one can define academics as training in the basic concepts of oral language, reading, writing, and math. These subdivisions are used to fulfill the purpose of special education which is to assist only those students who are classified as handicapped and who exhibit problems to the degree that they cannot be

133

TABLE 4–10   Model for Conceptualizing Social Education

THE SELF

Preschool Level

1. On request, the child can say his full name and age.
2. On request, the child can identify objects that belong to him and those that belong to others.
3. On request, the child can identify children who are taller, shorter, heavier, or lighter than he is.
4. When greeted by another person, the child will respond to the greeter either verbally, by gesture, or by facial expression harmoniously to the greeting.

Primary Level

1. Upon request, the child can say his home address and telephone number.
2. In a verbal discussion, the child can name each member of his family and tell two facts about each.
3. Given a self-help task such as putting on boots, brushing teeth, working zippers, buckling, buttoning, or tying, the child will respond correctly.
4. Upon request, the child will be able to wash his face, neck, ears, hands, arms, feet, and legs.
5. Upon request, the child will participate in the selection of games, food, clothing, and friends.
6. Given a task to perform, the child can determine when the task has been completed.

Intermediate Level

1. Given a youngster with whom he is unfamiliar, the child will be able to make at least one acceptable gesture to become acquainted, such as: being able to name the child, play a game with him, or engage in conversation.
2. Given five pictures labeled as showing the emotions of anger, sadness, happiness, hostility, or fear, the student can identify the pictures.
3. When discussing abilities, the child will be able to choose from a list of descriptive words, those which describe his feelings when he performs well and those which describe his feelings when he performs poorly.
4. Given a law at his level of experience, the child will be able to state why it is important to obey it.
5. In a role-playing situation, the student can verbally state the difference between satisfactory and unsatisfactory behavior of the antagonists.
6. The child can participate in group discussions without arguing.

Prevocational Level

1. When verbally given the sentence started "I can," the student can tell five things he is able to do.
2. When verbally given the started sentence "I like" or "I do not like," the student can name five things for either sentence.
3. Given a situation involving the belongings of others, the student returns the property intact after every use.
4. When given a compliment, the student will respond positively with "Thank you" or a smile.
5. Given a situation in which the student is involved in a fight or becomes angry, the student will be able to verbalize what alternative actions might have been possible.

TABLE 4–10 (*cont.*)

6. Given a situation involving a disagreement with another person, the child will be able to accept the situation as evidenced by his willingness to talk to or work with the other person.
7. Given a situation in which he is confronted with constructive criticism, the student will be able to respond without arguing or denying the criticism.

Vocational Level
1. When someone offers to assist him, the student accepts the offer in an appropriate manner.
2. When shown pictures of interaction among people, the student will be able to identify those who exhibit cooperative behavior.
3. Given a task in which he has previously made errors, the student will be able to identify the errors and the reasons for the errors.
4. When in a social dance situation, the student can demonstrate the proper behavior for the situation.

IN THE SCHOOL

Preschool Level
1. After demonstration, when asked by teacher, the child can pour liquid into a glass or cup and drink when asked.
2. After demonstration, the child can put food into a bowl and use either a fork, knife, or spoon when asked.
3. After demonstration, the child can feed, water, and clean the home of classroom pets whenever asked.
4. On request, the child can verbally state the basic classroom rules and give a reason why.
5. In a structured classroom activity, the child will accept the decisions of the person in authority without leaving the activity.
6. Within the school environment, when the teacher exhibits a positive verbal or physical response toward the child, the child's attempts to co-operate will increase.

Primary Level
1. Given a new situation, the child will respond with a behavior commonly acceptable in the situation.
2. Given a daily assigned chore at school, the child will be able to perform the task without complaining or having to be reminded.
3. Given the responsibility of checking out a library book the child will return the book at the stated time to the stated place.
4. Given adequate previous training or experience in a specific exercise, the child will be able to lead others in the exercise.
5. In an unstructured situation, the child will demonstrate that he identifies the rights of others by allowing them to make choices and decisions and to express themselves.
6. During free time, the child will join an activity of his own volition and/or invite other children to join him in a play activity.
7. When shown ten pictures showing interaction among people, the student can differentiate those who show cooperating behavior from those who do not.

TABLE 4–10 (*cont.*)

Intermediate Level

1. The student can participate in a group project without arguing or fighting.
2. Upon request, the student can verbally state five ways school experiences help people prepare for everyday living.
3. Upon request, the student can verbally state five reasons why he should practice good health habits.
4. Upon request, the student can verbally state five reasons why he should practice good habits of grooming.
5. Upon request, the student will be able to say the names of the school principal, teacher, nurse, and secretary.
6. Given an academic task that the child fails, he will not physically or verbally abuse or disrupt others but rather will seek assistance in an acceptable manner.
7. Upon receiving a reasonable request for help from a peer for a classroom task, he will fulfill the request.

Prevocational Level

1. Given a situation in which the rights of another are being violated, the student will recognize that the rights are being violated, be able to determine an appropriate course of action, and take definite action that will defend those rights.
2. Given a set of school rules he is capable of following, the student will be able to abide by them without having to be reminded of them more than once.
3. Given a classroom situation where other students are involved, the student will be able to demonstrate an interest in the activity of others as demonstrated by taking part in the activity without distracting or disrupting those involved.
4. In group discussions and gatherings, the student will voluntarily contribute at least one idea, thought, or feeling during the time of the meeting.
5. Given an assigned work task involving two or more students, they will work together until the task is completed.
6. During a structured situation in which two students who have expressed a dislike for each other must work next to each other, the student will be able to work without teacher correction.
7. Given a competitive situation, the student will be able to contribute as a member of a team by demonstrating his ability to follow the rules of the game.

Vocational Level

1. Given a social situation, the student will be able to select the clothing proper for the occasion and verbally offer two reasons to support the selection.
2. Upon request, the student will be able to state verbally five principles of grooming and relate them to employment or social situations.
3. In a given social situation, the student will be able to state verbally the appropriate graces called for and defend his selection of the behaviors named.
4. Upon request, the student will be able to define honesty, truthfulness, and tolerance, and cite examples of each.

TABLE 4–10   (*cont.*)

5. Upon request, the student will be able to state a set of moral standards and explain and defend them.
6. Upon request, the student will be able to explain and demonstrate his understanding of the need for sharing in maintaining good relations with fellow employees.
7. Upon request, the student will be able to explain verbally the differences between the role of leader and worker in an employment situation.
8. Given a situation, the student will be able to set up committees and other groups necessary for organization in order to accomplish a goal.

THE HOME, NEIGHBORHOOD, AND COMMUNITY
Preschool Level
1. Given an assigned home task that he can perform, the child will accomplish it to the satisfaction of the parents and will be able to state when he has done it well.
2. Given a written note or a verbal message the child will deliver it to the designated person.
3. Upon request, the child will be able to state verbally three things about the work of his father, mother, or surrogates.

Primary Level
1. Upon request, the child will be able to tell the location of stores and public buildings with reference to his house.
2. Upon request, the child will be able to prepare a simple breakfast of cereal, milk, and toast.
3. Upon request, the child will be able to use a vacuum cleaner, dust pan and broom, can opener, dust cloth, mixer, mop and scrub brush, and stove.
4. Upon request, the child will be able to state reasons for starting work on time and putting things away when home chores are finished.
5. In role playing, the child will be able to ask a stranger for directions while maintaining a cautious distance and cordial behavior.
6. Upon request, the child will be able to state verbally two behavior rules that apply to each situation of being at the movies, riding on a bus or subway, in a restaurant, swimming pool, or library.
7. Upon request, the child will be able to describe at a simple level the need for each of the community helpers: police, firemen, garbage collector, bus driver, or subway conductor.
8. Upon request, the child will be able to describe at a simple level the need for each of the family service persons: doctors, dentists, nurses, clergymen, druggists, welfare worker.

Intermediate Level
1. Upon request, the student will be able to find the telephone numbers of the Police Department and Fire Department in the local telephone book.
2. Given a public transportation system, the student will be able to describe which bus or subway he would use to go from his home to a downtown shopping area.
3. Upon request, the student will be able to name five local businesses, five occupations, and five different jobs people perform.

TABLE 4–10   (*cont.*)

4. Upon request, the student will be able to name five historical figures and describe the contribution of each.
5. Upon request, the student will be able to name the mayor, governor, and president.

Prevocational Level
1. Upon request, the student can verbally state three responsibilities of a wage earner in a family.
2. Upon request, the student can verbally state five responsibilities of a homemaker in a family.
3. Upon request, the student will be able to supply three effects companions have on each other.
4. Given a map of the state, the student will be able to identify and briefly describe each of the major geographical areas.
5. When a state government division is named, the student will be able to tell its major function.
6. Upon request, the student will be able to identify each of the major utilities that serve houses.

Vocational Level
1. When questioned, the student will be able to state his obligations as a family member and cite examples.
2. Upon request, the student will be able to differentiate between benefits and nonbenefits of neighborhood life.
3. Given either pictures of traffic signs or the signs themselves, the student will be able to describe their meaning.
4. Given a road map, the student will be able to identify the directions north, south, east, and west.
5. Given a road map, the student will be able to produce a route from any given point to another.
6. Upon request, the student will be able to identify agencies providing help in cases of specific family emergencies and describe how to secure the help.
7. Upon request, the student will be able to cite examples of behaviors that reflect the responsibilities, duties, and rights of citizens.
8. Upon request, the student will be able to plan and prepare a proper breakfast, lunch, or dinner.
9. Given a bundle of dirty clothes, the student will be able to sort and wash the clothes, using the appropriate settings for kinds and colors.
10. Given a basket of newly washed clothes, the student will be able to iron them, using the proper settings for each item of clothing.

SOURCE: Kolestoe, O. *Teaching educable mentally retarded children.* New York: Holt, Rinehart and Winston, 1976. Used with permission of publisher.

educated successfully in the regular classroom. Therefore, any student for whom academic education is needed through special education must first be instructed in the basic skills necessary to matriculate into society and school. Attention to auxiliary academic areas (such as history, sciences, and literature) is elaborative and in most instances a waste

TABLE 4–11   Normalization Model

| LEVELS OF ACTION | DIMENSIONS OF ACTION | |
	Interaction	*Interpretation*
Person	Elicting, shaping, and maintaining normative skills and habits in persons by means of direct physical and social interaction with them	Presenting, managing, addressing, labelling, and interpreting individual persons in a manner emphasizing their similarities to rather than differences from others
Primary and intermediate social systems	Elicting, shaping, and maintaining normative skills and habits in persons by working indirectly through their primary and intermediate social systems, such as family, classroom, school, working setting, service agency, and neighborhood	Shaping, presenting, and interpreting intermediate social systems surrounding a person or consisting of target persons so that these systems as well as the persons in them are perceived as culturally normative as possible
Societal systems	Eliciting, shaping, and maintaining normative behavior in persons by appropriate shaping of large societal social systems, and structures such as entire school systems, laws, and government	Shaping cultural values, attitudes, and stereotypes so as to elicit maximal feasible cultural acceptance of differences

SOURCE: Wolfensberger, W. *Normalization*. Toronto: National Institute on Mental Retardation, 1972. Used with permission of publisher.

TABLE 4–12.   Basic Constructs of Language

	Receptive	*Expressive*
Phonology	The ability to differentiate individual sounds heard	The ability to produce or reproduce individual sounds
Morphology	The ability to understand differences in word meanings when endings, prefixes, etc., are utilized	The ability to utilize appropriate endings, prefixes, etc.
Syntax	The ability to understand sentences using various grammatical forms	The ability to utilize various grammatical forms in one's own speech
Semantics	The ability to understand meanings of words and sentences spoken	The ability to utilize words and sentences to express appropriate meaning

of the student's time. Instruction in more advanced academic areas can and should be provided to those intellectually and emotionally capable handicapped students through the regular classroom.

The concept of academic education as defined here, which is applicable to all handicapped youngsters, begins with establishing a system of oral language and continues through being able to express oneself in writing and perform complex mathematical operations. Each of these academic curricular areas has been defined and taught in many ways, but, unlike the areas of self-help, vocational, and behavioral education, the general format varies only slightly. For the most part, persons who have conceptualized academic curricula have arranged concepts and specific skills within a format referred to as a scope and sequence. The scope and sequence is a two-dimensional array of skills organized according to constructs or divisions within each curriculum area and levels representing increasing complexity within each construct. Some examples are given below to aid the reader in developing his/her own ideas regarding constructs and levels within each curricular area of education.

Language. Traditionally, the area of language is divided into two major components: listening and speaking (referred to as receptive and expressive language). In many instances, each of these constructs is in turn divided into the subcategories of phonology, morphology, semantics, and syntax. Phonology is the study of the individual phonemes or sounds that constitute spoken language. Morphology is the study of the smallest meaningful units in language. For example, the word "boats" has two morphemes—"boat" and "s," a plural marker. The arrangement of individual words into meaningful phrases and sentences is referred to as syntax. Syntax can be thought of as the grammatical system of a language. Semantics refers to the underlying meaning of words and sentences (Wallace and Larsen, 1978). Table 4–12 (p. 139) displays the relationship between these constructs and receptive and expressive language.

Bartel and Bryen (1978) have developed an extensive scope and sequence chart of language development sequenced from birth to six years of age (see Table 4–13, pp. 142–163). Constructs emphasized by Bartel and Bryen include the characteristics of a child's language at each age period, sounds made at the various ages (phonology), acquired intonation at the various ages, meaning (semantics and morphology), and grammar (syntax) skills. Readers may wish to use this table to ascertain the various receptive and expressive elements of normal language development appropriate at different age levels.

Lee (1974) conceptualized the area of syntax in a complex assessment device designed to measure a child's use of the various grammatical aspects of the English language (Table 4–14, pp. 164–167). In each of the various parts of speech, Lee delineates simplest to most complex forms. Although the Developmental Sentence Analysis shown in Table 4–14 is actually an assessment device, the chart may be useful in formulating one's own ideas of the skills involved in oral language education. Other aspects of language frequently needing attention in handicapped children include the areas associated with written language, that is, reading and writing.

Reading. The academic area of reading is generally of great concern to special educators. Approximately 80 to 90 percent of students needing special assistance in academics are referred primarily because of reading problems. Reading problems are generally categorized as either comprehension problems or word-recognition problems. Frequently, both types of problems exist concurrently. Occasionally, word-recognition skills are so deficient that it is impossible even to measure reading comprehension skills. However, there are also handicapped students who are able to call words but do not comprehend the meaning. Guszak (1972) provides diagrams representing one way of conceptualizing the aspects of reading word recognition and comprehension (Figure 4–1, p. 162). Chall (1967) similarly defined the following eight measures of reading ability:

1. Word pronunciation—ability to read (pronounce) words on a list.
2. Connected oral reading—ability to read a selection aloud.
3. Phonics—knowledge of letter-sound correspondences.
4. Spelling—skill in writing words from dictation.
5. Vocabulary—knowledge of word meaning.
6. Silent reading comprehension—ability to understand material read.
7. Rate of reading—how quickly the child reads silently.
8. Interest, fluency, expression. (1969, pp. 104–105)

This model includes aspects of the child's oral reading such as rate, fluency, and so on, as well as spelling. For the most part, educators center reading concerns around recognition and comprehension.

Word recognition skills are those necessary for a student merely to read the word, including memory for sight words and analysis skills such as phonics, structural analysis, configuration, and context analysis. Of the major skills defined by Guszak, the first area mentioned is context analysis. Context analysis refers to using the context or meaning of the sentences or selection around a particular word in order to recognize the word itself. Generally context analysis is used in conjunction with particular phonic analysis skills. Phonic analysis entails using sounds of letters or letter groups in generating a particular word. A list of phonic skills taught in various basal reading programs is given in Table 4–15

141

TABLE 4–13. Scope and Sequence of Oral Language

Characteristics of the Period	*Sound Making*

Birth to Six Weeks

Characteristics of the Period

A. Reflexive vocalization
1. Sounds produced from a column of air expelled from lungs and passed through tensed vocal bands (Berry and Eisenson, 1956)
2. Primary purpose of speech mechanism for breathing and eating (McCarthy, 1954)
3. Undifferentiated vocalization—first three weeks
   a. No intent, awareness, meaning, or purpose
   b. Total bodily expression in response to stimulus
      (1) No distinguishable response to cold, hunger, pain, etc.
      (2) Variety in intensity (Berry and Eisenson, 1956)
      (3) Total emotional response (Anderson, 1953)
4. Differentiated vocalization—second three weeks
   a. Vocalization related to stimulus
   b. Muscle pattern sets for different cries (Berry and Eisenson, 1956)

Sound Making

A. Grunts, sighs, gurgles, glottal catch
1. Similar to swallowing movements
2. Present in whimpering rather than in crying (Van Riper, 1963)
B. No sex difference (Irwin, 1952)
C. Nasalization (Van Riper, 1963)
D. Average of seven phoneme-like sounds (Irwin, 1952)
1. Monosyllablic cries
2. Predominantly front vowel-like sounds
   a. Average of 4.5 distinguishable sounds (Irwin, 1952)
   b. /ae/ most predominant sounds (Berry and Eisenson, 1956)
   c. Other sounds: /ɪ ɛ ʌ ʊ/ (Irwin, 1948)
3. Predominantly glottal and velar consonant-like sounds
   a. Average of 2.7 sounds
   b. Predominantly plosive and fricative /h/ sounds (Irwin, 1947a, 1947b)
   c. Other sounds: /k g h/ (Irwin, 1947a, 1947b)

Six Weeks to Three Months

Characteristics of the Period

A. Beginning of babbling period (Berry and Eisenson, 1956)
1. Sounds made "for their own sake"
   a. Satisfaction from utterance
   b. Different from comfort sounds
   c. Play with sounnds (Lewis, 1963)
2. Spontaneous production of sounds
   a. Encompass more sounds than spoken by parents
   b. Indicate pleasurable mood (Anderson, 1953)
   c. Self-initiated vocal play (Berry and Eisenson, 1956)
   d. Random production of sounds

Sound Making

A. Coos, gurgles, squeals, sighs of contentment (Berry and Eisenson, 1956)
B. Monosyllabic utterances (Shirley, 1933)
1. Combination of consonant- and vowel-like sounds (McCarthy, 1954)
2. Little repetition (Berry and Eisenson, 1956)
3. Nasalization of sounds
   a. Vowel-like sounds—displeasure
   b. Consonant-like sounds—pleasure (Berry and Eisenson, 1956)
C. Average of thirteen to fourteen different sound types (Irwin, 1952)

Intonation	*Meaning*	*Grammar*
A. Variety in intensity Berry and Eisenson, 1956)	A. Beginning of crude vocabulary (Berry and Eisenson, 1956)	
B. Fundamental frequency of infant cry: 556 Hz (Fairbanks, 1942)	B. Response to other's voice (McCarthy, 1954)	
	C. Response of crying when other babies cry (Lewis, 1963)	
A. Variation in pitch	A. Vocalizes for pleasure or displeasure (Berry and Eisenson, 1956)	
B. Variation in loudness (Berry and Eisenson, 1956)	B. Reacts to sounds made (Berry and Eisenson, 1956)	
	C. Smiles at mother's voice (Lewis, 1963)	

(*continued*)

TABLE 4–13. (*cont.*)

	Characteristics of the Period	*Sound Making*
Six Weeks to Three Months	(1) /a/ produced at length (2) Most sounds not repeated (Berry and Eisenson, 1956) e. Predominantly noncrying sounds (Berry and Eisenson, 1956) f. Self-enjoyment from sound making (Berry and Eisenson, 1956) B. Sound making still essentially reflexive (Berry and Eisenson, 1956)	

A. Continuation of the babbling period

Three Months to Six Months

A. Continuation of the babbling period
1. Associated with pleasure, contentment
2. Autistic enjoyment (Mowrer, 1952)
3. Self-imitation
   a. Occurs while child is alone
   b. Disappears when distracted by someone else (Templin, 1957)
4. No longer reflexive
   a. Source from internal stimulation
   b. Hearing not important (Berry and Eisenson, 1956)

A. Some control over oral region (Irwin, 1952)
B. Disyllabic utterances (Shirley, 1933)
1. Consonant-like plus vowel-like sounds (Irwin, 1952)
2. Average of seventeen different sound types (Irwin, 1952)
   a. Predominantly vowel-like sounds
      (1) More frequent front and mid sounds
      (2) A few back sounds
      (3) Distinguishable sounds: /ɪ ɛ ʌ ʊ u/ (Irwin, 1948)
   b. Consonant-like sounds
      (1) Predominantly glottal /h/ and velar sounds
      (2) Appearance of labial sounds (Irwin, 1947b)
      (3) Appearance of nasals, plosive, and glide types (Irwin, 1947a)

Six Months to Nine Months

A. Lalling stage—repetition of vocal play
1. Expression of self
2. Association of hearing with sound production
   a. Ear reflex—circular response involving hearing and sound production
   b. Repetition of selected heard sounds
   c. Imitation as incentive for repetition (Berry and Eisenson, 1956)
B. Accompanying motor responses to vocalizations

A. Frequent change in syllable repetition (Van Riper, 1963)
B. Consonant-vowel-type combinations reduplicated (Weir, 1966)
C. Predominantly vowel-like sounds
1. Front sound 92 percent of the time (Irwin, 1948)
2. Some back vowels: /v ʊ o/ (Weir, 1966)

144

A. Intonation—infant cry of similar pressure waveform, much as the expiratory form of adult utterances (Lieberman, 1967)

A. Babbling—speech without content (Bullowa, 1967a, 1967b)
  1. Dental and labial sounds expressive of contentment
  2. Velar sounds expressive of distress (Lewis, 1963)
B. Noises—rudiments of vocal response (Lewis, 1963)
C. Systematic response to specific stimuli (Lewis, 1963)
D. Awareness of human speech (Shirley, 1933)

A. Pattern of intonation heard over a number of syllables
B. Little pitch variation within a single syllable (Weir, 1966)
C. Expressive intonation
  1. Dominating factor
  2. Discrimination among different patterns of expression (Lewis, 1963)
    a. Questions or commands

A. Application of vocalization
  1. For getting attention
  2. For socialization
    a. Support rejections
    b. Express demands (Van Riper, 1963)
  3. Re-creation of sound to replace or recall a pleasurable situation or object (Mowrer, 1952)
B. Response to human

(continued)

TABLE 4–13. *(cont.)*

	Characteristics of the Period	*Sound Making*
Six Months to Nine Months	1. Particular sounds accompany motor response (Berry and Eisenson, 1956) 2. Arm movements more meaningful than mouth movements (Van Riper, 1963) C. Language problems evident at this age through lack of lalling behavior; the deaf, retarded, aphasic, emotionally deprived (McCarthy, 1954)	

Nine Months to Twelve Months	A. Echolalic stage
	1. Repetition of sounds made by others
	   a. Sounds confined to those of native language (Berry and Eisenson, 1956)
	   b. Awareness of sound patterns of native language
	   c. Fixation of these sounds in vocalization (Anderson, 1953)
	2. Sounds devoid of meaning (Berry and Eisenson, 1956)
	3. Vocally fluent (Lewis, 1963)
	B. Imitation
	1. Perpetuation of sounds that interest him (Weir, 1966)
	2. Rudimentary imitation—speaks on hearing someone else speak (Lewis, 1963)
	3. Regularity in response to particular sounds (Lewis, 1963)
	C. Vocal play
	1. Production of vegetative sounds without demand
	2. Vocalization while playing (Weir, 1966)
		A. Consonant-like sounds beginning to exceed vowel-like sounds
		1. Front and mid vowel-like sounds less frequent
		   a. Most frequent types: /ɪ ʊ ʌ/
		   b. Back sounds appearing (Irwin, 1948)
		2. Glottal and velar sounds frequent
		   a. Appearance of postdental and labial types (Irwin, 1947b)
		   b. Additional semivowel and fricative types (Irwin, 1947a)

Twelve to Eighteen Months	Characteristics of the period—true speech A. Period of silence between babbling and true speech (Jakobsen and Halle, 1956) B. Intentional use of speech 1. First word—accident of vocal play (Berry and Eisenson, 1956) 2. Approximation of sound	Sound making—developing of phonological system A. Acquisition built on system of contrasts 1. /pa/ universal syllable (Jakobsen and Halle, 1956) 2. Consonants more frequent than vowels (Irwin, 1952) a. Nasal/oral distinction made (Jakobsen and Halle, 1956)

Intonation	*Meaning*	*Grammar*
b. Elicit surprise (Van Riper, 1963) D. Use of rhythm in vocal play (Van Riper, 1963)	speech by smiling or vocalizing C. Distinction between angry and pleasant sounds D. Beginning of imitation of parental uttterances (Van Riper, 1963)	
A. Discrimination among different patterns of expression (Lewis, 1963) B. Development of stress/unstress pattern (Weir, 1966) C. Fundamental frequency 1. 340 Hz when with father 2. 390 Hz when with mother 3. Higher frequency when crying (Lieberman, 1967)	A. Beginning of single-word usage 1. First word a crude approximation (McCarthy, 1954) 2. Babblings shortened into words (Irwin, 1952) 3. Manipulation of others through sound making (Lewis, 1963) B. Understanding of a few words and gestures (Myklebust, 1957) 1. Listens with selective interest (McCarthy, 1954) 2. Responds discriminatingly to adult verbalizations (Van Riper, 1963)	
A. Intonation and pitch dominating over phonetic form (Lewis, 1963) B. Marking of sentence boundaries by intonation contours (Weir, 1966) 1. Referential breath groups as phonetic	A. Development of vocabulary 1. One to three words (*bye-bye, no,* etc.) (Lewis, 1963) 2. Adaptation of child's primary experience to adult form of words (Lewis, 1963)	A. Holophrastic utterances 1. Single-word utterances 2. Ambiguous in meaning—broad and diffuse (McNeill, 1966) 3. Meaning derived from the situation

(*continued*)

TABLE 4–13. *(cont.)*

	Characteristics of the Period	*Sound Making*
Twelve Months to Eighteen Months	through echolalia (Lewis, 1963) 3. Strengthening of word through repetition (Berry and Eisenson, 1956) C. Accompanying motor activity or gestures to aid in understanding and stabilizing speech (Van Riper, 1963)	b. Labial/nonlabial contrast (Leopold, 1953–1954) c. Consonant used in initial position most frequently rather than medial or final (Irwin, 1952) 3. Vowel system 1. High/low contrast 2. Front/back contrast (Weir, 1966) B. Monosyllabic or disyllabic words—some onomatopoeic in character (*bow-wow*) (Irwin, 1952) C. Girls' achievement greater than that of boys (Irwin, 1952) Intonation
Eighteen Months to Twenty-Four Months	A. Acquisition of new words 1. Perception of new experiences 2. Manipulation of object or activity 3. Introduction of word by adult (Van Riper, 1963) B. Use of echolalia 1. Used in private (Van Riper, 1963); monologue-type speech (Weir, 1963) 2. Prolongs sounds 3. Occurs instantly and unconsciously (Van Riper, 1963) C. Use of jargon 1. Purposeful to child 2. Provides for fluency (Van Riper, 1963) D. Beginning of primitive grammatical system (McNeill, 1966) E. Motor activity 1. Much activity with speech	A. Many variants in child's system 1. Vowels most changeable (Metreaux, 1950); more front vowels than back (Irwin, 1952) 2. Instability of voicing feature (Weir, 1963) 3. Rare use of medial and final consonants (Metreaux, 1950; Irwin, 1947a) B. Articulation change under pressure of adult responses (Lewis, 1963) C. Periods of practice in perfecting sounds (Weir, 1963)

Intonation	*Meaning*	*Grammar*

markers of complete sentences (Lieberman, 1967)
2. Juncture evident in utterances (Weir, 1963)
C. Stress pattern: stress/unstress (Weir, 1963)
	3. Words learned through associated actions (Lewis, 1963)
	4. Names objects (Bayley, 1935)
	5. Performative utterance—names what he is doing at the time (Bullows, 1967a, 1967b)
	6. Begins to apply words to categories (Brown, 1965)
	B. Verbal understanding greater than production (McCarthy, 1954)
	1. Responds to commands (McCarthy, 1954)
	2. No understanding of questions
	  a. At times no response (Bellugi, 1965)
	  b. At times imitation or repetition of question (Bellugi, 1965)
		(Berry and Eisenson, 1956)
		B. Parts of speech (adult grammar)
		1. Nouns most common
		2. A few verbs and adjectives (McNeill, 1966)

A. Earliest feature acquired (Weir, 1963)
B. Indication of contrastive elements of stress (Weir, 1966)
1. Inconsistent use
2. Overuse of stress on syllables other than correct one (Weir, 1966)
Pitch rise at end of sentence (Metreaux, 1950)
Voice control—unstable
1. Variation from good modulation to straining
2. Much experimentation (Metreaux, 1950)
Fluency—frequent repe-
	A. Twenty- to 100-word vocabulary (Irwin, 1952)
	1. Prominence of meaningful words (McCarthy, 1954)
	2. General referents (*cookie* refers to anything similar) (Van Riper, 1963)
	3. One fourth of utterances understood by others (Van Riper, 1963)
	4. Beginning of substitution of words for physical acts (Lewis, 1963)
	  a. Extension of use of words (*pay*
		A. Beginning of structure
		1. Two-word sentences—words in juxtaposition (McNeill, 1966)
		2. Telegraphic utterances
		  a. Result of limited memory span
		  b. Inclusion of informational content of message
		  c. Omission of auxiliaries, prepositions, articles, verbs, and inflections (Brown and Fraser, 1964)
		3. Use of nouns, a few verbs, adjec-

(*continued*)

TABLE 4–13.   (*cont.*)

Characteristics of the Period   *Sound Making*

2. Overflow in lips, jaw, tongue,
   eyes, head (Metreaux, 1950)

Eighteen Months to Twenty-Four Months

A. Period of preoccupation with
   sound (Weir, 1966)
B. Rapid increase in language growth
   1. Use of speech for self-assertion,
      self-awareness, and as safety
      valve (Van Riper, 1963)
   2. Growth in grammatical capacity
C. Demand of response from others
   1. Demand from adults
   2. Kicks and screams with peers
      (Metreaux, 1950)
D. Motor activity
   1. Able to speak before he acts
   2. Acts in relation to task at hand
      (Metreaux, 1950)

A. Mastery of two thirds of adult
   speech sounds (Irwin, 1952)
   1. Vowels—90 percent correct (Irwin, 1948)
   2. Specific pronunciation for most
      consonants
      a. Most correct—plosives
      b. Slighting of medial consonants (Irwin, 1952)
      c. Overpronunciation of some
         words—*flonwer* for *flower*
         (Metreaux, 1950)
B. Distinctive features in production
   and recall
   1. Voicing and nasality best maintained
   2. Continuancy and stridency least
      maintained
   3. Sounds differing in one feature
      (especially continuancy) most
      difficult (d for ð)
   4. Nonperipheral sounds more difficult than peripheral (Menyuk, 1968)

Two Years to Three Years

Intonation	Meaning	Grammar

tition of words and syl-
lables—unforced and
easily terminated
(Metreaux, 1950)

for anything that
flies)
b. Rudiment of gen-
eralization (*tee*
for *cat* as well as
dog) (Lewis,
1963)
5. Naming of objects in
books (Shirley,
1933)
B. Reportive utterances—
description of things in
environment without
accompanying action
(Bullowa, 1967a,
1967b)
C. Lower boundary for be-
ginning of semantic
system (McNeill, 1966)

tives, and some
pronouns of adult
categories (Mc-
Carthy, 1954)
B. Average of 1.7 words
per utterance (Mc-
Carthy, 1954)

A. Intonational pattern becoming subordinated to
phonetic (Lewis, 1963)
B. Voice—unstable pattern
1. Range from high to
low
2. Presence of nasality
3. Straining and forc-
ing (Metreaux,
1950)
C. Fluency—broken
rhythm
1. Repetition of sounds,
words, phrases
2. Use of starters
3. Echoic of others
(Metreaux, 1950)

A. Two-hundred-and-fifty-
word vocabulary (Ir-
win, 1952)
1. Words still general
in content (Me-
treaux, 1950)
2. Assignment of each
referrent to a cate-
gory (McNeill,
1966)
3. Categories learned
from actions rather
than names of words
(Brown, 1965)
4. Children's definitions
of words in terms of
action
5. Order of learning ad-
verbs—locative, tem-
poral, manner (Mil-
ler and Ervin, 1964)
B. Period of compiling a
word dictionary in
building of semantic
system (McNeill, 1966)

A. Two-word utterances
—primitive grammar
1. Selection not ran-
dom
2. Patterned arrange-
ments in sequen-
tial order
3. Missing elements
a. Auxiliaries, arti-
cles, determin-
ers, pronouns,
prepositions, in-
flections
b. Small-sized cat-
egorical classes
c. Words predict-
able from con-
text
d. Intermediate
words in adult
constructions
(Brown and
Fraser, 1964)
4. Elements retained
in imitation of
adult
a. Initial and final
words
b. Reference-mak-
ing forms

(*continued*)

TABLE 4–13. *(cont.)*

Characteristics of the Period	Sound Making

Two Years to Three Years

c. Nonpredictable forms
d. Words with heavier stress
e. Expandable classes (Brown, 1964)

5. Development of word classes based on privilege of occurrence (Brown, 1964)
   a. Class distinction into pivot and open word classes
      (1) Pivot—distinct category similar to function words (McNeill, 1966)
         (a) Few members
         (b) Frequent use
         (c) Heterogeneous selection on basis of adult grammer (articles, greetings, adjectives, verbs)
      (2) Open class—similar to nounlike categories
         (a) Many members
         (b) Less frequent use of each member (Brown and Fraser, 1964)
   b. Predictable structure of utterance
      (1) Pivot plus open (*pretty shoe, see mommy*)
      (2) Open plus open (*daddy shoe*)—similar to adult possessive form (McNeill, 1966)

B. Later constructions
   1. Mean word length per utterance is 3.5 words (McCarthy, 1954)
   2. Original pivot class reduced by subdivision
   3. Treatment of demonstrative pronouns and adjectives as unique classes to yield *a that horsie*
   4. Development of hierarchical structure
      a. Structure of noun phrase
      b. Structure of verb phrase
      c. Ultimate combination of noun phrase and verb phrase to form adultlike grammar (McNeill, 1966)

(*continued*)

TABLE 4–13. (*cont.*)

Characteristics of the Period	Sound Making

Two Years to Three Years

C. Transformations
  1. Stages of negative structure development
     a. *No* or *not* plus primitive structure (*no wash*)
     b. Addition of *can't* and *don't* as vocabulary items contained in primitive structure
     c. Indication of adult rule
        (1) Use of auxiliary in affirmative (*I can see it*)
        (2) Use of auxiliary with *n't* (*I can't see it*)
     d. Copular *be* optional (*I not big enough*)
     e. Appearance of double negative (*He never made no trip*) (Bellugi, 1964)
  2. Stages of interrogative structure development
     a. No use of questions or comprehension of question
        (1) no response or inappropriate response
        (2) Imitation of question
     b. Intonational question (*See doggie?*)
     c. Use of interrogative words—*who, what, where*
        (1) Initial word (*How you do it?*)
        (2) *Why not* a single vocabulary item
        (3) Better comprehension of adult questions
     d. Approaching of adult form
        (1) Use of auxiliaries
        (2) Use of interrogative words as replacement for missing element in sentence (Bellugi, 1965)
D. Inflections—latter part of second year
  1. Use of present progressive
  2. Use of present indicative (Miller and Ervin, 1964)

(*continued*)

Characteristics of the Period

A. Becomes linguistic adult
   1. Acquires adult syntax
   2. Is versatile in use of language (McNeill, 1966)
      a. To express emotions
      b. To manipulate associates
      c. To express relations
      d. To satisfy needs
      e. To seek verification (*What's this?*)
      f. To express dependency
      g. To entertain self (Templin, 1957)
      h. Verbalizes as he acts (Lewis, 1963)
B. Can be controlled by language (Metreaux, 1950)
C. Learns to whisper (Metreaux, 1950)
D. Squeals, sputters, laughs, sighs (Metreaux, 1950)
E. Accompanies speech with tongue protrusion, lip smacking, tongue clicks (Metreaux, 1950)
F. Continues to use echolalia
   a. When speech becomes difficult
   b. To assimilate associations (Myklebust, 1957)

Sound Making

A. 90 percent of vowels and diphthongs mastered (Templin, 1957)
B. 60 percent of consonants mastered (Templin, 1957)
   1. By manner of articulation
      a. Nasals—92.5 percent
      b. Plosives—79.1 percent
      c. Fricatives—41.0 percent
   2. By position
      a. Initial sound—70 percent
      b. Medial sound—68 percent
      c. Final sound—52 percent (Templin, 1957)
   3. By mastery of specific sounds— /p b m w h/ (Poole, 1934)
   4. Inconsistent production (Metreaux, 1950)
C. Greatest change in articulatory ability
   1. Between 3 and 3.5 years for girls
   2. Between 3.5 and 4 years for boys (Templin, 1957)

Three Years to Four Years

Intonation	Meaning	Grammar
A. Well patterned (Van Riper, 1963)	A. 900-word vocabulary (Berry and Eisenson, 1956)	A. Mean word length per utterance: four words (Templin, 1957)
B. Normal loudness and tone	B. Use of linguistic symbols in dealing with situations (Lewis, 1963)	B. Mean number of different words per fifty utterances
C. Breathiness	C. Use of language in imaginative play (Lewis, 1963)	1. 92.5 at three years
D. Nasality with soft voice		2. 104.8 at three and and one-half years (Templin, 1957)
E. Faster rate	D. Self-centered explanations	C. Acquisition of adult grammar
F. Fluency	a. Egocentric speech	1. Well-formed utterances but not always grammatical (Brown and Fraser, 1964)
1. Recurrence of compulsive repetitions	b. No apprehension of information requirement of others (Piaget, 1960)	2. 48 percent of utterances grammatically correct (Templin, 1957)
a. Tonic blocks on initial syllables	E. Few semantic markers for words (McNeill, 1966)	3. Copular *be* optional (Brown and Fraser, 1964)
b. Grimacing, puffing		4. Incorporation of rules of grammar
2. Use of starters (Metreaux, 1950)		a. Understand and produce sentences
		b. Has difficulty in repetition of structure complexity and not because of sentence length (Menyuk, 1963)
		D. Inflectional rules
		1. Use of past tense
		a. Omission (*push* for *pushed*)
		b. Redundancy (*pushted* for *pushed*) (Menyuk, 1963)
		2. Use of present progressive (Bellugi, 1964)
		3. Use of present indicative (Belugi, 1964)

(*continued*)

Characteristics of the Period

A. Language a facile tool
  1. Commands giving way to spontaneous speech
  2. Questions other's activity (Metreaux, 1950)
B. Girls exceed boys in linguistic ability at four and one-half years (Templin, 1957)
C. Motor activity
  1. Tension at a minimum
  2. Overflow in gross activity
  3. Less verbalization with activity (Metreaux, 1950)

Sound Making

A. Consonant production 90 percent correct by four and one-half years (Templin, 1957)
  1. Percent of correct scores by manner of articulation
    a. Nasals—95 percent
    b. Plosives—90 percent
    c. Semivowels—85 percent
    d. Fricatives and combinations —60 percent (Templin, 1957)
  2. Percent of correct scores by position
    a. Initial—88 percent
    b. Medial—86 percent
    c. Final—74 percent (Templin, 1957)
  3. Substitution of /w/ for /l/ and /r/ (Metreaux, 1950); example of hierarchical development of distinctive features (Menyuk, 1968)
  4. Additional mastered sounds— /d t n g k ŋ j/ (Poole, 1934) (Templin, [tʃ] 1957)
B. Production more stable (Metreaux, 1950)

Four Years to Five Years

Five Years to Six Years

A. More sophisticated use of language
B. More use of language
C. More comprehensible
D. Increased speech in social interaction
E. Less repetition of adults (Brown, 1965)

A. 98 percent of vowel production correct (Templin, 1957)
B. 88 percent of consonant production correct (Templin, 1957)
  1. Percent of correct production by manner of articulation
    a. Nasals—95 percent

Intonation	Meaning	Grammar
A. Imitation of parent's intonation pattern (Metreaux, 1950)	A. Rapid increase in vocabulary (Berry and Eisenson, 1956)	A. Mean number of words per uttterance: 5½ (Templin, 1957)
B. Voice well modulated and firm	B. Speech egocentric in nature (Piaget, 1960)	B. Mean number of different words per utterance: 2½ (Templin, 1957)
1. Subdued at times (Metreaux, 1950)	C. Use of descriptive types of explanations in word definitions (Feifel and Lorge, 1950)	C. Mean number of different words per fifty utterances:
2. Whining at times (Metreaux, 1950)	D. Word association studies	1. 120.4 at 4 years
C. Rate—186 words per minute (Metreaux, 1950)	1. Multiple-word responses	2. 127.0 at 4½ years (Templin, 1957)
D. Fewer repetitions	2. Excessive number of syntactic responses	D. More complicated sentence structure (Anderson, 1953)
1. For emphasis at times	3. Excessive number of noun responses (Entwisle et al., 1964)	E. Use of rules for forming simple plural, present progressive, and possession when expanded to new words never heard before
2. Continued blocking and grimacing (Metreaux, 1950)		1. Unable to expand /ed/ to new words when final sound is /t/ or /d/ for past tense
		2. Operate on rule: "A voiceless sibilant after a voiced consonant and a voiced sibilant after all other sounds makes a word plural" (Berko, 1958)
		3. Use plural for counting nouns (Bellugi, 1964)
		F. No awareness of separate elements of compound words (Berko, 1958)
A. Continued improvement in fluency and intonation	A. Vocabulary of 2000 words (McCarthy, 1954)	A. Mean number of words per utterance: 5.7 (Templin, 1957)
B. Hesitations, pauses, and slower rate evident in speech requiring explanation rather than de-	B. Word-association studies	B. Mean number of different words per fifty utterances: 132.4 (Templin, 1957)
	1. Percentage of noun responses decreases	

(*continued*)

TABLE 4–13 (*cont.*)

Characteristics of the Period	*Sound Making*

Five Years to Six Years

b. Plosives and semivowels—85 percent
c. Fricatives—68 percent
d. Combinations—60 percent (Templin 1957)
2. Percent of correct production by position
a. Initial—90 percent
b. Medial—84 percent
c. Final—80 percent (Templin, 1957)
3. Additional sounds mastered: /f v s z/ (Poole, 1934)
C. Occasional reversals of sound (Van Riper, 1963)

Six Years to Seven and Beyond

A. Language more socially oriented (Piaget, 1960)
B. Language as instrument for growth of individual personality (Lewis, 1963)
C. Different languages
1. Of elders
2. Of peers
3. Of reading and writing (Lewis, 1963)

A. Boys' requirement of additional year for mastery of sounds (Poole, 1934)
B. Six-year-old status
1. Correct production by manner of articulation
a. Nasals and plosives—98 percent
b. Semivowels—92 percent
c. Fricatives—75 percent
d. Combinations—65 percent
2. Correct production by position
a. Initial—92 percent
b. Medial—91 percent
c. Final—90 percent
3. Additional sounds mastered: /v ð ʒ ʃ l/; loss of /s z/ (Poole, 1934)
C. Seven-year-old status
1. Correct production by manner of articulation
a. Nasals—99 percent
b. Plosives—98 percent
c. Semivowels—95 percent
d. Fricatives—88 percent
e. Combinations—70 percent (Templin, 1957)
2. Correct production by position
a. Initial—100 percent
b. Medial—98 percent
c. Final—100 percent (Templin, 1957)
3. Additional sounds mastered: /r θ hw/ with recurrence of /s z/

Intonation	Meaning	Grammar

Intonation	Meaning	Grammar

scription(Levin et al., 1967)	2. More paradigmatic responses to verbs and adjectives (Entwisle et al., 1964)
	3. Children less able to take advantage of semantic consistency in sentences when shadowing speech than an eight-year-old group (McNeill, 1965)
		C. Improved syntax (Van Riper, 1963)
		D. Perfecting of rules for forming inflections
		  a. Use of possessive
		  b. Use of third person singular (Berko, 1958)
		E. Production and recall of nongrammatical material not different from grammatical (Menyuk, 1965)

A. Fundamental frequency for seven-year-old boys: 294 Hz; for eight-year-old boys: 297 Hz.
B. Fundamental frequency for seven-year-old girls: 281 Hz; for eight-year-girls: 288 Hz.
C. Upward and downward voice breaks common to all groups (Fairbanks, 1950)
	A. Mean number of words per utterance
	  1. 6.4 words for six years
	  2. 7 words for seven years
	  3. 7.7 words for eight years
	B. Mean number of different words per fifty utterances
	  1. 147 at six years
	  2. 157.7 at seven years
	  3. 166.5 at eight years
	C. Grammatical system well established (Slobin, 1966)
	  1. Evaluation of passive, negative, and negative passive sentences by six-year-olds
	  2. More time required for evaluation of complex structure (Slobin, 1966)
	  3. Percentage of correct grammatical utterances
	    a. 73.7 by six-year-olds
	    b. 76.1 by eight-year-olds (Templin, 1957)
		A. Basic estimated vocabulary
		  1. 13,000 words (2000 spoken) at six years
		  2. 21,600 words at seven years
		  3. 28,300 words at eight years (Templin, 1957)
		B. More discriminate use of vocabulary (Lewis, 1963)
		C. Definitions of words
		  1. By use of description below six or seven years
		  2. By synonym at eight to eleven years
		  3. By categorical description or explanation above eleven years
		D. Language taking on idiosyncrasies (Lewis, 1963)
		E. Word association studies
		  1. Primarily syntagmatic responses at six years (McNeill, 1965)
		  2. Decrease in per-

TABLE 4-13 *(cont.)*

Characteristics of the Period   *Sound Making*

(Poole, 1934); /d/ (Templin, 1957)

D. Eight-year-old status
 1. Correct production by manner of articulation
    a. Nasals—100 percent
    b. Plosives—98 percent
    c. Semivowels—98 percent
    d. Fricatives—98 percent
    e. Combinations—75 percent
 2. Little difference in percentage of correct production by position with the exception of difficulty with fricatives in final position (Templin, 1957)

Six Years to Seven and Beyond

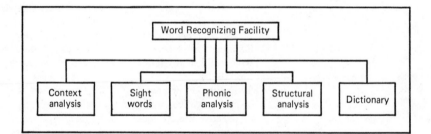

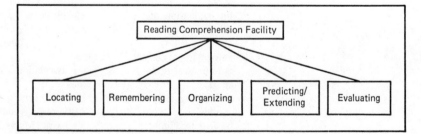

FIGURE 4-1 Major Components of Reading
SOURCE: Guszak, F. *Diagnostic reading instruction in the elementary school.* New York: Harper & Row, 1972. Used with permission of publisher.

Intonation	Meaning	Grammar
	4. Learning tasks and recall easier with grammatical material than with non-grammatical material (Menyuk, 1965)	centage of noun responses from six to eight years (Entwisle, et al., 1964) 3. Increase in percent of paradigmatic responses for verbs F. Continuation in developing of semantic markers in child's word dictionary (McNeill, 1966)

SOURCE: Bartel, N. R., and Bryen, D. N. Problems in language development. In D. D. Hammill and N. R. Bartel. *Teaching children with learning and behavior problems*, (2nd ed.), pp. 284–297. Boston: Allyn and Bacon, 1978. Used with permission of publisher.

(pp. 169–170). These skills include the phonic rules governing consonant sounds, vowel sounds, blends, and so on. Higher-order recognition-analysis skills, generally referred to as structural analysis skills, include using syllabication, root words, prefixes, suffixes, and so on. Often dictionary use is also considered a structural analysis skill. Occasionally these last two skill areas—structural analysis and dictionary skills—are conceived as part of reading comprehension. A last concept underlying word recognition is the recognition of words by sight or memory. Often sight-word skills are applied to words where few phonic analysis skills would apply. These sight words, generally termed irregular, rarely if ever are totally irregular. For most of the words, consonant sounds are regular enough to apply some degree of phonic analysis such as beginning or ending consonant sounds. However, the ability to recognize words is only a small part of the reading process. While a necessary prerequisite to understanding words in written text, this skill of recognizing words is not the primary goal of reading instruction.

Ultimately, the goal of reading is the ability to secure information through printed or brailled materials. This can only be accomplished when the student *comprehends* the material she/he has learned to recognize. Unlike recognition, the component of reading comprehension has many different meanings when viewed in relation to instruction. Guszak (1972) divides this area into the abilities to (1) locate informa-

163

TABLE 4–14   Conceptualization of Syntax in Language Development

	Noun Modifiers	Pronouns	Main Verbs	Secondary Verbs
1	it, this, that	1st and second person: I, me, my, mine, you, your(s)	A. Uninflected verb: I *see* you. B. copula, is or 's: *It's* red. C. is + verb + ing: He *is coming.*	
2		3rd person: he, him, his, she, her, hers	A. -s and -ed: *plays, played* B. irregular past: *ate, saw* C. Copula: *am, are, was, were* D. Auxiliary *am, are, was, were*	Five early-developing infinitives: I wan*na see* (want *to see*) I'm gon*na see* (going *to see*) I got*ta see* (got *to see*) Lemme [to] see (let me [*to*] *see*) Let's [to] play (let [us *to*] *play*)
3	A. no, some, more, all, lot(s), one(s), two (etc.), other(s), another B. something, somebody, someone	A. Plurals: we, us, our(s), they, them, their B. these, those		Non-complementing infinitives: I stopped *to play.* I'm afraid *to look.* It's hard *to do* that.
4	nothing, nobody, none, no one		A. can, will, may + verb: *may go* B. Obligatory do + verb: *don't go* C. Emphatic do + verb: I *do see.*	Participle, present or past: I see a boy *running.* I found the toy *broken.*
5		Reflexives: myself, yourself, himself, herself, itself, themselves		A. Early infinitival complements with differing subjects in kernels: I want you *to come.* Let him [*to*] *see.* B. Later infinitival complements: I had *to go.* I told him *to go.* I tried *to go.* He ought *to go.* C. Obligatory deletions: Make it [*to*] *go.* I'd better [*to*] *go.* D. Infinitive with wh-word: I know what *to get.* I know how *to do* it.

164

Negatives	Conjunctions	Interrogative Reversals	WH-Questions
it, this, that + copula or auxiliary is, 's, + not: It's *not* mine. This is *not* a dog. That is *not* moving.		Reversal of copula: *Isn't it* red? *Were they* there?	
			A. who, what, what + noun: *Who am* I? *What is* he eating? *What book* are you reading? B. where, how many, how much, what . . . do, what . . . for *Where* did it go? *How much* do you want? *What* is he *doing*? *What* is a hammer *for*?
	and		
can't, don't		Reversal of auxiliary be: *Is he* coming? *Isn't he* coming? *Was he* going? *Wasn't he* going?	
isn't, won't	A. but B. so, and so, so that C. or, if		when, how, how + adjective: *When* shall I come? *How* do you do it? *How* big is it?

TABLE 4–14 (cont.)

	Noun Modifiers	Pronouns	Main Verbs	Secondary Verbs
6		A. Wh-pronouns: who, which, whose, whom, what, that, how many, how much I know *who* came. That's *what* I said. B. Wh-word + infinitive: I know *what* to do. I know *who(m)* to take.	A. could, would, should, might + verb: *might come, could be* B. Obligatory does, did + verb C. Emphatic does, did + verb	
7	A. any, anything, anybody, anyone B. every, everything, everybody, everyone C. both, few, many, each, several, most, least, much, next, first, last, second (etc).	(his) own, one, oneself, whichever, whoever, whatever Take *whatever* you like.	A. Passive with *get,* any tense Passive, with *be,* any tense B. must, shall + verb: *must come* C. have + verb + en: *I've eaten* D. have got: *I've got* it.	Passive infinitival complement: With *get:* I have *to get dressed.* I don't want *to get hurt.* With *be:* I want *to be pulled.* It's going *to be locked.*
8			A. have been + verb + ing had been + verb + ing B. modal + have + verb + en: *may have eaten* C. modal + be + verb + ing: *could be playing* D. Other auxiliary combinations: *should have been sleeping*	Gerund: *Swinging* is fun. I like *fishing.* He started *laughing.*

SOURCE: Lee, L. *Developmental sentence analysis.* Evanston, Ill.: Northwestern University Press, 1974. Used with permission of publisher.

Negatives	Conjunctions	Interrogative Reversals	WH-Questions
	because	A. Obligatory do, does, did: *Do they* run? *Does it* bite? *Did*n't *it* hurt? B. Reversal of modal: *Can you* play? *Wo*n't *it* hurt? *Shall I* sit down? C. Tag question: It's fun, *isn't it*? It isn't fun, *is it*?	

All other negatives:
A. Uncontracted negatives:
I can *not* go.
He has *not* gone.
B. Pronoun-auxiliary or pronoun-copula contraction:
I'm *not* coming.
He's *not* here.
C. Auxiliary-negative or copula-negative contraction:
He was*n't* going...
He has*n't* been seen.
It could*n't* be mine.
They are*n't* big.

why, what if, how come
how about + gerund
Why are you crying?
What if I won't do it?
How come he is crying?
How about coming with me?

A. where, when, how, while, whether (or not), till, until, unless, since, before, after, for, as, as + adjective + as, as if, like, that, than
I know *where* you are.
Don't come *till* I call.
B. Obligatory deletions:
I run faster *than* you [run].
I'm as *big as* a man [is big].
It looks *like* a dog [looks].
C. Elliptical deletions (score O):
That's *why* [I took it].
I know *how* [I can do it].
D. Wh-words + infinitive:
I know *how* to do it.
I know *where* to go.

A. Reversal of auxiliary have:
Has he seen you?
B. Reversal with two or three auxiliaries:
Has he been eating?
*Could*n't *he have* waited?
Could he have been drying?
*Would*n't *he have been* going?

whose, which, which + noun
Whose car is that?
Which book do you want?

167

tion in reading, (2) remember what was read, (3) organize what was read, (4) predict events, sequences, and so on, and extend thoughts beyond what is actually written, and (5) evaluate material read (see again Table 4–15). In addition, these skills can be further specified by grade levels. An example of this is given in Table 4–16 for the level of second grade. Goals for reading comprehension are generally listed in each basal reading program such as the one shown in Table 4–17. Once goals such as these have been accomplished, the student probably no longer needs special education assistance in reading.

Because of the paramount importance placed upon reading in the school environment and the necessity of reading in daily life, it is necessary for educators to develop fully special reading curricula containing all the skills possible in reading in order to provide appropriate instruction to students. These skills are generally thought to precede the ability to express oneself in writing.

Written expression. Written expression is an academic performance area that is highly complex and involves several constructs. The constructs included in written expression are spelling, handwriting (or some other form of production such as typing or brailling), and conceptual writing. Many educators deal with the areas of spelling and handwriting separately from the conceptual writing curriculum, but they do all encompass the act of written expression. Spelling skills entail instruction in the relationship between phonological structures (sounds) and their grapheme counterparts (letters). Generally these skills are viewed along a continuum of most regular, that is, one sound to one letter (such as *bat*), to the more irregular forms that to a great extent must be memorized (such as *phone*). Table 4–18 (p. 176) represents a scope and sequence of spelling that reflects certain graphemes or grapheme structures (such as consonants, vowels, blends and digraphs) as the constructs of spelling. The structures are then sequenced along levels of complexity similar to grade equivalents.

Handwriting or penmanship generally is defined in terms of actual movements required to produce a letter or letters. One such listing of handwriting movements is provided in Table 4–19. Penmanship is often a difficult skill for certain special education students because of poor fine-motor coordination and/or actual physical impairments. Frequently typewriters are needed to allow the student to compensate for motor problems. Other mechanical devices such as those used for brailling and recording may also be required to assist a child in handwriting or in acquiring handwriting skills.

The actual expression of ideas in writing encompasses several additional constructs. Table 4–20, which is one such conceptualization, initially breaks the concept of written expression into two dimensions—the mechanical aspects and the compositional aspects. In this model Hammill and Poplin (1978) note the mechanical aspects involved are punctuation and capitalization. One might also include spelling and handwriting as mechanical skills. Compositional skills involved in written expression are not as easily defined. In the example provided in Table 4-20 the constructs of compositional skills include:

- vocabulary—the child's supply of words that she/he comprehends and uses in speaking and writing
- word usage—the appropriateness of the words selected for use
- grammar—the way in which groups of words are structured or organized
- sentence construction—the organization of all of the above and inclusion of a thought
- paragraph construction—the organization of one idea formulated with several sentences

One can see from the diagram presented here that the educational area of written expression is quite complex. For this reason, instruction in written expression is not appropriate for many students for the first few years of their education. It is important for special educators to remember that the areas of oral language, reading, and written expression are to a large extent intertwined and dependent upon one another. For many handicapped children this interface of skills in the language arts can be adventitious if commonalities among these constructs are stressed. For example, when reading and spelling vocabulary are the same or similar, more exposure to a single word is provided.

Mathematics. The educational performance area of mathematics is the simplest academic area to conceptualize. Unlike the constructs involved in reading comprehension, language, and writing, mathematical constructs are fairly well determined by the very nature of the subject. For purposes of special education, one may break the pertinent areas of math into (1) operations, (2) measurements, and (3) concepts and reasoning. Operations include numeration, addition, subtraction, multiplication, and division. These operations are essential to using measurements and concepts; therefore, generally they are considered paramount in the instruction of students with basic math problems. Measurements include such concepts as time, money, space, volume, and line measures. Concepts and reasoning range from the simplest concepts of same-different, equal to–greater than to the higher concepts involved in trigonometry and geometry. In order to examine the constructs of math more

TABLE 4–15 Major Phonic Elements in Five Programs *

Grade	Bloomfield System	Phonetic Keys to Reading	Hay-Wingo †	Phonovisual Method ‡	Scott, Foresman (1956)
Readiness & preprimers	Letters of alphabet; left-to-right visual progression Single consonants Short vowels	Long vowels Vowel digraphs Short vowels Single consonants Consonant digraphs Consonant blends (several)	Short vowels 10 single consonants	Single consonants Consonant digraphs Long vowel *ee*	Auditory perception of initial consonants
Primer (1–1)	Consonant blends Consonant digraphs Vowel digraphs Diphthongs	Consonant blends Diphthongs Silent letters	Single consonants Consonant digraphs Consonant blends	Short vowels Consonant blends Long vowels	Visual-auditory perception of single initial consonants
First (1–2)	New sounds for letters taught (semiregular) Long vowels	Irregularities	Long vowels Vowel digraphs Diphthongs Silent letters	Vowel digraphs Diphthongs No silent letters	Visual-auditory perception of final consonants. Consonant digraphs

Second (2–1)	Silent letters Irregularities	Review and irregularities	Consonant blends Long and short *i, y, a* Long and short, *e, o, u* Diphthongs Vowel digraphs Silent letters Alphabet in sequence (for alphabetizing)
Second (2–2)		Same as above	

SOURCE: Chall, J. *Learning to read: The great debate.* New York: McGraw-Hill, 1967. Used with permission of publisher.

* There is considerable overlapping in the teaching of these elements from one level to the next; this breakdown is intended to give a general view of sequence.

† The breakdown of lessons at each level was based on the researcher's estimate and the authors' suggestion that each page of this book constitutes one lesson.

‡ This system does not define lessons. The breakdown here is based on the authors' statement that all the sounds should be learned in first grade.

TABLE 4-16 Outline of Reading Comprehension Skills—Grade Two

Predicting/Extending	*Locating Information*	*Remembering*	*Organizing*	*Evaluating Critically*

Predicts convergent outcomes from:
  pictures
  picture and title
  title
  oral description
  story situations
	Locates specifics within written materials
	  phrase(s)
	  sentence(s)
	  paragraph(s)
	  page numbers
	  parts of a story (beginning, middle, end, etc.)
		Remembering simple sentence content	Retells:
			  sentence
			  sentence set
			  paragraph
			  story
				Makes judgments about the desirability of a:
				  character
				  situation

Predicts divergent outcomes	Locating information with book parts
	  titles
	  stories
	  table of contents
		Remembering the content of two or more simple sentences in sequence	Outlines orally the sequence of the story	Makes judgments about the validity of a:
				  story
				  description
				  argument, etc.
				  by making both *external* and *internal* comparison

Explain story character actions
Explain gadget operations
Generalizes from sets of information in story(ies)
(Include task of identifying an unstated *main idea*).
	Locating information with reference aids
	  picture dictionaries
	  maps (political)
	  dictionaries
		Remembering the factual content of complete and complex sentences and sentence sets
		
		Remembering paragraph content
		
		Remembering story content
			Reorganizes a communication into a:
			  cartoon
			  picture
			  picture sequence
				Making judgments about whether stories are fictional or non-fictional by noting:
				  reality
				  fantasy
				  exaggeration

Restores omitted words in context				
Labels feelings of characters, i.e. sad–glad				

Source: Guszak, F. J. *Diagnostic reading in the elementary school.* New York: Harper & Row, 1972. Used with permission of publisher.

TABLE 4–17   Comprehension Skills Taught in a Basal Reader Program

---

Identifying the meaning of a word or phrase in specific context
Identifying story problem
Making and checking inferences about what is read
Grasping implied ideas
Anticipating action or outcome in a story
Perceiving relationships (analogous, cause-effect, general-specific, class, sequence, time, place, or space, size)
Forming sensory images (visual, auditory, kinesthetic, tactile)
Sensing emotional reactions and inferring motives of story characters
Evaluating actions and personal traits of story characters
Following story sequence and plot
Recognizing plot structure
Comparing and contrasting
Interpreting figurative, idiomatic, and picturesque language
Identifying elements of style
Making judgments and drawing conclusions
Identifying author's purpose or point of view
Comprehending author's meaning
Organizing and summarizing ideas
Generalizing
Reacting to story content, linking it to personal experience, and applying ideas gained through reading
Using aids to memory:
  Association
  Sensory imagery
  Sequence
  Cause-effect relationships
  Size relationships
  Organization of ideas
Achieving effective oral interpretation, including sensitivity to pitch, intonation, stress, and rate

---

SOURCE: Robinson, H. M.; Artley, A. S.; Aaron, I. E.; Monroe, M.; Huck, C. S.; and Weintraub, S. *Reading comprehension skills in Scott Foresman Basic Readers.* Chicago: Scott Foresman, 1965. Used with permission of publisher.

thoroughly, we have included here (1) a discussion of certain readiness tasks purported to be prerequisite to the acquisition of math skills, (2) a suggested outline of arithmetic skills by mental age, and (3) a scope and sequence chart taken from a commercial math series.

With regard to readiness for mathematics, Bartel (1978) has identified seven concepts purported to be basic to developing arithmetic-related abilities. These include the concepts of:

- Classification—the grouping of objects according to some common characteristic.

173

TABLE 4-18 Scope-and-Sequence of Spelling

	Auditory		Auditory Plus Visual				Conceptual	
Test Level	1	2	3	4	5	6	7	8
Avg. Grade Level	K–3	1–4	2–5	3–6	4–7	5–8	6–9	7–10
Consonants	b d f g h l m n p r t v y	s z w	c j k x qu			c: city g: germ		ph: phrase ch: ache i: stadium i: companion
Beginning Blends	dr- gr- tr- pl- fl- y	sw- sp- sl- st- str- spr- spl-						
Ending Blends	-mp -nd -ft -lt -nt	-st -nt -lf -nd -mp						
Digraphs		ch sh th ng	wh					
Vowels	short a e i o u	short a e i o u	ai, ay, a-e ee, ea, e-e igh, y, i-e, ind oa, ow, o-e, old	u-e: cube	u-e: rule -y: envy	ie: field ei: receive schwa(ə): *	y: system	
Vowel Digraphs				oo: pool	oo: hood ea: ready	au: sauce		
Dipthongs				oi: join ou: cloud ow: down aw: claw	oy: joy ew: chew			
"r" & "l" control				ar, er, ir, ur er, ear are, ire, ore all				
Prefixes				un- re-	pre- en- mis- ex- a- in-	con- per- com-		Derivational Doubling: immature
Suffixes		-s: chops	-s: wheels -ing	-er -est -ly -ful	-tion -ive	-ent -en -ant	-ment -ous -ness	-ance -ence -ible -able

Endings					-et: target -ic: public -al: signal -le: poodle	-ey: kidney	-us: cactus	ti: cautious ci: social tu: future
Syllables: ** open and closed							open: ti-ny closed: gos-sip	
Generalizations								
Advanced phonics						ck-k ch-tch ge-dge		
Contractions							mustn't they've	
Rules							1. Dropping e: hope-hoping 2a. Doubling final consonants (monosyllabic): hop-hopping 3. Changing y to i: funny-funnier	2b. Doubling final consts (polysyllabic): open-opening begin-beginner
Sample Words	lap rug flop yet mint	sang chops brush spent bathtub	mean loaded junk painting waxes	refuse smartest fired join loudly	loyal ahead expensive strangle prescribe	loosen freckle computer belief launched	skinny scaring cloudiness sympathy enormous	fortunately immortal forbidden phrase architect
Total Test Words	20	20	40	40	40	40	40	40

Source: Cohen, C. R., and Abrams, R. M. *Spellmaster, spelling: testing and evaluating book one.* Exeter, N.H.: Learnco Inc., 1976. Used with permission of publisher.

* The "schwa" is a neutral vowel sound in an unaccented syllable.

** Open syllable ends in a vowel making the vowel long: mo/ment, pu/pil. Closed syllable ends in a consonant making the vowel short: sad/dle, pup/py.

TABLE 4–19 Movements Involved in Handwriting

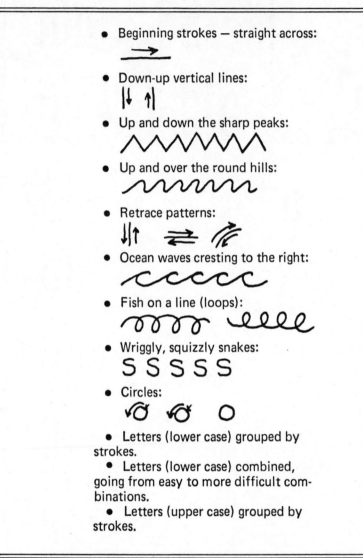

- Beginning strokes — straight across:

- Down-up vertical lines:

- Up and down the sharp peaks:

- Up and over the round hills:

- Retrace patterns:

- Ocean waves cresting to the right:

- Fish on a line (loops):

- Wriggly, squizzly snakes:

- Circles:

- Letters (lower case) grouped by strokes.
- Letters (lower case) combined, going from easy to more difficult combinations.
- Letters (upper case) grouped by strokes.

SOURCE: Madison, B. D. A kinesthetic technique for handwriting development. In J. L. Arena (ed.), *Building handwriting skills in dyslexic children.* San Rafael, Calif.: Academic Therapy, 1970. Used with permission of publisher.

- One-to-one correspondence—the ability to match one object to one object, involving two or more equal sets.
- Many-to-one correspondence—the ability to match or relate one object to a set of objects, involving two or more sets, one set of which is a multiple of the other.

- Seriation or ordering—the ability to arrange in ascending or descending sequence according to some common characteristic such as size, number, length, and height.
- Space and spatial representation—understanding the concept of distance and position between and among objects.
- Flexibility—the ability to classify objects on the basis of more than one common characteristic, for example, size and then regroup by color.
- Reversibility—understanding the ability of objects to return to original state.
- Conservation—the understanding that quantity of a set or object remains constant regardless of appearances, such as conservation of weight, space, volume, shape, and length.

Bartel (1978) also cautions that the ability to increase a student's performance in these skills through instruction remains unvalidated. The reader is cautioned that these conservation tasks may or may not actually preclude a child's ability to profit from other math instruction such as operations and counting.

A developmental chart for the acquisition of certain math skills is presented in Table 4–21. In this table, Brueckner and Bond (1955) provide a delineation of the constructs involved in math arranged by developmental ages. These mental ages purportedly represent the age at which the majority of students are able to master the listed concepts. The concepts themselves are broken into those dealing with whole numbers, fractions, and decimals. This table represents a developmental organization of math constructs as opposed to the traditional math skills sequenced by grade levels.

A traditional and more specific organization of the educational area of mathematics is presented in Table 4–22 (pp. 188–191). This table formulated by Wallace and Kauffman (1973) represents a scope and sequence chart of math skills from kindergarten through sixth grade. The constructs defined here include:

- Readiness—conservation tasks and many tasks involved in numeration skills such as one-to-one correspondence.
- Mathematical concepts—the student's comprehension of such terms as greater than, less than, minus, and multiples.
- Sets—an understanding of the concepts of grouping elements, adding them (union), subsets (subtraction), and equal groups vs. non-equal.
- Whole numbers—constituting skills in counting by one's, two's, three's, ten's, and so on.

TABLE 4–20   Scope and Sequence of Conceptual Writing Skills

	Grade 1	Grade 2	Grade 3
Capitalization	The first word of a sentence The child's first and last names The name of the teacher, school, town, street The word "I"	The date First and important words of titles of books the children read Proper names used in children's writings Titles of compositions Names of titles: Mr., Mrs., Miss	Proper names: month, day, common holidays First word in a line of verse First and important words in titles of books, stories, poems First word of salutation of informal note, as "Dear" First word of closing of informal note, as "Yours"
Punctuation	Period at the end of a sentence which tells something Period after numbers in any kind of list	Question mark at the close of a question Comma after salutation of a friendly note or letter Comma after closing of a friendly note or letter Comma between the day of the month and the year Comma between name of city and state	Period after abbreviations Period after an initial Use of an apostrophe in a common contraction such as isn't, aren't Commas in a list
Vocabulary	New words learned during experience Choosing words that describe accurately Choosing words that make you see, hear, feel	Words with similar meanings; with opposite meanings Alphabetical order	Extending discussion of words for precise meanings Using synonyms Distinguishing meanings and spellings of homonyms Using the prefix un and the suffix less

Grade 4	Grade 5	Grades 6, 7, and 8
Names of cities and states in general	Names of streets	Names of the Deity and the Bible
Names of organizations to which children belong, such as Boy Scouts, grade four, etc.	Names of all places and persons, countries, oceans, etc.	First word of a quoted sentence
Mother, Father, when used in place of the name	Capitalization used in outlining	Proper adjectives, showing race, nationality, etc.
Local geographical names	Titles when used with names, such as President Lincoln	Abbreviations of proper nouns and titles
Apostrophe to show possession	Commercial trade names	
Hyphen separating parts of a word divided at end of a line	Colon in writing time	Comma to set off nouns in direct address
Period following a command	Quotation marks around the title of a booklet, pamphlet, the chapter of a book, and the title of a poem or story	Hyphen in compound numbers
Exclamation point at the end of a word or group of words that make an exclamation	Underlining the title of a book	Colon to set off a list
Comma setting off an appositive		Comma in sentences to aid in making meaning clear
Colon after the salutation of a business letter		
Quotation marks before and after a direct quotation		
Comma between explanatory words and a quotation		
Period after outline Roman numeral		
Dividing words into syllables	Using antonyms	Extending meanings; writing with care in choice of words and phrases
Using the accent mark	Prefixes and suffixes; compound words	In writing and speaking, selecting words for accuracy
Using exact words which appeal to the senses	Exactness in choice of words	Selecting words for effectiveness and appropriateness
Using exact words in explanation	Dictionary work; definitions; syllables; pronunciation; macron; breve	Selecting words for courtesy
Keeping individual lists of new words and meanings	Contractions	Editing a paragraph to improve a choice or words
	Rhyme and rhythm; words with sensory images	
	Classification of words by parts of speech	
	Roots and words related to them	
	Adjectives, nouns, verbs—contrasting general and specific vocabulary	

TABLE 4–20 (*cont.*)

	Grade 1	Grade 2	Grade 3
Word Usage	*Generally in oral expression* Naming yourself last Eliminating unnecessary words (my father he); use of *well* and *good* Verb forms in sentences: is, are did, done was, were see, saw, seen	*Generally in oral expression* Double negative Use of *a* and *an*; *may* and *can*; *teach* and *learn* Eliminating unnecessary words (this here) Verb forms in sentences: rode, ridden took, taken grow, grew, grown	Use of *there is* and *there are*; *any* and *no* Use of *let* and *leave*; *don't* and *doesn't*; *would have,* not *would of* Verb forms in sentences: throw, threw, thrown drive, drove, driven wrote, written tore, torn
Word Usage	ate, eaten went, gone came, come gave, given	know, knew, known bring, brought drew, drawn began, begun ran, run	chose, chosen climbed broke, broken wore, worn spoke, spoken sang, sung rang, rung catch, caught
Grammar	Not applicable	Not applicable	Nouns: recognition of singular, plural, and possessive Verbs: recognition

Grade 4	Grade 5	Grades 6, 7, and 8
Agreement of subject and verb	Avoiding unnecessary pronouns (the boy he . . .)	Homonyms: *its,* and *it's; their, there, they're; there's, theirs; whose, who's*
Use of *she, he, I, we,* and *they* as subjects	Linking verbs and predicate nominatives	
Use of *bring* and *take*	Conjugation of verbs, to note changes in tense, person, number	Use of parallel structure for parallel ideas, as in outlines
Verb forms in sentences:		
blow, blew, blown	Transitive and intransitive verbs	Verb forms in sentences:
drink, drank, drunk		beat, beat, beaten
lie, lay, lain	Verb forms in sentences:	learn, learned, learned
take, took, taken	am, was, been	leave, left, left
rise, rose, risen	say, said, said	lit, lit, lit
teach, taught, taught	fall, fell, fallen	forgot, forgotten
raise, raise, raise	dive, dived, dived	swing, swung, swung
lay, laid, laid	burst, burst, burst	spring, sprang, sprung
fly, flew, flown	buy, bought, bought	shrink, shrank, shrunk
set, set, set	Additional verb forms:	slid, slid, slid
swim, swam, swum	*climb, like, play, read,*	
freeze, froze, frozen	*sail, vote, work*	
steal, stole, stolen		
Nouns, common and proper; noun in complete subjects	Noun: possessive; objective of preposition, predicate noun	Noun: clauses; common and proper nouns; indirect object
Verb in complete predicate	Verb: tense; agreement with subject; verbs of action and state of being	Verb: conjugating to note changes in person, number, tense; linking verbs with predicate nominatives
Adjectives: recognition		
Adverbs: recognition (telling how, when, where)	Adjective: comparison; predicate adjective; proper adjective	
Adverbs modifying verbs, adjectives, other adverbs	Adverb: comparison; words telling how, when, where, how much; modifying verbs, adjectives, adverbs	Adjective: chart of uses; clauses; demonstrative; descriptive, numerals; phrases
Pronouns: recognition of singular and plural		Adverb: chart of uses; clauses; comparison; descriptive; *ly* ending; modification of adverbs; phrases
	Pronouns: possessive; objective after prepositions	
	Prepositions: recognition; prepositional phrases	Pronoun: antecedents; declension chart—person, gender, case; demonstrative; indefinite; interrogative; personal; relative
	Conjunction: recognition	
	Interjection: recognition	Preposition: phrases
		Conjunction: in compound subjects and predicates; in subordinate and coordinate clauses

(*continued*)

TABLE 4–20 (*cont.*)

	Grade 1	Grade 2	Grade 3
Sentences	Write simple sentences	Recognition of sentences; kinds: statement and question Composing correct and interesting original sentences Avoiding running sentences together with *and*	Exclamatory sentences Use of a variety of sentences Combining short, choppy sentences into longer ones Using interesting beginning and ending sentences Avoiding run-on sentences (not punctuation) Learning to proofread one's own and others' sentences

Grade 4	Grade 5	Grades 6, 7, and 8
		Interjection: placement of, in quotations
		Noun: antecedent of pronouns; collective nouns; compound subject; direct object; indirect object; object of preposition
		Verb: active and passive voice; emphatic forms; transitive and intransitive; tenses, linking verbs
		Adverb: as modifiers; clauses; comparing adverbs; adverbial phrase, use of *well* and *good*
		Adjectives: as modifiers; clauses; compound adjectives
		Pronouns: agreement with antecedents; personal pronoun chart; indirect object; object of preposition; objective case, person and number; possessive form
		Preposition: in phrase
		Conjunction: coordinate; subordinate, use in compound subjects; compound predicates; complex and compound sentences
Command sentences Complete and simple subject; complete and simple predicate Adjectives and adverbs recognized; pronouns introduced Avoiding fragments of sentences (incomplete) and the comma fault (a comma where a period belongs) Improving sentences in a paragraph	Using a variety of interesting sentences: declarative; interrogative; exclamatory; and imperative (*you* the subject) Agreement of subject and verb; changes in pronoun forms Compound subjects and compound predicates Composing paragraphs with clearly stated ideas	Development of concise statements (avoiding wordiness or unnecessary repetition) Indirect object and predicate nominative Complex sentences Clear thinking and expression (avoiding vagueness and omissions)

TABLE 4–20 (*cont.*)

Grade 1	Grade 2	Grade 3
Not applicable	Not applicable	Keeping to one idea
		Keeping sentences in order; sequence of ideas
		Finding and deleting sentences that do not belong
		Indenting

Paragraphs

- Operations (whole numbers)—delineate addition, subtraction, multiplication, and division skills and properties of these operations with regard to whole numbers (0, 1, 2, 3, 4, . . . 1005, 1006, 1007, . . .).
- Fractions—involves the operations again only with regard to non-whole numbers written as fractions.
- Measurements—skills in time, money, and measure of length, degrees, weight, and so on.
- Geometry—skills involved in mathematical manipulations of various shapes.

As with other special education areas (academic and otherwise), the manner in which one conceptualizes the area of mathematics is not

Grade 4	Grade 5	Grades 6, 7, and 8
Selecting main topic	Improvement in writing a paragraph of several sentences	Analyzing a paragraph to note method of development
Choosing title to express main idea	Selecting subheads as well as main topic for outline	Developing a paragraph in different ways: e.g., with details, reasons, examples, or comparisons
Making simple outline with main idea	Courtesy and appropriateness in all communications	Checking for accurate statements
Developing an interesting paragraph	Recognizing topic sentences	Use of a fresh or original approach in expressing ideas
	Keeping to the topic as expressed in title and topic sentence	Use of transition words to connect ideas
	Use of more than one paragraph	Use of topic sentences in develoving paragraphs
	Developing a four-point outline	Improvement in complete composition—introduction, development, conclusion
	Writing paragraphs from outline	Checking for good reasoning
	New paragraphs for new speakers in written conversation	Use of bibliography in report based on several sources
	Keeping lists of books (authors and titles) used for reference	

SOURCE: Hammill, D. D., and Poplin, M. S. Problems in writing. In D. D. Hammill, and N. R. Bartel. *Teaching children with learning and behavior problems,* (2nd ed.), pp. 186–191. Boston: Allyn and Bacon, 1978. Used with permission of publisher.

as crucial as the idea that educators have developed a concept of the pertinent areas of special education. This concept need only define the constructs of a particular area broadly and thoroughly enough to include all the possible skills in which a handicapped child might need instruction.

Summary

Following the discussion presented here, the extensive range of performance areas pertinent to the education of handicapped students becomes obvious. Prior to any educational planning, such as establishing present levels of performance, annual goals, and objectives, it is imperative that educators understand for themselves exactly what constitutes the various areas of educational performance likely to be needed by any handicapped student. Until and unless this has been accomplished in

TABLE 4–21 Developmental Chart of Math Skills

Mental Age	Whole Numbers	Fractions	Decimals
6–7	1. Counting 2. Identifying numbers to 200 3. Writing numbers to 100 4. Serial idea 5. Using numbers in activities of all kinds	1. Contacts in activity units and in simple measurements	1. Tens as basis of number system
7–8	1. Reading and writing numbers to 1,000 2. Concept development 3. Addition and subtraction facts to 6	1. Recognizing fractional parts	1. Place value 2. Zero as a place holder
8–9	1. Addition and subtraction facts and simple processes 2. Multiplication and division facts through 3 3. Multiplication by one-place numbers 4. Related even division by one-place numbers	1. Extending uses of fractions in measurements 2. Finding part of a number	1. Reading money values 2. Addition and subtraction of dollars and cents 3. Multiplication and division of cents only
9–10	1. Completion of all multiplication and division facts 2. Uneven division facts 3. All steps with one-place multipliers and divisors	1. Extending use and meaning of fractions 2. Easy steps in addition and subtraction of like fractions by concrete and visual means 3. Finding a part of a number	1. Computing with dollars and cents in all processes
10–11	1. Two-place multipliers 2. Two-place divisors—apparent quotient need not be corrected 3. Zeros in quotients	1. Addition and subtraction of like fractions; also the halves, fourths, eighths	1. Addition and subtraction through hundredths

TABLE 4–21 (*cont.*)

Mental Age	Whole Numbers	Fractions	Decimals
11–12	1. Three- and four-place multipliers 2. Two-place divisors; apparent quotient must be corrected	1. Addition, and subtraction of related fractions, as 1/3 and 1/6; also of easy unrelated types, 1/2 and 1/3 2. Multiplication 3. Division of whole numbers and mixed numbers by fractions	1. Addition and subtraction extended to thousandths 2. Multiplication and division of decimals by whole numbers

SOURCE: Brueckner, L. J., and Bond, G. L. *The diagnosis and treatment of learning difficulties*, pp. 206–207. Englewood Cliffs, N.J.: Prentice-Hall, 1955. Used with permission of publisher.

each of the four areas of education pertinent to special education—self-help/basic living, career/vocational, sociobehavioral, and academics—educational planning can only be haphazardly undertaken. In fact, most handicapped students have needs in more than one or in all four of these areas. For instance, a student in need of the self-help skills of feeding and dressing may also need language training, an academic skill. For this reason it is recommended that persons in each school or education agency research each of these areas presented in this section and define for themselves the performance areas and constructs that constitute special education. Examining the examples presented here and other sources can assist educators in conceptualizing each area of special education in order to determine possible annual goals. At the risk of being redundant, it is necessary to underscore the value in personalizing these concepts in order that education agencies may (1) better represent local needs and concerns, (2) provide educators within the agency an opportunity to re-examine their present educational programs for handicapped children and youth in light of other programmatic possibilities, and most importantly (3) develop both confidence and competence within individual educators regarding the tasks involved in teaching.

Once these areas have been examined and defined, the IEP team can begin deliberations concerning specific children. These deliberations should be taken in light of all the possible constructs involved in defining the areas, along with the student's unique needs as derived from a number of sources. The factors that should be involved when selecting performance areas for individual children are described below.

TABLE 4-22 Scope and Sequence of Elementary Mathematics

	Grade						
	K	1	2	3	4	5	6
I. *Readiness for Mathematics*							
Classification	•	•	•	•	•	•	•
One-to-one correspondence	•	•	•	•	•	•	•
One-to-many correspondence				•	•	•	•
Seriation or ordering	•	•	•	•	•	•	•
Space and spatial representaion	•	•	•	•	•	•	•
Flexibility and reversibility	•	•	•	•	•	•	•
Conservation	•	•	•	•	•	•	•
II. *Mathematical Concepts*							
Same, equal, as much as	•	•	•	•	•	•	•
More than, greater, greatest, larger, largest	•	•	•	•	•	•	•
Bigger, biggest, longer, longest	•	•	•	•	•	•	•
Less than, fewer, fewest, smaller, smallest	•	•	•	•	•	•	•
Shorter, shortest, most, least	•	•	•	•	•	•	•
Enough, not enough, more than enough	•	•	•	•	•	•	•
Left, right		•	•	•	•	•	•
Above, below, up, down, next to, between		•	•	•	•	•	•
Putting together, add, plus		•	•	•	•	•	
Take apart, take away, subtract, minus		•	•	•	•	•	
How many in all? How many are left?		•	•	•	•	•	
Odd, even			•	•	•	•	•
Open, closed			•	•	•	•	•
=, >, <			•		•	•	•
Factors, primes, multiples							•
III. *Sets*							
Definition	•	•	•	•	•	•	•
Elements of sets	•	•	•	•	•	•	•
Kinds of sets							
Identical	•	•	•	•	•	•	•
Equal and equivalent	•	•	•	•	•	•	•
Unequal and nonequivalent						•	•
Empty set			•	•	•	•	•
Union of sets (addition)			•	•	•	•	•
Subset (subtraction)			•	•	•	•	•
Intersection of sets						•	•
IV. *Whole Numbers*							
Abstracting idea of cardinal number from equivalent set	•	•	•	•	•	•	•
Counting: one through ten	•	•	•	•	•	•	•
Concepts and counting: numbers above ten		•	•	•	•	•	•
Concept of zero	•	•	•	•	•	•	•
Skip counting by twos, threes, fives, tens		•	•	•	•	•	•
V. *Operations on Whole Numbers: Addition and Subtraction*							
Properties							
Closure and nonclosure			•	•	•	•	•
Commutativity and noncommutativity			•	•	•	•	•
Associativity and nonassociativity			•	•	•	•	•

TABLE 4–22   (*cont.*)

	Grade K	1	2	3	4	5	6
Inverse relation of addition and subtraction		•	•	•	•	•	•
Ways of conceptualizing							
Union of sets or forming of subsets		•	•	•	•	•	•
Number line		•	•	•	•	•	•
Addition and subtraction with zero		•	•	•	•	•	•
Addition and subtraction with horizontal notation		•	•	•	•	•	•
Addition and subtraction with vertical notation		•	•	•	•	•	•
Addition and subtraction without regrouping							
One-place numbers	•	•	•	•	•	•	•
Two-place numbers		•	•	•	•	•	•
Three-place numbers			•	•	•	•	•
Numbers with more than three digits				•	•	•	•
Addition and subtraction with regrouping							
Two-place numbers			•	•	•	•	•
More than two-place numbers				•	•	•	•
Column addition		•	•	•	•	•	•

VI. *Operations on Whole Numbers: Multiplication and Division*

	Grade K	1	2	3	4	5	6
Properties							
Commutativity of multiplication			•	•	•	•	•
Associativity of multiplication				•	•	•	•
Distributive property of multiplication and division over addition				•	•	•	•
Inverse relationship of multiplication and division			•	•	•	•	•
Ways of conceptualizing							
Union of sets or partitioning into equivalent sets			•	•	•	•	•
Repeated addition or successive subtraction			•	•	•	•	•
Arrays			•	•	•	•	•
Number line				•	•	•	•
Multiplication and division with horizontal notation			•	•	•	•	•
Mutliplication and division with vertical notation			•	•	•	•	•
Use of zero in multiplication and division			•	•	•	•	•
"One" as the identity element			•	•	•	•	•
Multiplication and division with 10's, 100's, etc.				•	•	•	•
Computation without regrouping							
One-place factor or divisor, one-place sums, dividend			•	•	•	•	•
One-place factor or divisor, two-place sums or dividends			•	•	•	•	•
Computation without regrouping							
One-place factor or divisor, two- or three-place sums or dividends				•	•	•	•
Two-place factors or divisors, any number sums or dividends					•	•	•
Three- or four-place factors or divisors							•
Multiple multiplication				•	•	•	•

(*continued*)

TABLE 4–22   (*cont.*)

	K	1	2	3	4	5	6
				Grade			
VII. Fractions							
Definition		•	•	•	•	•	•
Ways of conceptualizing							
Number line				•	•	•	•
Arrays or subsets				•	•	•	•
Geometric figures		•	•	•	•	•	•
Computation							
Addition and subtraction of simple fractions with common denominators				•	•	•	•
Addition and subtraction of simple fractions with mixed denominators					•	•	•
Addition and subtraction of mixed fractions with common denominators				•	•	•	•
Addition and subtraction of mixed fractions with mixed denominators					•	•	•
Multiplication and division							•
Decimal fractions							•
VIII. Measurement							
Measurement of length (inch, foot, yard, mile, metric)		•	•	•	•	•	•
Measurement of area (English and metric units)						•	•
Measurement of weight (ounce, pound, ton, metric units)					•	•	•
Measurement of liquids (cup, pint, quart, metric units)	•	•	•	•	•	•	•
Dry measures (quart, peck, bushel, metric units)				•	•	•	•
Measurement of quantity (dozen, gross)				•	•	•	•
Measurement of temperature (Fahrenheit, Celsius)				•	•	•	•
Measurement of time (clock, calendar)	•	•	•	•	•	•	•
Measure of money (coins, paper bills)	•	•	•	•	•	•	•
IX. Geometry							
Geometric shapes (circle, square, rectangle, triangle)	•	•	•	•	•	•	•
Geometric shapes (pentagon, hexagon, octagon, parallelogram)				•	•	•	•
Spatial relationships	•	•	•	•	•	•	•
Point, line, line segment, ray, intersection					•	•	•
Parallel line, curved line, straight line						•	•
Radius, diameter					•	•	•
Angles, arc degrees							•
Closed-line plane, open-line place						•	•
Area and perimeter						•	•
Three-dimensional shapes (sphere, cube, cone)						•	•

Source: Wallace, G., and Kauffman, J. *Teaching children with learning problems.* Columbus: Charles E. Merrill, 1973. Used with permission.

SELECTING APPROPRIATE
EDUCATIONAL PERFORMANCE AREAS

Once educators have examined and conceptualized the performance areas and constructs that constitute the categories of self-help/basic living, academic, career/vocational, and sociobehavioral education, the IEP team can begin to select appropriate performance areas and constructs pertinent for individual children. Determining those areas of special education upon which to construct a particular student's individualized educational program constitutes the general direction of that particular child's education. In addition, determining pertinent educational performance areas, such as grooming, multiplication, reading comprehension, or values, calls attention to any additional evaluations that may need to be conducted in order to document the child's present levels of educational performance. Selecting those areas of performance pertinent to each child defines more clearly the intent of that child's instruction and gives form to selecting annual goals and objectives. This documentation is very similar to that used to select required annual goals except that in most instances establishing appropriate educational areas provides an *ultimate goal or goals* for the child's education. This, in turn, also provides a cohesive structure for long-range educational planning. As with all aspects of a child's individualized education program, the selected area of educational performance is subject to review and revision as necessary.

There are several factors to consider when establishing appropriate educational performance areas for each student: (1) the referral and screening data, (2) the evaluation for diagnosis and placement, (3) the age of the student, (4) the severity of the handicap, (5) the unique restrictions placed upon a particular student by his/her handicapping condition, (6) the environment where the child is presently expected to function, (7) the next least-restrictive environment, and (8) parent and child expectations. It is helpful to give each of these considerations some attention while selecting those areas of educational performance most appropriate for a particular student. This information also leads directly to determining the types of additional assessments that may be needed in order to document present levels of functioning. The following paragraphs exemplify the ways in which each of these factors influences the selection of educational performance areas.

Referral and Screening Data

The referral and screening process is often the single best source for determining pertinent educational areas because the referral is most often made by an individual or individuals who observe the child regularly in an environment where the child is expected to function such as home, school, nursery. This individual expresses particular concerns regarding the child's development through the referral. Along with further screening data, the initial concern forms a base of information that is indicative of what is expected of a child his/her age. Therefore, the IEP team should examine these unfulfilled expectations as a possible guide in establishing the general direction the child's education should take. The usefulness of these data in establishing general directions is obvious in the cases of Bobby and Charles. Bobby is a nine-year-old student referred by his regular classroom teacher for behavior problems. The screening committee determined that his disruptive behavior was pervasive throughout all situations in which Bobby found himself, that is, home, school, and with peers. From these data the IEP team could conclude that an appropriate general direction for special services would be in the area of sociobehavioral skills. Charles, however, was referred by his parents. The parent referral form indicated that, at the age of three, Charles had still not begun talking. Screening conducted found that Charles' babysitter and playschool teacher had noticed the same deficit in language and, in addition, noted some coordination problems. However, they had concluded that Charles was possibly just shy around strangers. The obvious initial educational area of primary concern was language development.

Once screening and referral information has been analyzed by the IEP team, evaluation data collected during the placement phase should be reviewed for further clues as to the educational needs of handicapped children and youth.

Formal Evaluation Data

Diagnostic data collected during the *evaluation for placement* discussed in Chapter 3 are also helpful in supplying clues as to the student's potential for benefiting from various areas of educational emphasis. In many instances these evaluation data allow the IEP team to choose immediately to exclude certain educational concerns, as well as direct the team in further evaluation efforts. For example, Bobby's evaluation indicated he was of normal intelligence and somewhat behind in the academic areas of reading, spelling, and written expression. This information can lead to the conclusion that additional educational areas of concern should be the academic area of written language. Charles, on the other hand, was evaluated with two intelligence scales (one of which was nonverbal). On both scales Charles scored in the mentally retarded range.

Evaluation of adaptive behavior skills indicated a deficiency as well. Several conclusions can be drawn upon review of the evaluation data concerning Charles. First of all, with the exception of early language development skills, Charles did not at this time possess the potential for performing academic skills. In addition to language development, it can be determined that Charles needed instruction in developing certain social and behavioral skills. Because of Charles' generally retarded development, the IEP team will need to examine self-help and basic living skills, an area neglected during evaluation for placement. In addition to the handicapping condition itself, one must consider the age of the student involved when defining important areas of educational performance.

Age of Student

The age of the particular student has a great deal to do with the appropriateness of certain education directions. For example, were either Charles or Bobby much older, educators and parents might well be concerned with training them in certain skills that would enable them to obtain employment. With Bobby, of course, social skills as well as vocational skills would be a concern. On the other hand, Charles would still need self-help and basic living skills along with particular vocational skills that might allow him to enter a sheltered workshop experience. Age is a crucial and, for the most part, an obvious factor in setting educational performance areas to deal with. In addition to age and handicap, a great deal of educational direction depends on the severity of the given condition.

Severity and Multiplicity of Handicap

The severity of certain handicapping conditions is often a more critical variable in educational planning than is the type of handicapping condition itself. Frequently, this is reflected in the diagnostic data accumulated for placement. For example, consider, if Bobby's disruptive behaviors were so severe as to preclude most traditional instruction, academic areas might not be designated as a concern regardless of the academic problems demonstrated throughout his evaluation. Educational concerns might by necessity center solely around developing rapport with Bobby and determining and implementing an appropriate reinforcement system or merely getting Bobby to attend classes. The severity of the behavior problem in this case would cause less emphasis to be placed on academic performance areas. In the case of sensory handicaps, for example, the degree of residual vision determines whether or not low-vision utilization should be an area of educational emphasis.

Other Disabling Effects

Unfortunately, the severity, multiplicity, and type of handicapping condition do not adequately predict the way in which the handicap affects a particular individual. For reasons about which one can only guess, the identical handicap does not manifest itself with the same problems in any two persons. Perhaps this is because present instrumentation is not yet sensitive or sophisticated enough to note differences, or that certain immeasurable personality factors are involved, or that the past experiences of a child influence the effect of a given handicap to a large degree. In any event, one can be sure that, for example, two deaf students with identical measured intelligence and residual hearing do not necessarily have the same educational needs. For instance, one student may require a great deal of social skill development while the other may be able to compete in a traditional academic environment with little assistance. Even the degree of effective utilization of auditory input may not be similar in the two children. The characteristics that are unique to individual students must be examined in an effort *not* to exclude or overlook pertinent educational needs. In addition, the environment in which a child is expected to function has a great deal to do with the performance of an individual and, thus, the establishment of educational areas of concern.

Present Environment

The environment in which a child is expected to function gives team members further clues as to the appropriateness of certain educational performance areas. For instance, for a mentally retarded student residing in an institutional setting, pertinent social skills would be different from the kinds of social skills expected of a mentally retarded child residing at home and attending the public school special classes. Another important environmental consideration is involved when training students in vocational skills who would probably remain within their own communities and/or homes for most of their lives. It is imperative that the kinds of vocational skills introduced to students must be applicable in the geographical areas in which they reside. Job markets must be evaluated and general directions set appropriately. However, with handicapped students there must always be attention focused on the next least-restrictive environment. The next most "normalized" setting where the student might function would also be a consideration when establishing general directions for education.

Next Least-Restrictive Environment

The least-restrictive environment concept is an important consideration for the IEP team throughout educational programming and must first be considered when establishing pertinent educational performance areas. This concept forces educators and parents to look ahead to the results of certain educational directions. For instance, the goal for a student placed in an institution may be ultimately to return to his/her community, to a half-way or group-home setting. In this case, educational performance must be concentrated on the sociobehavioral, self-help/basic living, and vocational skills necessary to matriculate back into society. Wolfensberger (1972) describes in detail a more comprehensive process of this sort (discussed earlier in this chapter) that is defined as normalization. The process of moving handicapped individuals into a less restrictive environment has often been misconstrued as meaning "back to the regular classroom." This is often not the case; but, where regular classroom performance is desirable, students must acquire the specific sociobehavioral and academic skills necessary for success in the classroom. This concept is further discussed in Chapter 7 regarding establishing appropriate services. In determining educational performance concerns with regard to the present environment and next least-restrictive environment, one must also consider the expectations of parents and students themselves regarding their ultimate goals of education.

Parental and Child Expectations

In the past special educators have often neglected to investigate the concerns and *expectations of parents* for their children's futures, as well as the students' own expectations and aspirations. Very likely this will not be the case with the advent of parent, and sometimes student, participation on the IEP team. Often parents can give educators insight regarding their perceptions of the child's abilities. In many cases, parents see an entirely different child at home than educators see in a competitive school environment. When they exist, discrepancies between expectations of parents and potential as exhibited in school should be investigated. Once these discrepancies are assessed, school personnel can then either assist parents in developing new and different expectations or adjust the child's educational directions to approximate more closely the student's real (as opposed to measured) potential. An example of discrepant expectations would be John, a three-year-old perceived as being without language who was referred by his playschool teacher. John was then evaluated as having little language and qualified as being mentally retarded. His parents, it was later discovered, felt John was a normal three-year-old and had foreseen no problems. Upon investigation it was found that at home John did talk intelligently, interacted, and displayed normal adaptive behavior. It may then be surmised that socialization may be a more appropriate direction for further educational planning along with language stimulation. One would hope that these discrepancies would be noted during screening; however, often parents may not feel free to voice objections or educational directions of their choice.

Probably many conflicts between school-perceived expectations and those of parents center around academic education versus vocational education. Often parents hold sincere desires that their children have the opportunity to continue formal education upon graduation. This is equally true of parents of handicapped youngsters. Where these expectations are viable, they must be attended to and where there appear to be gross misconceptions, efforts must be made immediately to assist parents in developing new and productive expectations.

Students' expectations can also be an insightful predictor of unrealized student potential and interests, as well as an indication of the student's reinforcement system and self-confidence. At this point, it is essential to deal with and resolve any differences in expectations and aspirations. Once resolved and understood, the IEP team members can define those areas of educational performance that reflect the present and future needs of the student by combining his/her interests and potential for achievement with realistic educational expectations.

Systematic investigation of all these factors—parent-child expectations, handicapping condition, severity, complicating factors, referral, screening and evaluation data, age, and present and projected environmental placements—allows the IEP team to determine all the educational performance areas pertinent to the individual student at this time. This determination constitutes the basic general directions that the child's education should follow and forms the basis for subsequent educational planning and programming. At this point the IEP team can formally begin IEP document development, the first step of which is to document present levels of performance in each defined performance area of special educational concern.

ESTABLISHING PRESENT LEVELS OF EDUCATIONAL PERFORMANCE

Once appropriate areas of educational performance have been defined for a given handicapped child, the IEP team must, by law, document his/her present level of performance within each of the areas outlined. This statement constitutes the first *mandated* component of the IEP document and serves to establish the child's present functioning levels in pertinent special educational areas. There are essentially two purposes to be fulfilled by documenting present performance levels. These are establishing data for (1) program entry and planning and (2) program evaluation.

The first purpose of documenting present levels of performance is accomplished by providing the IEP team with a general place in which to begin programming the student's educational program. That is to say, educational planners should have some idea of the degrees to which the student has or has not mastered certain skill areas. This documented entry point for special education programming also fulfills the second purpose—program evaluation. The performance levels at which a student is found to be functioning provide educators an initial measure that can be repeated periodically in order to ascertain the amount of pupil progress being made. Through this periodic evaluation educators can determine the success of individual programs as well as the need for revision and updating.

These purposes can only be accomplished when the present levels of performance are documented by using reliable and valid instrumentation. The instrumentation must measure adequately the areas of educational performance constituting the child's special education program. At this point it is important to remind the reader that only those areas of education provided through special education and related services need present level documentation. Special education and related services may or may not constitute the child's total education program. Many times certain areas of the child's education program are provided through the regular classroom services. In these instances, it is necessary to document present levels of performance *only* in those areas that are the responsibility of special education and related services. For example, Sue, a fifth grader, was referred for problems in written language. The evaluation for placement resulted in her being classified as learning disabled. The academic areas of reading, spelling, and written expression were defined as educational performance areas of concern. However, with only slight regular classroom modifications (such as oral testing), Sue is perfectly capable of functioning in the regular classroom for math, social studies, and science. Therefore, in Sue's case, present levels of functioning are defined only for the areas of reading, spelling, and written

197

expression. Though not stated, it is assumed that Sue's performance in the areas where she attends regular classroom instruction closely approximates that of her peers, and that general goals and objectives set for those classes are also appropriate for Sue. Therefore, the IEP team need only document performance levels for educational areas that are the responsibility of special education and related services. While this documentation is a relatively simple process when the areas of concern are within academic curricula, the process for documenting performance levels in other areas can become quite complex.

To a large degree, the instrumentation needed to document present levels of educational performance would already have been administered during the referral, screening, and evaluation for placement process (see Chapter 3). This is particularly true in instances like Sue's where placement procedures are conducted to determine the handicapping condition of learning disabilities since the criteria for placement alone require establishing performance levels in several areas of academic achievement. For example, Sue's present levels of functioning in reading, spelling, and written expression were established when it was determined that she did, indeed, qualify for special education placement. However, many test instruments used in the evaluation for placement procedures are not designed to yield *educationally pertinent* data (that is, data useful for educational programming). For example, the evaluation of certain physical and sensory disorders (such as degree of blindness, asthma, or crippling conditions), while certainly holding implications for education planners, does *not* yield present levels of *educational performance*. Intelligence tests are almost always administered to handicapped youngsters and are useful *predictive* measures; however, these tests also do not yield educational performance levels. For example, Billy was evaluated as mildly mentally retarded on the basis of an individual intelligence scale. The IEP team established the areas of educational concern to be certain self-help skills and preacademic tasks of oral language. Had the IEP team not conducted further assessments, they could not at this time document present educational performance levels. Therefore, often there is the need to conduct formal evaluations over and above those required for special education placement in order to formulate a statement(s) of present level(s) of educational performance.

When attempting to conduct evaluations that would yield appropriate present levels of educational performance, the IEP team must locate and conduct valid, reliable measures of performance so that educators not only have a point for program entry but also are able to utilize the data in evaluating student progress. Two types of evaluative measures can be used to document present functioning: standardized tests and, when standardized tests are not available, comprehensive data collection systems. Standardized, norm-referenced tests best fulfill these purposes. Data yielded from these instruments give grade, age, and, possibly, criterion levels so that entry points in educational programs can be established. Standardized instruments are also appropriate for repeated administration within certain time limits thus serving also to verify educational progress. However, it is not uncommon to have identified areas of educational pertinence for which there are no viable standardized instrumentation or areas where available instrumentation, though well-standardized, is inappropriate. In these instances, it is possible for educators to collect data that are reliable and to document present levels of educational performance. We next discuss both the careful selection of standardized performance or achievement measures and reliable alternative data collection systems, as well as recommend a format for the written statement of performance levels in the IEP document.

Standardized Measures of Educational Performance

When available, norm-referenced tests are the most reliable sources of performance-level data. When attempting to document present levels of educational performance, educators must re-examine the educational performance areas defined for the student in light of present-day standardized tests. When examining available instrumentation, there are two important considerations for educators to keep in mind that apply directly to the appropriateness of certain standardized measures in documenting present levels of educational performance: (1) many standardized instruments are not designed as performance measures but as predictive measures, and (2) standardized instruments often measure areas of educational performance so broadly that the resultant data are difficult to utilize. The authors discuss each of these issues prior to specifying some possible standardized performance measures in each of the four areas of special education.

Traditionally standardized testing has been utilized in special education primarily as a diagnostic tool, that is, to establish diagnosis for placement. As was discussed earlier, though standardized, these instruments do not yield educationally relevant data for programming. Most of these instruments can be thought of as "predictive," that is, the tests indicate potential problems or strengths but do not specifically define a level of educational performance. This consideration applies to several areas of evaluation—sensory, intellectual, medical history, and vocational testing. Sensory-acuity testing reveals gross problems for educators and documents a handicapping condition. This data is most useful in establishing the need for specific special services or for indicating the degree to which low vision or residual hearing training would be useful. Tests of intelligence are best utilized as predictors of whether or not a student can benefit from certain kinds of academic instruction. Medical histories often indicate possible sources of a disorder and special precautions or treatments that the student may need to continue. For educators these kinds of information are available and are often useful in more thoroughly understanding a student's particular problem. However, this data provides little or no information regarding a child's actual performance in pertinent special education areas. Career and vocational testing is another example of primarily predictive measurement. These instruments provide educators directions in channeling a student toward certain occupations but have little to do with present competence in occupational skills. These are several examples intended to caution the reader that establishing present levels must be directed toward special education *needs,* not prediction.

An additional consideration in selecting instrumentation is that many available tests document performance in a broad manner. For example, many of the early developmental scales provide levels for language, social, and motor skills, but these levels (usually given as developmental ages) are derived from an extremely limited number of items. Therefore, although documenting present levels, very little information is actually obtained regarding performance. With these considerations in mind, we now examine standardized instrumentation that is useful for documenting present levels of performance in each of the four areas of education for the handicapped.

Self-help and basic living performance. Generally, levels of self-help skills are assessed through standardized developmental scales, checklists, and motor scales. Often these developmental scales also assess certain areas of social and language concerns. The following table provides the reader with available instrumentation to investigate for use in documenting present levels of performance in self-help/basic living skills (see Table 4–23).

The reader may note that other special education areas are assessed in many of these devices. However, these measures do assess particular aspects defined earlier as representative of the area of self-help/basic living skills.

For the most part, the instruments listed in Table 4–23 give a very broad idea of general functioning in the constructs purported to be measured. There are times when the ability to perform specific tasks such as those involved in dressing or feeding may need to be assessed. These may, if desired, be assessed through data recording discussed later.

Social and behavioral performance. Sociobehavioral skill levels are also occasionally tapped in the developmental instruments listed in Table 4–24. These levels can also be defined in measures of adaptive behavior, personal interactions, and personality. Table 4–24 provides some additional instrumentation useful in documenting performance levels in social and behavioral skills, particularly those referred to as adaptive behavior.

In addition to assessing adaptive behavior, it is often desirous to obtain information regarding a socially or behaviorally maladjusted student's interactional patterns with peers and adults. These measures were discussed briefly in Chapter 3. Information gleaned from results of such assessments can be valuable in detecting differences in sociobehavioral performance from situation to situation. Wallace and Larsen (1978) provide a listing of those standardized instruments useful in assessing adult-child interactions and rating scales useful in measuring peer relationships. These are combined and included in Table 4–25 (p. 205–206). Both these devices and the adaptive behavior devices are useful in establishing levels of performance in socialization skills.

For students who exhibit primary behavior problems as opposed to just social maladjustments, educators may wish to administer personality tests or measures. These instruments give further information regarding the student but to a large degree are developed for prediction and diagnosis as opposed to educational performance. A list of such instrumentation has been developed by Salvia and Ysseldyke (1978) and is shown in Table 4–26 (p. 207). The self-concept tests and interests tests are also often used in assessing career/vocational skills.

Once again, for particular behaviors the team wants to investigate further, observational recordings can be a useful and reliable measurement of present performance. In many instances, a particular behavior problem may only be assessed by one or two items on a standardized instrument but may be debilitating enough to affect the child's entire interactional and performance abilities. In these instances, documentation of degree, frequency, duration, and so on, of the behavior should be assessed as part of the performance-level documentation.

Career/vocational performance. The area of career and vocational skill assessment is particularly difficult to assess with standardized measures. The reason for this is that standardized instruments in this area have been produced almost exclusively for prediction. This prediction takes the form of suggesting broad occupational areas to which the individual seems best fitted. Wallace and Larsen (1978) classify existing career assessment instrumentation as measuring aptitude, interest and attitude, and career maturity. In addition, desired measures in career/vocational programs often include self-image and concept tests. Table 4–27 lists some of the devices but the reader is cautioned that, for particular job-

201

TABLE 4–23 Examples of Standardized Tests Useful in Documenting Present Levels of Educational Performance—Self-Help/ Basic Living Skills

Test Name	Appropriate Ages	Constructs Purported to Be Assessed
Vineland Social Maturity (Doll, 1953)	Birth–30 yrs.	Self-help general, self-help eating and dressing, locomotion, occupation, communication, self-direction, socialization
Cain-Levine Social Competency Scale (Cain, Levine, and Elzey, 1963)	5–14	Self-help, initiative, social skills, communication
AAMD Adaptive Behavior Scale (Nihira, Foster, Shellhaas, and Leland, 1969)		Independent functioning—eating, toileting, cleanliness, posture, and clothing (appearance), care of clothing, dressing, transportation, and direction, telephone use Physical development—sensory and motor Economics—money, shopping Language development—expression, comprehension, social language Numbers and time Domestic activity—cleaning, food services Vocational activity Self-direction—initiative, perseverance, leisure Responsibility—personal belongings, general Socialization—appropriate vs. inappropriate Also measured are: Violent and destructive behaviors, untrustworthiness, antisocial behaviors, rebellious behavior, withdrawal, stereotyped behavior, inappropriate manners, poor vocal habits, unacceptable habits, self-abuse, hyperactivity, sexually aberrant behaviors, psychological disturbance, and the use of medication

Developmental Scales and Checklists

Category	Test	Ages	Areas
Scales and Checklists	Preschool Attainment Record (Doll, 1967)	1 mo.–6 yrs.	Personal social, fine motor, gross motor, language
	Denver Development Screening Test (Frankenburg and Dodds, 1970)	Elementary ages	Auditory comprehension, spoken language, motor coordination, orientation, personal-social behaviors
	The Pupil Rating Scale (Myklebust, 1971)		
	Meeting Street School Screening Test (Hainsworth and Sigueland, 1969)	5–0 to 7–5	Visual motor, language, gross motor
	First Grade Screening Test (Pate and Webb, 1969)	5–6	General knowledge, body image, perception of parental images, appropriate play, visual motor coordination, following directions, memory, and emotional maturity
	Cooperative Preschool Inventory (Caldwell, 1970)	3–6	Numerical and sensory concepts, personal-social responsiveness, vocabulary
Motor Proficiency	Lincoln-Oseretzky Motor Development Scale (Sloan, 1954)	6–14	Motor speed, balance, dynamic coordination, general coordination, jumping
	Bruininks-Oseretzky Test of Motor Proficiency (Bruininks, 1977)	3–18	Running speed and agility, balance, bilateral coordination, strength, upper-limb coordination, response speed, visual motor control, upper-limb speed, and dexterity
	Cratty Perceptual Motor Battery (Cratty, 1970)	4–10	Body perception, gross agility, balance, locomotor agility, tracking, throwing
	Fleishman Motor Ability and Fitness Scales (Fleishman, 1964)	12–18	Grip strength, throwing, running, pull-ups, broad jumps, sit-ups, and general agility
Other	Purdue Perceptual Motor Survey (Roach and Kephart, 1966)	6–10	Balance and posture, body image and differentiating, perceptual motor match, ocular control, form perception
	Visual Efficiency Scale (Barraga, 1970)		Degree of visual functioning

TABLE 4-24 Examples of Standardized Tests Useful in Documenting Present Levels of Educational Performance—Socio-behavioral Skills

Adaptive Behavior

Test Name	Appropriate Ages	Constructs Purported to Be Assessed
Vineland Social Maturity Scale (Doll, 1953)	Birth–30 yrs.	Self-help general, self-help eating and dressing, locomotion, occupation, communication, self-direction, socialization
Cain-Levine Social Competency Scale (Cain, Levine, and Elzey, 1963)	5–14	Self-help, initiative, social skills, communication
AAMD Adaptive Behavior Scale (Nihira, Foster, Shellhaas, and Leland, 1969)		Independent functioning—eating, toileting, cleanliness, posture and clothing (appearance), care of clothing, dressing, transportation and direction, telephone use Physical development—sensory and motor Economics—money, shopping Language development—expression, comprehension, social language Numbers and time Domestic activity—cleaning, food service Vocational activity Self-direction—initiative, perseverance, leisure Responsibility—personal belongings, general Socialization—appropriate vs. inappropriate Also measured are: Violent and destructive behaviors, untrustworthiness, antisocial behaviors, rebellious behavior, withdrawal, stereotyped behavior, inappropriate manners, poor vocal habits, unacceptable habits, self-abuse, hyperactivity, sexually aberrant behaviors, psychological disturbance, and the use of medication
Behavior Rating Profile (Brown and Hammill, 1978)	6–13	Peer relations Teacher perception (school) Parent perception (home) Child perception (home, school, peers)

TABLE 4–25   Peer Relations and Adult/Child Interaction Measures

INSTRUMENT	DESCRIPTION
Peer Rating Scales	
Russell Sage Social Relations Test (Damrin, 1956)	Provides information regarding the problem-solving skills of various classroom groups.
Syracuse Scales of Social Relations (Gardner and Thompson, 1959)	Pupil rates types of need relationships with classmates and others.
A Class Play (Bower, 1961)	Peer-rating instrument designed to indicate negative, neutral, and positive influences of others.
The Class Picture (Bower, 1961)	Given individually, this scale estimates how students are perceived by their peers.
Ohio Social Acceptance Scale (Ohio State Department of Education, 1944)	Consists of six headings: 1. My very, very best friends 2. My other friends 3. No friends, but okay 4. Don't know them 5. Don't care for them 6. Dislike them Each student is asked to place each of his or her classmates in one of these categories.
Minnesota Sociometric Status Test (Moore and Updegraff, 1971)	Measures social status or acceptance of students by peers. Testing materials on a board with photographs of every child in the peer group. Each student is interviewed and questioned about the photographs.
Adult-Child Interaction Systems	
Reichenberg-Hackett Teacher Behavior Observation System (Reichenberg-Hackett, 1962)	Focuses upon nursery school teachers and pupils. Teacher-behavior is coded according to five major categories.
Teachers Practices Observation Record (Brown, 1970)	Consists of 62 items grouped into seven categories. Requires little training of observers and possesses high reliability and validity.
Connors-Eisenberg Observation System (Connors and Eisenberg, 1966)	Is appropriate for use in nursery school and elementary grades. Yields three sets of scores that relate to "episodes," "activities," and "overall judgments."
The Purdue Teachers Observation Scale (Bentley and Starry, 1970)	Is designed to provide junior or senior high school teachers with an evaluation of their performance as seen through the eyes of students.
Classroom Observational Scales (Emmer, 1971)	Bases observations in 12 variables from "pupil attention" to "enthusiasm." Easily learned and administered.

(continued)

TABLE 4–25 (cont.)

INSTRUMENT	DESCRIPTION
Flanders' System of Interaction Analysis (Flanders, 1970)	Is intended to gather data on teacher behaviors that restrict or increase student freedom of action. Focuses upon categories of behavior.
Nonverbal Interaction Analysis	Provides a method of recording nonverbal behavior in classrooms. Designed to parallel the categories of verbal behavior in Flanders' System of Interaction Analysis.
Fuller Affective Interactions (Records 33) (Fuller, 1969)	Assesses interpersonal behaviors of pre-service teachers and their students. Utilizes five interpersonal dimensions.
Teacher-Child Dyadic Interaction (Brophy and Good, 1969)	Categorizes each teacher-student verbal interaction. Requires 20 hours of training to be used effectively. An excellent research tool.

ADAPTED FROM: Wallace, G., and Larsen, S. C. *Educational assessment of learning problems.* Boston: Allyn and Bacon, 1978. Used with permission of publisher.

related skills, some form of observational recording needs to be conducted. While the devices may not be appropriate for documenting a performance level that actually becomes a goal of instruction, they may lead educators into locating appropriate areas for assessment based on the student's abilities and interests in certain types of occupations that require specific skills. Those skills can generally be assessed separately.

Academic levels. The performance area of academics as was discussed earlier is perhaps the easiest area of education in which to document present levels of performance. This is due to the multitude of instruments designed specifically for this purpose. Many of the instruments utilized were discussed more thoroughly in Chapter 3; however, an additional listing is provided in Table 4–28. The table does not include the multitude of general group-achievement tests frequently given in the schools because of the inadequacy of these measures in assessing academically handicapped children's performance. The tests included here represent individual general achievement measures, comprehensive individual tests of language, reading, written language, and math. In locating appropriate instrumentation the reader may also find it useful to consult Wallace and Larsen (1978) and/or Salvia and Ysseldyke (1978).

While appropriate instrumentation is ample for documenting present levels of academic performance, this is obviously not the case in the educational areas of self-help/basic living, career/vocational, and sociobehavioral. When appropriate standardized tests are not available, educators must document performance levels through careful observational

206

TABLE 4–26   Tests of Personality, Interests, Traits, and Self-Concept

---

General Personality and Emotional Development
Bender Visual Motor Gestalt Test (Bender, 1938)
Blacky Pictures (Blum, 1967)
California Psychological Inventory (Gough, 1969)
California Test of Personality (Thorpe, Clark, & Tiegs, 1953)
Children's Apperception Test (Bellak & Bellak, 1965)
Draw-a-Person (Urban, 1963)
Early School Personality Questionnaire (Coan & Cattell, 1970)
Edwards Personal Preference Schedule (Edwards, 1959)
Edwards Personality Inventory (Edwards, 1966)
Eysenck Personality Inventory (Eysenck & Eysenck, 1969)
Family Relations Test (Bene & Anthony, 1957)
Holtzman Inkblot Technique (Holtzman, 1966)
House-Tree-Person (Buck & Jolles, 1966)
Human Figures Drawing Test (Koppitz, 1968)
Jr.-Sr. High School Personality Questionnaire (Cattell, Coan, & Belloff, 1969)
Minnesota Multiphasic Personality Inventory (Hathaway & McKinley, 1967)
Rorschach Inkblot Technique (Rorschach, 1966)
School Apperception Method (Solomon & Starr, 1968)
Sixteen Personality Factor Questionnaire (Cattell, Eber, & Tatsuoka, 1970)
Thematic Apperception Test (Murray, 1943)
Interests or Preferences
A Book About Me (Jay, 1955)
Kuder Personal Preference Record (Kuder, 1954)
School Interest Inventory (Cottle, 1966)
School Motivation Analysis Test (Sweney, Cattell, & Krug, 1970)
Personality or Behavior Traits
Burks' Behavior Rating Scale (Burks, 1969)
Devereux Adolescent Behavior Rating Scale (Spivack, Spotts, & Haimes, 1967)
Devereux Child Behavior Rating Scale (Spivack & Spotts, 1966)
Devereux Elementary School Behavior Rating Scale (Spivack & Swift, 1967)
Peterson-Quay Problem Behavior Checklist (Quay & Peterson, 1967)
Pupil Behavior Inventory (Vinter, Sarri, Vorwaller, & Schafer, 1966)
Walker Problem Behavior Identification Checklist (Walker, 1970)
Self-Concept
Piers-Harris Children's Self-Concept Scale (Piers & Harris, 1969)
Tennessee Self Concept Scale (Fitts, 1965)

Source: Salvia, J., and Ysseldyke, J. *Assessment in special and remedial education.* Boston: Houghton Mifflin, 1978. Used with permission of publisher.

TABLE 4–27 Examples of Standardized Tests Useful in Documenting Present Levels of Educational Performance—Career/Vocational

	Test Name	Ages/Grades Applicable	Constructs Purported to Be Measured
Aptitude	General Aptitude Test Battery (U.S. Department of Labor, 1970)	High school and up	General learning ability, verbal aptitude, numerical aptitude, spatial aptitude, form perception, clerical perception, motor coordination, finger dexterity, and manual dexterity
	Non-reading Aptitude Test Battery (U.S. Department of Labor, 1970)	High school and up	Same constructs as above through: picture-word matching, oral vocabulary, coin matching, design completion, tool matching, three-dimensional space, form matching, coin series, name comparison, and marking, training, assembling
	Differential Aptitude Test (Bennett, Seashore, and Wesman, 1969)	Grades 8–12	Verbal reasoning, numerical ability, abstract reasoning; space relations, clerical speed and accuracy, mechanical reasoning, and language usage
	Flanagan Aptitude Classification Tests (Flanagan, 1960)		Inspection, coding, memory, precision, assembling, scales, coordination, judgment and comprehension, arithmetic, patterns, components, tables, mechanics, expression, ingenuity, reasoning, vocabulary, and planning
Interest and Attitude	Strong-Campbell Interest Inventory (Campbell, 1974)	High school	Occupations, school subjects, activities, amusements, types of people, preference for activities and characteristics
	Kuder Occupational Interest Survey (Kuder, 1966)	High school	Measures individuals' likes and dislikes and in comparison to others in various occupations
	Reading Free Vocational Interest Inventory (Becker, 1975)	High school	Students select pictures taken from various occupations; developed for mentally retarded and semiliterate; nonprofessional occupations assessed
	Minnesota Vocational Interest Inventory (Clark and Campbell, 1966)	15 yrs. and up	Assesses interests and matches student to a nonprofessional job
Career Maturity	Career Maturity Inventory (Crites, 1972)	Grades 6–13	Involvement in career choice, orientation to work, independence in decision making, preference for career-choice factors, and concepts of choice process
	Super's Work Values Inventory (Super, 1970)		Altruism, creativity, intellectual stimulation, achievement, independence, prestige, management, economic returns,

recording techniques. The following section briefly discusses such methods.

Observational Recording

In attempting to document present levels of educational performance in an area where either there are no standardized test instruments or educational planners prefer to have more specific information than that provided by test results, it is necessary to collect reliable data through carefully planned observations. This information can serve the same two purposes as do standardized levels of functioning. Therefore, the data can be utilized as a beginning point in programming an individual's education and can serve as a point of reference upon which subsequent observations can be compared for evaluation purposes. In order to meet these purposes, one must organize and collect the necessary data carefully. Factors involved in the reliable and valid collection of observational data include defining the behavior(s), considerations and formats for recording, and comprehension of the limits of the data's usefulness.

Defining the behavior. Probably the most important step in observational recording is defining the behavior or set of behaviors that are of concern for establishing present levels of performance. There are two types of behaviors for which one might be interested in documenting levels: (1) behaviors desired to increase and (2) behaviors necessary to decrease. Each of these requires careful definition prior to data collection. When defining behaviors the most important factor to keep in mind is that a defined behavior must be observable directly so that any recorder would know immediately if the behavior were to occur and any two persons would record occurrences identically. For example, rather than attempting to measure or observe "hyperactivity," one must define what activities constitute the behavior of "hyperactivity," such as rocking, getting out of seat, running, and hitting. Different individual recorders are then able to recognize the act of running but educators' opinions of what constitutes hyperactivity vary greatly.

Often when documenting present levels of performance, one might wish to define a *set* of related behaviors. For example, personal appearance on the job may be defined in a list of desired characteristics such as clothing matches; clothing appropriately buttoned, snapped, etc.; clothing is clean; clothing pressed; clothing—sportshirt and slacks; hair clean, hair combed; no body odor present. This type of observational recording where the data are grouped makes interpretation more inclusive—and possibly more meaningful. Another example of grouping data might be with regard to a student's self-concept. One might define some

TABLE 4-28 Examples of Standardized Tests Useful in Documenting Present Levels of Performance—Academic Achievement

	Name of Test	Grades or Ages Appropriate	Constructs Purported to Be Measured
General	Peabody Individual Achievement Test (Dunn and Markwardt, 1970)	K–12 grades	Mathematics, reading recognition, reading comprehension, spelling, general information
	Wide Range Achievement Test (Jastak and Jastak, 1965)	5–12 yrs. 12 yrs. and up	Reading, spelling, arithmetic
Language	Test of Oral Language Development (Newcomer and Hammill, 1977)	4.0–8.11 yrs.	Receptive semantics, expressive semantics, two areas of receptive syntax, expressive syntax, and receptive and expressive phonology
	Houston Test of Language Development (Crabtree, 1963)	6 mos.–6 yrs.	I. Accent, melody of speech, gesture, vocabulary, sound articulation, dynamic content, and grammatical usage II. Vocabulary, auditory judgments, temporal content, syntax, self-identity
	Utah Test of Language Development (Mecham, Jex, and Jones, 1967)	1–15 yrs.	Repetition of digits, color names, picture names, copying designs, sentence length, vocabulary, following directions and reading
Reading	Woodcock Reading Mastery Tests (Woodcock, 1974)	K–12 grades	Letter identification, word identification, word attack, word comprehension, passage comprehension
	Gates McKillop Reading Diagnostic Tests (Gates and McKillop, 1962)		Oral reading, words (flash presentation), words (untimed), phrases (flash presentation), knowledge of words parts, recognizing visual forms of words, auditory blending

210

Area	Test	Grades	Content
Reading	Durrell Analysis of Reading Difficulty (Durrell, 1955)	K–6 grades	Oral reading, silent reading, listening comprehension, word recognition and analysis, naming letters, visual memory of words, sounds, learning rate
	Test of Reading Comprehension (Wiederholt, Brown, and Hammill, 1978)		Following written directions, reading comprehension in science, math, social studies
Arithmetic	Key Math (Connolly, Nachtman, and Pritchett, 1971)	K–8 grades	Content—numeration, fractions, geometry, and symbols Operations—addition, subtraction, multiplication, division, mental computation, numerical reasoning Applications—word problems, missing elements, money, measurement, time
	Stanford Diagnostic Arithmetic Test (Beatty, Madden, and Gardner, 1966)	1–12 grades	Number system and numeration, computation, applications
Written Expression	The Test of Written Language (Hammill and Larsen, 1978)	3–8 grades	Spelling, word usage, capitalization, punctuation, sentences, vocabulary, parts of speech, creativity
	Picture Story Language Test (Myklebust, 1965)	1–6 grades	Productivity, correctness, meaning
Spelling	The Test of Written Spelling (Larsen and Hammill, 1976)	1–6 grades	Predictable and unpredictable words
	Spellmaster (Cohen and Abrams, 1974)	K–10 grades	Regular and irregular words, homonyms

of the following behaviors as undesirable, that is, indicative of a poor self-concept; head down, shoulders slouched, makes negative statements about self. These are examples of grouped data recording that might need to be collected over an extended period of time.

Recording data. Once behaviors for observational recording are defined, specific considerations necessary include the factors involved in recording the dimensions of a behavior. In general, these dimensions define the intensity or severity of a particular behavior. The degree to which a certain behavior or set of behaviors is present can be measured when one considers such factors as:

- frequency—how often a behavior occurs
- rate—how often within a given amount of time a behavior occurs
- duration—how long it lasts
- intensity—how much it affects others
- situational—where or when the behavior occurs or with whom

When studying these factors, one might wish to review Gropper et al.'s (1975) criteria listed in Table 4–9. It is important to note that not all the factors are applicable to a given behavior or set of behaviors. For example, for the behavior of eye contact, it is only appropriate to consider such things as frequency, rate, duration, and situation. In the example of criteria defined for personal appearance on the job, one might wish to measure only the extent to which the criteria were true once daily. Intensity and duration would be irrelevant in this instance; the situation is defined as on-the-job only; and rate would be most appropriate in terms of week(s).

Once the appropriate factors for a given behavior have been determined, educators can establish a format for observational recording based on the extensiveness of the data desired and the specific behavior to be observed. Brown (1978) lists six techniques for recording observations. Of these, four are recommended for documenting present levels of performance—event recording, duration recording, interval recording, and time sampling.

Event recording is simply a documentation of the number of times a defined behavior occurs. This type of recording is appropriate for counting behaviors that are measured continuously and can be easily noted. It is best when event recording is documented in terms of the time recorded, that is, daily, from 9:00–4:00, weekly, and so on. For example, one might measure appearance on the job as the number of

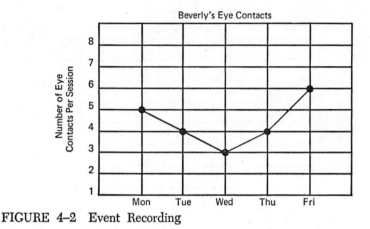

FIGURE 4–2   Event Recording

days per week the student was appropriately dressed (dressed according to criteria set forth in the behavioral definition of "appropriately dressed"). Another example of event recording might be in recording the number of times during a given 10 minute session that a student maintained eye contact. A graph illustrating a format for event recording is given in Figure 4–2.

Duration recording is the observation of time in which a specific behavior is present. This type of recording is important when event recording is not descriptive enough to document the intensity of a behavior or when the goal is to increase the length of time a specific behavior lasts. An example of when duration recording may be desirable is in measuring the length of time a given child maintains eye contact. Event recording, in this instance, might lead to the erroneous assumption that the behavior was well-established when in fact events of eye contact may only denote glances. Figure 4–3 illustrates a format for recording duration of behavior. It is obvious that the data accumulated regarding Beverly's eye contacts are more revealing in Figure 4–3 when duration was timed than in Figure 4–2 where only the event was recorded.

Interval recording measures both events and duration and is particularly useful when continuous duration recording is impractical or impossible and event recording inappropriate. In interval recording one must establish a length and frequency of time by which to record behavior, for example, every 10 minutes for 2 minutes or once every 30 seconds. In these cases, only during specified regularly scheduled times would the behavior be observed and recorded. By then dividing the period of time observed into the period when a behavior existed, one can derive an approximate percentage of time a behavior exists. For instance,

213

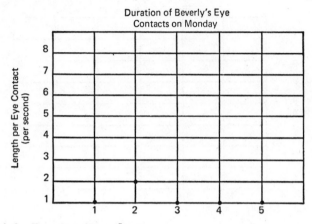

FIGURE 4–3   Duration Recording

on-task behavior (eyes on paper and working) might be observed 10 seconds in each minute during a 10-minute seatwork assignment. Each of the blocks illustrated in Figure 4–4 would represent a second in the 10-second period. One can then divide the number of times the behavior was observed by the number of seconds observed (in total) to arrive at a percent of on-task behavior.

Time sampling is much like interval recording, except that the observer is not required to observe the entire period; instead the behavior is recorded once each specified amount of time. For example, instead of observing for 10 seconds each minute, one would only mark the presence

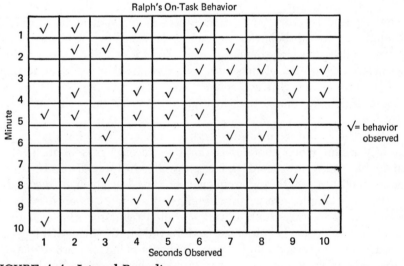

FIGURE 4–4   Interval Recording

of a behavior the first second of each 10 seconds for 10 minutes. Here again, a percentage may be obtained (see Figure 4–5).

Limitations of observational recording. When using observational recording, several cautions must be kept in mind in order to ensure the reliability and validity of the data collected. Because of the subjective nature of observation and the possible bias, it is necessary to validate data recording. The most common procedure for validating observation recording is to employ two recorders at the same time on several occasions to observe and record identical behaviors. If the same or similar results are obtained by each recorder (that is, 90 percent interrater agreement), one can be assured that the data has not been subjected to the biases of the recorder. In the event of discrepancy, there are two major possibilities: either the recorder(s) was biased or the behavior was not well defined and thus subject to recorder interpretations.

A last note of caution regarding observational data is that the data collected are extremely limited. This narrowness of data obtained is, of course, the result of the necessity of defining behaviors specifically. For instance, if on-task behavior is measured as "eyes on paper," one must remember the limits involved in this description. This factor makes observational recording less appropriate than standardized testing considering that present level of educational performance calls for only a broad, general statement of performance level as opposed to specific data. Undoubtedly, however, in most instances observational data are more useful in educational programming than data obtained on test instruments.

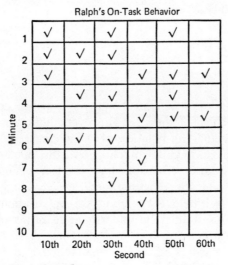

FIGURE 4–5 Time Sampling

Documenting present levels of educational performance can, therefore, be accomplished through two valid and reliable types of measurement. The first and simplest type of measurement consists of standardized achievement tests that measure educational performance in each of the specific areas of concern. When not available, educators can develop and conduct reliable and valid measurements by using specific observational recording devices. Once any additional evaluations (evaluations over and above placement information) necessary have been conducted, the team is ready to draw up the statement of present levels of educational performance.

Recommended Format for Documenting Present Levels of Educational Performance

The authors recommend that present levels of performance information, as well as evaluation for placement information, be contained in the first section of the IEP called an introduction. This introductory section consists of these data and other background and present information. The introduction to the IEP is similar in appearance to traditional psychological reports, following a format shown in Table 4–29. This format is largely listing; however, it should contain two or three brief paragraphs summarizing referral information, background information, and diagnostic data. It should conclude with a statement of conclusions regarding the child's general educational direction. At the conclusion of this text are two case studies that include sections on present level of educational performance.

SUMMARY

Documenting present levels of educational performance constitutes the first mandated component of the IEP. However, there are several steps prerequisite to the actual formulation of a statement of present performance levels for an individual student. First, this documentation can be accomplished only after educators have a clear definition of what presently constitutes education for the handicapped. These broad areas of special education—self-help/basic living, career/vocational, academic, and sociobehavioral—must then be understood in terms of the performance areas and constructs involved in each. Once these concepts have been mastered by educators, they are then utilized to further define educational problems exhibited by individual students.

TABLE 4-29   Suggested Format for Initial Phase of IEP Document

Individualized Education Program

Name:	Parent:
Birthdate:	Address:
Present age:	Phone:
School:	Examiner(s):
Teacher(s):	Date of examination(s):

Introduction

A brief narrative containing:

Referral Information. Who referred the student? With whom did the screening committee work? What was the observed or stated problem? Where should efforts need to be concentrated? Brief report of screening committee meeting if desired.

Background Information. Age. Sex. Family (parents and siblings). Brief physical description. School history—attendance patterns, grade in school, repeated grades. Any other history that might seem pertinent.

Present Levels of Educational Performance. Results of tests and observational data used to document performance levels. Any other recent test results available (within the past 2 years). Has the student ever been diagnosed as handicapped; when and by whom? Results of vision and hearing screening.

Name of Test, Date Given:	Name of Test, Date Given:
Results:	Results:
Results:	Results:
Name of Test, Date Given:	Name of Test, Date Given:
Results:	Results:
Results:	Results:
Observational Data:	Observational Data:

General Direction for Child's Education. A brief summary of conclusions drawn from above data and previous investigations that state generally the special, regular, and related services needed. In addition, broad goal areas and services should be delineated.

When determining which educational performance areas are appropriate for an individual student, there are several factors to consider including: (1) referral and screening data, (2) evaluation for diagnosis data, (3) age of the student, (4) the severity of the disability, (5) any unique restrictions placed on a student, (6) present environment, (7) next least-restrictive environment, and (8) parent and student expectations. Once pertinent areas have been determined for the individual student, educational planners can develop a statement of present levels of performance in each area.

In order to document present levels of performance in areas of concern, the IEP team might need to conduct further evaluations, over and above those conducted for special education placement. In these instances, educators must locate and administer standardized tests designed to measure educational performance. When none are available, educators must develop a data recording system and collect the present levels of functioning through reliable and valid observations.

The purposes accomplished by documenting present levels of performance are twofold. First, educators will have a general idea of where, in any given educational area, to begin planning and programming. Second, educators will have a reference point by which to compare future evaluations. This will serve as an accountability measure in assuring the success of a given program and/or signaling the need for change in an unsuccessful program.

Each of the preparatory steps discussed in this section and the actual statement of present levels of performance simplify subsequent educational programming. The reader can more clearly see just how this information serves to simplify the process when attempting to develop annual goals, the second mandated component of the IEP.

References

Bailey, L. J., and Stadt, R. W. *Career education: New approaches to human development.* Bloomington, Ill.: McKnight Publishing Company, 1973.

Barraga, N. *Visual efficiency scale.*

————, *Visual handicaps and learning: A developmental approach.* Belmont, Calif.: Wadsworth, 1976.

Barsch, R. H. A movigenic curriculum. Bulletin No. 25, Bureau of Handicapped Children. Madison, Wisc.: State Department of Public Instruction, 1965.

Bartel, N. R. Problems in mathematics achievement. In D. D. Hammill and N. R. Bartel, *Teaching children with learning and behavior problems.* (2nd ed.) Boston: Allyn and Bacon, 1978.

————, and Bryen, D. N. Problems in language development. In D. D. Hammill and N. R. Bartel, *Teaching children with learning and behavior problems.* (2nd ed.) Boston: Allyn and Bacon, 1978.

Beatty, L.; Madden, R.; and Gardner, E. *Stanford diagnostic arithmetic test.* New York: Harcourt Brace Jovanovich, 1966.

Becker, R. L. *Reading free vocational interest inventory.* Washington, D.C.: American Association on Mental Deficiency, 1975.

Bennett, H.; Seashore, G.; and Wesman, A. *Differential aptitude tests.* New York: Psychological Corporation, 1969.

Brolin, D. E. *Vocational preparation of retarded citizens.* Columbus: Charles E. Merrill, 1976.

Brown, L. L. Teacher strategies for managing classroom behaviors. In D. D. Hammill and N. R. Bartel, *Teaching children with learning and behavior problems.* (2nd ed.) Boston: Allyn and Bacon, 1978.

Brown, L. L., and Hammill, D. D. *Behavior Rating Profile.* Austin, Tex.: Pro-Ed. 1978.

Brueckner, L. J., and Bond, G. L. *The diagnosis and treatment of learning difficulties.* Englewood Cliffs, N.J.: Prentice-Hall, 1955.

Bruininks, R. G. *Bruininks-Oseretzky test of motor proficiency.* Circle Pines, Minn.: American Guidance Service, 1977.

Cain, Levine, and Elzey. *Cain-Levine social competency scale,* 1963.

Caldwell, B. M. *Cooperative preschool inventory.* Circle Pines, Minn.: American Guidance Service, 1970.

Campbell, D. P. *Strong-Campbell interest inventory.* Stanford, Calif.: University of Stanford Press, 1974.

Chall, J. *Learning to read: The great debate.* New York: McGraw-Hill. 1967.

Clark, K., and Campbell, D. *Minnesota vocational interest inventory.* New York: Psychological Corporation, 1966.

Cohen, C. R., and Abrams, R. M. *Spellmaster.* Exeter, N.H.: Learnco, 1974.

Connolly, A.; Nachtman, W.; and Pritchett, E. *Key math diagnostic arithmetic test.* Circle Pines, Minn.: American Guidance Service, 1970.

Crabtree, M. *The Houston test for language development.* Houston: Houston Test Company, 1963.

Cratty, B. J. *Perceptual and motor development in infants and children.* New York: Macmillan, 1970.

Crites, J. *Career maturity inventory.* Monterey, Calif.: CTB/McGraw-Hill, 1973.

Doll, E. *Preschool attainment record.* Circle Pines, Minn.: American Guidance Service, 1967.

———, *Vineland social maturity scale.* Minneapolis: Educational Test Bureau, 1953.

Dunn, L., and Markwardt, F. *Peabody individual achievement test.* Circle Pines, Minn.: American Guidance Service, 1970.

Durrell, D. *Durrell analysis of reading difficulty.* New York: Harcourt Brace Jovanovich, 1955.

Flanagan, J. *Flanagan aptitude classification tests.* Chicago: Science Research Associates, 1960.

Fleishman, E. A. *The structure and measurement of physical fitness.* Englewood Cliffs, N.J.: Prentice-Hall, 1964.

Frankenburg, W. K., and Dodds, J. B. *Denver developmental screening test.* Denver: LADOCA Project and Publishing Company, 1970.

Frostig, M. *Movement education: Theory and practice.* Chicago: Follett Educational Corporation, 1970.

Gates, A., and McKillop, A. *Gates-McKillop reading diagnostic tests.* New York: Bureau of Publications, Teachers College Press, Columbia University, 1962.

Gray, R. *Assessment of the handicapped learner: A review.* Unpublished manuscript. Austin: The University of Texas at Austin, 1978.

Gropper, G. L.; Kress, G. C.; Hughes, R.; and Pekich, J. Training teachers to recognize and manage social and emotional problems in the classroom. In H. Dupont (ed.), *Educating emotionally disturbed children.* (2nd ed.) New York: Holt, Rinehart and Winston, 1975.

Guszak, F. J. *Diagnostic reading instruction in the elementary school.* New York: Harper & Row, 1972.

Hainsworth, P. K., and Sigueland, M. L. *Early identification of children with learning disabilities: The Meeting Street School screening test.* Providence, R.I.: Crippled Children and Adults of Rhode Island, 1969.

Hammill, D. D., and Larsen, S. C. *The test of written language.* Austin, Tex.: Pro-Ed, 1978.

—— and Poplin, M. S. Problems in writing. In D. D. Hammill and N. R. Bartel, *Teaching children with learning and behavior problems.* (2nd ed.) Boston: Allyn and Bacon, 1978.

Harmin, M., and Simon, S. B. Values. In H. Kirschenbaum and S. B. Simon (eds.), *Readings in values clarification.* Minneapolis: Winston Press, 1973.

Hewett, F. *The emotionally disturbed child in the classroom.* Boston: Allyn and Bacon, 1968.

Humphrey, J.; McEntire, B.; and Saski, J. *Administrative strategies for secondary special education programs.* Austin, Tex.: Texas Education Agency, 1978.

Jastak, J., and Jastak, S. *Wide range achievement test.* Wilmington, Del.: Guidance Associates, 1965.

Keller, L. J. Career development—An integrated curriculum approach, K–12. In K. Goldhammer and R. Taylor (eds.), *Career education: Perspective and promise.* Columbus: Charles E. Merrill, 1972.

Kirschenbaum, H. Beyond values clarification. In H. Kirschenbaum and S. B. Simon (eds.), *Readings in values clarification.* Minneapolis: Winston Press, 1973.

Knapp, C. E. Teaching environmental education with a focus on values.

In H. Kirschenbaum and S. B. Simon (eds.), *Readings in values clarification.* Minneapolis: Winston Press, 1973.

Kolestoe, Oliver. *Teaching educable mentally retarded children.* New York: Holt, Rinehart and Winston, 1976.

Kuder, K. *Kuder occupational interest survey.* Chicago: Science Research Associates, 1966.

Larsen, S. C., and Hammill, D. D. *Test of written spelling.* Austin, Tex.: Pro-Ed, 1976.

Lee, L. *Developmental sentence analysis.* Evanston, Ill.: Northwestern University Press, 1974.

Madison, B. D. A kinesthetic technique for handwriting development. In J. L. Arena (ed.), *Building handwriting skills in dyslexic children.* San Rafael, Calif.: Academic Therapy, 1970.

Madsen, C. H.; Becker, W. C.; and Thomas, D. R. Rules, praise and ignoring: Elements of elementary classroom control. In H. Dupont (ed.), *Educating emotionally disturbed children.* New York: Holt, Rinehart and Winston, 1975.

Mecham, M.; Jex, J.; and Jones, J. *Utah test of language development.* Salt Lake City: Communication Research Associates, 1967.

Meyen, E. *Developing units of instruction.* Dubuque, Iowa: William C. Brown, 1972.

Myklebust, H. R. *Development and disorders of written language.* New York: Grune & Stratton, 1965.

———— *The pupil rating scale.* New York: Grune & Stratton, 1971.

Newcomer, P., and Hammill, D. D. *Test of oral language development.* Austin, Tex.: Pro-Ed, 1977.

Pate, J. E., and Webb, W. W. *First grade screening test.* Circle Pines, Minn.: American Guidance Service, 1969.

Roach, E., and Kephart, W. *The Purdue perceptual motor survey.* Columbus: Charles E. Merrill, 1966.

Robinson, H. M.; Artley, A. S.; Aaron, I. E.; Monroe, M.; Huck, C. S.; and Weintraub, S. *Reading comprehension skills in Scott Foresman Basic Readers.* Chicago: Scott Foresman and Company, 1965.

Roe, A. *The psychology of occupations.* New York: John Wiley and Sons, 1956.

Salvia, J., and Ysseldyke, J. *Assessment in special and remedial education.* Boston: Houghton Mifflin, 1978.

Saski, J. *Competencies for teachers of the handicapped adolescent.* Unpublished manuscript. Austin, Tex.: The University of Texas at Austin, 1977.

Sloan, *The Lincoln-Oseretzky motor development scale,* 1954.

Stark, E. S. *Special education: A curriculum guide.* Springfield, Ill.: Charles C. Thomas, 1969.

Super, D. The work values inventory. In D. E. Zytowski (ed.), *Contemporary approaches to interest management.* Minneapolis: University of Minneapolis Press, 1973.

U.S. Department of Labor. *General aptitude test battery.* Washington, D.C.: U.S. Government Printing Office, 1970.

—— *Nonreading aptitude test battery.* Washington, D.C.: U.S. Government Printing Office, 1970.

Wallace, G., and Kauffman, J. *Teaching children with learning problems.* Columbus: Charles E. Merrill, 1973.

—— and Larsen, S. C. *Educational assessment of learning problems: Testing for Teaching.* Boston: Allyn and Bacon, 1978.

Wiederholt, J. L., Brown, V., and Hammill, D. D. *Test of reading comprehension.* Austin, Tex.: Pro-Ed, 1978.

Wolfensberger, W. *Normalization.* Toronto: National Institute on Mental Retardation, 1972.

Woodcock, R. *Woodcock reading mastery test.* Circle Pines, Minn.: American Guidance Service, 1974.

5

Annual Goals
and General Objectives

Perhaps more than any other statement within the actual IEP document, establishing annual goals and general objectives determines the success of a handicapped child's education. The degree to which educators (1) select appropriate and comprehensive goals, and (2) identify all the skills necessary to achieve those annual goals (general objectives) directly influences the effectiveness of the individualized education program. Utilizing these concepts, annual goal and general objectives require educators to use their own conceptualization regarding the educational performance areas as specified in Chapter 4. Together these components lend specific direction to the child's special education instruction. In addition, goals and general objectives lead directly to establishing short-term instructional objectives that define instruction even more specifically (see Chapter 6). Although "annual goals including short-term instructional objectives" are actually mandated in the law, educators find it necessary to define general objectives prior to establishing short-term instructional objectives. Because of the impact on instruction provided by these two components, it is essential that their development be conducted primarily by instructional personnel. This chapter presents: (1) definitions of the concepts of annual goals and general objectives, (2) suggested outlines of a process for their comprehensive development, and (3) specific selection procedures in determining goals and objectives for individual handicapped children and youth.

ANNUAL GOALS

The second mandated component of any individualized education program is determining annual goals. Annual goals constitute those goals appropriate for the child's immediate education and projected to be accomplished within the present school year. These goals do represent projections and are not to be considered a legally binding contract. They are also only representative of those educational goals to be attempted through the provision of special education and related services. Establishing annual goals serves to coordinate and direct the subsequent programming efforts such as objectives and services and provides a projection from which annual evaluations can be devised. Establishing annual goals determines to a great extent exactly what short-term instructional objectives and services to program. As discussed in a subsequent section of this chapter, each annual goal has its own series of general objectives which constitutes the basis for defining short-term instructional objectives, the third mandated component of the IEP. In addition, these goals or projections of progress provide some very general criteria upon which to evaluate the success or failure of a given IEP. While goals, by definition, do not have to be measurable directly, annual goals are such that standardized testing or observation such as that conducted to document present levels of performance would, for the most part, provide excellent measures of yearly progress. The type of standardized tests generally used to document performance levels are appropriate to re-administer once or twice per school year. We will now examine (1) the general content of annual goals, (2) a suggested procedure for selecting goals for individual students, and (3) annual goals for the various areas of concern.

The actual content of annual goals depends entirely upon the team or district's conceptualization of the areas of education. This should have been determined previously as set forth in Chapter 4. In many instances, lists of annual goals are already a part of the special education curriculum guidelines. In effect, these goals are statements regarding projected or desired improvements within the various constructs defined as constituting a given special education area. For example, in the area of self-help/basic living skills, a construct that would be an appropriate annual goal might be establishing self-feeding or toileting skills. In academic areas one might project a student to increase word recognition skills by one year. The individual sections that follow the discussion of factors involved in goal selection demonstrate examples of the way in which the authors have conceptualized the various areas into annual goals. Once again, readers are encouraged to develop their own concepts in order to develop possible annual goals in each area.

Selecting Appropriate Annual Goals

The actual determination of which annual goals are appropriate for an individual child is derived from several sources. First, the selection and evaluation of appropriate performance areas is the major source from which to draw annual goals. Remember, the selection procedure for educational performance areas involves the analysis of eight factors—age, expectations, evaluation, data, referral, and so on. Second, annual goals are determined while examining any newly acquired evaluation information during the documentation of present levels of performance. A third factor in determining which annual goals to select for any given year depends to some extent on the desires and expertise of each member of the IEP team. A collective list of each factor that determines the particular annual goals selected for an individual student is given below:

1. Goal was indicated appropriate during referral and screening.
2. Goal is appropriate in light of evaluation for placement data.
3. Goal is appropriate in light of present levels of performance.
4. Goal is age appropriate.
5. Goal is appropriate to the severity of the handicapping condition.
6. Goal is not in conflict with additional student restrictions that are either separate from or a by-product of the condition itself.
7. Goal is appropriate within present environmental contexts.
8. Goal will assist in performance in the next least-restrictive environment
9. Goal is in concert with parent expectations.
10. Goal is in concert with student expectations.
11. Goal is viewed as appropriate by other IEP team members.

Each factor is important for the IEP team to consider when determining which annual goals from the accumulated goals in each area are most appropriate for an individual student at the present time.

By the very nature of handicapping conditions, one generally finds an extraordinary number of desired goals. In addition, for most special education students, goals are defined in two or more of the four educational areas. All the goals within each area may be legitimate; however, generally it is necessary to narrow the desired goals so they may be accommodated appropriately within any given school year. Therefore, in addition to delineating possible goals in each area, we suggest a method for selecting the most appropriate goals. This procedure uses the 11 above factors in an attempt to organize goals from most to least urgent for any given year. The format presented in Table 5–1 utilizes a checklist of the 11 factors involved in goal selection. Once the relevant factors for each appropriate goal have been checked, the IEP team can determine the degree of urgency or appropriateness of each goal. Goal statements receiving the most checks in the first 10 columns and those receiving the largest number of priority rankings in column 11 are those of greatest concern and probably the most important for the upcoming year. An example of the way the goals checklist may be presented and used is illustrated in Table 5–1.

The portion of a goals checklist shown here represents the area of self-help/basic living skills for Rich. To the far left is denoted a performance area of self-help skills called "Personal Skills." Constructs or goals indicated and listed under this area include feeding, toileting, and dressing. The right-hand columns refer specifically to the 11 factors delineated earlier as necessary to select annual goals. Therefore, a check in column 1 next to feeding skills means that the skills involved in feeding were indicated as a possible problem (goal) during referral and screening. We can see that dressing skills were not mentioned during this period. These numbered columns correspond to the delineation of factors on page 226. Column 11 is somewhat different. Each column within column 11 is assigned to a member of the IEP team. In this particular case there were four members of the team. Members were asked to rank what they considered the top ten annual goals for Rich (this also included goals in career/vocational, academics, and sociobehavioral skills). From this one can see that the skills of feeding and toileting were ranked consistently as a priority area among all four members, as well as being indicated appropriate throughout factors 1 to 10. Although receiving lower total appropriateness checks, dressing still was ranked among the top five skill areas needed. Although not shown here, no goals were ranked on the career/vocational chart and only few checked. Oral language was the only aspect of academic performance

TABLE 5–1 Format for Analyzing Factors in Goal Selection

Area: Self Help/Basic Living	Name: Rich									Date:		
Performance Area	Construct/Goal	Factors in Goal Selection											
		1	2	3	4	5	6	7	8	9	10	11
Personal Skills	Feeding Skills	√	√	√	√	√	√	√	√	√	√	1 2 1 2
	Toileting Skills	√	√	√	√	√	√	√	√	√	√	2 1 2 1
	Dressing Skills	√	√	√	√	√	√					4 3 5 4

areas receiving numerous checks and rankings. Peer relations was the goal selected as most appropriate for Rich in the area of sociobehavioral education. With this selection procedure in mind we can now specify possible performance areas and annual goals for self-help/basic living, academic, sociobehavioral, and career/vocational.

Developing Comprehensive Annual Goals

It is essential that each local or intermediate education agency initiate developing a comprehensive list of annual goals for the areas of special education. This provides the base from which to select specific goals for individual children. In order to identify possible goals, educators should define for themselves the performance areas and constructs involved in each of the four areas of special education. The following section exemplifies the manner in which the constructs of particular educational performance areas can be used to generate comprehensive annual goals in the areas of self-help/basic living, academics, sociobehavioral, and career/vocational education.

Self-help and basic living goals. Goals or constructs involved in self-help and basic living education may be classified under three major performance areas: personal skills, motor and mobility, and independent living skills. Personal skills are those directly related to the welfare of the child's own body. Motor and mobility deal with the movement of one's body and the ability to move from place to place within one's environment. The ability to maintain a household encompasses the area of independent living. Appropriate annual goals involved in the three performance areas of self-help and basic living education are listed in Table 5–2. These goals are listed in the same format as given earlier so that decisions can be made regarding the appropriateness of each goal with respect to individual children.

When actually stating the self-help/basic living goals selected for a child's education program document, educators generally include: (1) the construct and (2) a phrase regarding projected performance increase. Some examples of annual goal statements would then be:

- Jim will *increase* his understanding of family responsibility.
- Sally will *improve* her posture.
- Harold will *improve* grooming habits.
- Rich will *be toilet trained* by May.

This kind of statement personalizes the constructs of the various educational performance areas and makes them appear more "goal-like" rather

227

TABLE 5-2 Performance Areas and Annual Goals—Self-Help/Basic Living Education

Area _Self Help/Basic Living_ Name_____ Date_____											
Performance Area	Construct/Goal	Factors in Goal Selection									
		1	2	3	4	5	6	7	8	9 10	11
Personal	Feeding										
	Dressing										
	Health & Hygiene										
	Grooming										
Motor & Mobility	Posture										
	Gross Motor Movement										
	Fine Motor Movement										
	Spatial Orientation										
	Special Motor Skills										
Independent Living	Meal Preparation										
	Clothing										
	Transportation										
	Money Management										
	Leisure Time										
	Housekeeping										
	Civic Activities										
	Home Furnishings										
	Family Responsibilities										
	Community Resources and Services										
	Personal Communication										

than merely the recording of constructs in a checklist format; however, the checklist alone may be desired.

Academic education goals. Prior to defining the major performance areas involved in academic education, one must first divide this special education area into the four separate areas of language, reading, written expression, and math. This division is necessary because of the variance between the sets of constructs contained in each academic content area. Therefore, both performance areas and goals are defined for each of these areas. Oral language entails performance areas of receptive and expressive language while reading involves both word recognition and comprehension. Written expression includes sets of goals for spelling, penmanship, and conceptual writing. Goals or constructs of mathematics are defined under the performance areas of operations, measurements, and concepts. Appropriate annual goals for each performance area within the four content areas of academic education are delineated in Tables 5-3, 5-4, 5-5, and 5-6. Once again the format is such that specific goals may be easily identified for individual children's programs.

TABLE 5–3   Performance Areas and Annual Goals: Academics–Oral Language

Area __Academic–Language__ Name_____ Date_____												
		Factors in Goal Selection										
Performance Area	Construct/Goal	1	2	3	4	5	6	7	8	9	10	11
Reception	Phonology											
	Morphology											
	Syntax											
	Semantics–Command											
	Semantics–Question											
	Semantics–Statement											
Expression	Phonology											
	Morphology											
	Syntax											
	Semantics–Command											
	Semantics–Question											
	Semantics–Statement											

TABLE 5–4   Performance Areas and Annual Goals: Academics–Reading

Area __Academics–Reading__ Name_____ Date_____												
		Factors in Goal Selection										
Performance Area	Construct/Goal	1	2	3	4	5	6	7	8	9	10	11
Reading Recognition	Sound–Symbol Correspondence											
	Consonants											
	Short Vowels											
	Consonant Blends and Diagraphs											
	Long Vowels											
	Vowel diagraph											
	Irregular Consonant											
	Irregular Vowel											
	Compound Words											
	Sight Words											
	Structural Analysis											
Reading Comprehension	Vocabulary											
	Fact											
	Main Idea											
	Conclusion											
	Inference											
	Judgement											
	Literary Interpretation											
	Reference											

TABLE 5–5   Performance Areas and Annual Goals: Academics—Written Expression

Area___Academic—Writing___ Name_____ Date_____

Performance Area	Construct/Goal	Factors in Goal Selection										
		1	2	3	4	5	6	7	8	9	10	11
Spelling	Phoneme/Grapheme Correspondence											
	Consonant Blend and Diagraphs											
	Short Vowels											
	Long Vowels											
	Irregular Consonants											
	Irregular Vowels											
	Compound Words											
	Structural Analysis											
Penmanship	Process											
	Product											
Conceptual Writing	Capitalization											
	Punctuation											
	Vocabulary											
	Word Usage											
	Grammar											
	Sentence											
	Paragraph											
	Thesis											

TABLE 5–6   Performance Areas and Annual Goals: Academics—Mathematics

Area___Academics—Math___ Name_____ Date_____

Performance Area	Construct/Goal	Factors in Goal Selection										
		1	2	3	4	5	6	7	8	9	10	11
Operations	Numeration											
	Addition											
	Subtraction											
	Multiplication											
	Division											
Measurements	Time											
	Money											
	Measures											
Concepts	Sets											
	Correspondence											
	Conservation/ Relationships											
	Geometry											
	Fractions											
	Decimals											
	Written Problems											
	Reasoning											

Because of the relatively well-defined nature of the constructs of the various academic performance areas, goal statements occasionally include not only a statement of desired increase and the construct, but the projected grade level of attainment. Some examples of typical goal statements for the areas of academics include:

- Becky will increase reading vocabulary to the second-grade level.
- Jim will increase skills in fractions to the third-grade level.
- Greg will utilize syntax up to three-year level.
- Diane will write sentences.
- Beth will understand short vowels in reading and spelling.

Academic goals are one of the easier areas to select and define for individual handicapped students because of the accessibility of curricula and measurements.

Sociobehavioral goals. The constructs or goals of sociobehavioral education are defined most appropriately as social skills desirable to increase and/or behaviors to decrease. Essentially there are three areas in which one might define behaviors desirable to increase: self-awareness, social skills, and task-related behaviors. Self-awareness goals involve building the child's image of him/herself while socialization includes the child's relationships to others. Task-related behaviors define the child's behaviors with regard to his/her performance at school or job. An additional performance area of importance to educators in defining sociobehavioral education is identifying undesirable behaviors. This consists of a list of goals regarding behaviors to be extinguished.

Often it is possible to match two goals so that the behavior to increase automatically results in a decrease of an undesirable behavior. For example, the goal of decreasing distractibility is essentially the same as the goal of increasing attention. However, with such behaviors as destroying property there may be numerous behavior options to choose from. Because of this, both the performance areas of desirable and undesirable behaviors are defined. This allows educators the flexibility to match goals to individual students by defining both sets from which to choose. By necessity goal statements then would indicate (1) direction of progression desired, that is, decrease versus increase and (2) the specific construct. When goals are designed to offset each other they should be listed together as "increasing while decreasing." Therefore, sample goal statements for children needing sociobehavioral education might be:

- Connie will increase independent behaviors and decrease dependency.

TABLE 5–7   Performance Areas and Annual Goals—Sociobehavioral Education

Area Social/Behavioral	Name	Date										
Performance Area	Construct/Goal	Factors in Goal Selection										
		1	2	3	4	5	6	7	8	9	10	11
Self-Awareness	Physical											
	Values											
	Limitations											
	Strengths											
Socialization	Courtesies											
	Relations—Public											
	Relations—Peers											
	Relations—Superiors											
Task-Related	Attention											
	Respect											
	Flexibility											
	Completion											
	Independence											
Undesirable Behaviors	Destruction Person											
	Destruction Property											
	Disruption											
	Disassociation											
	Disobedience											
	Distraction											
	Dependency											

- Linda will decrease disruptions.
- Rich will improve relations with peers while decreasing disassociative behaviors.
- Sue will increase attention to task behaviors.

Though broad, these statements provide direction for identifying more specific objectives that define precise, observable behaviors to increase or decrease.

Career/vocational goals. The area of career/vocational education is often defined to include goals previously delineated under self-help/basic living, academic, and sociobehavioral. Rather than appear repetitive, for purposes of this discussion goals for career/vocational education exclude topics covered previously. Obviously, these goals may easily be selected regardless of the area under which they have been grouped. For example, self-awareness, leisure time, and numerical skills may be necessary career/vocational goals also and should not be overlooked. Once excluding these redundancies one finds the area of career/vocational education divided into three major performance areas: (1) occupational exploration, (2) occupational application, and (3) occupational preparation, maintenance, and change. Table 5-8 specifies the constructs under each of these three performance areas. Occupational exploration involves goals related to the awareness of various jobs, their characteristics, prerequisite skills, and so on. Application includes those skills necessary to locate, apply, and obtain a job that is appropriate to a particular individual. The ability to acquire additional job-specific skills, maintain a particular job, and change occupations when necessary is delineated under the construct of occupational preparation, maintenance, and change.

Career/vocational goals are highly individual, particularly under the construct of preparation and maintenance, because of the widely variant abilities and interests of individual handicapped students. Thus, they are limited to specific occupational interests and needs. Career-exploration goals are more similar among students since the overall goal is to provide the child with an awareness of *all* occupational possibilities. The goal of application is also similar in that form requirements, interviews,

TABLE 5–8   Performance Areas and Annual Goals—Career/Vocational Education

Area____Career/Vocational____ Name_____ Date_____

Performance Area	Construct/Goal	Factors in Goal Selection										
		1	2	3	4	5	6	7	8	9	10	11
Occupational Exploration	Occupational Clusters											
	Job Characteristics											
	Occupational Opportunities											
	Prerequisite Working Skills											
Occupational Application	Possibilities											
	Search											
	Application											
	Interview											
Occupational Preparation Maintenance and Change	Physical—Manual Skills											
	Expression											
	Administration Skills											
	Talents											
	Personal Skills											
	Computation											

and so on, vary only slightly in the different occupations. Sample career/ vocational skills are given below:

- Jim will develop interview skills.
- Carol will understand various occupational clusters.
- Sue will increase computational skills.
- Anne will improve job application skills.

Summary. The preceding delineation of performance areas and goals has provided but one example of how educators define for themselves the constructs of the special education areas of self-help/basic living, career/vocational, academic, and sociobehavioral. When developed, these constructs must be comprehensive enough to encompass all the skills in each of the various areas. However, the names and divisions of the constructs or goals defined may vary from person to person and between education systems. Once all the possible annual goals are defined, educators must begin to identify each of the necessary skills. This is done in the form of general objectives and facilitates selecting and constructing short-term instructional objectives.

GENERAL OBJECTIVES

Following defining the various performance areas of special education and selecting annual goals in each of these areas, the general objectives that underlie each goal should be defined. While not mandated by law, this process provides an *essential* intermediate step between annual goals and short-term instructional objectives. Most of the confusion that currently surrounds the concept of short-term instructional objectives can be avoided by first establishing general objectives. General objectives can be defined as those skills that, once accomplished, result in attainment of a goal. Consequently, for each goal specified in an individual education program there should be a series of general objectives from which to choose. Because the skills leading to an annual goal are essentially the same regardless of how they are to be taught, it is recommended that, as with annual goals, each education agency define the gamut of general objectives for each goal or construct outlined during the previous section. The first portion of this section discusses the actual formation of general objectives. Once developed, educators can use the comprehensive listing of skills as reference for the individual selection of pertinent objectives much like the completed list of annual goals. These two components, goals and objectives, provide a basic structure

234

for developing special education curricula and simplifies developing the IEP.

In order to organize defined goals and objectives, the second part of this section presents the concept of *curricular maps*. Curricular maps are developed directly from the goals and objectives delineated and provide educators with structure for special education curriculum guides, important reference points for individual programs, and a guide for assessing student needs and progress. Curricular maps should be developed for each performance area defined under the four areas of special education (self-help/basic living, career/vocational, academic, and sociobehavioral). Specific examples of possible maps for each area are provided in a third section of the chapter.

The four basic topics covered in this chapter include: (1) developing general objectives, (2) construction and purposes of curricular maps, (3) specific examples of maps and objectives in each area of special education, (4) a procedure for assessing and selecting general objectives for individual children, and (5) a special discussion on the appropriate application of the concepts of general objectives and curricular maps. The single most important link in developing appropriate educational programs for handicapped students lies within careful and comprehensive development of general objectives and subsequent curricular maps. All other portions of any IEP, no matter how well formulated, are instructionally useless if a continuum of instructional objectives is not developed and followed. General objectives and curricular maps promise to fulfill this purpose; that is, provide *content* to annual goals and *meaning* to short-term instructional objectives.

Developing General Objectives

General objectives consist of the skills involved in attaining a given goal. They provide an intermediate step between annual goals and short-term instructional objectives in an individual child's written educational program. Although not a mandated component, educators find it helpful to include these in the child's program document. In addition, general objectives (1) simplify developing short-term instructional objectives, a mandated component of the IEP, (2) serve to clarify and define goal statements, (3) provide a continuum of special education curricula, and (4) assist in assessing student performance and progress. To accomplish these purposes one must thoroughly understand the manner in which general objectives are developed. In order to generate appropriate objectives for each goal, one must understand the characteristics of general objectives that distinguish them from broader goals and short-term instructional objectives and procedures for generating, refining, and sequencing objectives. Each of these is discussed below.

Characteristics of general objectives. There are several unique characteristics of general objectives that serve to distinguish them from annual goals and short-term instructional objectives. The eight points to keep in mind while developing general objectives include:

1. There is a set of general objectives for each educational construct or goal outlined under the four general areas of special education.
2. General objectives within each set *can be sequenced* either (a) developmentally, or (b) from simplest to most complex, or (c) from least to most important.
3. General objectives *do not specify a particular behavior* a child is required to perform.
4. General objectives *do not specify criteria* for success.
5. General objectives generally can be written in *three or four words* and generally do not constitute a complete statement.
6. General objectives *do not state desires for improvement* increase, understanding, improvement . . . , as do annual goals.
7. General objectives *are not time specific*, that is, mastering one general objective may involve hours or years.
8. When selecting general objectives for individual students, it is *generally not appropriate to define all the general objectives involved in one goal* for one year.

We will next examine several sets of general objectives in light of the eight above factors. For example, consider the special education area of academics and the performance area of math. One construct or goal involved in mathematics is *addition*. A few of the general objectives in addition are listed below:

Special Education Area: *Academics*
  Performance Area: *Math*
    Construct or Goal: *Increase ability in addition*
      General Objectives:
        1. Two whole numbers, sums less than 10.
        2. Two whole numbers, factors less than 10.
        3. Two two-digit whole numbers without carrying.
        4. Three one-digit whole numbers that sum less than 10.
        5. Three two-digit numbers without carrying.

Examining these few general objectives in light of the eight factors, it can be determined that:

1. There is an extensive set of general objectives that can be defined for the goal of addition.
2. These can be sequenced from simple to difficult. Obviously, adding two one-digit numbers with a sum of less than 10 is much easier than adding two two-digit numerals.
3. There is no behavior stated in these objectives; therefore, one cannot determine how the child is required to respond, for example, to write the answers to written problems, respond orally to flash cards, or oral presentation.
4. There is nothing to indicate how often the child must get the answer correct before she/he is considered to have mastered each skill.
5. There are only a few descriptive words specifying the skill involved in each general objective of addition.
6. A desire to increase, understand, and so on, within the general objective is not necessarily stated; however, in goals a desire to increase performance is stated.
7. No time lines are set for each objective. Objective number 3 may require a full year, half year, or day to accomplish.
8. Consider that one of the last objectives is adding "mixed fractions with unlike denominators." One would certainly not expect a child for whom addition was a goal to go from the first objective to the last in one year.

While mathematics is a relatively simple area to define and understand as it relates to general objectives, performance areas involving independent living skills present a more complex proposition. The problems associated with this area are due largely to its uniqueness within the traditional concept of education rather than the actual complexity of the skills involved. However, the same eight characteristics apply to general objectives within every construct of special education. For example, consider the following goal and objectives for the area of self-help/basic living.

Special Education Area: *Self-Help and Basic Living*
   Performance Area: *Independent Living*
      Construct or Goal: *Meal Preparation*
         General Objectives:

1. Food categories	3. Nutritional considerations
2. Recipes and directions	4. Cost considerations

237

5. Amount considerations
6. Shopping
7. Storing
8. Preparing
9. Cooking
10. Timing
11. Serving
12. Left-overs
13. Clean-up
14. Meal-planning nutrition, amount, cost
15. Meal shopping
16. Meal preparation
17. Meal cooking
18. Meal timing
19. Meal serving
20. Left-overs
21. Clean-up
22. Weekly planning

In light of the eight basic characteristics we find that this listing of general objectives also satisfies the criteria for constructing objectives. Analyzing this one finds:

1. There is an extensive set of objectives or skills involved in the goal or ability to prepare meals.
2. These objectives begin with identifying food items and move into objectives involved in preparing one item, preparing a meal, and preparing and planning several meals.
3. No activity such as *cutting* vegetables or *placing* in pots is stated.
4. There are no criteria (such as number of times) stated for success of objectives such as serving and shopping.
5. Objectives here are written in two-word descriptions of skills.
6. There is no statement of increased or desired performance.
7. No time lines are given for accomplishing each objective.
8. All 22 objectives may or may not be appropriate for one year.

Annual goals, in each of the examples discussed here, represent merely a broad statement of an educational construct within a given performance area where educators hope to increase a given child's performance. The examples of goals used here were to increase math performance in addition and to increase the student's ability to prepare meals. By contrast, short-term instructional objectives would not be so broad as to use the verb "increase," rather they might say "the child will record answers to 25 vertical addition problems with 90 percent accuracy, three days in succession," or, "the child will select, wash, peel, cut, and place in a bowl three vegetables that go into a tossed salad." Therefore, general objectives provide educators with a structure from which to derive short-term instructional objectives from annual goals. Once educators understand the primary characteristics of general objectives, it is necessary to establish a process for generating such objectives within each annual goal.

Generating general objectives. The process of generating general objectives for defined annual goals is much like the process described in Chapter 4 for defining educational performance areas and annual goals. Essentially that process was accomplished through careful research of curricula that had been established previously. Once the necessary research has been conducted, the IEP team or group of educators can now begin to *brainstorm* all the skills that might possibly be involved in any given annual goal. Once brainstorming has been accomplished, educators must select a set of general objectives by deleting those repetitions and irrelevant skills mentioned during brainstorming, adding any additional ones needed, and sequencing the objectives in an orderly fashion. Before discussing actual selection and sequencing, it is necessary to examine a method for brainstorming.

Brainstorming objectives. Brainstorming is a group activity where ideas of individual members (in this instance regarding skills that constitute a goal(*s*)) are orally expressed and recorded for later use. The session is conducted under special conditions established to avoid any discussion, criticism, or analysis (Harris and Bessent, 1969). The primary purpose of conducting brainstorming sessions with educators is to generate an extensive data base of objectives needed to accomplish a specific goal. It is important to assimilate as much professional expertise regarding a specific educational area as is possible. Therefore, when forming a brainstorm team, the more professional interests represented, the more comprehensive will be the obtained results. Appropriate expertise may be found primarily with regular educators of various grade levels and special educators trained in various areas of special education; others include: parents, social workers, psychologists, remedial teachers, curriculum supervisors, and related service personnel, to mention but a few. The success of brainstorming in developing objectives is directly related to the number of unrestricted contributions by the members of the team.

Harris and Bessent (1969) define six purposes of brainstorming. Each of these is discussed and related to establishing general objectives:

1. To inform all participants of ideas held by others regarding what skills constitute a particular goal.
2. To stimulate the development of numerous general objectives.
3. To provide an inventory of the ideas or skills for later use, i.e., selection, sequencing and organizing objectives in curricula, and IEPs.

4. To suggest a variety of alternative approaches to the content of general objectives.
5. To influence the opinions and attitudes of other members of the group regarding the skill constitution of a goal.
6. To cultivate positive attitudes towards various general objectives and alternative approaches to a given goal. (p. 36)

In order to accomplish these purposes it is necessary to follow certain procedures carefully. First, the goal to be brainstormed is presented to the group by a leader and the group is instructed to think of all the skills in accomplishing the goal. Generally a short period (two or three minutes) is provided for the group to brainstorm silently. A time period should be established for the entire session; however, when ideas are no longer being expressed, the session should be terminated. Expressing ideas or skills freely, quickly, and openly is encouraged. Each skill or idea must be recorded in writing, preferably where all members can view it (chalkboards are excellent—except they also should be recorded permanently). The leader generally repeats the skill or objective as he/ she records it providing feedback and clarification. Silence is permitted between skill generation periods and should not indicate termination of the activity. Often silence is quite productive as well as essential to further elaboration of skills. Probably the most important part of the procedure is to allow spontaneous expression. In order to promote this flow of expression, Harris and Bessent (1969) suggest the following six rules:

1. All ideas related to the focus (goal) in any direct way are desired.
2. A maximum number of related ideas (objectives or skills) is desired.
3. One idea (skill) may be modified, adapted, and expressed as another. idea (objective). This is sometimes called "hitch-hiking" on ideas.
4. Ideas (related skills) should be expressed as clearly and concisely as possible.
5. No discussion of ideas (skills or objectives) should be attempted.
6. No criticism of ideas (objectives) is accepted. (p. 235, parentheses added)

It is essential that each group member understand these ground rules before beginning the brainstorming session. Successful brainstorming in each education agency undoubtedly results in developing the most appropriate general objectives because they reflect local needs, are comprehensive and, most importantly, are understood by those involved in their development and implementation. The resultant general objectives should be screened carefully to select and refine a set of pertinent objectives that lead to attaining annual goals.

Refining objectives. In order to establish a viable set of general objectives from the brainstormed list, the team of educators or members of the team that participate in the brainstorming session must carefully examine and analyze the resultant list with respect to various factors. This selection process can be accomplished by the same group of persons involved in the brainstorming or by a smaller committee of individuals. In some instances, a brainstorming group may wish to consider two or more annual goals in one sitting. The general objectives derived from this process may be refined more efficiently by dividing the group into subcommittees who assume responsibility for a particular annual goal and its general objectives. Regardless of the division of responsibilities, each member must be cognizant of the factors involved in defining the set of objectives for each goal.

The factors involved in refining brainstorm activities lead educators to establishing the set of skills or general objectives necessary for each goal. The factors include:

1. Defining brainstormed ideas according to the characteristics given for general objectives (as outlined previously).
2. Eliminating repetitive skills or objectives.
3. Broadening or combining ideas brainstormed that were too specific to be general objectives (that is, those that include activities similar to instructional objectives).
4. Separating ideas containing more than one skill.
5. Eliminating skills which will be irrelevant to special education students or skills involved in other goals.
6. The constant awareness of possible difficulties encountered in a given area to signal the need for developing additional general objectives.

These six considerations can be exemplified with the following example.

After brainstorming a group of educators had recorded the following list of skills or objectives in addition:

1. Simple addition
2. Addition sums to 10
3. 3-digit numbers
4. 2-digit numbers
5. 1-digit numbers
6. Addition with zeroes
7. Addition with carrying
8. Addition of fractions
9. Addition with like denominators (fractions)
10. Addition with unlike denominators (fractions)
11. Addition of decimals no carrying
12. Addition of decimals with carrying
13. Addition orally (in your head)
14. Written problems with addition

15. Horizontal addition	24. Using cuisenaire rods
16. Timed addition facts	25. Additive inverse
17. Flash cards	26. Adding time
18. Addition of objects	27. Adding money
19. One-to-one correspondence	28. Adding measurements
20. Counting	29. Knowing the addition sign
21. Adding on fingers	30. Addition worksheets
22. Using abacus	31. Story problems
23. Using number lines	

This composite list demonstrates several aspects of brainstorming such as how one idea "hitch-hiked" upon another in several instances (see 3–5 and 26–28). However, the most important thing for the committee of educators to do is to refine and complete this listing of skills. Following down the six factors involved in refinement, we can see how each objective was considered and finally resulted in a list of general objectives.

1. *Defining skills in proper format* Obviously ideas #17 and 21–24 defined specific *materials* not appropriate for general objectives. These may be important for short-term instruction objectives, thus they will be recorded for use later. #29 is an important objective but is stated as a goal— a general objective might be merely "addition or plus sign." Skill #13 also is useful as an instructional objective but defines a behavior and thus is not appropriate for consideration as a general objective.

2. *Eliminating repetitious skills* #1 and 2; 14 and 31 state essentially the same skills, therefore, #31 can be omitted; we will examine #1 and 2 again later.

3. *Grouping too specific skills* if using various devices was considered important enough for a special objective, #21–24 could be combined as "use of manipulative aids."

4. *Separating broad objectives* #1 and 7 involve various skills that could be separated along the same lines as #3, 4, and 5 so that one might have: simple addition one-digit numerals, simple addition two-digit numerals . . . , and addition with carrying two-digit numerals, addition with carrying three-digit numbers. . . . The same might be true of objectives #11 and 12.

5. *Eliminating unnecessary skills* The skill or objective of

counting, #20, probably would be dealt with under the goal of numeration so it can be eliminated or referred to the committee working on numerations. Likewise, objectives 19, 26, 27, and 28 should be dealt with elsewhere. Number 25 represents an interesting dilemma for special educators that frequently needs to be dealt with. Additive inverse $(2 + \underline{\hspace{1em}} = 6)$ is a concept taught in most regular math programs; however, for students with computational problems, skills such as this can result in a waste of valuable instructional time, and may, in fact, never be accomplished. However, it may be left on the list to indicate to special educators that it is, in fact, a skill needed for the student to be matriculated back into regular classroom mathematics. When these questions arise, it is recommended that the skill in question be included but marked so that the possible need to move ahead in the continuum without mastery of that particular objective is indicated.

6. *Awareness of possible difficulties* Brainstormed skills #6 (addition with zeroes), #15 (horizontal addition), #16 (timed facts), and #30 (worksheets) are important to attend to because they signal potential difficulties. The fact is a child may be able to add simple one-digit numbers vertically and not horizontally, or add ten correctly in a given time period but not complete 30 per page. In addition the use of zeroes often compounds student difficulties. Many of these potential problems should be represented during the brainstorm sessions and set aside but remembered so that they can be considered later in specifying short-term instructional objectives. However, pointing up the difficulty between two-digit addition with carrying and without carrying is a significant enough consideration to attend to while establishing general objectives.

The following is the list of general objectives for addition after expansion and elimination of brainstormed objectives:

1. Plus sign
2. Simple one-digit addition, sums to 10
3. Simple one-digit addition, sums to 18
4. (Additive inverse)
5. Three one-digit simple addition, sums to 18
6. Simple two-digit addition
7. Written problems with simple additions

8. Two-digit addition carrying
9. Simple three-digit addition
10. Three-digit addition with carrying
11. Addition fractions (like denominators)
12. Simple addition of decimals
13. Four-digit addition with and without carrying
14. Addition fractions with different denominators
15. Addition mixed fractions
16. Addition unlike-digit decimals
17. Addition decimals with carrying
18. Written problems requiring addition with carrying fractions and decimals.

Several potential problem areas were set aside for later consideration during short-term instructional objective formation. These included the concepts of numbers of problems per page, horizontal versus vertical addition, addition orally, use of manipulatives, and use of zeroes. Each of these ideas was recorded during the brainstorming session and is helpful later when identifying specific behaviors for short-term instructional objectives. In addition, the concepts of adding money, time, measure; counting; and one-to-one correspondence were recorded and given to the various committees working on time, money, measure, and numeration. As the preceding example demonstrates, information retrieved during brainstorming sessions is extremely useful in generating general objectives and is applicable to developing short-term instructional objectives as well. Following refinement, educators must arrange the general objectives in an appropriate sequence.

Sequence objectives. There are essentially three ways in which to sequence objectives: (1) from simplest to most complex, (2) according to the developmental patterns of skill acquisition, or (3) from least to most important. Addition objectives are among the best examples of skills that need to be ordered from *simple to complex*—acquiring one skill is necessary in order to develop the next. Obviously a student must know how to add two one-digit number sums to 18 before acquiring skills in carrying in addition of two-place numbers.

Developmentally sequenced objectives generally are employed in areas where skills are acquired at very early ages. There appears to have been more and better research conducted on the developmental sequences of very young children. Oral language acquisition is a prime example of using developmental ages in ordering objectives and skills, such as the chart shown in Chapter 4, Table 4–4. Many motor skills and early self-help skills are also approached in this respect. For example, balance is acquired developmentally prior to speed and agility.

Arranging objectives in order of importance is the most common way of sequencing sociobehavioral and career/vocational objectives. Sociobehavioral objectives are generally arranged beginning with those behaviors most needing immediate extinction or with those social skills needed at any given time. For example, behaviors that result in injury to others are generally high priority for immediate intervention. Social skills involving using telephones generally are assigned to later ages because they have a lower priority than social skills of thanking adults or playing with peers. In the career/vocational education areas, skills are arranged by priority on the basis of predictive and interest tests that help determine possible career choices. Based on these choices, skills are sequenced according to those most needed for specific occupational clusters.

In order to sequence established general objectives one must be cognizant of the manner in which it would be most appropriate to order particular sets of skills, that is, by developmental stages, by complexity, or by priority. Occasionally, there is no apparent sequence in which to order skills. In these instances, it is common to find the sequence in which the skills are selected for individual students varying from one child to the next, making specific ordering unnecessary. Often when attempting to sequence objectives, it is helpful to examine the list of skills and determine the most complex (or lowest priority) objective and proceed toward the most simple (or most important). When determining which general objective should be listed last, it is helpful to look for the one or two objectives that, if accomplished, would be indicative of mastering a particular goal. In any event, attempts should be made to sequence general objectives under each goal so that an orderly progression of educational objectives exists. Examples of the various types of sequencing are included in the section of this chapter that provides sample lists of general objectives in each of the four special education areas.

Once general objectives have been defined, refined, and sequenced, educators need a structure by which to manage these objectives effectively. The format for recording general objectives, called curricular maps, provides an overview of all general objectives involved in a given performance area, as well as a structure for curriculum development in special education.

Developing Curricular Maps

The basic structure around which general objectives are organized is the curricular map, which is a two-dimensional array of skills (general objectives) involved in a particular performance area. It is organized by the educational goals and sequenced by levels of development, difficulty, or priority. It is possible to construct a curricular map for each performance area defined within the four areas of special education—self-help/ basic living, sociobehavioral, career/vocational, and academic. Therefore, each special education area requires several curricular maps; for example, self-help/basic living requires three curricular maps. The curricular maps should include personal skills, independent living skills, and motor-mobility skills—the primary performance areas of self-help/ basic living education. The particular goals involved in each of these areas form the basic constructs for the particular map. Whenever possible, the constructs or goals of a given performance area should also be sequenced by complexity, priority, or developmental stages. For instance, within the performance area of personal skills some of the constructs (or goals) are feeding, toileting, and dressing. These would be the constructs of the curricular map for personal skills. Figure 5–1 graphically displays the concept of the curricular map structure.

The second dimension of any curricular map involves grouping the previously *sequenced* general objectives. Therefore, each block shown in the graph contains several objectives distributed across levels (see Figure 5–2). For example, block A (level I, goal 1) contains the initial objectives outlined for the first goal, block B contains another series of objectives. However, the objectives in B (under level II, goal 1) are more complex, later to develop, or lower in priority than those contained in block A. The division into levels can be representative of developmental ages, grade levels, or merely indicative of increasing priority or complexity. Often academic skills are grouped by grade levels so that

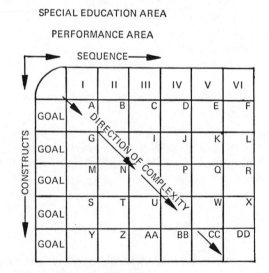

FIGURE 5–1   Graph of Curricular Map

246

block G (see Table 5–1) might contain a group of general objectives that are generally taught under that particular goal in first grade, while block H would represent objectives taught in second grade. For many areas of special education, however, grade levels are inappropriate for effective instructional sequencing. Nonetheless, an attempt should be made to order objectives within levels so that each objective in level I could be appropriate during a given time period. That is, all objectives in level I might be considered appropriate for one year's (month or semester) program. This definition and brief discussion of the two-dimensional array of skills (constructs and sequence) called curricular maps are applied to each of the four areas of special education in a later section. However, it would be profitable for the reader to examine (1) several important characteristics of curricular maps, and (2) the specific purposes for which they are developed. Following these discussions, examples of maps and objectives in each area are included.

Characteristics of curricular maps. Three characteristics of properly constructed curricular maps that should be examined include (1) the general direction of complexity, (2) the absence of some skills at certain levels, and (3) the necessary overlap between performance areas and maps. When both the constructs and levels outlined are sequenced developmentally or by complexity, the *general direction of increasing complexity* of a given curriculum is a diagonal from the upper left-hand corner to the lower right (see Figure 5–1). In other words, block A contains the simplest objectives in this particular performance area and block DD contains the most complex. Whenever possible, this charac-

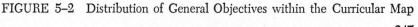

FIGURE 5–2   Distribution of General Objectives within the Curricular Map

247

teristic of curricular maps should be obtained because it lends a general order to the special education curriculum.

A second characteristic of curricular maps is that in some cases there is *no set of general objectives for a particular goal* at every level. This most frequently occurs when both constructs and levels are sequenced from simple to complex. The reason for this is that some constructs become so complex in and of themselves that they are inappropriate to remediate at an early level or time within the educational program. In these instances, it is frequently found that blocks such as S, T, AA, and BB (Figure 5-1) are devoid of any objectives. However, if a particular curricular map becomes too devoid of objectives or skills, it is probably because the goals or constructs have been broken down too specifically. This results in too few objectives distributed across all levels. For instance, if the construct of vowel sounds in reading recognition were broken into short vowels, long vowels, and irregular vowel sounds, one would find the five short vowel sounds covering at most the first two levels, long vowels a third level, and so on. Combining these constructs into one such as vowel sounds would solve the problem.

In constructing a thorough map of all the objectives or skills that could possibly be contained in a goal or performance area, some *overlap* of general objectives does occur. For instance, some of the more complex personal skills probably would overlap with initial independent living skills. Initial reading comprehension skills may include a level of listening comprehension causing overlap to occur between these skills and the most complex skills involved in oral language comprehension. Figure 5-3 graphically illustrates this repetitious use of general objectives in constructing curricular maps. This is a natural outgrowth of the process of curricular mapping and should not be considered negative. In fact, this continuous overlapping probably indicates the rigors with which a map was constructed. It also assists educators in establishing for themselves the degrees to which much of education is virtually inseparable and encourages integrating curriculum areas.

These three characteristics of curricular maps including the general direction of skill complexity, the necessary absence and overlap of various general objectives along with the definition given earlier form the basis from which to examine their purposes which we discuss in the following section.

Purposes of curricular mapping. The primary purposes for developing curricular maps are to provide (1) educators with knowledge of the needed curriculum and components of special education in a form applicable to curriculum guides; and thus (2) handicapped students with a continuum of education within a number of curricular possibilities for assessment and instruction. The first purpose or outgrowth of the re-

248

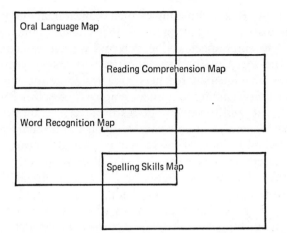

FIGURE 5-3   Illustration of Skill Overlap

search, brainstorming, defining, writing, and organizing that goes into developing curricular maps is the growth of the professionals involved. Each educator involved adds to his/her own understanding of the various special education skills needed within each curriculum area. This is the major reason it is crucial to involve regular classroom and special education teachers in curriculum development for it is ultimately only *their* knowledge of children's needs and curriculum objectives that make the difference in a handicapped child's education program. The following section more clearly illustrates just how these differences can be made by developing curricular maps in special education.

Perhaps the most devastating aspect of special education in the past has been the lack of well-established curricula that would direct educators in taking a handicapped student from where she/he is presently functioning and lead the child back into the "mainstream" of education or to the next least-restrictive special education environment. This lack of curricula or guides probably led Dunn (1968) to note the untenable fact that most children placed in special education were never dismissed from special services; a fact that special educators in the late 70s are still attempting to overcome. In order to move handicapped students to a more "normal" environment, special educators *must* devise a complete curriculum that leads to mastery of those skills needed in the next least-restrictive environment, be it society, regular classroom, or community home. This is the major purpose to be accomplished by constructing curricular maps which outline skills from a very low functioning level up to those needed in society or regular education.

Establishing a thorough curriculum in special education provides handicapped pupils a continuum in their educational programs that is all too often absent in current practice. It is not uncommon for a handicapped child to enter special education and receive remedial academic training as the focus of his/her education for a few years. However, changing special education teachers may result in the entire focus of his/her education changing to a major emphasis on self-help/basic living skills. In the past, and to some degree still today, a handicapped child's education has depended almost entirely upon the preferences and often limited curriculum training of the individual special educator. One reason for this occurrence is because special educators frequently have walked into a classroom for the first time with little more provided to them in the way of materials than a stick of chalk and empty bulletin boards. In addition, they may have been provided with individual educational programs written by support staff who have seen the student only a very limited length of time. These individual programs have often alluded to vague educational objectives and materials that may not even exist within the confines of the school district. To a large extent, this problem is avoided in the regular classroom through the uniform adoption and provision of basal materials that, when followed, automatically progress along a continuum of objectives. While providing uniform texts and material is certainly not appropriate for special education where student needs are much too diverse, it does allow regular educators the security of a continuous curriculum without having to conceptualize curriculum areas for themselves. Once curricular maps have been established for and by special educators there is a guide for the continuous selection of objectives within each area. Only then are special education teachers no longer dependent upon narrow skills taught them in their college or university training programs in special education and an orderly continuum of educational programs for the handicapped can become the rule rather than the exception.

Constructing curricular maps in all areas of special education provides a variety of educational objectives that educators can follow in programming instruction for any given handicapped child. Providing this variety in curriculum selection and guides promises handicapped students a more thorough educational program. It is then possible to program goals and objectives for the kinds of diverse needs a handicapped pupil may exhibit from low-level self-help skills to complex academic tasks. Therefore, any educational need identified for an individual child should have corresponding sets of general objectives easily located within a given curricular map.

Curricular maps also provide educational planners with a comprehensive view of skills involved in a given performance area so that it not only allows for thorough programming, but also a comprehensive scope for assessment. This kind of assessment of general objectives can be conducted prior to placement and programming in a particular goal. Appropriate general objectives are then located for programming, as well as for evaluating progress made toward attaining general objectives. In turn, this assessment of progress serves as a guide for programming future objectives. A procedure for assessing the general objectives contained within a given curricular map is discussed following an examination of sample curricular maps and general objectives within each of the four areas of special education.

Curricular Maps and General Objectives

In each of the areas of special education, attempts should be made to develop comprehensive maps of general objectives. Once accomplished, individual education programs can be developed with ease. There should be a separate map of objectives developed for each performance area defined by the school when conceptualizing the four areas of special education. Goals under each performance area constitute the constructs around which to develop the map. General objectives under each construct are brainstormed, refined, and sequenced into levels. Once completed, educators have both the basis for special education curriculum planning and individual student programming. Examples of the ways in which annual goal conceptualizations can be used in developing curricular maps and general objectives in each area of special education are given below. The reader should note the importance here of the conceptualizations presented and developed earlier.

Self-help/basic living. Remember, in defining the goals of self-help/basic living education, three performance areas were identified—personal, motor and mobility, and independent living. Therefore, in the area of self-help/basic living education there should be three curricular maps of general objectives. According to the manner in which personal skills were conceptualized during goal development, the constructs of a curricular map in this area would appear as in Table 5–9. Sequences of general objectives are defined in developmental levels because age or grade development is not appropriate since the last skills in dressing generally are completed long before the final objectives of health and hygiene.

A suggested curricular map structure for curricular maps of general objectives involved in motor and mobility and independent living is shown in Table 5–10. In order to assist the educator in brainstorming general objectives under each construct, each goal is elaborated on below.

TABLE 5-9 Curricular Map—Personal Skills in Self-Help/Basic Living Education

	I	II	III	IV	V
Feeding	Being fed—liquids Being fed—solids Self-feeding—bottle Self-feeding—hands	Cup Spoon Fork and spoon	Knife, fork, spoon Drinking from cans, bottles	Table manners Food selection School luncheon	Restaurant dining
Dressing	Shoes Socks Coat Shirt	Pants Skirts Gloves Undergarments	Selecting appropriate colors Hose Selecting appropriate sizes	Selecting weather-appropriate clothes Appropriate for physical characteristics	Selecting appropriate styles Purchasing own wardrobe Accessories
Health and Hygiene	Toilet training Face washing Hand washing	Regular bathing Deodorant	Medical and dental when needed Menstruation	Medical and dental care—regular Use of over-the-counter drugs	Regular hygiene Use of prescription drugs Medical and dental emergencies
Grooming	Combing hair Brushing teeth	Washing and drying Washing clothes	Shaving Curling hair Ironing	Care of nails Special skin care Simple repair of clothing	Make-up Styling hair

TABLE 5-10 Suggested Outline for Curricular Maps—Motor and Mobility and Independent Living Skills in Self-Help/Basic-Living Education

	I	II	III	IV
Posture				
Gross Motor				
Fine Motor				
Spatial Orientation				
Special Motor Skills				

	I	II	III	IV
Meal Preparation				
Clothing				
Transportation				
Money Management				
Leisure Time				
Housekeeping				
Civic Activities				
Home Furnishings				
Family Responsibilities				
Safety				
Community Resources and Services				
Personal Communications				

PERSONAL SKILL GOALS

- *Feeding* involves general objectives beginning with the intake of food from others to the appropriate and mannerly skills involved in eating a meal in public.
- *Dressing* includes general objectives from activities in dressing and undressing to the ability to dress and undress oneself completely as well as selecting appropriate attire.
- *Health and hygiene* activities cover general objectives such as toileting, washing, bathing, administering medication, care of personal hygiene during menstruation, and so on.
- *Grooming* involves general objectives, other than dressing and cleansing, needed to improve one's appearance, and include fixing one's hair, shaving, and using makeup.

MOTOR AND MOBILITY

- *Posture* involves the range of abilities from a child's holding his/her head up to the skills involved in standing erect and holding one's head up and shoulders back.
- *Gross motor skill* involves utilizing the large muscles necessary for such movements as crawling, walking, and running with balance, rhythm, strength, and agility.
- *Fine motor skill* involves using the small muscles in tactual-kinesthetic movements such as grasping, gripping, throwing, and catching.
- *Spatial orientation* includes body awareness, directing one's body toward sound, light, and movement. Later spatial orientation skills involve knowledge of right, left, north, south, east, west.
- *Special motor skills* are taught with regard to special equipment such as prosthetic devices, wheelchairs, walkers, and braille type, needed by children with physical or motor problems.

INDEPENDENT LIVING

- *Meal preparation* involves the skills of classifying foods, planning recipes, shopping, and cooking one item to cooking and serving entire meals and planning weekly menus.
- *Clothing* involves selection, purchase, and care of appropriate clothes for various life activities.
- *Transportation* involves the ability to utilize public transportation facilities or to transport oneself within a community.
- *Money management* includes the range of skills from budgeting, planning purchases, and buying with small allowances to the ability to budget, expend, pay taxes, and so on, for an entire household.

- *Leisure time* involves the ability to plan and follow through with activities for entertainment and relaxation ranging from free time at school to vacation planning.
- *Housekeeping* includes skills of cleaning furniture, appliances, floors, and so on, in a given household.
- *Civic activities* involve a student's ability to locate and participate in community affairs, both voluntary and mandated, such as obtaining licenses and paying taxes.
- *Home furnishings* include skills of selection, purchase, and care of furniture and appliances.
- *Family responsibilities* include the understanding of responsibilities involved in marriage and parenting.
- *Safety* involves those skills necessary to prevent accidents.
- *Community resources and services* involves skills necessary to locate and obtain assistance available in the community.
- *Personal communication* involves using communication vehicles such as services provided by radio and television and using the telephone, telegraph, and postal system.

Academics. In the area of academic education there are 10 performance areas so 10 different curricular maps should be developed; one each for: receptive language, expressive language, reading recognition, reading comprehension, spelling, penmanship, conceptual writing, mathematical operations, mathematical measurement, and mathematical concepts. Table 5–11 graphically displays a format for each of these ten maps. Each construct involved in the various maps can be further defined and sequenced into a series of general objectives.

The academic areas of receptive and expressive language may well be represented by the same map of general objectives. The difference would be in whether or not the linguistic structure defined as a skill

TABLE 5–11   Suggested Outlines for Curricular Maps—Academics

Spelling	I	II	III	IV	V	VI
Phoneme/Grapheme Correspondence						
Consonant Blends and Diagraphs						
Short Vowels						
Long Vowels						
Irregular Consonants						
Irregular Vowels						
Compound Words						
Structural Analysis						

Penmanship	I	II	III	IV	V	VI
Process						
Product						

Reading Recognition	I	II	III	IV	V	VI
Sound-Symbol-Correspondence						
Consonants						
Short Vowels						
Consonant Blends and Diagraphs						
Long Vowels						
Voewl Diagraphs						
Irregular Consonant						
Irregular Vowel						
Compound Words						
Sight Words						
Structural Analysis						

Conceptual Writing	I	II	III	IV	V	VI
Capitalization						
Punctuation						
Vocabulary						
Word Usage						
Grammar						
Sentence						
Paragraph						
Thesis						

Language—Expression	I	II	III	IV	V	VI
Phonology						
Morphology						
Syntax						
Semantics—Command						
Semantics—Questions						
Semantics—Statement						

Reading Comprehension	I	II	III	IV	V	VI
Vocabulary						
Fact						
Main Idea						
Conclusion						
Inference						
Judgment						
Literary Interpretation						
References						

Math—Operations	I	II	III	IV	V	VI
Numeration						
Addition						
Subtraction						
Multiplication						
Division						

Language—Reception	I	II	III	IV	V	VI
Phonology						
Morphology						
Syntax						
Semantics—Command						
Semantics—Question						
Semantics—Statement						

Math—Measurements	I	II	III	IV	V	VI
Time						
Money						
Measures						

Math—Concepts	I	II	III	IV	V	VI
Sets						
Correspondence						
Conservation/Relationship						
Geometry						
Fractions						
Decimals						
Written Problems						
Reasoning						

within the map is to be understood by the student or expressed by him/her. An example of general objectives that might be outlined for the construct or goal of morphology is shown in Table 5–12.

The area of reading contains two curricular maps of general objectives. Objectives defined under the construct of consonant blends and graphs in reading recognition might include something similar to those in Table 5–13. Table 5–14 represents general objectives involved under the construct of reference skills.

Table 4–20 in Chapter 4 displayed a sample of a completed curricular map of conceptual writing skills organized as were the goals in Table 5–5. One last example of general objectives in the area of academics is provided in Table 5–15. This table delineates general objectives for the construct of time in the mathematical measurement map.

These examples should provide a basis from which educators can expand and develop the remainder of the curricular maps for the various areas of academics. It may be helpful to review the procedure and characteristics of general objectives once again prior to further curriculum development.

Sociobehavioral. Sociobehavioral education can be divided into four different curricular maps: self-awareness, socialization, task related, and undesirable behaviors. Table 5–16 displays curricular map structures for organizing general objectives. Because the constructs of sociobehavioral education are not as well defined as those of academics, each construct is discussed briefly below so as to provide the reader a basis from which to begin developing general objectives.

SELF-AWARENESS GOALS

Physical awareness objectives involve the student's building accurate perceptions regarding his/her physical appearance and abilities. Knowledge of hair color, height, weight, and so on, are initial skills of physical awareness while knowledge of physical strength, health, and endurance are later general objectives.

TABLE 5-12 General Objectives as Outlined in Curricular Map for the Construct of Morphology—Oral Language

I	II	III	IV
root words—noun	s (plural)	're (are)	'll (will)
root words—verb	ing (progressive)	is (possessive)	've (have)
root words—adjective	-er, -est (comparisons)	en, ed (past tense)	's (has)
root words—adverb		verb + s (third person singular)	n't (negative)
		compound words	

V	VI	VII
prefixes	*suffixes*
ing (gerund)	re- (again)	-ant, -ent (one who)
ly (adverb)	be- (near)	-ive (that performs an action)
ing (adjective)	dis-	-ion (an act)
ly (adjective)	a-, an-	-less (not having)
y (adjective)	in-, un-, ir- (not) il-	-ness (quality, state)
	non-	-ful, -ous (full of)
	mis-	-ish (relating to)
	anti- (against)	-ment (noun)
	pro- (for)	-able, -ible (state of being)
	com-, col-, con- (together)	-ance, -ence (action or process)
	pre- (before)	
	de- (down)	
	sub- (below)	
	post- (after)	
	mini-, micro- (small)	
	uni-, bi-, tri- (number)	
	ex- (out from)	
	trans- (across)	

Morphology

TABLE 5-13 General Objectives as Outlined in Curricular Map for the Construct of Consonant Blends and Digraphs Reading Recognition

	I	II	III	IV	V
Consonant Blends and Digraphs	Initial consonant digraphs sh, ch, th	Initial consonant digraph wh	Final consonant blends st, ng, ng, sp, rt	Initial consonant digraphs ph, wr, kn	Initial and final blend combinations in medial position
	Initial consonant blends bl, br, cl, cr, dr, fl, fr, gl, gr, pl, pr, st, sl, tr	Final consonant digraphs sh, ch, th, ck		Final consonant digraph gh	Initial and final digraphs in medial position
		Initial consonant blends spr, str, sw, tw, sm, sn		Final blends ft, lt, lp, rp	

259

TABLE 5-14 General Objectives as Outlined in Curricular Map for the Construct of Reference Skills—Reading Comprehension

	I	II	III	IV
	Alphabetizing	Using encyclopedia	Skimming	Using almanac
	Reading to follow directions	Using library	Taking notes	Using Atlas
		Using card catalog	Using indexes	Using pronunciation keys
Reference Skills	Using dictionary	Using table of contents	Using glossary	Using charts and graphs
				Using library services call slips, etc.

TABLE 5-15 A Curricular Map for Math Measurement Time

	I Days of week	II Time by hour	III Seasons	IV Hrs. and mins.	V Time zones	VI Adding days months, yrs.
Time	Months of year	Date of month	Half hours	Minutes till hour	Adding hrs. and mins.	Subtracting days, months, yrs.
	Hours of day— general year	Using calendar	Quarter hours	A.M. v. P.M.	Subtract hrs. and mins.	24-hr. clock

SOURCE: Adapted from Hoover, L. S., and Sherman, S. *Arithmetic instructional map*. Unpublished manuscript, University of Texas at Austin, 1978.

TABLE 5–16 Suggested Outlines for Curricular Maps—Sociobehavioral

Self-Awareness	I	II	III	IV	V	VI
Physical						
Values						
Limitations						
Strengths						

Undesirable Behaviors	I	II	III	IV	V	VI
Destruction—Person						
Destruction—Property						
Disruption						
Disassociation						
Disobedient						
Distraction						
Dependency						

Socialization	I	II	III	IV	V	VI
Courtesies						
Relations—Public						
Relations—Peers						
Relations—Superiors						

Task Related	I	II	III	IV	V	VI
Attention						
Respect						
Flexibility						
Completion						
Independence						

Values objectives involve skills in the construct of values and initially entail knowledge of likes and dislikes, friends, and so on. Later value objectives involve defining values for oneself such as honesty and integrity.

Limitations objectives involve an awareness of limitations describing skills necessary for a student to understand limits of his/her own physical, mental, and social characteristics and skills. Initially physical limitations are simplest to determine. Acceptance and planning around these limitations is also a part of skills in this area.

Strengths are similar to limitations. Emphasis is placed on utilizing these strengths in home, school, and work. Objectives begin by defining things one is proud of, things one does well, and so on. Later skills to develop are the ability to perceive strengths in relating to people and evaluating special talents and skills.

SOCIALIZATION GOALS

Courtesies are those skills not necessarily essential to successful living but that may promote one's interests. These objectives begin with such things as saying thank you and you're welcome and follow to courtesies in specific places such as elevators and on telephones.

Relations—public are those skills needed by an individual in order to be "socially acceptable" in public. These include skills of conversing with strangers, normalized behaviors of knowing important timely social trends, and being able to obtain and utilize information from the public in general.

Relations—personal include general objectives designed to promote close personal relations from early playmates to marital partners and close friends. The objectives may be as simple as listening to others or as complex as those involved in dating.

Relations—superiors are primarily centered on establishing those conventional skills that assist a person in relating to teachers, employers, and other officials. They involve accepting responsibility when assigned and displaying respectful behaviors when interacting with superiors. To some degree courtesies and relations with the public objectives are appropriate here also.

TASK-RELATED GOALS

Attention is a highly valued construct, particularly during school. Objectives include initially such things as eye contact and orientation to speech. Later skills in attention include maintaining attention to task or direction and the ability to exclude or ignore irrelevant stimuli.

Respect as related to tasks entailing both pride in property and material as well as in accomplishment and team efforts. General objectives begin with material care and proceed to more pride and honor and being part of a team.

Flexibility includes objectives that promote the individual's ability to change tasks or kinds of tasks without upset. This also entails the ability to continue trying after early failure.

Completion includes a set of general objectives that delineates specific types of tasks that increase in complexity and time required to complete.

Independence includes the gradual reduction of cues, prompts, and models or supervision necessary for a task to be attempted or accomplished.

UNDESIRABLE BEHAVIORS. These behaviors are defined in general objectives ranging from most to least severe for amelioration.

Destructive—personal includes behaviors ranging from most physically destructive to those which are not physically destructive but cause others' feelings to be hurt, embarrassed, and so on. These behaviors may be troublesome to self or others.

Destructive—property includes behaviors that result in damage to material or property rather than persons. Once again the range is from most severe to least damaging behaviors.

Disruption includes behaviors that result in major classroom or societal disruption ranging from minor disruptions to self and others upward.

Disassociation involves behaviors that describe students completely detached from surroundings, withdrawn, or merely shyness.

Disobedience includes severe problems with conformity to all rules and commands as well as less severe problems with specific rules or demands.

Distraction involves problems with attention to task. Severity usually is determined by time of attention and complexity of task.

Dependency involves behaviors ranging from sudents who perform no exploratory behaviors to students who are situationally dependent.

Once the sociobehavioral skills to be developed and/or extinguished are outlined, educators can more easily plan specific behavioral management techniques to apply all socialization objectives for instruction. For further clarification Table 5–17 delineates a set of comprehensive general objectives within sample constructs of two curricular maps—self-awareness (values) and undesirable behaviors (disassociation).

Career/vocational. General objectives in the area of career/vocational education can be placed in three curriculum maps, one each for: occupational exploration; occupational application; and occupational preparation, maintenance, and change. Table 5–18 provides an outline of these maps. Below are some content suggestions for goals under these general objectives.

OCCUPATIONAL EXPLORATION

Occupational clusters contain objectives designed to increase the students' awareness of the wide range of occupational opportunities.

Job characteristics sequence the various aspects of specific occupations such as hours, salary, benefits, and travel.

Occupational opportunities examine opportunities in the local area and possibilities in the future as well as acquainting pupils with certain job requirements.

Prerequisite working skills are designed to promote healthy work attitudes and prerequisite skills such as task responsibility and completion and reward.

OCCUPATIONAL APPLICATION

Possibilities deal with an extension of examining various job possibilities with regard to individual abilities and talents.

Search emphasizes the students' knowledge of the various ways in which one can locate potential jobs.

Application involves securing necessary forms and collecting or developing needed data for prospective employers.

TABLE 5–17 Sample General Objectives in Values and Disassociation—Sociobehavioral Education

				Most Normal
Values	Examining value behaviors	Expressing likes and dislikes (behavioral)	Choosing by consequences	Expressing actions by feelings	
	Modeling others	Choosing from alternatives	Prizing—nonmaterial	Choosing freely	
	Expressing likes and dislikes (material, physical)	Prizing material or physical	Expressing concerns	Acting consistent with expressed values	
	Describing friends	Expressing pride	Acting by consequences		
	Expressing feelings	Acting on feelings	Matching behaviors, values and feelings (not self)		
	Most Severe				*Most Normal*
Disassociation	Attends only to objects	Observes others	Verbal interaction—adults	Verbal and physical interaction—adults	Interacts with peers
	Verbalizes to objects	Eye contact with adults	Maintains physical separation—adults	Verbal interaction—peers	Shares with peers
	Physically isolates self	Physically separate but part of general environment	Eye contact—peers	Maintains physical separation—peers	Takes turns with peers

TABLE 5–18 Suggested Outlines for Curricular Maps—Career/Vocational Education

Occupational Exploration	I	II	III	IV	V	VI
Occupational Clusters						
Job Characteristics						
Occupational Opportunities						
Prerequisite Working Skills						

Occupational Application	I	II	III	IV	V	VI
Possibilities						
Search						
Application						
Interview						

Occupational Preparation, Maintenance, and Change	I	II	III	IV	V	VI
Physical—Manual Skills						
Expression						
Administration Skills						
Talents						
Personal Skills						
Computation						

Interview includes the skills necessary to present oneself appropriately physically and socially and communicate interests and abilities to prospective employers.

OCCUPATIONAL PREPARATION, MAINTENANCE, AND CHANGE

Physical-manual skills are similar to the skills delineated in motor and mobility and are job specific. These skills are particularly important to specify for students involved in occupations requiring dexterity or strength.

Expression involves abilities to express oneself orally or in writing. These skills, too, are job specific.

Administrative skills include specific skills involved in managing and coordinating other persons.

Talent encourages and develops abilities already present in an individual student, such as musical or artistic skills, which can be developed into an occupational talent.

Personal skills entails the ability to interact with peers or the public as it relates to specific job requirements. The degree to which personal skills are necessary often depends upon the type of job involved.

Computation involves mathematical skills directly related to the ability to perform certain job functions. These are also job specific.

Once again several examples of comprehensive general objectives in several areas may serve to clarify further the construction of curricula maps. Table 5–19 provides an example of general objectives necessary for occupational clusters under occupational exploration and job search under occupational application, as well as physical-manual skills under occupational maintenance. Note that particularly the physical-manual skills are not sequenced in terms of complexity but are merely delineated for selection. This is true for most job-specific objectives.

Once curricular maps and general objectives have been defined for each performance area in the four special education areas, educators have a comprehensive base for special education curriculum planning and individualized educational programming. However, in order to avoid several pitfalls of skills merely listed one after another, one must understand several basic unique qualities of general objectives and curricular maps. These differentiating characteristics are presented in the following section as cautions in order to assure appropriate use of maps and general objectives.

Appropriate Uses of Curricular Maps and General Objectives

At this point in the discussion of general objectives and curricular maps it becomes necessary to interject several cautions. In addition to the purposes already described, these cautions define more clearly the appropriate use of general objectives and maps. The cautions involve the important distinctions between (1) general objectives and instructional methods, and (2) curricular maps and scope and sequence charts. Understanding the distinguishing characteristics can prevent misusing the concepts of objectives and maps presented in this chapter.

Although general objectives represent specific skills involved in a particular curriculum area, they do not mandate or suggest a "skills approach" to instruction. Much controversy exists in many areas of education between advocates of a "natural approach" to learning concepts and skills as opposed to a traditional step-by-step skill-building approach. Regardless of the way in which educators *instruct* students in acquiring new behaviors and knowledge, the fact remains that specific skills are necessary to perform certain tasks. General objectives are developed to identify these skills. The method of instructing these abilities probably is left to the individual teacher's own philosophies and strengths. Instructional methodology is not dictated by delineating skills

TABLE 5-19 Examples of General Objectives in Occupational Clusters, Job Search, and Physical-Manual Skills—Career/Vocational Education

I	II	III	IV
Service Workers Policemen Firemen	Professionals Teachers Doctors	Professionals Lawyers Scientist	Other Employee Directors
Government President Governor Mayor	Service Workers Waitress Barber Grocer	Government other Elected Officials Agency Employees	Professionals Engineers Psychologists
Craftsmen Carpenters Auto Mechanics Plumbers	Clerical Secretary Typist	Clerical Bookkeepers File Clerks Reception	Craftsmen Artists Musicians
	Craftsmen Electricians Other Mechanics	Operators Drivers Delivery Machinery	Operators Technicians Computer Programmers
	Sales Buyers Stockers Salesmen	Craftsmen Welders Builders Plasterers	

Occupational Clusters

Job Search	Community possibilities	Uses Newspaper	Uses Local Public	Specific Inquiries
	Telephone book	Uses vocational rehabilitation services	Uses private employment agencies	Searches other locally
	Dictionary of Occupational Titles		Uses other public agencies such as manpower	

Physical-Manual Tasks	Fine Motor	Large Machinery	Wood Working	Electrical
	Printing	Driving	Sawing	Motor repair
	Typing	Sewing	Nailing	Welding
	Manipulating small devices	Weighing	Drilling	Wiring
	Drawing	Moving	Painting	
	Musical Instruments		Finishing	
			Carving	

involved within various areas of education. It is the authors' contention that instructional methodology is best selected by individual teachers as they interact with particular children and that neither approach is always applicable to the education of handicapped children. In fact, the approach may even vary among objectives taught to a single student. It is quite likely that the most appropriate instructional method used to develop certain skills or objectives in individual children is that approach in which an individual educator has most confidence. Therefore, identifying a series of general objectives does not dictate instructional methodology.

The accumulation and structure of general objectives within curricular maps also differs from the traditional scope and sequence charting in several ways. First of all, a traditional scope and sequence chart specifies only those objectives presented in a particular set of materials or program. Often these are constructed by commercial material producers where no attempt is made to include and organize *all* skills or objectives possible in a given curriculum area. Curricular maps may be thought of as the ultimate accumulation and organization of many scope and sequence charts in a given area. Also, in the past scope and sequence charts have often been used to pass or promote children to next grade levels. This is not an appropriate use of curricular maps whose sole purpose is to promote successful education programming. There are no lock-step levels of attainment or sequences of objectives. Many students do not need each objective and certainly many cannot acquire skills in the traditional order. Of course, by the definition and the need of special education services, handicapped children already have been found not to fit the traditional "scope and sequence" of education. *Curricular maps and general objectives are developed to define more clearly possible avenues of instruction. Methods and materials are chosen after needed objectives are identified rather than having methods and materials dictate the objectives to be taught.* In order, then, to select general objectives appropriately, educators must develop a manner in which to assess general objectives. Once these are assessed, educators can define those most appropriate but unaccomplished objectives for the student's individualized program.

Assessing General Objectives

Assessing the degree to which a particular child has mastered a given set of general objectives is a highly complex process. The complexity is a result of the fairly subjective nature of general objective assessment. In fact assessing objectives accomplished is conducted most efficiently through observation. Observing a skill being performed spontaneously without assistance, prompting, cueing, or modeling is the single best assurance that a general objective has been attained. The degree to which the assessment of needed general objectives is successful directly corresponds to the educational assessor's understanding of the concept of mastery. The concept of mastery is also essential to developing short-term instructional objectives presented in the following chapter.

Mastering an educational objective exists only when the skill can be and is performed without prompting—clues, models, primes, cues, directions, or partially completed tasks. Performing the skill must be consistent to be sure the act does, in fact, indicate mastery as opposed to being accidental. In most cases mastery of general objectives is fairly obvious. For instance, one can observe whether or not an individual can cook a meal, dress himself, cook a single dish, or fill out a job application. However, the existence of certain sociobehavioral objectives must be interpreted such as what criteria to use to establish when a behavior is no longer considered disruptive or how often and when the student must say "thank you" in order to have accomplished an objective involved in courtesies. In academic education, for example, often a student is asked to complete a worksheet on short vowel sounds. Does successful completion of the given worksheet mean the student can apply the short vowel sounds to words he/she needs to decode in the environment? The answer is a resounding no. Until the handicapped child applies the skills to given situations in his/her life, a skill is not mastered. These concepts of mastery are extremely important to remember when attempting to assess those general objectives that a student has mastered and those that need instructional intervention of some kind.

For each of the hundreds of general objectives identified as special education concerns, there exist several ways of conceptualizing mastery. The primary considerations are the goal to which the objective belongs, the specific purpose the objective fulfills for the individual student, and the kind of observation that can be made. Without going into the details of plotting short-term instructional objectives, we will examine several questions useful to ask when determining whether or not a student has mastered a given objective. These questions include:

1. Was the skill performed spontaneously by the child to benefit himself?
2. Has it been performed spontaneously before?
3. Was the skill observed exactly as stated in the general objective rather than "almost"?
4. Did the student perform the task without prompting or assistance of any kind?

5. Did the given material or direction not assist the student in accomplishing the task in any way?
6. Could this be considered a natural response or habit of the student's?
7. Can the student perform the skill in the environment where it is most needed?

If the answer to these seven questions is "yes," the objective may be considered accomplished. Otherwise, the general objective in question may be considered for selection in the child's individualized education program.

In order to select appropriate general objectives for individual students, one must consider both the goal priority and sequence of objectives. Objectives listed under goals receiving high-priority rankings are, of course, selected first. In choosing general objectives under a specific goal, educators should look to the simplest (or highest priority) objectives not yet accomplished. Many times appropriate general objectives are those in which the student has demonstrated some degree of proficiency but has not yet mastered. A progression of objectives leading to mastery are defined later as short-term instructional objectives.

Documenting those general objectives selected for individual educational programs can often be best accomplished by the entire IEP team. First of all, documentation requires the collective efforts of the entire IEP team—parents included. The concept of mastery must first be discussed in depth. Then general objectives pertinent to selected goals are given to each member who is to mark those objectives he/she knows have been mastered by the child in question. In some few cases, further observation of specific situations or even special designing of situations may be necessary. For example, a parent may wish to give the child a certain amount of money to spend and observe his/her purchase in order to ascertain mastery of general objectives in math measurement-money. Special education teachers or other personnel should probably (if not already) observe certain of the child's behaviors in the regular classroom. From these observations, educators and parents can plan the next most appropriate objectives in which to intervene. Obviously, the subjective nature of this evaluation warrants careful attention by all team members. Instructional staff trained in diagnosis and observation can be very effective in this role.

The format for recording accomplished and/or appropriate objectives can take the form of recording on the curricular map itself, a checklist constructed from the map, or pertinent objectives only can be transferred to the IEP document. Often recorders can mark objectives that have been mastered on the curricular map itself. These may or may not be transferred later to the format shown in Table 5–20. This table sug-

TABLE 5–20 Format for Recording Annual Goals and General Objectives in Individualized Education Programs

Special education area _____

Performance area _____

Annual goal _____

   General objective _____

   General objective _____

   General objective _____

   General objective _____

Annual goal _____

   General objective _____

   General objective _____

   General objective _____

   General objective _____

Annual goal _____

   General objective _____

   General objective _____

   General objective _____

   General objective _____

Special education area _____

Performance area _____

Annual goal _____

   General objective _____

   General objective _____

   General objective _____

   General objective _____

gests a means by which educators may document annual goals and general objectives in the IEP. In addition, once curricular maps are developed, a checklist can be devised of skills listed either by levels or by constructs. These checklists can then become a part of the IEP document itself. Once those general objectives appropriate for the child's immediate education have been located, steps can be taken to develop short-term instructional objectives that lead to mastery.

In any event, assessing which general objectives are to be outlined in a given child's annual program depends largely upon educators' abilities to know and observe mastery. The selected objectives depend upon goal appropriateness, sequence, and priority. These general objectives lead educators directly to establishing short-term instructional objectives.

SUMMARY

In summary, annual goals and general objectives provide special educators with content for special education curricula. Once special education curricula are defined as goals and objectives, individual student programming may be conducted. Organized within curricular maps by constructs and sequences, these goals and general objectives assure a continuum of instruction that heretofore has been absent from the education of handicapped youngsters. In addition, developing comprehensive curricula ensures that educators make decisions regarding instruction as opposed to materials or program producers. These decisions are made as educators in local districts or schools conceptualize the areas of special education and develop these concepts into annual goals and general objectives. A framework for organizing these is referred to as a curricular map. This organizational structure aids the IEP team in the appropriate selection of annual goals and general objectives for individual handicapped students.

Annual goals should be developed for each area of special education by defining the performance areas and constructs involved in the education of handicapped youngsters. When defining these constructs, it is important to utilize the vast resources available through professionals in the local school area as well as in the special and regular education literature. Once all the possible goals that may be involved in any given handicapped student's education are identified, the IEP team may begin selecting particular goals for individual children.

Annual goals are selected for individual education programs by examining certain factors regarding the handicapped child that were collected during screening, evaluation, and present-level documentation.

These factors investigate the applicability of various curriculum constructs to a particular student's characteristics and needs including age appropriateness, severity of condition, parent and student expectations, present level of performance, and reason for referral. Once individual goals are developed, educators must examine general objectives that lead to accomplishing particular goals.

General objectives can best be developed for each goal stipulated under the four areas of special education through a process of brainstorming. Objectives that are brainstormed are later refined and sequenced so that each goal has its individual set of skills to be accomplished. As objectives are defined and sequenced, they are organized within a framework by goals and levels of complexity or priority. This organization results in developing special education curricular maps. Developing general objectives and curricular maps provides a continuum of curriculum skills and more clearly delineates specific instructional directions for all handicapped students.

Selecting appropriate general objectives for individual handicapped students follows investigation of those skills that have been mastered. In order to accomplish this purpose, educators must understand the concept of mastery and be able to observe and recognize behaviors indicative of mastery. This assessment generates those objectives not yet accomplished and allows educators to select the next most important and least complex objectives for immediate instructional intervention. At the conclusion of this assessment, the IEP team must begin to identify short-term instructional objectives that lead to mastering the selected general objectives.

References

Dunn, L. Special education for the mildly retarded—Is much of it justifiable? *Exceptional Children*, 1968, 35:5–22.

Harris, B. M., and Bessent, W. *Inservice education: A guide to better practice.* Englewood Cliffs, N.J.: Prentice-Hall, 1969.

6

Short-Term Instructional Objectives

An additional mandated requirement for the individualized education program is documenting short-term instructional objectives. These objectives are by far the most useful component of the child's IEP for instructional personnel. Short-term instructional objectives represent sets of specific tasks that, if sequenced and presented well, lead to mastering a general objective. Therefore, for each general objective stipulated in any curricular map, it is possible to define a set of short-term instructional objectives that, when accomplished, result in attaining the individual general objective or skill. Each short-term objective contains essentially two components: (1) a behavior and (2) criteria for success. That is, instructional objectives must state a directly observable behavior to be performed by the student and must define the criteria by which one can determine if the student has accomplished that specific task successfully. The criteria often define a number of times, a percentage of correct responses, or situation where application must be observed as it relates to the specific behavior defined as an objective. Only when both criteria and behavior are present can an objective be considered truly a short-term instructional objective.

There are two major purposes to be served by specifying short-term objectives. These purposes are almost impossible to differentiate completely once applied in a classroom. First, short-term instructional objectives provide specific direction for instruction and, second, allow for continuous assessment of reattaining specific skills. Once instructional objectives have been specified in a particular student's written program, educators need only provide appropriate instructional activities and materials in order to have daily classroom planning accomplished. However, it is important to note that the goal of providing direct instruc-

276

tional assistance is not the same as planning daily activities. Instructional activities depend on a given teacher's methods and materials. Instructional objectives do not attempt to dictate these specific aspects of instruction. Methods and materials used may deviate markedly from student to student or class to class but short-term instructional objectives leading to *mastery* of a given general objective will not. In other words, while the approach to mastery may differ, instructional objectives remain the same. Therefore, once sets of instructional objectives have been defined for each general objective, educators can employ them uniformly. Developing comprehensive short-term instructional objectives, then, gives *specific* direction to the daily instruction of all handicapped students.

The second purpose to be accomplished by identifying short-term objectives is to provide a means whereby student progress can be monitored continuously. The mere listing of short-term instructional objectives allows for this type of continuous evaluation. Because criteria for success are an inherent part of the objective, there is no question as to when an objective has been accomplished. In addition, short-term instructional objectives provide a basis whereby educators may easily construct and administer teacher-made criterion tests. However, most often special instruments do not need to be devised since the process of instruction itself creates evaluative data for a keen observer. The only important thing for educators to keep in mind during the construction of instructional objectives is to develop the list of objectives in a format that encourages the automatic recording of progress. Sample formats are shown later in this chapter.

In order to develop and use to their fullest potential appropriate short-term instructional objectives, educators must become fully acquainted with several processes: (1) the ways in which to consider the concept of mastery, (2) the major characteristics of appropriately designed objectives, and (3) the actual construction of instructional objectives from a given general objective, with sample formats and objectives in each area of special education. Since the pervasive goal of developing short-term objectives is to guide a student to mastery of any general objective through instruction, educators must be aware of the ways in which the concept of mastery may be approached. The following section is devoted to this topic.

MASTERY AS A CONCEPT

The concept of mastery in education means to have command of or to have acquired a specified skill. With regard to short-term instructional objectives, mastery can be defined as performing a set of behaviors that are indicative of attaining a general objective or skill. There are three primary ways in which progress toward mastery has been applied to education; these include (1) a well-defined taxonomy of educational objectives, (2) task analysis, and (3) cue reduction. The taxonomy of educational objectives defines an ideal classification system for objectives leading to mastery of intellectual, psychomotor, and affective domains. This hierarchical classification system moves students along a continuum from concrete, simple, external behaviors to more complex, abstract, internalized ones. Task analysis is the process of breaking an objective down into subtasks. These subtasks represent single behaviors that, when sequenced as steps, result in performing given objectives. The concept of cue reduction can be defined as the initial performance of a behavior or set of behaviors with assistance. As indicated by the term itself, this assistance is reduced gradually, finally leaving the entire performance of the behavior to the child him/herself. Each of these three ways of conceptualizing steps to mastery is examined in the following section so that either one or several may be considered when actually constructing short-term instructional objectives.

Taxonomy of Educational Objectives

Bloom (1956) and Krathwohl, Bloom, and Masia (1964) outlined a strategy for developing educational objectives that would gradually lead to mastery. The first published taxonomy dealt with the cognitive domain. Its hierarchy goes from requiring the student to perform behaviors involving rote recall to behaviors demanding complex manipulation, sequencing, and combining of materials and information in order to solve problems. The taxonomy of objectives in the cognitive domain, then, defined the major categories or steps to mastery as:

1. *Knowledge objectives*—require retention of previously presented information, that is, memory and recall.
2. *Comprehension objectives*—demand the student perform behaviors that indicate his/her understanding of the meaning of acquired information.
3. *Application objectives*—require behaviors in which learned material is applied to new situations.
4. *Synthesis objectives*—students must put previously learned information together in new ways to form a new whole.
5. *Evaluation objectives*—demand students be able to perform behaviors whereby information or materials are judged.

278

This classification of objectives demonstrates an inherent increase in task complexity. With regard to specific behaviors that may be defined under each of the five categories of objectives toward mastery of cognitive objectives, Gronlund (1970) provided examples of how each level could be operationalized into behaviors (see Table 6–1). Being able to transform these concepts into behaviors that lead to mastery of a given objective is extremely important when beginning to construct short-term instructional objectives. The reader should note that any of the behaviors listed in the second column of Table 6–1, e.g., states, predicts, diagrams, categorizes, or explains, are appropriate for the stated behavior in short-term objectives.

The taxonomy of educational objectives for the affective domain has been categorized by Krathwohl et al. (1964). These objectives emphasize feelings, emotions, or degrees of acceptance or rejection. The progression toward mastery is particularly important when developing short-term instructional objectives for sociobehavioral education. The five categories involved in mastering affective objectives include:

1. *Receiving (attending) objectives*—require the student to perform behaviors indicative of his/her sensitization to the existence of certain phenomena.

2. *Responding objectives*—demand students exhibit behaviors indicative of an active willingness to commit him/herself to an objective.

3. *Valuing objectives*—require students exhibit behaviors that demonstrate that a thing, phenomenon, or behavior has worth.

4. *Organization objectives*—suggest that the students are able to systematize their own values and demonstrate behaviors that indicate the student has established relationships between and priorities among certain values.

5. *Characterization objectives*—demand the student's values be so internalized regarding certain things, situations, and phenomena that these things no longer arouse emotion when presented; the student merely behaves accordingly.

Behaviors defined for each of the classifications defined above have been outlined by Gronlund (1970) and are shown in Table 6–2.

Although the taxonomy of the psychomotor domain is still under development, Gronlund (1970) has developed illustrative objectives and behaviors for the domain involving fine and gross motor movements. These objectives and behaviors are illustrated in Table 6–3.

The taxonomies or hierarchy of objective classification and example

279

TABLE 6–1 Examples of General Instructional Objectives and Behavioral Terms for the Cognitive Domain

	Illustrative General Instructional Objectives	Illustrative Behavioral Terms for Stating Specific Learning Outcomes
Knowledge	Knows common terms Knows specific facts Knows methods and procedures Knows basic concepts Knows principles	Defines, describes, identifies, labels, lists, matches, names, outlines, reproduces, selects, states
Comprehension	Understands facts and principles Interprets verbal material Interprets charts and graphs Translates verbal material to mathematical formulas Estimates future consequences implied in data Justifies methods and procedures	Converts, defends, distinguishes, estimates, explains, extends, generalizes, gives examples, infers, paraphrases, predicts, rewrites, summarizes
Application	Applies concepts and principles to new situations Applies laws and theories to practical situations Solves mathematical problems Constructs charts and graphs Demonstrates correct usage of a method or procedure	Changes, computes, demonstrates, discovers, manipulates, modifies, operates, predicts, prepares, produces, relates, shows, solves, uses
Analysis	Recognizes unstated assumptions Recognizes logical fallacies in reasoning Distinguishes between facts and inferences Evaluates the relevancy of data Analyzes the organizational structure of a work (art, music, writing)	Breaks down, diagrams, differentiates, discriminates, distinguishes, identifies, illustrates, infers, outlines, points out, relates, selects, separates, subdivides
Synthesis	Writes a well organized theme Gives a well organized speech Writes a creative short story (or poem, or music) Proposes a plan for an experiment Integrates learning from different areas into a plan for solving a problem Formulates a new scheme for classifying objects (or events, or ideas)	Categorizes, combines, compiles, composes, creates, devises, designs, explains, generates, modifies, organizes, plans, rearranges, reconstructs, relates, reorganizes, revises, rewrites, summarizes, tells, writes
Evaluation	Judges the logical consistency of written material Judges the adequacy with which conclusions are supported by data Judges the value of a work (art, music, writing) by use of internal criteria Judges the value of a work (art, music, writing) by use of external standards of excellence	Appraises, compares, concludes, contrasts, criticizes, describes, discriminates, explains, justifies, interprets, relates, summarizes, supports

SOURCE: Gronlund, N. E. *Stating behavioral objectives for classroom instruction.* New York: Macmillan, 1970. Used with permission of publisher.

TABLE 6-2   Examples of General Instructional Objectives and Behavioral Terms for the Affective Domain

	Illustrative General Instructional Objectives	*Illustrative Behavioral Terms for Stating Specific Learning Outcomes*
Receiving	Listens attentively Shows awareness of the importance of learning Shows sensitivity to human needs and social problems Accepts differences of race and culture Attends closely to the classroom activities	Asks, chooses, describes, follows, gives, holds, identifies, locates, names, points to, selects, sits erect, replies, uses
Responding	Completes assigned homework Obeys school rules Participates in classroom discussion Completes laboratory work Volunteers for special tasks Shows interest in subject Enjoys helping others	Answers, assists, complies, conforms, discusses, greets, helps, labels, performs, practices, presents, reads, recites, reports, selects, tells, writes
Valuing	Demonstrates belief in the democratic process Appreciates good literature (art or music) Appreciates the role of science (or other subjects) in everyday life Shows concern for the welfare of others Demonstrates problem-solving attitude Demonstrates commitment to social improvement	Completes, describes, differentiates, explains, follows, forms, initiates, invites, joins, justifies, proposes, reads, reports, selects, shares, studies, works
Organization	Recognizes the need for balance between freedom and responsibility in a democracy Recognizes the role of systematic planning in solving problems Accepts responsibility for his own behavior Understands and accepts his own strengths and limitations Formulates a life plan in harmony with his abilities, interests, and beliefs	Adheres, alters, arranges, combines, compares, completes, defends, explains, generalizes, identifies, integrates, modifies, orders, organizes, prepares, relates, synthesizes
Characterization	Displays safety consciousness Demonstrates self-reliance in working independently Practices cooperation in group activities Uses objective approach in problem solving Demonstrates industry, punctuality and self-discipline Maintains good health habits	Acts, discriminates, displays, influences, listens, modifies, performs, practices, proposes, qualifies, questions, revises, serves, solves, uses, verifies

SOURCE: Gronlund, N. E. *Stating behavioral objectives for classroom instruction.* New York: Macmillan, 1970. Used with permission of publisher.

TABLE 6–3   Examples of General Instructional Objectives and Behavioral Terms for the Psychomotor Domain

Taxonomy Categories	Illustrative General Instructional Objectives	Illustrative Behavioral Terms for Stating Specific Learning Outcomes
(Development of categories in this domain is still underway)	Writes smoothly and legibly	Assembles, builds, calibrates, changes, cleans, composes, connects, constructs, corrects, creates, designs, dismantles, drills, fastens, fixes, follows, grinds, grips, hammers, heats, hooks, identifies, locates, makes, manipulates, mends, mixes, nails, paints, sands, saws, sharpens, sets, sews, sketches, starts, stirs, uses, weighs, wraps
	Draws accurate reproduction of a picture (or map, biology specimen, etc.)	
	Sets up laboratory equipment quickly and correctly	
	Types with speed and accuracy	
	Operates a sewing machine skillfully	
	Operates a power saw safely and skillfully	
	Performs skillfully on the violin	
	Performs a dance step correctly	
	Demonstrates skill in driving an automobile	
	Repairs an electric motor quickly and effectively	
	Creates new ways of performing (creative dance, etc.)	

SOURCE: Gronlund, N. E. *Stating behavioral objectives for classroom instruction.* New York: Macmillan, 1970. Used with permission of publisher.

behaviors presented here should assist educators in the appropriate development of short-term instructional objectives. For an extensive treatment of this subject, the reader is referred to Bloom, Hastings, and Madus (1971). It may also be helpful to examine another approach taken to developing instructional steps designed to lead to mastering educational objectives. This second approach to mastery is commonly referred to as task analysis.

Task Analysis

Task analysis is defined as a process whereby a specific skill, that is, general objective, is broken down into small, successive steps that once attained result in mastery of the general objective. This process involves designating sequential steps beginning with the most simple or basic act and gradually increasing the complexity of the behavior required to be performed. The last or resultant behavior is indicative of the way in which educators have defined mastery of a given general objective. In recent years, the task analysis approach has become a fairly common method of designing instruction for the handicapped. The purpose of the task analysis approach is to prevent the learner from experiencing failure by ensuring that each task involves learning only a minute additional element. In other words, each task defined under a given general objective is itself a successive approximation of mastering the objective. Several considerations are important when conducting task analysis of a general objective:

1. Consideration should be given first to the behavior or set of behaviors that constitute mastery.
2. Working backward from the defined set of behaviors, educators must progress toward the most basic or simplest behavior that is a part of the entire objective.
3. The resultant defined set of specific behaviors must be sequenced from simplest to most complex.
4. Each defined specific behavior should require no more than one additional element or behavior to be acquired.
5. One should avoid including irrelevant specific behaviors or tasks.
6. Care should be taken to ensure that tasks are being accumulated so as to result in mastery of the given general objective.

These six considerations are particularly helpful when developing short-term instructional objectives that are appropriate to task analysis. Table 6–4 provides an example of task analysis applied to the general objective of dialing the telephone. The six considerations outlined above may be examined in light of the example.

Factors five and six of those just listed are of particular importance because the efficacy of task analysis has been questioned on the basis that such organization tends merely to emphasize the acquisition of specific and seemingly unrelated subskills within a student's repertoire of behaviors. Opponents of this approach suggest that these subskills are never consolidated or applied by the student in appropriate situations. It may be for this reason that, particularly with very early skills and more severely involved students, the approach to mastering a given general objective should also utilize cue reduction.

TABLE 6–4   Examples of Task Analysis

The task: The learner will be able to dial a given number on a telephone without making errors and without assistance.

Steps in the task:

1. Can recognize numerals 0–9.
2. Can recognize alphabet letters A–Z.
3. Can differentiate between left and right direction.
4. Can pick up receiver and demonstrate how to hold it.
5. Can point to the dial and show how to put fingers in holes.
6. Can point to the stopper.
7. Can turn the dial with his finger until it is stopped by the stopper.
8. Can put his finger in the hole matching a number he is given and move his finger to the stopper (he has dialed one number).
9. Can dial two numbers in proper order when he is given the two numbers.
10. Can dial more and more numbers in the proper order until he has dialed all seven numbers in a given telephone number.
11. Can repeat step 8 while holding the receiver to his ear.
12. Can repeat steps 9 and 10 whole holding the receiver to his ear.
13. Can repeat step 12 going in correct left-to-right order when he is given a written number. (pp. 22–23)

Source: Cartwright, C. A., and Cartwright, G. P. *Developing observation skills.* New York: McGraw-Hill, 1974. Used with permission of publisher.

Cue Reduction

An additional approach to designing instructional objectives that lead to mastery is referred to as cue reduction. Although very similar to task analysis, cue reduction proponents take a somewhat different approach to acquiring skills for mastery. Cue reduction techniques begin with accomplishing all those behaviors defined as mastery for a particular task. The behaviors are performed with extensive assistance from other person(s). This assistance (or cueing) is gradually withdrawn until the student is in fact performing the set of behaviors that constitute mastery independently. The concept of cueing can be considered as a series of prompt(s) set within the continuous performance of a behavior(s). It would be helpful to examine the various kinds of prompts that may be utilized.

Prompts may be either physical, verbal, or nonverbal cues directed to the student to assist in successfully completing a task. Several classes of prompts or cues are given below.

1. Imitation—the student is directly asked to imitate a behavior.
2. Modeling—the student is assisted by first being provided a model executing the task he/she will be asked to perform.

3. Verbal instruction—the student is provided verbal instructions or explanations that assist in task completion.
4. Verbal rehearsal—the student memorizes or repeats verbal instructions that assist him/herself in task completion.
5. Nonverbal instructions—the student is given a signal that he/she understands as a clue as to when or how to respond.
6. Prompting—the first portion of the task is begun by assisting the child directly in performing the behavior.
7. Physical priming—the teacher physically guides the student through movements required to perform a given behavior(s).
8. Emphasis—the student is given clues to his/her response through teacher emphasis on certain aspects of directions, instructions, and presentations.
9. Mnemonics—the student is provided physical or verbal mnemonic devices to assist in performing a behavior.

For further information on applying these methods to instruction, the reader is referred to Becker, Englemann, and Thomas (1975).

The concept of prompting may, in fact, be as applicable to defining the criteria for performing a task as to the behavior itself. Because cues are designed to be faded out gradually, independent accomplishment of a task may be defined as the behavior. Prompts could then be defined as situational criteria for the gradual mastery of an objective. Objectives applied to cue reduction techniques are generally more specific than those objectives defined through task analysis or the taxonomy of objectives to mastery.

There are several ways in which steps to mastery of a given general objective may be defined, that is, by using a taxonomy of objectives, task analysis techniques, or cue reduction approaches. Using these designs can assist educators in the appropriate development of short-term instructional objectives. Each of the approaches defined in the preceding section provides a framework for conceptualizing the steps to *mastery* of a given general objective, that is, the basic purpose for developing short-term instructional objectives. All three approaches seek essentially the same end and vary only slightly in actual practice. Their effects, if any, upon actual differences between sets of short-term objectives are minimal. However, these approaches provide their own distinctive approach to designing instructional objectives for mastery. The reader should find each of the three concepts useful in defining short-term objectives for different kinds of general objectives. It is important to note that usually combinations of these approaches are used and may be most effective. For example, often cue reduction techniques are applied to specific instructional objectives as criteria once task analysis is accomplished. A form of task analysis has also been applied to such areas as literary comprehension and art appreciation. Once each of these concepts of mastery have been examined, educators can begin the actual construction of short-term instructional objectives.

CHARACTERISTICS OF SHORT-TERM INSTRUCTIONAL OBJECTIVES

Well-constructed sets of short-term instructional objectives are essential to providing appropriate education to handicapped children and youth. These sets of objectives should guide classroom instruction in the direct selection of activities for daily intervention strategies. They should also be written in a format conducive to continuous recording of progress. The actual writing of instructional objectives for each general objective in the areas of special education should be the task of educators familiar with the area of concern who have recently had experience working with handicapped youngsters. These professionals invariably hold insights into the (1) behaviors required of children and (2) deviations of the behaviors presented by handicapped youngsters in the various general objectives or skills. This knowledge allows educators to construct series of short-term instructional objectives that have potential problem areas built into the sequence of the objectives. Once again it is recommended that this component of the IEP be designed previous to actually selecting specific short-term objectives for individual students. This preparation undeniably simplifies IEP development to a great extent. Prior to actually presenting sample instructional objectives in each area of special education, the reader should examine a step-by-step approach to the constructing of these objectives. The following sections present an overview of the basic characteristics of instructional objectives necessary to examine prior to actual attempts to construct viable short-term objectives and criteria for success.

There are several characteristics that can be used to identify appropriate short-term instructional objectives. When examining these factors involved in adequate short-term objective development, the reader should obtain a more thorough understanding of the concept and purposes of delineating these objectives in individual education programs. It is for this reason that a discussion of these characteristics is provided as a prelude to developing specific instructional objectives. Dillman and Rahmlow (1972) identified six points, relevant to this discussion, to consider when writing instructional objectives:

286

1. Level of specificity,
2. Principal performance,
3. Overt behavior,
4. Evaluation or performance criteria,
5. Relevant conditions, and
6. Student-directed performance. (p. 5)

In addition to these six characteristics, the following discussion also considers the factors of:

7. Length of time involved, and
8. Applicability to various methods and materials.

Each of these characteristics influences the development of appropriate short-term instructional objectives and is examined below.

Levels of Specificity

Levels of specificity is the characteristic of instructional objectives that assures the task developed is meaningful. In order to check a short-term objective for the level of specificity, Dillman and Rahmlow (1972) suggest the question be asked—Is the stated objective too broad or too specific to carry meaning? Short-term instructional objectives that are too broad appear more like the general objectives or annual goals discussed previously. Examples of objectives stated too broadly would include the following:

- Rich will improve his *attention.* (an annual goal)
- Rich will improve his ability to *attend to seatwork assignments.* (a general objective)

An appropriate short-term objective might be

- Rich will *focus his eyes upon seatwork* for 75 percent of the given assignment time.

Another problem associated with levels of specificity can be that the objective defined is stated too specifically or narrowly. This occurrence takes away the flexibility of instructional staff to use their own methods and materials for the actual activity of instruction. Examples of objectives written too narrowly are given below followed by an appropriate short-term instructional objective.

- Greg will *circle* all first words in a sentence.
- Greg will be able to *identify* first words in a sentence.
- Jon will *point to* a picture representing the value of honesty.
- Jon will *recognize* an act representative of the value of honesty.
- Lee will *stack pictures* of persons on the job into three occupational clusters.
- Lee will be able to *categorize* pictures of various jobs into appropriate clusters.

The characteristic of maintaining appropriate levels of specificity is a difficult task to accomplish when creating short-term instructional objectives. Nonetheless, it is important to keep in mind.

Principal Performance

An instructional objective should state clearly exactly what performance is the principal behavior desired (Dillman and Rahmlow, 1972). The behavior that is the purpose of the objective must be stated. Other behaviors may be applicable to certain activities but generally only "indicate" the actual desired behavior. This consideration of instructional objectives is closely related to the error of stating an objective too specifically. Consider the following examples.

1. Anne will *draw* a picture of a cat when shown the word cat.
2. George will *sing* the alphabet song.
3. Sue will *color* pictures of jobs she might enjoy.

The behaviors stated here—draw, sing, and color—do not appear to be the principal performance behaviors desired. Objective number 1 may mean Anne can *give an example* that demonstrates that she understands the letters c-a-t as a word or object. Objective number 2 may be more appropriate if George were asked to *recite* the alphabet and Sue might *select* jobs she would enjoy. In this way the principal behavior of concern is named without having to state a series of activities or indicator behaviors. Generally, these are left to the discretion of the individual educator.

Overt Behavior

An important factor to remember in writing short-term instructional objectives is that each behavior defined in the written objective must be overt. That is, the behavior described must be observable. This is the primary characteristic that differentiates instructional objectives from general objectives and annual goals. Verbs such as "know," "understand," and "comprehend" must be avoided. The verb used to state a behavior must be an action verb capable of being directly observed without further explanation. Examples of objectives constructed without stating overt behaviors are given below, followed by an adequate correction.

- Jane will *know* how to take turns.
- Rick will *appreciate* music class.
- Brian will *understand* the uses of a fork.

- Jane will *wait* until her turn in line.
- Rick will *tell* the music teacher thank you.
- Brian will *use* the fork to eat fruits, vegetables, and soft meats.

Defining overt behaviors assists instructional personnel in determining what is acceptable and leads to structuring situations that elicit the desired behavior.

Evaluation of Performance Criteria

An additional characteristic, as well as a component of each short-term instructional objective, is the statement of criteria. The criteria define the performance of an overt behavior according to how or when it is to be considered successful. Dillman and Rahmlow (1972) suggest that criteria are most important to include for open-ended objectives such as—the student will write a paragraph about the field trip. Unless criteria for successful accomplishment of the task are established, mastery will be an extremely subjective proposition. Several ways in which criteria could be applied to the above example include:

- Jim will write a paragraph about the field trip consisting of at least *three complete sentences.*
- Beth will write a paragraph about the field trip *in 30 minutes or less,* or
- Becky will write a paragraph about the field trip that will *contain at least three things observed.*

Because of the importance of stating appropriate criteria as a component or characteristic of instructional objectives, an entire section is devoted to the topic at a later time.

Relevant Conditions

Conditions that are important to specify in order for a behavior to be performed successfully is another characteristic of short-term instructional objectives that may also be considered a component. This is a particularly important characteristic to remember if material aids or cues are to be provided in accomplishing the objective behavior. Examples of short-term objectives where describing relevant conditions is essential are given below.

- Donald will add two one-digit numbers *with the aid of the number line.*
- Virginia will be able to say her name and parent's phone number *when asked by a stranger.*
- Harold will be able to put on his shirt *without any assistance at home.*

In many instances, relevant conditions are either obvious from the stated behavior or not important to delineate separately. However, when conditions are relevant to the objective, this too becomes a component as well as a characteristic of instructional objectives. A more detailed discussion of applying relevant conditions to instructional objectives follows in a later section.

Student-Directed Performance

Instructional objectives derived from general objectives are directed at the student's ability to perform a task. Therefore, short-term objectives should state observable behaviors that the student is asked to perform as opposed to those performed by the teacher in instruction. Teacher-directed instructional objectives would state specific activities and methods used by the educator him/herself. These activities are inappropriate to define within an individual student's education program document.

Length of Time Involved

An interesting characteristic of short-term instructional objectives is the variance that can be noted in both the amount of time involved in acquiring one instructional objective and in acquiring a set of short-term objectives. The phrase "short-term" is less descriptive than the phrase "instructional objectives." The adjective short-term can be misleading unless the educator is aware of the possibility of time variance. The following set of instructional objectives exemplifies the time-related characteristic.

General objective: Capitalization of first word in a sentence.
Short-term instructional objectives:
1. Student can recognize first words in given sentences.
2. Student identifies errors in capitalization of first words in given sentences.
3. Student corrects errors in given sentences.
4. Student capitalizes first words in dictated sentences.
5. Student automatically capitalizes first words of original sentences.

Although none of the individual objectives listed above, with the possible exception of #4, appear to be extremely lengthy, the progression from #1 to #5 may in fact require years to accomplish. While objectives 1 to 3 can possibly be instructed in a single year or less, objective 4 cannot be accomplished until the student has developed a repertoire of words that he/she can spell. Objective 5 will not be possible before the student actually begins to construct original sentences. The importance of outlining each instructional objective becomes painfully apparent when we consider that most standardized tests and regular classroom materials assume mastery at the second and no later than third objective. Unfortunately, accomplishing the third objective may occur several years before attaining the fifth.

Applicability to Methods and Materials

A last characteristic of well-constructed, short-term instructional objectives is that they should lead the teacher directly to selecting appropriate methods and materials. However, whenever possible, specific materials should not be stated within the context of the instructional objective. There would be some objectives, however, that deal directly with the ability to utilize specific materials, such as an abacus, number lines, specific on-the-job tools, or prosthetic devices. In these instances, objectives must contain the use of materials to expedite instructional planning.

With regard to educational methods for instruction, it is often more difficult to avoid indicating specific teaching techniques when delineating short-term instructional objectives. This, too, should be avoided if possible. While one can avoid dictating "the child will circle . . ." by utilizing the objective "the child will identify . . . ," it is often more difficult to prevent overselecting very basic methodologies over others. The

291

mere delineation of specific discrete behaviors that lead to skill mastery appears to favor a skills-oriented and task-analysis approach to instruction. However, delineating specific skills can be used as merely an assessment tool when methods are applied that do not conform to the stated sequence of short-term instructional objectives. For example, there are basically three different approaches to reading instruction—language experience, phonics, and linguistics. Language experience approaches emphasize the child's own oral and/or written language to develop reading skills. The child may dictate or write a story to be used in his/her reading instruction. Phonics approaches emphasize acquiring sound-symbol relationships and blending sounds to form the *given* word presented to the child for reading. Methods referred to as linguistic reading approaches present grapheme (letter) combinations to the child for memorization and application to other similar combinations. Now consider the following short-term instructional objectives:

Consonant Digraphs—the student will be able to read with 90% accuracy:	*Recognizes and Can Name*	*Write from Dictation*	*Uses Word in Original Sentences*
1. Words with ch-v-c			
2. Words with sh-v-c			
3. Words with th-v-c			
4. Words with wh-v-c			
5. Words with c-v-sh			
6. Words with c-v-ch			
7. Words with c-v-th			
8. Words with sh-v-c-v			
9. Words with ch-v-c-v			

Each of the objectives might be taught directly in either a phonic or linguistic approach. Phonic instruction would emphasize the sound blends aspects of the consonant digraphs, short or long vowels, and other consonants. Linguistic instruction would present various words time and again in various activities that were identical in structure to those outlined above. Therefore, although the particular *instructional activities* for these two *methods* might differ to a great extent, short-term objectives would be identical. The activities involved in instructing a student through the language experience method of teaching reading would differ to an even greater extent. In fact, instructional activities may never be designed specifically toward the skill acquisition of being able to read or write consonant-vowel-consonant digraph words. Nevertheless, consonant-vowel-consonant digraph words do exist and must be read and understood. In this particular method, however, the short-term instructional objective guides the teacher more in assessing the child's performance during language experience–reading activities than in structuring activities. This format of listing specific word combination skills would still be of much utility in organizing a structure for diagnosing particular problem areas. In this way a teacher using the language experience methods is still tuned into the various ways of organizing written language to be read or written by the child. Therefore, when developing short-term instructional objectives, every attempt should be made to avoid the specificity that would dictate actual method of instruction. This is particularly true when school districts or agencies attempt to develop short-term objectives for all general objectives and annual goals. Otherwise, specifying the method in the actual objectives prevents its being adequately flexible to meet various handicapped student's needs.

Essentially the same phenomena exist when considering such things as methods of decreasing socially inappropriate behaviors. Both the behavior and criteria should indicate steps to extinguish a given behavior; however, methods of reinforcement should not be dictated except as individual children are considered. Therefore, to avoid including methodology in stating short-term instructional objectives for sociobehavioral education, attempts should be made to state the objectives by increasing the criteria for success. That is, negative behaviors should be stated and the criteria (duration, frequency, and intensity) lowered gradually. In this manner the method will be determined by the individual educators concerned with a particular student rather than dictated in the curriculum.

One last example of avoiding including methods can be examined in the area of self-help/basic living skills. For instance, although short-term instructional objectives for the general objective of washing hands may be stated as below (without criteria included), the method of instruction is not.

1. Shows interest in playing in the water; permits hands to be washed and dried
2. Shows interest in faucet and stopper
3. Locates sink
4. Locates faucet
5. Turns water on

6. Wets one hand
7. Wets both hands
8. Locates soap
9. Gets soap on hands
10. Rubs soap on hands
11. Rinses hands
12. Locates faucet
13. Turns water off
14. Locates towel
15. Takes towel
16. Dries hands
17. Locates waste basket
18. Washes and dries hands and throws towel away or hangs it up

These eighteen steps may be instructed through cue reduction beginning with performing the final completed task each time in its entirety, or by a task analysis approach in which the objectives can be used successively. Even though the complete task is accomplished during each instructional lesson, cue reduction would still require the child to gradually perform one or more of the tasks independently. Task analysis methods may attempt to teach each skill separately. Of course, most of the time both methods are employed. In any event, the short-term instructional objectives should be written so that there is a progression or accumulation of behaviors toward mastery that would assist educators in the appropriate selection and application of methods and materials. When short-term objectives are being developed for application to a large group of students, it is essential to avoid specific mention of methods and materials. The following section presents a consolidated, step-by-step approach to developing short-term instructional objectives in the various areas of special education.

CONSTRUCTING SHORT-TERM INSTRUCTIONAL OBJECTIVES

There are three major components of short-term instructional objectives that must be designed while constructing specific objectives: the behavior, any relevant conditions, and the criteria for success. While a behavior and criteria for success are essential elements, there are only certain circumstances that require delineation of relevant conditions. One can remember from the previous discussion that the stated behavior must be overt, that is, observable without further explanation and not so specific as to dictate teaching method. The criteria states the frequency or duration of a behavior that must be observed before considering the objective accomplished. Relevant conditions must be stated when mastery involves using certain aids or accomplishment under certain situations, for example, time limits and locations. The step-by-step development of each of these elements will be discussed below. To provide the reader a broad perspective with regard to the various areas of special education that need to be addressed, the discussion follows the development of appropriate short-term instructional objectives for four dissimilar general objectives. These four general objectives, selected from each area of special education, include:

1. Adding two one-digit numerals. (Academic—Math—Operations)
2. Hair care. (Self-Help/Basic Living—Personal Skills—Grooming)
3. Eye contact. (Sociobehavioral—Undesirable Behaviors—Disassociation)
4. Using local public employment agency. (Career/Vocational—Occupational Application—Job Search)

The actual construction of short-term instructional objectives begins with the selection of general objectives such as those just listed. The process of instructional objective development entails (1) developing an instructional objective indicative of mastery, (2) delineating steps from mastery back to a level of little or no proficiency, and (3) refining any content problems that may be noted after the delineation of a given set of short-term instructional objectives, and (4) developing a format for simplified recording. Each of these steps is discussed below in light of the above discussions and the four selected general objectives.

Defining Mastery

The first step in developing a set of short-term instructional objectives for a given general objective is to define what behavior(s), relevant condition(s), and criteria indicate mastery of the general objective. This statement of mastery forms the last or final short-term instructional objective. Educators should keep in mind the concepts of mastery that deal with the student's ability to (1) apply a skill to his/her own life or circumstances, (2) perform a skill without assistance, and (3) consolidate several discrete behaviors into one act in order to perform a skill. These points are essential to the definition of mastery. Let us consider each of the specified general objectives in light of mastery.

Adding two one-digit numerals. Let us assume that the ultimate ability in this objective is determined by the student's ability to perform in the regular classroom math class. One must then be cognizant of the kinds of behaviors necessary for successful completion of this task within the regular classroom curriculum. These considerations, as well as relevant issues uncovered during general objective brainstorming, lead us to several conclusions. First, the student needs to be able to add many combinations of one-digit numerals at one time on a given page. Answers need to be recorded in writing and meet some set percentage of correctness. In addition, the student should be asked to record answers to problems given in both vertical and horizontal forms. Therefore, with these considerations in mind an appropriate final short-term instructional objective would be:

> The student will add and record, in writing, answers to 25 addition problems given in horizontal or vertical form in 30 minutes with 90 percent accuracy.

Because of the large number of relevant conditions to consider if the child is to be placed in the regular classroom math program, this last objective becomes rather lengthy.

Hair care. Appropriate hair grooming is an essential skill in normalizing handicapped children and increases their acceptance in many social situations. In the instance of hair care, the short-term instructional objective defining mastery must delineate the entire *set* of behaviors, criteria, and any relevant conditions necessary to care for one's hair. Criteria in this instance probably deal with the frequency of hair care. The only relevant condition is that the student eventually accomplish the task independently without direct assistance or prompting. An appropriate final objective might be stated as:

> The student will wash, set, dry, and style hair, independently, twice weekly.

Stipulating several discrete behaviors that result in one act is not an uncommon occurrence in final instructional objectives, particularly in the areas of self-help/basic living and career/vocational education. The general objectives defined for these areas frequently require the accumulation of several discrete behaviors into one act.

Eye contact. A general objective in sociobehavioral education that is frequently selected for development with handicapped children is eye contact. In defining mastery of the ability to maintain eye contact, one must consider the behavior, duration, and additional situational conditions. For instance, one may consider eye contact important "during conversation," "with superiors," "with peers," and so on. In selecting mastery, these kinds of situations must be examined and the most difficult combination of situations selected as the final instructional objective. An appropriate short-term instructional objective for mastery might be:

> The student maintains eye contact during a conversation with a stranger, 50 percent of the time when other person is speaking and 50 percent of the time when the student is speaking.

These kinds of relevant conditions serve to direct educational attention to potential problem areas such as eye contact when speaking or spoken to. The percentage of time allows flexibility so that the objective may be applicable to a number of situations.

Using local public employment agencies. The ability to use local public employment agencies is particularly important to many handicapped students. In order to define mastery, an overt behavior(s), relevant condition(s), and criteria for success must be stated. Once again, we find a general objective that is actually an accumulation of several behaviors. The condition is, in fact, stated in the objective when the agency is delineated. Criteria for success may be merely accomplishing the task independently once. One way of stating an appropriate short-term instructional objective is given below.

> The student will locate a local public employment agency, set up an appointment, an interview, apply, and follow up, independently.

When delineating actual behaviors for preceding steps to mastery of this act, we find several discrete behaviors necessary for "locate," "interview," and "apply." Many of these specific behaviors are also treated individually in other aspects of career/vocational education and can be, themselves, considered objectives to an end.

Steps to Mastery

The second step in constructing appropriate short-term instructional objectives involves stating (1) a beginning behavior and criteria that initiate instruction in a given general objective, and (2) the intermediate steps leading to mastery, as stated above. The statement of initial behavior and criteria form the first in the series of instructional objectives for a given general objective. Here again, relevant conditions may need to be stated. Constructing subsequent instructional objectives is facilitated by the existence of the first and last objectives. These objectives too must be consistent with the characteristics specified previously. The following sections present initial and subsequent instructional objectives that lead to mastery of the general objective, that is, the final short-term instructional objective delineated above.

Adding two one-digit numerals. In attempting to determine the initial behavior for the skill of adding two one-digit numbers, one must consider those relevant conditions and criteria stated in the instructional objective denoting mastery, that is, recording in writing, 25 answers, horizontally and vertically, in 30 minutes, with 90 percent accuracy. One may wish to maintain the 90 to 100 percent accuracy criteria throughout all subsequent objectives to ensure that each instructional objective is accomplished successfully. The following objectives are listed sequentially from simplest to most complex. The student will add and record with 90 to 100 percent accuracy:

1. Two one-digit numerals, sums less than 10, listed vertically (15 per page).
2. Two one-digit numerals, sums less than 10, listed vertically (10 per page).
3. Two one-digit numerals, sums less than 19, listed vertically (5 per page).
4. Two one-digit numerals, sums less than 19, listed vertically (10 per page).
5. Two one-digit numerals, listed vertically, 15 per page in 30 minutes.
6. Two one-digit numerals, listed vertically, 20 per page in 30 minutes.
7. Two one-digit numerals, listed horizontally (5 per page).
8. Two one-digit numerals, listed horizontally (10 per page).
9. Two one-digit numerals, listed vertically and horizontally, 10 per page in 30 minutes.
10. Two one-digit numerals, listed vertically and horizontally, 20 per page, in 30 minutes.
11. Two one-digit numerals, listed vertically and horizontally, 25 per page, in 30 minutes.

An additional dimension that may be added later in developing a format for recording would be stipulating any aids or assistance given the student. Mastery would be the last objective accomplished without assistance.

Hair care. Because the final objective for care of one's hair stated several discrete behaviors, initial and subsequent objectives must develop each of these behaviors. In addition, the condition for mastery included accomplished each task independently; therefore, in stating other behaviors assistance may need to be withdrawn gradually. The stated criteria of twice weekly probably would not be applicable to all subsequent instructional objectives listed for the general objective of hair care. The following sequence of short-term instructional objectives takes these considerations into account. The student will:

1. Use comb and brush on others
2. Admire own hair when groomed
3. Comb (brush) hair down on sides
4. Comb (brush) hair down in back
5. Comb (brush) hair, voluntarily, once per day
6. Comb (brush) hair, voluntarily, twice per day
7. Comb (brush) hair, voluntarily, three times daily
8. Clean out brush with comb
9. Take off clips, bands, pins, etc.
10. Wash hair with assistance
11. Wash hair by self
12. Dry hair with blow dryer
13. Wash and dry hair
14. Roll and dry hair
15. Wash, set, dry, and style hair, with assistance, twice weekly
16. Wash, set, dry, and style hair, independently, twice weekly

The reader should note that each discrete behavior has been delineated separately as well as in combined form.

Eye contact. Developing eye contact with handicapped youngsters is often a very slow proposition. Sequences of objectives center primarily upon the slow progression of contact duration. In addition, it must be considered that achieving and maintaining eye contact with a familiar person is a simpler task than with a stranger. Many times developing such skills requires extensive reinforcement strategies. These strategies, representing specific instructional methods, may be added to individual children's programs, when needed. The following sequence is representative of appropriate short-term instructional objectives for developing eye contact.

With a familiar adult, the student will

1. Glance at face
2. Glance at face, several times, during conversation
3. Glance at eyes, several times, during conversation
4. Look at eyes for 2 to 3 consecutive seconds, during conversation
5. Look at eyes for 5 seconds at a time
6. Maintain eye contact 10 percent of the time involved in conversation
7. Maintain eye contact 25 percent of the time when spoken to and 25 percent of time when speaking
8. Maintain eye contact 50 percent of time when speaking and spoken to

With a peer, the student will

9. Glance at face
10. Glance at face, several times, during conversation
11. Glance at eyes, several times, during conversation
12. Look at eyes for 2 to 3 consecutive seconds, during conversation
13. Look at eyes for 5 seconds at a time
14. Maintain eye contact 10 percent of the time involved in conversation
15. Maintain eye contact 25 percent of the time when spoken to and 25 percent of time when speaking
16. Maintain eye contact 50 percent of the time when speaking and spoken to

With a stranger, the student will

17. Glance at face
18. Glance at face, several times, during conversation
19. Glance at eyes, several times, during conversation

20. Look at eyes 2 to 3 consecutive seconds, during conversation
21. Look at eyes for 5 seconds at a time
22. Maintain eye contact 10 percent of the time involved in conversation
23. Maintain eye contact 30 percent of the time when spoken to and 20 percent of time when speaking
24. Maintain eye contact 50 percent of the time when speaking and spoken to

Using local public employment agencies. In order to state the initial and subsequent instructional objectives for being able to use a local public employment agency, one must examine each of the discrete behaviors necessary to accumulate. These behaviors must then be sequenced from simplest to most complex. Once again relevant conditions must be stated and criteria where appropriate. A suggested sequence of objectives is provided below.

The student will:

1. Locate the local public employment agency in the phone book for six different cities and towns ranging in size from 3,000 to 1,000,000 populations.
2. Call the appropriate number and set an appointment.
3. Locate appropriate public or private transportation.
4. Dress appropriately.
5. Utilize transportation system to arrive on time.
6. Ask directions to find appropriate interviewer.
7. Complete interview.
8. Obtain needed forms.
9. Complete necessary forms or applications.
10. Return forms.
11. Respond to further interactions by using the above skills.
12. Be able to locate the local public employment agency, set an appointment, an interview, apply, and follow up, independently.

This same sequence of steps may be followed for vocational rehabilitation services, private agencies, and so on. Just completing necessary forms contains a series of short-term instructional objectives under a previous general objective in career/vocational education. Obviously this particular general objective calls for coordinating and applying many previously stated objectives.

Once an appropriate sequence of short-term instructional objectives has been established, educators must develop a format in order to use the objectives most efficiently. This format must also be applicable to simplified transfer into an individual student's programs. The following section is designed to present several formats that may be utilized in generating viable options for recording short-term instructional objectives.

SAMPLE FORMATS FOR ORGANIZING INSTRUCTIONAL OBJECTIVES

Two considerations must be taken into account when delineating short-term instructional objectives. First, one must determine the way in which the sequential listing of skills can be simplified into a checklist format. Second, educators must determine the manner in which to record short-term instructional objectives along with annual goals and general objectives in each individual education program. There are several ways in which the listing of objectives can be simplified into a checklist format. The added component of the column for marking objectives when accomplished often allows for condensing criteria or relevant conditions. Examples are given below utilizing the objectives delineated above.

Adding Two One-Digit Numerals

The student will add and record written answers with 90–100% accuracy to problems that utilize:

Objective	5 per page	10 per page	20 per page	25 per page
1. Two one-digit numerals, sums less than 10, vertically arranged				
2. Two one-digit numerals, sums less than 19, vertically arranged				
3. Two one-digit numerals, sums less than 10, horizontally arranged				
4. Two one-digit numerals, sums less than 19, horizontally arranged				
5. Two one-digit numerals, sums less than 19, arranged both horizontally and vertically				

Note to teacher: Initial and date as each objective is accomplished and proceed to appropriate next step.

The reader should note that the starred objective above denotes mastery and that there can be as many as 20 instructional objectives in this series. The format here allows for continuous recording as well as directing instruction. Another example of an instance where pertinent conditions can be used to form a checklist follows.

Hair Care				
The student will be able to:	*With Verbal and Physical Assistance*	*With Verbal Assistance*	*With Prompting*	*Independently*
1. Use comb and brush on others				
2. Admire own hair when groomed				
3. Comb (brush) hair down on sides				
4. Comb (brush) hair down in back				
5. Comb (brush) hair once per day				
6. Comb (brush) hair twice per day				
7. Comb (brush) hair three times daily				
8. Clean out brush with comb				
9. Take off clips, bands, pins, etc.				
10. Wash hair				
11. Dry hair with blow dryer				
12. Wash and dry hair				
13. Roll and dry hair				
14. Wash, set, dry, and style hair, twice weekly				

Note to Teacher: Date and initial as objective is accomplished.

The relevant condition utilized in the checklist above involves the cue reduction technique where a skill is taught through the gradual elimination of assistance. Mastery, again, would be accomplished when lower right hand box is initialed and dated. The following two examples are similar in format and each will simplify the delineation of short-term instructional objectives.

Eye Contact			
The student will:	*With Familiar Adult*	*With Peer*	*With Stranger*
1. Glance at face			
2. Glance at face several times during conversation			
3. Glance at eyes several times during conversation			
4. Look at eyes for 2–3 consecutive seconds during conversation			
5. Look at eyes for 5 seconds at a time			
6. Maintain eye contact 10% of the time involved in conversation			
7. Maintain eye contact 25% of the time when spoken to and 25% of time when speaking			
8. Maintain eye contact 50% of time when speaking and spoken to			

Using Local Public Employment Agencies		
The student will:	*With Assistance*	*Without Assistance*
1. Locate the local public employment agency in the phone book for six different cities and towns ranging in size from 3,000 to 1,000,000 population		
2. Call the appropriate number and set an appointment		
3. Locate appropriate public or private transportation		
4. Dress appropriately		
5. Utilize transportation system to arrive on time		
6. Ask directions to find appropriate interviewer		

(*continued*)

The student will:	*With Assistance*	*Without Assistance*
7. Complete interview		
8. Obtain needed forms		
9. Complete necessary forms or applications		
10. Return forms		
11. Respond to further interactions by using above skills		
12. Be able to locate the local employment agency, set an appointment, an interview, apply, and follow up, independently		

TABLE 6–5 Alternative Format for Recording Annual Goals, General Objectives, and Short-Term Instructional Objectives

Special education area: _____

_____

Performance area: _____

Annual goal: _____

General objective #1 _____

Short-term instructional objective A

1.
2.
3.
4.
5.
6.
7.

Short-term instructional objective B

1.
2.
3.
4.
5.

General objective #2 _____

Short-term instructional objective A

1.
2.

Once short-term instructional objectives have been developed and organized in an appropriate and efficient format, the IEP team concerned with particular students must delineate specific sets of instructional objectives within the IEP document. It is recommended that, for each area of special education from which appropriate annual goals and objectives are selected, a separate section of the IEP be developed. This format would delineate each annual goal followed by general and short-term objectives. In many instances this may require several pages. *However, if general and instructional objectives have been determined previously, it is possible to merely duplicate the appropriate materials.* That is, pages in an appropriate curriculum document can be merely referred to in the IEP. A sample page of the IEP document containing annual goals and general and short-term objectives is shown in Table 6–5.

SUMMARY

An important instructional component that must be included in each individualized education program is the delineation of short-term instructional objectives. These objectives underlie attaining each general objective selected for instruction. This element of the IEP serves to give specific direction to the education of handicapped children. Appropriate delineation of short-term instructional objectives aids educators providing appropriate instructional activities and materials selection. In addition to guiding instructional personnel in developing activities and materials, appropriate development of short-term instructional objectives provides a structure for continuous monitoring of pupil progress.

In beginning the process of developing instructional objectives educators must first examine the various ways in which the concept of mastery in education is conceptualized. Taxonomies that characterize objectives according to the level of mastery required have been developed. These are helpful to educators when developing final instructional objectives. Task analysis is a procedure by which some educators define a sequence of steps to mastery of an objective. An additional process used to guide instructional activities is cue reduction. Cue reduction is a process through which assistance to the student in accomplishing a task is gradually withdrawn. With these concepts in mind, educators can begin actual construction of short-term instructional objectives. This process involves: (1) defining a behavior, criteria, and relevant conditions for mastery, (2) delineating sequential objectives leading to the final objective, and (3) developing an appropriate format. Delineating appropriate objectives in proper formats undeniably simplifies instructing the handicapped child, as well as the IEP development.

References

Becker, W. C.; Englemann, S.; and Thomas, D. R. *Teaching 2: Cognitive learning and instruction.* Chicago: Science Research Associates, 1975.

Bloom, B. S. (ed.) *Taxonomy of educational objectives: The classification of educational goals. Handbook 1. Cognitive domain.* New York: McKay, 1956.

Bloom, B. S.; Hastings, J. T.; and Madus, G. F. *Handbook and formative and summative evaluation of student learning.* New York: McGraw-Hill, 1971.

Cartwright, C. A., and Cartwright, G. P. *Developing observation skills.* New York: McGraw-Hill, 1974.

Dillman, C. M., and Rahmlow, H. P. *Writing instructional objectives.* Belmont, Calif.: Lear Siegler, Inc./Fearon Publishers, 1972.

Gronlund, N. E. *Measurement and evaluation in teaching.* New York: Macmillan, 1971.

Krathwohl, D. R.; Bloom, B. S.; and Masia, B. B. *Taxonomy of educational objectives: The classification of educational goals. Handbook 2. Affective domain.* New York: McKay, 1964.

7

Educational Services

Selecting the most appropriate educational services to be afforded the handicapped child is developed in conjunction with the statement of the child's present levels of educational performance, annual goals, general objectives, and short-term instructional objectives. The educational services delineated for a given child are predicated upon these goals and objectives and his/her age, severity and type of handicap, and the various related factors that negatively influence the disability. Whatever services are provided to the disabled youngster, they must permit the child to be educated to the maximum extent appropriate with children who are not handicapped or less handicapped. In order to plan and implement educational services for handicapped youngsters, it is necessary to become thoroughly conversant with the rules and regulations governing the concepts of *special education, related services,* and *least-restrictive environment.* In addition, policies of the state and local school systems as well as available educational placements must be explored. The purpose of this chapter is to define and discuss each of these aspects of the individualized educational program. The projected dates for initiation and duration of the services provided the handicapped child are also addressed.

SPECIAL EDUCATION

The concept of special education is central to the individualized education program. This is particularly true in light of the fact that the child cannot be considered handicapped unless he/she needs the services provided in special education. In addition, the definition of "related services" depends upon the need for special education in that a related service must be necessary in order for a youngster to benefit from a special education placement. Consequently, if a child is not judged to be handicapped to the degree that special education is needed, no related services are required, at least under the structure provided by PL 94–142. Under the rules and regulations governing PL 94–142, special education means

Specially designed instruction, at no cost to the parents, to meet the unique needs of a handicapped child; including classroom instruction, instruction in physical education, home instruction, and instruction in hospitals and institutions. (Implementation of Part B of the Education of the Handicapped, 1977, p. 42480)

The term "special education" also includes speech pathology and special vocational education if these services consist of specially designed instruction, at no cost to the parents, to meet the unique needs of a handicapped child. The phrase "at no cost" is interpreted to mean that the special and/or related services are made available free of charge. Only those incidental fees that are normally charged to non-handicapped students or their parents as a part of the regular education program may also be charged to the handicapped person or his/her legal guardians.

Repeatedly throughout discussion regarding special education, the phrase "specially designed instruction" is used to denote the type and quality of education to be provided the handicapped child. Specially designed instruction refers to those statements of annual goals, general objectives, short-term instructional objectives, and special services that have been devised to attenuate the disabilities exhibited by the handicapped youngster. Implementing these goals and objectives through the most appropriate placements constitutes special education. Chapters 5 and 6 have defined and outlined annual goals, general objectives, and short-term instructional objectives in the areas of self-help/basic living, academic, career/vocational, and sociobehavioral. If carried out in appropriate instructional arrangements, these educational strategies most certainly represent *specially designed instruction.*

It is important to note that not only must a public agency devise, initiate, and maintain special instructional arrangements or services to meet the unique needs of the handicapped child, but also must *document* the extent to which the child is able to participate in regular education programs. The concept that the interests of handicapped youngsters are best served by being educated with normal children whenever possible has been termed *least-restrictive environment.* It is axiomatic that specially designed instruction is of limited benefit unless the culmination of such instruction facilitates the disabled child in leading the most satisfying and productive life possible. To achieve this end, the special instruction provided must be conducted in such a fashion that it allows the child to interact with and experience the "mainstream." In this case, the mainstream means those nonhandicapped children, programs, and settings that constitute regular education. To be most effective, the instructional opportunities afforded handicapped children must permit participation in regular education to the fullest degree possible. The following section discusses the concept of least-restrictive environment and the alternative placements necessary to accommodate the diverse types and severity of handicapping conditions.

Least-Restrictive Environment

Least-restrictive environment is best understood as a process rather than a product. By regarding it as a process, it is possible to consider "least-restrictive environment" as a continuum of alternative educational placements flexible to the degree that *all* handicapped children are educated to the maximum extent appropriate with students who are not handicapped or less severely handicapped. In addition, Section 121a.550 of the rules and regulations governing the implementation of Part B of the Education of the Handicapped Act states

> That special classes, separate schooling or other removal of handicapped children from the regular education environment occurs only when the nature and severity of the handicap is such that education in regular classes with the use of supplementary aids and services cannot be achieved satisfactorily. (p. 42497)

In order to be in compliance with the rules and regulations of PL 94–142 as they relate to the individualized educational program, statements must be made (i.e., documentation) regarding the manner and degree with which the handicapped child will be incorporated into regular education, if at all.

It is important to note that some educators and lay persons have misconceived the real intent of the concept of least-restrictive environment. This misconception seems to center around the belief that *all* handicapped children are to be educated in regular education programs to some extent. This erroneous belief has caused much consternation among many persons, and rightfully so. It is untenable to think that a severely and profoundly retarded person is able to participate meaningfully in the regular classroom regardless of the activity. To try to institute such a placement would undoubtedly be educationally unwise and deprive the youngster of valuable time when instruction could be appropriately directed to his/her unique needs. In some instances, this type of placement would be obviously inappropriate and would result in interactions that would be detrimental to the child's well-being. Obviously, discretion must be exercised when determining the educational placement that best meets the needs of the handicapped child.

To be more specific, the concept of the least-restrictive environment must be employed in such a way that the child is placed in that setting that permits attainment of the stated goals and objectives constituting an appropriate education. If a child is placed in a special day school initially because it has facilities to accommodate the particular needs exhibited by the youngster, it is not implied that he/she *must* participate in regular programming. This would be desirable only if regular education activities provided some assistance in accomplishing the goals and objectives specified in the IEP and if the child were capable of benefiting from the services offered. More likely, a youngster placed in a special day school would be moved gradually to a self-contained classroom placement to interact with children who exhibit less pervasive handicapping conditions. This, of course, would represent a move to a "less-restrictive environment." Only after a series of such placements would the child gradually move to a situation where he/she could participate realistically in regular classroom activities. While the merits of regular education placement should be considered on an individual basis for specific children, educators and parents would be well advised to consider their concept of least-restrictive environment and be sure that the educational needs of handicapped children is the first consideration in determining the most appropriate placement possible.

The specificity with which an IEP team is able to document participation of the handicapped youngster in the least-restrictive environment depends upon the continuum of alternative placements available to the public agency. To a great extent, the responsibilities of the public agency as to the continuum of services that *must be offered to the handicapped* have been already delineated in the rules and regulations interpreting PL 94–142. Explicitly, the service placements required to be afforded the handicapped child include instruction in regular classes, special classes, special schools, home instruction, and instruction in hospitals and institutions. Public agencies must also provide additional services to be administered in conjunction with regular class placement (such as a resource room or itinerant instruction). In reality, the continuum of alternative placements made available by most public agencies includes (from least to most restrictive): (1) regular class placement with special assistance; (2) resource rooms; (3) integrated classrooms;

(4) self-contained classrooms; (5) special day schools; and (6) hospital, home, and residential placement.

The proper interpretation of the least-restrictive environment concept has been amply described elsewhere (Reynolds, 1962; Deno, 1970). In essence, the least-restrictive environment is grounded in the belief that the placements provided handicapped children should be extensive enough to permit an individual to be provided specially designed instruction geared to their unique needs and to be included in as many regular education activities as feasible. It is apparent that the types and severity of the handicapping conditions and the age and relevant educational characteristics of the many and varied disabled children necessitates a wide range of placement alternatives. The primary criteria governing which educational placement is most beneficial to a given child are determined by many factors. The two primary criteria, however, include that the youngster (1) be afforded (and profit from) the specially designed instruction that has been delimited in the statement of annual goals, general objectives, and short-term instructional objectives, and (2) not seriously interfere with the educational opportunities provided other handicapped or normal children. The *least-restrictive* educational setting that permits attainment of these criteria constitutes the best placement for a given youngster.

In some cases, the least-restrictive environment best suited to a handicapped individual is not immediately apparent. In these instances, it is good educational practice to place the child initially in the setting that provides both a good chance for educational success and allows for the greatest interaction with the regular education environment. That is to say, if there is some question as to whether a youngster can profit from placement in a resource room or integrated classroom, he/she should be placed initially in the resource room since it usually permits at least 50 percent of the school day to be spent in the regular classroom. If, upon follow-up evaluation, it is found that the child is not benefiting from specially designed instruction and is badly disrupting regular classroom activities, he/she may be placed in the integrated classroom. In other words, a good rule of thumb to follow in placement decisions is to give handicapped children the "benefit of the doubt" and allow them to demonstrate their readiness to profit from whatever placement is initially chosen. Alternative placements are always available if, in fact, an error is made in the placement of a youngster (that is, he/she may be moved to the next least- or most-restrictive environment). The parent must be notified whenever there is a modification in the child's educational placement. If this change in placement is necessary and successful for a child, the public agency usually can be assured that they have located that setting best geared to the idiosyncratic needs of the youngster. In addition, written *documentation* as to why the child was not

312

able to be retained in the less-restrictive environment serves to, in part, meet the requirements mandated within the individualized educational program and Sections 121a.550–554 of Part B of the Education of the Handicapped Act.

The continuum of placements that typically represents least-restrictive environments has been stated above. Figure 7–1 lists the various alternatives, from least to most restrictive. The lines between the placements are meant to indicate that transition, from one to the other, should be fluid and easily made. It is crucial to note that, regardless of the placement chosen for handicapped children, the specially designed instruction that has been formulated for them must be carried out to the fullest extent possible. The characteristics of each placement alternative are discussed below.

Regular classroom with special assistance. Some handicapped children with mild to moderate disabilities can be maintained full time within the context of the regular classroom with appropriate assistance from special education personnel. The services provided by the special education teacher entail consultation with the regular classroom teacher and direct teaching, treatment, and/or materials given the handicapped child. In some schools, the professional who works in this capacity is called the helping or visiting teacher and may be assigned to a particular school full time or be itinerant (that is, travels from school to school). In any event, the responsibility of this person is to ensure that the handicapped youngster is afforded specially designed instruction in accordance with the goals and objectives specified in the individualized educational program.

Children placed in the regular classroom with special assistance

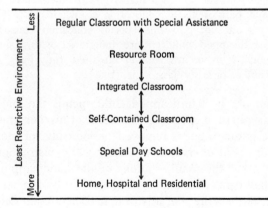

FIGURE 7–1.

should exhibit quite mild manifestations of their handicapping conditions. By virtue of their placement, such youngsters spend the entire school day with nonhandicapped children. They also are given academic instruction with their regular classes. The helping teacher tutors the child in areas where he/she is experiencing particular problems, manages behavior that is potentially disruptive, or locates special techniques and materials needed to fully integrate the child in classroom activities. For example, deaf, hard-of-hearing, or visually handicapped children with normal intelligence and social skills may be able to profit from regular class instruction if provided specialized materials. Using braille and large print texts, amplification devices, preferential seating, consultation with the regular teacher, etc., may all be necessary in some cases to educate sensorily impaired children in the regular classroom. Mild to moderate manifestations of specific learning disabilities, mental retardation, physical handicaps, and emotional disturbance may be handled adequately in the regular class with the assistance of the special educator. This arrangement, when successful, is most preferable since it is as closely aligned to the "mainstream" as possible. Not surprisingly, many handicapped children manifest disorders that do not permit education in the regular class. Their disabilities are such that more restrictive environments are necessary in order to provide specially designed instruction and to not interfere significantly with the education of the other handicapped and nonhandicapped children.

Resource room. The resource room is an educational placement that has gained wide popularity across the United States. In their very thorough discussion of the resource concept, Wiederholt, Hammill, and Brown (1978) define the resource room as:

> A resource room is any setting in the school to which a child comes to receive specific instruction on a regularly scheduled basis, while receiving the major part of his/her education elsewhere. . . . Therefore, resource rooms are not part-time special education classes where, for example, handicapped children are integrated with regular students only for lunch, gym, or art. Neither are they study halls, discipline or detention centers, or crisis classrooms. (p. 4)

In this environment, the handicapped child spends the majority of the school day (somewhere in excess of 50 percent of his/her time in school) in the regular classroom, but is removed periodically for more intensive academic and/or social intervention. Choosing this instructional strategy usually indicates that the manifestations of the handicapping condition are such that they cannot be managed effectively by the services of the helping teacher. Rather, the specially designed instruction deemed necessary for the handicapped youngster demands that he/she be seen at certain specified times for either individual or small-group teaching.

The amount of time a child spends in the resource room varies depending on the severity of the academic and/or social problem. In some cases, the child requires intervention only in the curricular area of mathematics and needs to see the resource teacher for approximately one hour, five times a week. Other children with more pervasive disabilities need longer periods of instruction in a wide range of areas in order to permit effective interaction with regular programs and students. As with all special education placements, care must be extended to ensure that a child's entry into whichever one is selected is done on an *individual basis*. Evaluating both the characteristics of the child *as well as* the programs available must be continual to document that the handicapped youngster is indeed being provided specially designed instruction that meets his/her unique needs.

While the resource room placement option has become very popular, it is not without its potential problems. In some cases, when applied in a pellmell fashion, the resource concept has defeated the purpose for which it was intended. When they do arise, most problems are directly relating to *scheduling*. The purpose of the resource room is to provide expert instruction in those areas in which the child is notably deficient while allowing regular class participation to the greatest extent possible. This is done not only to attenuate the problem areas, but also to assist the child in experiencing success in the regular class. Inversely, participation in the resource room should limit significantly the failure a child experiences in the regular classroom environment. Obviously, if a student is being taken to the resource room for special instruction in mathematics, he/she should receive this instruction when the regular class is also having a grade-level mathematics class. However, because of scheduling problems, some handicapped students must sit through the regular mathematics lessons (where failure is bound to occur) and be absent from activities where he/she can be successful. When scheduling problems arise, the IEP team is well advised to reconsider the applicability of the resource room to meet the child's special needs. Where the scheduling problem cannot be worked out, it is apparent that additional special education teachers need to be hired, the regular classroom schedule revised, or modification of the helping teacher concept devised and implemented. It is imperative that the participants of the IEP team continually remind themselves that the child must (1) be educated as much as possible with nonhandicapped children; (2) be provided specially designed instruction in whatever placement is chosen; and (3) be allowed to experience as much academic and/or social success as is possible within the mainstream of education.

Integrated classroom. Integrated classrooms represent an intermediate step between the resource room and the self-contained classroom. Placement in an integrated classroom usually is reserved for handicapped children who, because of the nature and extent of their disability, must spend the majority of the school day in a self-contained unit. However, it is important to note that they can be placed in resource rooms with mildly involved youngsters or with nonhandicapped children in the regular classroom for certain, carefully chosen, activities.

An illustration of how an integrated classroom may be well used is Ann, a 10-year-old child found to be seriously emotionally disturbed. Throughout much of Ann's academic career, she has consistently demonstrated an inability to foster satisfactory interpersonal relationships with peers and teachers, a persistent mood of unhappiness, and learning problems that cannot be explained by intellectual, sensory, or health reasons. As a result of these symptoms, Ann was placed in an integrated classroom in order to facilitate academic achievement and to develop coping skills that would permit realistic and productive relations with both children and adults. It was hoped that, if these goals were accomplished, her moods would shift to where she could reasonably expect some measure of happiness in her daily life. It was also noted that Ann possessed significant artistic ability and could work with certain teachers in this one academic activity. The school in which Ann was located did have an itinerant art teacher who had taken some course work in special education. When approached by Ann's teacher, the art instructor indicated willingness to include Ann in her class. Both teachers decided to try the integration on a trial basis for one month. Ann would attend art class three times a week for 30-minute sessions. At the conclusion of the month, the art teacher stated that Ann had completed two class projects. More important, she had gradually come to initiate a friendship with a girl in the class who was not handicapped. Ann's friend was encouraging her to come to physical education as well as art. The teacher of the integrated classroom was considering this possibility if the PE teacher and principal were amenable. Ann's special education teacher had also reported that her achievement was noticeably improved since establishing her friendship with the nonhandicapped child. However, long-term intensive remediation would still be necessary before it would be reasonable to expect Ann to be able to manage the majority of academic and emotional demands present in the regular classroom; that is to say, before it would be possible to place Ann in a resource room or in the regular classroom with special assistance.

Like the example just presented, handicapped children placed in the integrated classroom usually exhibit moderate levels of disabilities. In virtually every category of handicapping condition some children can benefit from a placement in an integrated classroom. It is self-evident

316

that, whatever non-special education activities are selected for the handicapped child to participate in, they must afford adequate opportunities for successful and satisfying experiences. In addition, close supervision and evaluation of the disabled child in the non-special education environment is of paramount importance. As stated previously, *fluidity* is essential to the concept of the least-restrictive environment. If a handicapped child is experiencing significant difficulties in the regular program, he/she should be removed immediately as a prelude to more successful program placement.

Self-contained classrooms. Most public agencies provide self-contained classrooms for handicapped children who are so severely impaired that regular class participation is impractical. Most youngsters placed in this setting manifest severe handicapping conditions and require intensively administered specially designed instruction in order to gain either academic or social proficiency. However, it should not be thought that self-contained classrooms are applicable only to the trainable mentally retarded, autistic, deaf-blind, severely involved multihandicapped, and so on. Indeed, self-contained placement for these types of handicapping conditions is frequently required, but children and/or adolescents who suffer from other conditions may also profit from this instructional arrangement.

Many professionals have formed the erroneous concept that certain disabilities are universally mild and can be managed effectively within the context of the resource room or through the services of the helping teacher. The area where this trend is most pronounced is that of learning disabilities. In fact, some school systems afford learning-disabled children only these types of placement opportunities. Learning disabilities, like all handicapping conditions, range in severity from mild to severe. In situations where the learning disability is severe, as in the example of an adolescent (with normal or near normal intelligence, sensory acuity, and emotional development) who is achieving below a second-grade level in reading, mathematics, and written expression, intensive and long-term remediation is necessitated. The goal for such an adolescent is initially to foster functional adult-level academic performance and career knowledge. To accomplish this, it is highly probable that he/she should be placed in a self-contained classroom in order to receive the full extent of the specially designed instruction defined in the individualized educational program. Interaction in the mainstream of regular education is largely useless unless he/she can be made ready to join the "world of work" when formal education has been terminated. In such cases, the individual characteristics of the student determine where he/she might best be placed. However, it is not in the best interests of the handicapped person to promote mainstreaming in regular education (even if possible) at the expense of providing to the fullest extent the specially designed instruction considered necessary to educate the student.

Special day schools. Typically, special day schools are used for children with relatively severe problems and low-incidence handicapping conditions (such as blind, deaf, or deaf-blind). Special schools may be geared to one particular type of handicapping condition (such as mentally retarded, or seriously emotionally disturbed) or to educating a diversity of severely disabled youngsters. The type of instruction provided is usually of a specialized nature that cannot feasibly be given in the normal school building. For example, some orthopedically impaired and other health-impaired children require special education or related services that are not available in neighborhood schools. Extensive physical therapy, occupational therapy, and associated medical necessities may all be factors in selecting a special school for a given child. Deaf, deaf-blind, and visually handicapped youngsters may also be placed in a special day school if their disorder is severely debilitating to their education. Seriously emotionally disturbed children are also sometimes placed in special schools as a means of meeting their idiosyncratic educational needs.

Using special day schools, by definition, precludes any significant interaction between a handicapped child and regular education. While interaction may occur on special days or for unusual activities, it would be unrealistic to expect frequent planned matriculation between the pupils of a special and a regular school. For this reason, placement in a special school must be considered with great care to ensure that such a restrictive environment is indeed required to attain the goals and objectives specified in the individualized educational program. It is also necessary to project (as is discussed later in this chapter) how long the youngster should need the services provided in the special school and when he/she will either terminate his/her education or be moved to the next most least-restrictive environment.

Home, hospital, and residential. In cases of exceedingly severe handicaps, some children may require instruction in the confines of the home, hospital, residential school, or group home. When such placement is desired, it is usually because the child's medical, intellectual, or social handicap can only be managed effectively in isolated settings. Usually home instruction is used where the youngster exhibits severe medical problems (such as bone tuberculosis or severe asthma) that make school attendance impossible. Either a "homebound teacher" or some audiovisual communication between home and school is required to provide specially designed instruction. It is hoped that home-based instruction may be relatively temporary and the child can be placed in a more least-restrictive environment when able.

Hospital and residential schools are available in all states of the union and, historically, have been the major means by which handicapped children have been educated. Factors such as extreme isolation, removal of the child from his/her home and neighborhood, impersonalized atmosphere, infrequent release have all led to de-emphasizing the service arrangement. This is not to say that hospital and residential schools are no longer needed. On the contrary, for some handicapped children removal from the home and neighborhood is the only viable alternative, at least for some period of time. Hospital settings provide the ongoing medical supervision necessitated by some handicapping conditions. Other disability areas such as severe forms of multihandicap, autism, schizophrenia, and deaf-blind require 24-hour specialized care in order to stimulate the youngster or to keep him/her from seriously being hurt or hurting others.

Hospital and residential placements are by far the most restrictive of all environments available to the handicapped child. Placement should be considered as a last step, and, when used, should be reevaluated continually to permit the child to move back into his/her home and neighborhood as soon as possible. Very likely, special education will witness a change in the ways in which hospitals and residential schools have been used in the past and are continuing to be used today. The rules and regulations governing PL 94–142 stipulate that, unless the handicapped child's individualized education program requires some other arrangement, the child must be educated in the school that he/she would attend if not handicapped. Through the ministrations of PL 94–142, school systems are being required to offer increasingly more sophisticated placements for their handicapped youngsters. Consequently, children who once were referred and placed in residential and hospital schools in a routine manner may now stay in their local school systems for appropriate educational alternatives. Ideally, only the most severely involved children will continue to use and benefit from hospitals and residential schools. It should be kept in mind that, when this instructional arrangement is employed, the local school system in which the child resides is responsible for developing an appropriate IEP and for its full implementation.

Additional Regulations Concerning the Least-Restrictive Environment

The responsibility for monitoring public agencies' compliance with the requirements governing the least-restrictive environment is given to the state education agency (SEA). The SEA must ensure that public agencies' placement of each handicapped child is (1) determined at least annually, (2) based upon his/her individualized education program, and (3) as close as possible to the child's home. In addition, a wide range of placements must be available to the extent necessary to implement the individualized educational program devised for the particular child. In selecting the most appropriate least-restrictive environment, consideration must be given to any potentially harmful effects on the child or on the quality of services he/she receives.

Additional requirements include that, at all possible times, handicapped children must be integrated with students in regular programs in *nonacademic* as well as academic settings. This means that such extracurricular activities as recess, lunch, athletics, clubs, and special interest groups must be made available to the handicapped when appropriate and feasible. Obviously, this requirement is especially beneficial with disabled children who must be contained with other handicapped youngsters during most of the day. Handicapped children placed in the integrated class, self-contained class, special school, and hospitals and residential settings would all profit if, when advisable, they were permitted to participate with regular programs and youngsters in a variety of nonacademic settings.

State education agencies must also make arrangements with public and private institutions as may be necessary to implement the concept of least-restrictive environment. Since institutional placement (hospitals and residential schools) is the most restrictive, it is crucial to provide all possible integration with regular classrooms. Regardless of why a youngster was institutionalized, no child who is so placed and is capable of education in a regular public school setting may be denied access to an education in that setting. Of course, this would include those children whose disability is such that special schools or self-contained classrooms would meet their educational needs. These placements may be used advantageously to test a child's ability to be educated in environments other than hospitals or residential schools.

It is also the responsibility of the state education agency to provide technical assistance, training, and monitoring activities to document that teachers and administrators are providing a least-restrictive environment to the handicapped children placed under their care. If an agency is found not to be in compliance, the SEA shall review the public agency's justification for its actions and assist in planning and implementing any necessary in-service teacher training or other types of corrective action. Technical assistance and training necessary to assist them in their effort to be in accordance with the provision of least-restrictive alternatives must also be made available. SEAs can well expect that, as parents of handicapped children become knowledgeable in the rules and regulations governing PL 94–142, increased pressure will be exerted to ensure that these youngsters receive their rights granted under the law. In order to provide all handicapped children with the least-restrictive environment available, state education agencies will, in some locations, need to offer extensive technical assistance and training. All professionals should be aware of those situations that are not providing least-restrictive environments to their handicapped children and take appropriate steps to facilitate the provision of such services at all possible costs.

RELATED SERVICES

As has been stated elsewhere in this book, the individualized educational program requires that a statement be made as to the specific special education and related services to be provided the handicapped child. In the previous section of this chapter, special education was defined as specially designed arrangements to provide instruction in the annual goals, general objectives, and short-term instructional objectives specified in the individualized education program. *Related services* are those activities necessary for a child to benefit from special education. More specifically, related services means:

> transportation and such development, corrective, and other supportive services as are required to assist the handicapped child to benefit from special education, and includes speech pathology and audiology, psychological services, physical and occupational therapy, recreation, early identification and assessment of disabilities in children, counseling services, and medical services for diagnostic and evaluation purposes. The term also includes school health services, social work services, and parent counseling and training. (Implementation of Part B of the Education of the Handicapped Act, 1977, p. 42479)

In essence, related services are those ancillary programs and activities that *may* be needed in order for a handicapped youngster to profit most from his/her special education program. Figure 7–2 graphically illustrates the interrelationship between special education and related services. In order to demonstrate fully the scope of special education, the primary placement options depicting least-restrictive environment are also incorporated in the figure.

Cursory perusal of this figure shows that the instructional placements and related services flow from special education. That is, a child must be judged handicapped prior to being placed in one of the many instructional alternatives that depict least-restrictive environments or being provided related services. Once the child is evaluated and found handicapped, has an IEP written that takes into account his/her individ-

321

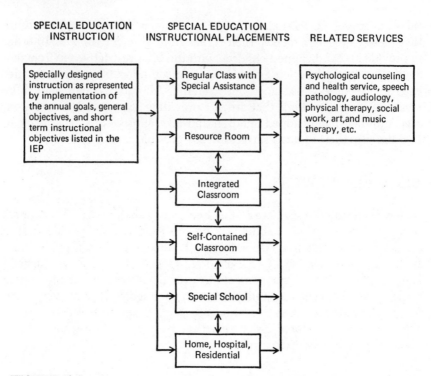

FIGURE 7–2.

ual learning needs, and is placed in an appropriate instructional alternative, it is possible to document the related services necessary to assist the youngster in benefiting from special education. The myriad possibilities given in the definition of related services should not be considered exhaustive. Virtually any developmental, corrective, or supportive services offered in a school or other public agency may legitimately be considered a related service. That is, as long as the service is determined essential in order for the youngster to profit from special education experiences and programming.

While the numbers of related services possible depend on the size of the public agency, they may be grouped conveniently under seven major headings. These include speech and hearing, counseling, therapy, psychological services, health, transportation, and other. Each of these categories of related services is discussed below.

Speech and Hearing

Two obviously related services are speech pathology and audiology. It is apparent that, if a handicapped youngster is speech or auditorially

322

impaired, he/she cannot make maximum use of the special services provided. If the disorders are significant in severity, they will interfere with the child's integration into regular education and cause much of the instruction given in special education to be without its full value.

Among other things, speech pathology entails identifying and diagnosing speech and language problems. Specific procedures for how this may be done can be found in Chapter 3. In addition to identification and diagnosis, the qualified speech therapist may also provide speech and language remediation necessary for the prevention or habilitation of these disorders. In some instances, a speech therapist may counsel parents, teachers, and children regarding communicative disabilities.

Hearing specialists (audiologists) may also be quite helpful to the special educator in supplying specific types of related services. These professionals may identify and refer for medical intervention children who exhibit symptoms associated with the deaf and hard of hearing. Determining the range, nature, and degree of hearing loss as well as providing habilitative activities (such as speech reading and speech observation) falls under the purview of the audiologist. From an instructional viewpoint, hearing specialists can be crucial in determining the need for group or individual amplification, selecting and fitting an appropriate aid, and evaluating the effectiveness of amplification.

Counseling

Counseling services are frequently a necessary component of an efficiently functioning special education program. Counseling may be provided by qualified social workers, psychologists, special educators, school counselors, or other related professionals. The recipients of the counseling efforts may be (1) the parents of the handicapped child, (2) the handicapped child him/herself, and/or (3) the regular class teachers and children who may come into contact with the handicapped youngster. The purpose of counseling is invariably to help the teacher, parents, and child to understand the nature of the disability and the long-term effects that may be expected. In some cases, counseling should be maintained over the entire time the child is in need of special education. Public agencies should be prepared to respond to this need when it arises.

Therapy

Two facets of therapy that may have some educational utility are occupational and physical. Occupational therapy usually entails (1) improving, developing, or restoring functions impaired or lost through illness, injury, or deprivation; (2) improving ability to perform tasks for independent functioning when functions are impaired or lost; and (3) preventing, through early intervention, initial or further impairment or loss of function. Physical therapy means those habilitative or rehabilitative services that are provided by a qualified physical therapist.

Occupational and physical therapy probably would be employed most extensively with those handicapping conditions that are physical in nature. The orthopedically and other health-impaired children frequently benefit from the activities offered in these types of related services. If one of the primary goals of special education is to integrate, to the maximum degree possible, handicapped youngsters into the mainstream of society, adequate motor functions are certainly desirable. The services of the occupational and physical therapist help greatly to meet this end.

Psychological Services

Psychological services are an integral part of most school systems and other human-related public agencies. These related services can include administering psychological tests and other assessment procedures, interpreting assessment results, consulting with other staff members in planning programs for handicapped children, and planning and managing a sequence of psychological services (including counseling) for children and parents. The usual school psychologist is needed to administer intelligence tests that are typically conducted on most potentially handicapped children.

Psychological services may also be interpreted to include social work. Social workers sometimes prepare a social or developmental history on a handicapped child, working with problems in the child's living situation that adversely affect adjustment in school, and serving as a bridge between the school and the community to enable the child to receive maximum benefit from his/her individualized education program.

Medical Services

Medical services for diagnosis and evaluation are commonly necessary for many handicapped children. Medical services include those activities of a licensed physician to document a youngster's medically related handicapping conditions that result in a child's demonstrated need for special education and related services. In cases where the child is obviously physically handicapped, a physician must determine whether the disability is progressive, correctable, or amenable to specialized treatment. Information as to using orthopedic devices, amplification, chemotherapy, and so on, may be necessary to provide for a child's educational opportunities.

Transportation

Transportation is a vital concern of most special education programs. The expenses associated with this related service are frequently substantial and need to be addressed by all public agencies. Transportation includes travel to and from school and between schools, travel in and around school buildings, and specialized equipment such as special or adapted buses, lifts, and/or ramps. In other words, handicapped children must not be denied access to educational programs because of physical barriers or transportation problems. One must also consider that travel to and from school may include a child going from his/her home to a special or residential school many miles away. Of course, the local school system is responsible for these travel expenses. This would include expenses incurred when the child comes home for vacations and other appropriate visits.

Other Related Services

Other related services that may be needed by handicapped children include early identification, adaptive physical education, recreation (that is, leisure function and therapeutic recreation), school health services, dance and music therapy, and art. There is little doubt that all school-related activities may, in some instances, be categorized appropriately as related services. If a particular activity would be of help in reaching the goals and objectives specified in the individualized educational program, it would qualify as a related service. The IEP team must carefully select those services that are available in a given public agency and ascertain their potential role in attenuating the handicapping condition. If a related service is needed and not available, action must be taken to secure it in order to provide the child the best opportunities possible to overcome his/her diagnosed disability.

PROJECTED DATES FOR INITIATION AND DURATION OF SERVICE

In addition to stating the specific special education and related services to be provided the handicapped child and the extent to which he/she is to participate in regular education programs, the IEP team must also project the dates for initiation of services and the anticipated duration of the services. While the rationale for this stipulation is not stated, it is apparent that its primary function is to commit the public agency, in writing, to those dates on which to begin the needed services and the amount of time it should take to provide for the child's needs. Obviously, the special education and related services judged necessary for the effective amelioration of the handicapping condition must be implemented as soon as possible following the IEP meeting. The IEP generated on a particular handicapped child must also be reviewed at least annually to determine its continued adequacy. Continuous modifications of the individualized education program should be made to ensure that the child has a reasonable idea of when he/she will no longer need special education or related services. Readers are encouraged to consult Chapter 2 for an in-depth discussion of the specific requirements of the individualized education program, particularly as it relates to accountability.

SUMMARY OF EDUCATIONAL SERVICES

The requirements for the individualized education program mandate that, for each handicapped child, a statement be made regarding the specific special education and related services to be provided the child and the extent to which the child will be able to participate in regular education programs. In order to accomplish this task, specific special education and related services and the least-restrictive environment must be defined. Special education means instruction specifically designed to meet the unique needs of the disabled youngster. Specially designed instruction entails implementing the annual goals, general objectives, and short-term instructional objectives specified in the individualized education program.

There can be little doubt that, as a prelude to effective implementation of the stated goals and objectives, the most appropriate educational environment for the handicapped child must be determined. This environment should (1) permit the efficient use of the IEP, and (2) allow the child access to regular students and programming to the maximum extent possible. The alternative placements available in most public agencies include (from least to most restrictive) the regular classroom with special assistance, resource room, integrated classroom, self-contained classroom, special schools, and hospital or residential schools. In selecting the most beneficial setting for a given youngster, all due consideration must be devoted to determining which environment permits the maximum fulfillment of the goals and objectives stated in the IEP and permits the most interaction with regular classroom activities. If this is done on an individual basis, the requirement for providing the child with the least-restrictive environment will have been met.

In addition to the least-restrictive environment, IEP teams must also consider the related services that may be necessary to assist the child in meeting the stated annual goals, general objectives, and short-term instructional objectives designed to meet his/her educational needs. Related services means transportation and such developmental, corrective, and other supportive services as are required to assist a handicapped child to benefit from special education. In actuality, any activity offered through a public agency can potentially qualify as a related service. In any event, related services include speech pathology, audiology, psychological services, physical and occupational therapy, recreation, early identification and assessment of disabilities in children, counseling services, and medical services for diagnostic or evaluation purposes.

The individualized education program must also include a statement regarding the proposed dates for initiation and duration of services to be provided the handicapped child. This requirement is, in all probability, meant to document the fact that services are actually being provided and that the IEP is being continually evaluated to ensure that the disabled child is being given services appropriate to his/her needs. It is essential that the IEP team institute a system of *accountability* so as to demonstrate that handicapped children are, in fact, securing those services that have been determined necessary to assist him/her to overcome or circumvent the handicapping condition.

References

Deno, E. Special education as developmental capital. *Exceptional Children,* 1970, 37:229–237.

Reynolds, M. C. A framework for considering some issues in special education. *Exceptional Children,* 1962, 28:267–270.

Wiederholt, J. L.; Hammill, D. D.; and Brown, V. *The resource teacher: A guide to effective practices.* Boston: Allyn & Bacon, 1978.

8

Evaluating and Revising
Individualized Education Programs

Evaluating and revising individualized education programs represents one of the most important factors in providing a free and appropriate education to handicapped children. The reason for the importance of the educational evaluation is that, if carefully conceived and carried out, it yields relevant data regarding the progress a youngster is evidencing in actually attaining specified goals and objectives. Evaluating attainment of goals and objectives delineated in the IEP determines the ultimate feasibility of the program and indicates modifications that should be made either at the time of annual review or when the child is not making adequate progress. Regardless of whether the IEP is found successful and needs restructuring in order to continue movement toward increased functioning or is obviously inappropriate in content and design and requires immediate change, the evaluation does denote those curricular goals and objectives that need to be either supplemented or supplanted.

The emphasis placed upon educational evaluations as a means of ascertaining the quality and quantity of a child's achievement is a relatively new phenomenon. The primary reasons as to why evaluations were either done poorly or not at all in the past are many and varied. Perhaps the most pervasive cause centers around the fact that the evaluation outcomes commonly were seen as the basis for judgments made about the competency of the person assigned to teach the youngster. Consequently, they were not typically undertaken with much vigor or enthusiasm. An additional reason was that efforts at instruction with handicapped as well as regular students frequently were governed by general goals and were not structured by specifying instructional objectives that permit efficient observation and measurement. This lack of specificity as to what is to be learned by the child and the criteria by which content is to be mastered makes evaluation extremely difficult, if not impossible. Lack of interest, skepticism, and lethargy also contributed to educators being somewhat slow in evaluating the products of their efforts. It is important to note, however, that increased awareness and concern by lay persons, educators, and recent federal legislation have made it necessary for educational personnel responsible for the handicapped to develop and implement procedures to validate the effectiveness of instructional activities. In relation to the individualized education program, the rules and regulations of PL 94–142 state that the IEP must include "appropriate objective criteria and evaluation procedures and schedules for determining, on at least an annual basis, whether the short term instructional objectives are being achieved" (p. 42491). There can be no doubt that educational evaluations are now an integral part of most, if not all, meaningful instructional systems and are indispensable (that is, mandated) for those who attempt to educate handicapped youngsters.

Perhaps the most important fact to keep in mind when planning educational evaluation and revision is that it must not be viewed as being isolated and separate from ongoing instruction. On the contrary, evaluation (particularly of short-term instructional objectives) is most profitably seen as a *process* by which it is possible to judge the efficacy of each distinct component that goes into formulating the individualized education program. From discussions presented in preceding chapters, it should be abundantly clear that, in order to identify appropriate short-term instructional objectives, the IEP team must have determined the child's present level of educational performance, annual goals, and general objectives accurately. In addition, placing the youngster in viable educational settings also conceivably influences attaining short-term instructional objectives. In other words, evaluating the child's individualized education program must be considered in light of the adequacy of each aspect of the IEP and not simply focus upon performing short-term instructional objectives.

The reasons as to why it is essential to conduct evaluations and revisions as a process and not merely to center upon performing discrete skills are apparent. The primary reason is that the ultimate goal of education for the handicapped is to assist handicapped youngsters to become as self-sufficient as possible. To accomplish this task, teachers must continually remember and review the major *goals* they are striving to help the child reach. If the goal for a blind child is eventually to increase mobility skills to the point where it is possible to travel across town independently, all instructional activities must be directed at achieving this goal. Any tasks that do not lead to this goal should be carefully reviewed and possibly eliminated as irrelevant. The tendency of some educators to become mired in a morass of teaching a series of short-term instructional objectives without thought to attaining more broadly based goals is unfortunate and ultimately works to the disadvantage of the child. Instructing the youngster in this manner results in the possible accumulation of many specific skills, but does not culminate in significantly increased levels of performance that assist the student in actually becoming self-sufficient. Such teaching efforts have given rise to the frequently heard adage that some children are "well taught but have learned little." Consequently, the evaluation of a youngster's individualized education program must continually monitor not only the child's attainment of short-term instructional objectives, but also the distinct movement toward mastery of broad-based goals and increasingly sophisticated and appropriate behavior patterns.

A second and related reason for assessing all components of the IEP is in the case where there is an obvious breakdown in the instructional plan and the child is simply not progressing as expected. In this instance, it is necessary to not only consider the manner in which the short-term instructional objectives were presented to the child, but also the possibility that the general objectives and annual goals from which they were derived were inappropriate. Furthermore, the service arrangements in which the youngster was placed may be inadequate to meet his/her unique learning needs. Given the many and varied reasons for potential failure of an IEP, it is crucial that educators maintain a flexible attitude when probing for possible causes of the failure.

One other aspect that is commonly overlooked in the evaluation and revision of the IEP, particularly when it pertains to its initial development or when failure is encountered, is the overall *climate* of the school or setting in which the child is placed. Any experienced educator is aware of the fact that, if the atmosphere of the learning environment is encouraging, respectful, and provides emotional support, the child will evidence high levels of motivation and perform at levels commensurate with ability. On the other hand, if the learning climate of an instructional setting is punitive, threatening, and nonsupportive, even the best-written individualized education program will be largely ineffective. It is often of great benefit for educators to consider the pervasive effects of the climate of the learning environment when initiating or revising the individualized education program.

It is axiomatic that the educational evaluation should be planned and conducted with great care in order to ensure handicapped children appropriate educational opportunities. Assessing instructional activities that compose the IEP make possible the rendering of judgments as to whether these activities should be revised, deleted, modified, unchanged, or supplemented with additional instructional components. The purpose of this chapter is to discuss the features of the educational evaluation

330

that must be addressed when determining the viability of the individualized education program. The specific elements to be considered include the (1) schedules and responsibilities in evaluation and revision; (2) evaluating the instructional components of the IEP; and (3) assessing the instructional climate and services provided the disabled child.

SCHEDULES AND RESPONSIBILITIES IN EVALUATION AND REVISION

Perhaps the first step in conducting efficacious evaluations of individualized education programs is establishing a schedule by which to accomplish assessment of the various components and assigning responsibility to school personnel who will actually conduct the evaluation. This facet of the evaluation effort typically is undertaken during planning stages when the IEP is being formulated initially, or when it is being reviewed to ascertain whether its content and placement options remain appropriate. As was indicated previously in this chapter, one of the mandated components of the IEP entails establishing procedures and schedules for determining whether short-term instructional objectives are being attained. Obviously, to do this efficiently, specific members of the school staff must assume responsibility for assessing the overall viability of the IEP in general and short-term instructional objectives in particular.

In one sense, the rules and regulations of PL 94–142 have already established minimal standards as to when to evaluate the IEP. In effect, each public agency must initiate and conduct periodic meetings to review each child's individualized education program *on at least an annual basis*. It is important to note that the rules and regulations stipulate that only short-term instructional objectives be the focus of the evaluation effort. This, of course, is intended to ensure that the child is indeed making progress in acquiring needed skills. However, determining that the child is truly progressing, on a daily basis, requires evaluation to be virtually *continuous*. The concept that instruction must be assessed at the completion of each instructional session is not new and is a routine part of many programs designed to educate handicapped children. That is to say, the special learning needs of disabled youngsters require *consistent* monitoring of their mastery of specific tasks in order to avoid missing or passing over information that is essential to learning more complex tasks. Consequently, it is inconceivable for one year to pass prior to evaluating a given youngster's attainment of those short-term instructional objectives that constitute the bulk of all direct teaching activities. To do so would almost certainly result in an individualized education program that is poorly managed and does not serve to provide the youngster an appropriate education.

One of the primary reasons for evaluating short-term instructional objectives on a daily (or at least a weekly) basis is that their effective formulation requires specifying criteria that must be met before the child can be judged to have mastered the task. For example, if one short-term instructional objective for a child who needs to develop basic math skills is stated as "counts consecutively two groups of lines joined by a plus with 100 percent accuracy," it is easy to see that evaluating the mastery of this objective *must* be done immediately upon teaching the task and the child's attempt to perform the behavior. The criteria of "100 percent accuracy" dictates that, in order for the objective to be considered "learned," he/she must be able to accomplish it with no mistakes each time it is presented. If failure is encountered, the skill must be retaught until the youngster understands the task and can accomplish it to the desired level of proficiency. To not specify criteria for mastery and evaluate attainment of mastery *continuously* (daily or weekly) would make it impossible to know if the child could actually perform the task to a specified level and whether it was advisable to move on to other short-term instructional objectives.

While evaluating short-term instructional objectives must be accomplished as an integral part of the continuous teaching process, general objectives and annual goals probably should be evaluated at longer time intervals. General objectives, from which short-term instructional objectives are generated, should be reviewed on at least a six-month basis and more frequently if necessary. The reason for the longer period of assessment of general objectives is that their attainment is predicated upon the child's accomplishing a number of short-term instructional objectives. Depending on the child, the task, and his/her level of functioning, the number of short-term objectives leading to a general objective may be few or many. However, it is very important to evaluate movement toward general objectives on a set schedule so that, if there are any problems in the direction that the sequence of short-term objectives is taking, they can be noted and modified without a significant waste of time and energy.

Assessing annual goals, of course, must be done once a year. These educational statements are broad based and long term in nature and serve to provide perspective to the ultimate progress made by the child. Actual accomplishment of annual goals rests upon successfully attaining short-term instructional objectives and general objectives. Consequently, it takes considerable time on the part of both the teacher and the child to demonstrate sufficient progress so that it is possible to ascertain whether an annual goal has, in fact, been accomplished. In the well-conceived and conducted IEP, it is possible to estimate successful movement toward annual goals by the attainment of short-term and general objectives. Not until enough objectives have been mastered, however, is it advisable to determine formally whether the stated annual goals were feasible.

Evaluating special education placement and related services afforded the disabled child must be closely tied to *all aspects* of the evaluation effort. The ultimate utility of an instructional placement must be judged by how well the child is progressing toward attaining goals and objectives and the degree to which he/she is able to participate in regular education programs (if at all). This determination is subjective in nature and will be done at least annually. The primary determinants of the placement's viability focus on (1) the adequacy of instruction provided the student; (2) the length of instructional time spent in special or regular education and the extent of related services employed; (3) the learning climate of the settings in which the child is taught; (4) the availability of appropriate materials; and (5) the adequacy of the physical plant and location of the settings in which the child is instructed. Each of these factors represents important decision points in determining the efficacy of an individualized education program and serves to point up needed directions for change.

The responsibilities for who is actually to conduct the various levels of evaluation must also be understood and decided upon as a prelude to implementing an individualized education program. Table 8–1 lists the various components of the IEP, probable schedules for evaluation, and the most likely person(s) to conduct the evaluation. This table indicates that for short-term instructional objectives evaluation must be conducted

TABLE 8–1 Evaluation of the IEP

Component	Schedule for Evaluation	Person Primarily Responsible
1. Short-term instructional objective	Daily or weekly	Teacher(s)
2. General objective	Two to six months	Teacher(s), parents, and other staff
3. Annual goals	Once a year	Representative of public agency, teacher(s), and other staff
4. Delivery of service	Two to six months and at least once a year	Representative of public agency, teacher(s), parents, and other staff

by the personnel involved in *actually* instructing the child. Determining the youngster's mastery of these objectives (that is, the demonstration that he/she can perform the objective at a certain criteria level) is only feasible through the ongoing activities involved in direct teaching. The teacher(s) responsible for instructing the youngster is the only one with sufficient information to keep continuous records of progress and to note objectives that may or may not be mastered adequately.

Assessing general objectives can also be accomplished by the teacher(s), parents, and other school staff who have *direct* contact with the child. Evaluating general objectives tends to be subjective in that they do not specify behavioral criteria that must be demonstrated by the youngster in the course of instruction. Rather, general objectives must be observed and attainment of the objective inferred from the ongoing behavior patterns of the child. Evaluating these objectives must be done in as many settings as possible and under a variety of conditions. It is obvious that since parents have perhaps the most constant contact with the child, their input as to mastery of the general objective should be sought and considered when estimating progress.

Annual goals probably were formulated by using standardized tests that depicted the child's level of performance within a given curricular area and systematic observation as needed. These goals served to provide the groundwork upon which the general and short-term instructional objectives were devised. The manner in which the goal was established serves to determine the evaluation strategy to ascertain whether progress has been made. That is, the standardized measures or observational techniques employed to establish the annual goal may be readministered to denote whether positive changes of behavior have occurred. In some cases, different instruments may be used, but they must possess sufficient reliability and validity to be useful. They must also at least purport to measure the same content or constructs as the initial test in order to permit efficient evaluation of the attainment of annual goals. The person(s) who conducts this facet of the assessment process may be the representative of the public agency, a member of the public agency's evaluation team, the teacher(s), and/or other related school staff. Which individuals actually carry out the evaluation vary depending on the child and the type of disability exhibited. However, whenever possible, the person who originally administered the tests should conduct all further formal evaluation efforts.

Estimating the adequacy of the delivery of service to the child requires the combined efforts of the entire IEP team. Information as to attaining goals and objectives, emotional status of the child, behavior in the home, and peer and teacher relationships all work to provide an image of whether the youngster is receiving the instructional opportunities needed to acquire the self-sufficiency and emotional development needed to perform at levels commensurate with ability. The decision to change or continue with a particular educational placement and service delivery structure should be made by a group of persons who have had contact with the child throughout a wide variety of situations.

While the schedules and responsibilities of evaluation are important features in determining the adequacy of an individualized education program, they do not specify how to conduct the evaluation. The specific ways in which to assess the various components of the IEP are of vital concern to determine whether a handicapped child is being provided an appropriate education. The following section delineates the instructional components of the IEP and discusses how to evaluate and revise them in an advantageous manner.

EVALUATING INSTRUCTIONAL COMPONENTS

The single best measure of the success of a given child's total individualized education program is the degree to which annual goals, general objectives, and short-term instructional objectives have been attained. These three aspects of the IEP are considered the basic *instructional* components while other components of the IEP are directly related to services and service delivery. There are two primary purposes for comprehensive evaluation of goals and objectives. The first is to signal program deficiencies. Program deficiencies are noted when evaluation reveals insufficient progress toward accomplishing goals and objectives is being made. Although program deficiencies may lie in either the instructional or service delivery components, only instructional evaluation reveals potential problems. The second purpose to be served by evaluating annual goals, general, and short-term objectives is to provide data regarding the handicapped student so that a new or revised educational program can be developed. In the case of either adequate or insufficient progress noted during evaluation, the IEP must be continually updated. This update may consist of minor variations from the original IEP or an almost total rewrite. The manner in which to conduct an evaluation of the IEP's instructional components to fulfill these purposes is discussed in this section.

It will be remembered that initially evaluation was for the sole purpose of planning an educational program as opposed to evaluating the success of an existing one. This basic difference between initial assessment for programming and assessment for program evaluation is seen primarily in sequencing evaluative efforts. There will be few if any differences in the actual process of assessment. Evaluation for placement and programming began with the general examination of the student's disabilities, present performance levels, and appropriateness of goals. Later educators began to assess general and short-term instructional objectives to construct an appropriate program. Evaluation efforts conducted to measure program success are administered in the opposite manner. That is, program evaluation begins with the specific instructional components and proceeds toward the general. Therefore, short-term instructional objectives should be evaluated first (in fact, continuously), general objectives second, and annual goals third. Finally, evaluating the quantity and quality of services is performed, a topic discussed in a following section of this chapter.

Regardless of the differences in assessment direction between programming and program evaluation, each is continuous and involves the same types of evaluations. As was pointed out earlier and as became obvious in the suggested scheduling of evaluation, the evaluation cycle is a process (see Table 8–2). Note how both types of assessment merge at the point of developing and evaluating short-term instructional objectives. This graph illustrates the virtual indistinction between instruction and assessment which makes evaluation a process without end. Because program evaluation is so closely related to assessment for programming, the following discussions are reviews of previous procedures suggested for educational programming. In addition, potential causes of problems and possible solutions are discussed in the event that progress in a particular instructional component is insufficient. Suggestions are also given for updating each instructional aspect of the student's IEP beginning with short-term instructional objectives, general objectives, and, finally, annual goals.

Evaluating Short-Term Instructional Objectives

As discussed previously, evaluating short-term instructional objectives is a process continuous with teaching. Recording of this evaluation may be daily but certainly no less often than weekly because the "short" nature of these objectives makes immediate recording a necessity. Procedures for noting and recording accomplished short-term instructional objectives are fairly straightforward. In fact, if the instructional objectives have been developed and sequenced carefully, recording of accomplished objectives immediately leads to a smooth continuation of instruction because it forces educators to focus attention on the next objectives. Teaching and evaluation are simplified by the very delineation of and attention to short-term instructional objectives.

In order to note accomplishment of short-term instructional objec-

336

TABLE 8–2 Evaluation Process

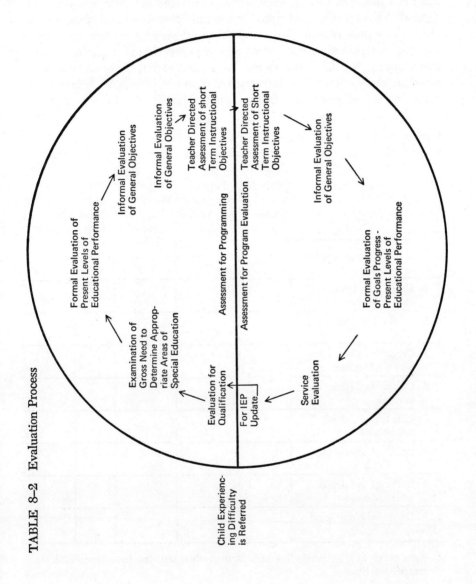

tives, one must observe the stated behavior in light of the criteria established for success. Noting the behavior itself does not mean the objective has been met. On the contrary, at minimum the behavior must be performed to the criteria level stated in the objective. It will be remembered, the criteria may require that an act be performed a certain number of times, a percentage of times correctly, a percent and/or number over a given number of days, and so on. To a great extent these situations develop as daily instruction is carried out. As an example, examine the following list of short-term instructional objectives.

General Objective—Drinking—Cup

	With Complete Physical and Verbal Prompt	With Physical Guidance and Verbal Help	Needs Only Slight Verbal and Physical Help	Only Verbal Cue	Independent
1. Drinks liquid when put in mouth					
2. Keeps liquid in mouth until swallowed					
3. Drinks liquid with straw in cup					
4. Drinks from cup when held for him/her					
5. Lifts cup off table to drink					
6. Lifts cup to drink independently					
7. Lifts and returns cup after drink independently					
8. Lifts cup and drinks with one hand					
9. Drinks with one hand and no spilling					

Place check in appropriate line and column when task has been completed ten consecutive times.

Both the behaviors and the criteria here are well defined. We can see that, to accomplish the last short-term instructional objective, the child must be observed to drink from a cup by removing it from the table with one hand and not spilling, independently, ten times, with no cues or prompts. If we must verbally cue him/her throughout accomplishing the task, this too is one of the latter short-term instructional objectives. Further criteria for each objective are noted by adding that it must be accomplished ten consecutive times before checking the behavior. This format for recording accomplished instructional objectives allows one behavior to have several criteria, providing the teacher many instructional objectives in little space. The simplified format for recording the accomplishment of objectives shown above actually contains 45 different instructional objectives. Table 8–3 provides another example of a format and criteria for recording accomplished behaviors. Note that the teacher initialed and dated each objective as accomplished. A space has also been provided for marking objectives that have been attempted and measured but not accomplished. These additional data will be helpful at the end of the school year by providing other instructional staff information regarding attempts to teach specific skills and general speed of skill acquisition. In constructing such evaluation devices it is important to plan for collecting all relevant information that will be helpful in guiding present and future instruction.

When locating short-term instructional objectives where little or no progress is being made, several possible factors must be examined. The first and most obvious factor to investigate is the degree of appropriateness of the established objectives. Educators must ask such questions as: Does the child have the ability to accomplish the objectives? Are there prerequisite skills that need to be developed? Are the objectives relative to his/her life and environment presently? Are the objectives sequenced appropriately? Are the criteria for success reasonable? Are objectives defined so that behaviors can easily be recognized? Questions such as these often uncover areas of difficulty which are hindering the child's progress. For instance, if the child is being asked to match upper and lower case letters, does he/she understand the words "match," "upper case," and "lower case letters"? Often failure to progress smoothly along a continuum of instructional objectives is the result of an inherent problem with the objective itself.

In the event that progress is insufficient and objectives do seem appropriate, it is necessary to explore the manner in which instruction is taking place. To some degree this subject is covered in a later section; however, specifically with regard to short-term instructional objectives, several aspects should be explored. Some of the considerations include the appropriateness of verbal and physical prompts and cues, the teacher's attitude regarding instruction, student's attitude, the appropriateness of the situation in which the behavior is to be elicited. These considerations prevent such things as instructing a child on how to drink from a cup immediately after a child has completed a bottle; or toilet training immediately after he/she has relieved him/herself. Social skills, in par-

339

TABLE 8–3 Evaluation and Instruction Device for Letter-Recognition Skills

Name: Rich Date: 1978–79	Can point to letter when given name		Can name letter when shown		Can make the sound when shown letter	
	Yes	No	Yes	No	Yes	No
A						
a						
B						
b						
C						
c						
D						
d						
E						
e						
F						
f						
G						
g						
H						
h						
I						
i						
J						
j						
K						

NOTE: Initial and date objective when achieved 90 percent accuracy or above over two-week period of time.

Can write letter when named		Can write letter when hears sound		Can match capital and small case	
Yes	No	Yes	No	Yes	No

NOTE: Initial and date objective when achieved 90 percent accuracy or above over two-week period of time.

ticular, are difficult if not useless to teach out of context. However, regardless of whether or not short-term instructional objectives have been met, periodically it is necessary to re-establish objectives for continued or future instruction.

While updating short-term instructional objectives is mandated at least annually, they may need revision more often particularly if progress is unusually slow or absent or unpredictably rapid. Any time progress toward instructional objectives is not seen for a period of weeks, some revision should be considered in light of the previous discussions and considerations regarding potential problems. Of course, children who sail through established objectives need new objectives delineated frequently. In these instances one can select a set(s) of instructional objectives from the next set of general objectives in a given goal. The advantages of good previous curriculum planning become even more obvious when updating and revising individualized education programming.

Continuous evaluation of short-term instructional objectives is accomplished by the teacher who observes and records when the stated objective behavior and criteria are reached. The format for recording progress toward short-term objectives can be adapted easily from lists of objectives delineated in the child's program and/or in special education curriculum guides. The importance of documenting accomplished instructional objectives lies in the fact that, for many general objectives and goals, although progress cannot be seen for long periods of time, in fact progress is being made. For example, if one only looks at the ability to drink independently from a cup, the ability to drink from a cup when assisted is overlooked. Drinking from a cup with some assistance represents a milestone with some handicapped children. However, general objectives also need to be assessed for evaluation and future programming.

Evaluation of General Objectives

General objectives are the second instructional component of the IEP to be evaluated. Evaluating the extent to which a child's general objectives have been met aids in locating program strengths and deficits and in determining future programming. General objective evaluation provides that extra, but essential, step between short-term instructional objectives. Although not capable of detecting as much specific progress as instructional objective evaluation, assessing general objectives does provide more information regarding the appropriateness of instruction than annual goal evaluation.

In order to evaluate the extent to which general objectives are being accomplished, educators and parents must again apply the concept of mastery. In many cases the last short-term instructional objective defines both the behavior and criteria for considering mastery, as was the case in drinking from a cup with one hand, independently, ten consecutive times. However, in cases such as the sound-symbol general objectives, we may wish to consider mastery only after the skills are begun to be *applied* to actual word recognition. The general objective of listening when others speak may only be recorded as mastered when observed in several environments with both peers and adults. At this point it may be helpful to review the seven considerations to keep in mind when evaluating progress toward general objectives.

1. Skill is performed spontaneously to benefit child's own self.
2. Skill has been performed before.
3. Skill was performed as stated.
4. No prompting, cueing, etc., was utilized.
5. Directions and/or materials given the student were not a factor in the success of the skill.
6. Skill appears to be a natural response or established habit.
7. Skill is performed in environment or situation where needed most.

It is most important to document mastery of general objectives when noted. Often general objectives are accomplished without actually instructing the student in each short-term instructional objective. Documenting accomplished general objectives may save valuable instruction time. Formats for recording the accomplishment of general objectives may vary from special checklists to curricular maps of objectives. Table 8–4 demonstrates both types of recording devices. More elaborate formats might include space for noting details of observations that led to the conclusion that the student had mastered the general objective.

In the event that general objectives are not being met, educators must re-examine the degree to which the short-term instructional objectives are leading to general objective mastery. It may not be uncommon to find that short-term objectives are being accomplished yet general objectives are not. There are two possible causes for this phenomenon: length and complexity of objective or incomplete short-term instructional objectives. First of all, this is not uncommon when mastery of a single general objective requires a great deal of time and instructional intervention. An example of this is given in the general objective and short-term instructional objectives listed below.

General Objective—Brushing Teeth—Grooming

Short-Term Instructional Objectives	*Criteria Levels*
1. Shows interest in brushing teeth or owning a toothbrush.	
2. Plays at brushing teeth	
3. Locates sink	
4. Gets toothpaste	
5. Takes cap off paste	
6. Gets brush	
7. Puts paste on bristles	
8. Puts brush into mouth	
9. Brushes teeth front, back, up, down	
10. Spits paste out	
11. Turns water on	
12. Gets cup	
13. Gets water in cup	
14. Rinses mouth and spits	
15. Rinses brush	
16. Turns off water	
17. Returns brush to proper place	
18. Puts cap on paste	
19. Returns paste to place	
20. Locates towel	
21. Wipes mouth	
22. Wipes hands on towel	
23. Brushes teeth at appropriate times	

Realistically, from initial instruction to mastery this one general objective can easily require more than one year. In fact, this objective is normally acquired over a period of more than one year. Educators should not attempt to check off general objectives prior to mastery. This results in learning only partial skills and ultimately harms the student's program. When concerned about the lack of mastery of general objectives, educators may want to document the percentage or fraction of short-term objectives reached within a given general objective rather

TABLE 8–4   Sample Formats for Recording Progress in General Objectives

Curricular Map Recording Device

	I	Check When Completed	III	Check When Completed
Feeding	Being fed—liquids		Knife, fork, spoon	
	Being fed—solids		Drinking from cans, bottles	
	Self-feeding—bottle			
	Self-feeding—hands			
Dressing	Shoes		Selecting appropriate colors	
	Socks			
	Coat		Hose	
	Shirt		Selecting appropriate sizes	
Health and Hygiene	Toilet training		Medical and dental when needed	
	Face washing			
	Hand washing		Menstruation	
Grooming	Combing hair		Shaving	
	Brushing teeth		Curling hair	
			Ironing	

General Objective Checklist

	5 per page	10 per page	15 per page	20 per page	25 per page
1. Simple one-digit addition, sums to 10					
2. Simple one-digit addition, sums to 18					
3. (Additive inverse)					
4. Three one-digit simple addition, sums to 18					
5. Simple two-digit addition					
6. Written problems with simple additions					
7. Two-digit addition carrying					
8. Simple three-digit addition					
9. Three-digit addition with carrying					
10. Addition fractions (like denominators)					
11. Simple addition of decimals					
12. Four-digit and addition with and without carrying					
13. Addition fractions with different denominators					
14. Addition mixed fractions					
15. Addition unlike-digit decimals					
16. Addition decimals with carrying					

than mastery. For example, in the previous objectives, the IEP team may want to state progress as follows:

General Objective	Date	Comment
Brushing teeth	12–16–78	14 of 23 short-term objectives met
Combing hair	12–16–78	10 of 24 short-term objectives met

This kind of recording prevents useless marking of mastery while denoting the progress that has been made toward the general objective.

The second factor to explore when short-term instructional objectives but not general objectives are being accomplished is the comprehensiveness of the short-term objectives. This is a more serious factor than the mere length or complexity of the general objective because it requires revising the instructional objectives. In order to determine the degree of comprehensiveness of short-term objectives, the IEP team need only define the behavior and criteria by which to measure a given general objective. If this behavior and criteria are more than is required by the last short-term instructional objective, the list of short-term objectives is incomplete. The objective stated as mastery should be added to the list and any other objectives needed to fill in between the previously stated last short-term objective. This solves the problem of incomplete sets of objectives. A related factor that could be involved would be that short-term instructional objectives require too much to be accomplished from one objective to the next. This situation is remedied by adding intermediate short-term objectives in those areas where accomplishment of one objective does not lead directly to the next.

Once the general objectives that have or have not been met are determined, the team may plan any revisions or updates for the next year or semester's programming. Program revisions may include restating the same objectives probably followed by a new set or revised list of short-term instructional objectives. The updated portion of the IEP's general objectives for a given goal should contain many possibilities for selecting new general objectives. The IEP team, parents included, can again determine which of these objectives are currently most appropriate for immediate intervention. Therefore, though much of the evaluation and planning of general objectives must be accomplished by well-trained observers who have a good concept of mastery, nonetheless it is an essential feature of the child's program. This component alone guides the child's education through a continuum of comprehensive special education curricula and unites the components of short-term instructional objectives and annual goals to provide a meaningful individualized education program.

Evaluating Annual Goals

The last instructional component of the IEP to assess is the degree to which annual goals have been met. These components should be evaluated approximately every year; however, because the school year contains only nine or ten months, most goals are assessed every nine to ten months maximum. Annual goals are evaluated to ensure that stipulated objectives are, in fact, contributing to goal attainment. While not mandated in law, this evaluation is essential for, without goal attainment, instructional objectives and strategies are useless. To evaluate and revise annual goals, present levels of educational performance must be reestablished and additional annual goals redesigned. The manner in which to accomplish these activities is presented below.

Prior to establishing annual goals, educators determine present levels of educational performance in each of the areas of special education determined pertinent to an individual student. Based upon these levels, educators develop a comprehensive set of annual goals. For the most part, evaluating the delineated annual goals can be accomplished by readministering standardized devices. Standardized tests are such that they may be used to measure broad-based goals and objectives and they may be administered every nine to twelve months. These devices generally yield grade and/or age levels that can be compared to levels attained on previous administrations. Selection criteria for appropriate standardized instruments are the same as those presented in Chapter 4. It will be remembered, however, that for many annual goals, particularly for the areas of sociobehavioral and career/vocational, there are few appropriate instruments available. The instruments in these areas often predict rather than evaluate performance. For these instances, present levels of educational performance are generally established by directly observing certain behaviors.

When evaluating the progress made toward the annual goals in which present levels were documented through direct observation, educators must attempt to observe and record the same behavior(s) as was collected initially. This observation should follow the identical format used previously—direct, continuous, or interval. In addition, the same defined behavior should be observed. Comparisons should be made between previous and current rate, frequency, duration, intensity, and so on, of the specified behavior. Goal progress is noted when the measured observations indicate that the desired direction of performance—increase or decrease in behavior—is being accomplished. If the

TABLE 8-5   Methods for Recording Progress toward Annual Goals

		Standardized Tests		
Language	*Test Name*	*Date*	*Results*	
Phonology	TOLD	5–20–78	Word articulation	5.3 yrs.
			Word discrimination	5.2 yrs.
Morphology	TOLD	5–20–78	Grammatic understanding	5.5 yrs.
Syntax	TOLD	5–20–78	Sentence imitation	6.2 yrs.
			Grammatic completion	5.0 yrs.
Semantics–Command	TOLD	5–20–78	Picture vocabulary	7.0 yrs.
Semantics–Question	TOLD	5–20–78	Oral vocabulary	5.5 yrs.
Semantics–Statement				

	Observational Recording		
Undesirable Behaviors	*Date Observed*	*Behavior*	*Result*
Destruction–Person	4–21–26–78	Hitting peers	Frequency—average 3 per day
			Duration—30 minutes
			Intensity—other children not injured
Destruction–			
Property			
Disruption			
Disassociation			
Disobedient			
Distraction			
Dependency			

increase or decrease is not yet to the desired level, of course the annual goal may be repeated and the observation for evaluation will become the new present level of performance. This is also true of new standardized data collected. Test results for program evaluation often suffice to document new performance levels for an annual goal continuation. Suggested methods for documenting or recording progress toward annual goals from standardized or observational data are presented in Table 8-5. Note the ease with which evaluative measures can become new present levels of performance.

In the event that evaluation of annual goals reveals little or no progress, several considerations should be examined. These considerations include investigating the appropriateness of (1) the goal itself,

348

(2) general objectives, (3) evaluation instruments, and (4) services and service delivery. One of the first questions to ask when no progress has been noted toward an annual goal is: To what degree was that goal appropriate to the individual student? Educators may wish to once again examine the eleven factors in goal selection. A particularly important factor to examine is the degree to which the goal meets with the student's own expectations and would assist him/her in the present environment. Often when goals are not perceived as relevant to the student within his/her own environment, no attempt is made on his/her part to attain the goal. However, if the goal itself appears to meet most of the factors involved in appropriate goal selection, educators should examine the general objectives designated as essential to the particular goal in question.

General objectives defined as composing a given annual goal may need to be re-examined as to their comprehensiveness and sequence. Often the best curricular maps should be revised periodically because of breakdowns noted during annual goal evaluations for students. These goals, when still unmet after completing many general objectives, shed light on areas of the curricular map that may need revision. Occasionally, the revision takes the form of merely changing the sequence of general objectives so that the simplest or highest priority objectives are listed first. However, many times breakdowns in annual goals are the direct result of pertinent general objectives that have been omitted. For example, in the curricular map of personal skills, several general objectives were first delineated under feeding skills. Only after application to a specific child's program was it noted that, while drinking from a cup was listed, drinking from a glass was not. This skill was found to be necessary since using a cup was found to be both a simpler and a different task from using a glass. Therefore, general objectives are another facet of the total IEP to examine when failure to reach stipulated annual goals occurs.

If accomplished general objectives continue to appear appropriate despite lack of progress toward annual goals, the manner in which the goal has been evaluated should be investigated. Any standardized test instruments used to evaluate goal attainment should be examined in light of the constructs that the test actually purports to measure. If the reported measurement is adequate, educators should examine reliability and validity data provided regarding the construction and administration of the particular test instrument. Poor reliability and validity can result in the over- or understatement of student progress. Of course, when problems such as this occur, it is best to locate a more appropriately constructed and standardized instrument for future assessments. Goal evaluation must then be based on the careful assessments of general and short-term objectives or direct observation. Observation instruments, too, must be screened carefully in order to assure that the measurement taken is representative of the entire set of goal behaviors. Often numerous related but different behaviors should be observed and recorded simultaneously in order to evaluate the entire scope of an annual goal. Once the goal itself, general objectives that comprise the goal, and evaluation instruments used to measure attainment have been examined, only one possible factor in the lack of goal progress remains to be investigated—the quantity and quality of services provided the handicapped student. Either not enough special services or poor quality services may result in a lack of achievement toward goal attainment. This concept is examined extensively in a following section of this chapter.

In order to re-establish appropriate annual goals for the following year, educators must re-examine possible goals in light of the criteria given in Chapter 4. In addition to locating new annual goals, it frequently is appropriate to continue a selected annual goal. However, this repeated goal probably has different general and short-term instructional objectives delineated under the goal heading. This process of restating a specific goal may continue for several years while progress toward actual mastery of the goal is being steadily made by accomplishing various objectives.

Once evaluation and revision of the instructional components of the IEP are completed, the IEP team must evaluate services and service delivery. Evaluation and revision of special, related, and regular education services completes the evaluation of the child's total education program. This evaluation leads to an even more successful special education program in the future. The following section discusses the purposes and components of service and service delivery evaluation.

EVALUATING EDUCATIONAL SERVICES

Evaluating educational services is an indispensable ingredient in the ongoing monitoring of a child's progress toward increasing self-sufficiency. As stated previously, educational services entail those activities afforded under the categories of special education, related services, and regular education programming. In actual practice, the delivery of whatever services are deemed necessary for a given handicapped youngster may be conceptualized conveniently as involving the components of (1) the *teacher* or *teachers* who directly instruct the student and (2) the *arrangements* in which the child receives appropriate educational opportunities. All aspects of educational services may be viewed as relating to these two elements. Consequently, evaluation efforts may endeavor to probe these variables when deficiencies in progress are noted and/or when the individualized education program is being reviewed as a prelude to establishing new goals and objectives. In either event, assessing the viability of currently utilized educational services must be undertaken to ensure the youngster the most appropriate education.

In order to evaluate services, it is necessary to delineate those aspects of the teaching methodology employed and the instructional arrangements that may influence attainment of stated goals and objectives. The elements of these variables that are of particular importance include the adequacy of instruction offered the child, length of instructional time spent in special or regular education, and the extent of related services used, learning climate of the setting(s) in which the child is taught, availability of appropriate materials, and adequacy of the setting in which the youngster is being instructed. All of these variables can and will significantly affect the child's progress toward increasingly sophisticated behavior patterns. The purpose of this section is to discuss each of these variables as they relate to the efficacious delivery of the best educational services to handicapped children.

Adequacy of Instruction

Perhaps the most obvious as well as important aspects of delivering educational services revolve around the adequacy of instruction provided the handicapped youngster. When discussing instruction from the standpoint of its demonstrated utility, it is important to note that the primary criteria for judgment can only be made by the amount of material a child has learned. That is, if teaching is to be deemed effective, it must result in *some* change in the behavior of a student. The factors that go into effective instruction are many and varied; however, the end product of the effort must be viewed in light of the child's movement toward attainment of appropriately selected and presented goals and objectives. Regardless of whether the instruction of interest is delivered in special or regular education or as a part of a related service, its efficiency must be seen in terms of how well the youngster is progressing in acquiring needed skills and abilities.

In order to provide appropriate instruction, several factors must be presented. The first of these is that the teacher(s) has developed or is provided with a curriculum that is geared to the child's unique learning needs. The curriculum that is employed must delimit specific goals and objectives that permit a continuous and smooth progression in skill attainment. If possible, the curriculum utilized should be thoroughly understood by the teacher(s) attempting to use it. Whenever feasible, it should be constructed by the teacher(s) as a basis for ensuring that

351

instructional activities will indeed address the problems exhibited by a particular child. If the teacher(s) does not have access to an adequate curriculum or is incapable of devising one for him/herself, instruction offered handicapped children must necessarily be spotty and not truly geared to the needs of the youngster.

A second factor of concern in determining the adequacy of instruction entails the manner in which the various curricular components are presented to the child. Even if a teacher(s) has access to a viable curriculum, the method chosen to present information to students influences the degree to which it will be mastered. For example, if a teacher(s) wishes to present the child with information about farms in general and common farm animals in particular to increase general knowledge, there are several ways in which it might be done. One teacher might elect to take field trips to several farms in order to permit the child to see farm animals and, hopefully, to understand and conceive of their size, odor, and so on. This "hands on" method may be appropriate if time permits and children are capable. However, it is likely that using extended field trips, in light of the relatively restricted and important instructional time available to disabled youngsters, may be undertaken primarily for humanitarian rather than educational purposes. Other teachers, cognizant of the *perspective* in which knowledge of farm animals relates to the child's general understanding of his/her world, may elect to use models, pictures, and/or movies to teach children these concepts. This instructional approach takes less time than field trips and can be built around short-term instructional objectives that allow measurement of a youngster's attainment of the presented information. It should not be interpreted that field trips are not a usable educational tool. Rather, teachers must be very judicious in selecting instructional activities to avoid wasting time that could be used profitably in teaching additional concepts. If a child is not making anticipated progress toward specified goals and objectives, it is wise to evaluate the *manner* in which the various instructional objectives are being presented and to determine if changes in presentation made could facilitate achievement.

A related variable that should be considered in determining the adequacy of instruction is the emotional climate present in the instructional setting and established by an educator during the course of teaching activities. In many instances the atmosphere of the learning setting and reinforcement methods employed either greatly increases the likelihood of mastering goals and objectives or seriously impairs the chances of their attainment. To some extent, the climate of a given setting may be beyond the control of single teachers in that the entire school or public agency may be nonconducive to providing for handicapped children. Regular teachers or related services personnel may not be willing to accommodate handicapped youngsters in the manner necessary to provide viable learning experiences. These individuals may consider the extra effort needed to plan and instruct the handicapped to be of "little value" and to detract from the time required to teach regular students. In these cases, it is unlikely that the educational services offered the child in special education can have their full and intended impact. This is particularly true when the student is capable of functioning in environments outside of special education to some extent.

Teachers responsible for instructing the handicapped must continually be on guard that all services afforded the child are given in a positive and supporting manner. The actual learning tasks presented to the youngster may be appropriate and well paced, but if he/she is anxious, fearful, or unsure of what is expected, failure is the common result. More in-depth discussions of techniques for evaluating the learning climate are provided later in this section. However, it should be recognized that, if a youngster is not experiencing expected gains in acquiring skills and knowledge, it is very important to consider and evaluate the adequacy of instructional opportunities. The viability of the curriculum and the climate in which it is presented greatly influence a child's progress. In most cases, these factors are within the control of school personnel and can be changed and modified to facilitate overall learning of handicapped children.

Educational Placement

The educational placement in which the handicapped child is provided instruction frequently needs to be assessed carefully when evaluating or reviewing the attainment of goals and objectives. The relationship between the amount and quality of service afforded in regular and special education as well as the extent of related services employed comprises the sum total of educational experiences that, hopefully, represent "appropriate educational opportunities." The degree of accommodation for each handicapped child in whatever placement(s) he/she finds him/herself and the viability of the related services used do much to facilitate or hinder progress toward improved skill development.

Determining the proper mixture of special education, regular education, and related services for a given youngster can be a difficult undertaking. For many children, the initial placement is exploratory in nature so as to ascertain the specific settings that best fit the needs of the child. For example, a student exhibiting serious emotional problems may be best placed in a self-contained classroom in order to bring deviant behavior patterns under control. After the pupil has evidenced sufficient progress, a move to a less restrictive environment may be con-

353

sidered. The feasibility of a part-time placement in a resource room or regular class can only be judged after the child has been given exposure to these settings. Educators must be continually alert to the possibility that the move may be precipitous and the youngster does not yet possess necessary control to function in these environments. Consequently, he/she may be placed in an alternative setting with more structure until such time that a placement in a less restrictive environment is once again indicated. The opportunity to "switch" placements with ease is indispensable to the well-functioning school setting and should be made on the basis of attaining goals and objectives and the ability of the child to exhibit acceptable behavior in that environment.

The quantity and quality of related services available to the child may also influence a child's educational and emotional development. Related services are defined as transportation and other supportive services as are required to assist a handicapped child to benefit from special education. These services include speech pathology and audiology, psychological services, occupational and physical therapy, health services, and so on. Obviously, many handicapped youngsters need to be provided a range of related services in order to profit the most from the specially designed instruction offered in special education. The availability of these services and the manner in which they are delivered is of major interest to those individuals who formulate or review the individualized education program. An inventory of the related services within a given public agency should be generated for purposes of information as well as permitting effective selection of those activities thought necessary to ensure a youngster the best educational opportunities. The climate or atmosphere in which related services are afforded and the competency with which they are provided significantly affects their true utility.

If a child is seen as making inadequate progress in mastering various goals and objectives, it is beneficial to evaluate both the type of placement and the extent of the related services being employed. In many instances, even slight modifications in either of these factors may do much to foster desired outcomes. The ultimate feasibility of the educational placement and related services can be seen in a handicapped child who is demonstrating increasing proficiency in educational tasks and is reasonably happy in the instructional setting(s) in which he/she is placed. In cases where failure is noted, changes in the instruction and services offered may be instituted to further probe whether alternative settings and strategies might result in expected gains. An inventory of available placements and related services permits the IEP team to make its decisions with relative speed and clarity. Educational placements and related services should be evaluated and reviewed routinely every six months or at least once a year.

Learning Climate of Educational Settings

One of the most frequently overlooked variables in evaluating the adequacy of educational services is the learning climate present in the educational settings in which handicapped children find themselves. When evaluating the climate of the total educational environment, the viability of such variables as communication patterns, role relationship and role perceptions, rewards and sanctions, and general rules and norms that operate within a given public agency must be determined. According to Fox, Schmuck, van Egmond, Ritvo, and Jung (1975), there are two basic indicators of a "healthy" learning environment—effective learning of students and personal satisfaction of the staff—that are directly involved with teaching the disabled youngster. Those educational settings with positive climates permit innovation and experimentation; consequently, educators gain a feeling of confidence and are motivated to begin and maintain satisfactory relationships with peers. On the other hand, if a learning climate is basically negative, there is evidence of job dissatisfaction, alienation, little or no creativity, frustration, and unusual conformity among staff members. Without doubt, in situations where the learning climate is not conducive to increasing self-esteem and productivity, disabled children's adjustment and achievement is adversely affected.

If school personnel judge it necessary to evaluate the learning climate of a given facility, there are a number of issues to address. The most important of these issues is the manner in which to collect the data. Whenever possible, the participants in the evaluation should be aware of the intent of the activity and how the data will be used. If the evaluation is viewed as punitive, it probably will be resisted with subsequent results made invalid. The following guidelines can provide a usable structure for conducting the assessment of the climate of the learning environment.

1. The people from whom the information is being gathered are aware of why it is being gathered.
2. The persons affected by the learning climate believe it is important to gather this information.
3. They know about and agree to the way the information is to be used.
4. They have helped to determine the need for gathering the information.
5. They have helped to determine the manner in which the information is being gathered.
6. They are helping to gather the information.

7. They are involved in analyzing and interpreting the information.
8. They are involved in considering actions that seem indicated by the evaluation.
9. The evaluation effort is being conducted at a time when it can be viewed constructively by all concerned, rather than as a threatening move by a faction of a potential conflict situation.
10. The evaluation effort is realistic in scope; it can conceivably contribute to an improvement effort.
11. The evaluation effort does not compete realistically with other time and energy demands.
12. The results of the evaluation are communicated to various groups in a manner that motivates constructive action, rather than mobilizing resistance to improvement. (Adapted from Fox, Schmuck, van Egmond, Ritvo, and Jung, 1975, pp. 149–140)

The primary way of collecting data revolves around written responses from various staff members, interviews, and observations. The structure of a given evaluation will vary depending on the public agency of interest and the characteristics of that setting. For example, variables such as staff responsibilities, resources, and related services are all possible areas of input. Parent and community involvement in the learning environment may also be of concern in some instances. Figure 8–1 pro-

FIGURE 8–1 Sample Form for Evaluating One Aspect of Staff Behavior

OUR TYPICAL BEHAVIOR

1. Suppose a teacher (let's call him Teacher X) disagrees with something B says at a staff meeting. If teachers you know in your school were in Teacher X's place, what would most of them be likely to do?

Would most of the teachers you know seek out B to discuss the disagreement?

( ) Yes, I think most would do this.
( ) Maybe about half would do this.
( ) No, most would *not*.
( ) I don't know.

Would they keep it to themselves and say nothing about it?

( ) Yes, I think most would do this.
( ) Maybe about half would do this.
( ) No, most would *not*.
( ) I don't know.

2. Suppose a teacher (let's call him Teacher X) feels hurt and put down by something another teacher has said to him. In Teacher X's place, would most of the teachers you know in your building be likely to . . .

FIGURE 8–1   *(cont.)*

. . . avoid the other teacher?

(   ) Yes, I think most would.
(   ) Maybe about half would.
(   ) No, most would *not*.
(   ) I don't know.

. . . tell the other teacher that they felt hurt and put down?

(   ) Yes, I think most would.
(   ) Maybe about half would.
(   ) No, most would *not*.
(   ) I don't know.

. . . tell their friends that the other teacher is hard to get along with?

(   ) Yes, I think most would.
(   ) Maybe about half would.
(   ) No, most would *not*.
(   ) I don't know.

3. Suppose you are in a committee meeting with Teacher X and the other members begin to describe their personal feelings about what goes on in the school. Teacher X quickly suggests that the committee get back to the topic, and keep the discussion objective and impersonal. How would you feel toward X?

(   ) I would approve strongly.
(   ) I would approve mildly or some.
(   ) I wouldn't care one way or the other.
(   ) I would disapprove mildly or some.
(   ) I would disapprove strongly.

4. Suppose you are in a committee meeting with Teacher X and the other members begin to describe their personal feelings about what goes on in the school. Teacher X listens to them and tells them his own feelings. How would you feel toward X?

(   ) I would approve strongly.
(   ) I would approve mildly or some.
(   ) I wouldn't care one way or the other.
(   ) I would disapprove mildly or some.
(   ) I would disapprove strongly.

5. Suppose Teacher X wants to improve his classroom effectiveness. In Teacher X's place, would most of the teachers in your building . . .

. . . ask another teacher to observe his teaching and then have a conference afterward?

(   ) Yes, I think most would do this.
(   ) Maybe about half would do this.
(   ) No, most would *not*.
(   ) I don't know.

. . . ask other teachers to let him (Teacher X) observe how the other teachers teach, to get ideas how to improve his own teaching?

FIGURE 8–1   (*cont.*)

(   ) Yes, I think most would do this.
(   ) Maybe about half would do this.
(   ) No, most would *not*.
(   ) I don't know.

. . . have a free and open discussion with his students about his teaching?

(   ) Yes, I think most would do this.
(   ) Maybe about half would do this.
(   ) No, most would *not*.
(   ) I don't know.

. . . ask the principal to observe his teaching and then have a conference afterward?

(   ) Yes, I think most would do this.
(   ) Maybe about half would do this.
(   ) No, most would *not*.
(   ) I don't know.

6. Suppose Teacher X disagrees with a procedure that the principal has outlined for all to follow. If Teacher X were to go and talk with the principal about his disagreement, how would you feel about it?

(   ) I would approve strongly.
(   ) I would approve mildly or some.
(   ) I wouldn't care one way or the other.
(   ) I would disapprove mildly or some.
(   ) I would disapprove strongly.

7. Suppose Teacher X disagrees with a procedure that the principal has outlined for all to follow. If X were to say nothing but ignore the principal's directive, how would you feel about it?

(   ) I would approve strongly.
(   ) I would approve mildly or some.
(   ) I wouldn't care one way or the other.
(   ) I would disapprove mildly or some.
(   ) I would disapprove strongly.

8. Suppose Teacher X develops a particularly useful and effective method for teaching something. If X were to describe the method briefly at a faculty meeting and offer to meet further with any who wanted to know more, how would you feel about it?

(   ) I would approve strongly.
(   ) I would approve mildly or some.
(   ) I wouldn't care one way or the other.
(   ) I would disapprove mildly or some.
(   ) I would disapprove strongly.

SOURCE: Fox, R. S.; Schmuck, R.; van Egmond, E.; Ritvo, M.; and Jung, C. *Diagnosing professional climates of schools.* Fairfax, Va.: NTL Learning Resources Corporation, 1975, pp. 71–72. Used with permission of publishers.

vides an illustration of one instrument designed to probe one aspect of "typical" staff behavior as it relates to the reactions of one member toward another. Using this device may yield some meaningful notion of the norms that tend to guide staff behavior in a particular learning environment.

Reviewing this figure, when completed by members of a public agency, provides considerable insight into the feelings and expectations of individuals operating within that environment. Interested parties will find it a relatively easy task to construct similar devices to probe other aspects of the learning environment. However, it should be pointed out continually that, if the staff is not agreeable to such an evaluation, there is little chance of attaining meaningful results.

In addition to determining the broad or general nature of a given situation, it also profitable to analyze directly the climate of specific settings (such as a classroom) where a handicapped child is receiving instruction. As has been stated repeatedly throughout this text, disabled youngsters achieve at an increased level in settings where goals and objectives are presented clearly, the child's affective needs are taken into consideration, and frequent monitoring of progress is undertaken. It is axiomatic that children who misperceive a teacher's intentions or who are placed in situations where their needs are not being met do not easily become involved in meaningful learning activities and fail to utilize their ultimate potential.

Figure 8-2 presents a scale that is meant to provide educators with how a youngster perceives the general status of a learning environment. The entire device can be administered in 10 to 15 minutes and may yield highly illuminating information regarding the climate of an instructional setting. Such an instrument is particularly helpful with students who are currently being "mainstreamed" in regular education programs. Of course, it could also be employed with youngsters in any setting within a given public agency. If the child does not have sufficient reading skills to complete the scale, it may be read to him/her and the answers given orally. Whether the child reads the form or it is read to him/her, the student should be assured of maximum privacy and be convinced that the resultant data will not be used in a punitive fashion.

As with every evaluation instrument utilized, the results should be viewed with caution. Educators can use the data from these or other devices to formulate hypotheses regarding the feasibility of some educational placements. Continued evaluations and observations should be conducted to determine finally if child responses are consistent over time. It is a wise practice to be alert to particularly unusual answers from an individual child in that immediate attention may be necessitated. It should never be overlooked that one of the most promising and reliable sources of evaluation data regarding the adequacy of educational settings

359

FIGURE 8–2 Sample Form for Evaluating the Child's Perception of the Learning Environment

Date _____

Your Number _____

Class _____

CLASSROOM LIFE

Here is a list of some statements that describe life in the classroom. Circle the letter in front of the statement that best tells how you feel about the class. *There are no right or wrong answers.*

1. Life in this class with your regular teacher has
   a. all good things
   b. mostly good things
   c. more good things than bad
   d. about as many good things as bad
   e. more bad things than good
   f. mostly bad things

2. How hard are you working these days on learning what is being taught at school?
   a. very hard
   b. quite hard
   c. not very hard
   d. not hard at all

3. When I'm in this class, I
   a. usually feel wide awake and very interested
   b. am pretty interested, kind of bored part of the time
   c. am not very interested, bored quite a lot of the time
   d. don't like it, feel bored and not with it

4. How hard are you working on schoolwork compared with the others in the class?
   a. harder than most
   b. a little harder than most
   c. about the same as most
   d. a little less than most
   e. quite a bit less than most

5. How many of the pupils in this class do what the teacher suggests?
   a. most of them do
   b. more than half do
   c. less than half do
   d. hardly anybody does

6. If we help each other with our work in this class, the teacher
   a. likes it a lot
   b. likes it some

FIGURE 8–2   (*cont.*)

---

   c. likes it a little
   d. doesn't like it at all

7. How good is your schoolwork compared with the work of others in the class?
   a. much better than most
   b. a little better than most
   c. about the same as most
   d. not quite as good as most
   e. much worse than most

8. How often do the pupils in this class help one another with their schoolwork?
   a. most of the time
   b. sometimes
   c. hardly ever
   d. never

9. How often do the pupils in this class act friendly toward one another?
   a. always
   b. most of the time
   c. sometimes
   d. hardly ever.

SOURCE: Fox, R.; Luszki, M. B.; and Schmuck, R. *Diagnosing classroom learning environments.* Chicago: Science Research Associates, Inc., 1966. Reprinted by permission of the publisher.

is the child him/herself. Scales such as the one presented in Figure 8–2 can be one technique to probe the feelings and attitudes of handicapped youngsters. Obviously, the educator's own astute observational skills used throughout the school day should also indicate whether children are participating in the most beneficial learning environments available.

Adequacy of Materials

The adequacy of materials available for use with handicapped children can sometimes be an important variable in the overall instructional effort. In many instances, the materials employed reflect the curriculum afforded the youngster. Knowledge of materials is a part of what constitutes competence in the field of education and assumes even greater significance when applied to teaching handicapped youngsters. In that virtually all aspects of instruction entail some use of materials, it behooves educators to be continually alert to which materials are being used and the manner and extent they are employed.

One of the most extensive evaluation schemas produced to assess the adequacy of materials has been developed by Brown (1975). The Q-Sheet is intended to improve the state of consumer and professional education in selecting and evaluating instructional materials. An abridged listing of Q-Sheet components is presented below.

(1) What is the stated rationale for developing the program?

Look for one or more statements of: (a) definition of the content area under study, e.g., reading; (b) philosophy regarding instruction in the area; or (c) dissatisfaction with specific aspects of other programs, or perhaps a previous program by the same publisher.

(2) What is the rationale for selection of program elements or content?

Look for comments on: (a) tradition; (b) experimental determination (always check this out in greater detail); (c) logic of the subject matter; (d) survey of other programs and their elements; or (e) the assumptions made concerning the content area, such as the linguistic base in a reading program.

(3) How can the quality of the content be checked?

This question is difficult. Usually some credence is given to the reputations of authors and publishers, as well as to supporting reference material. Usually "expert" opinion is needed in addition to a determination of the internal consistency of *all* program elements.

(4) What is the scope of the program?

Scope is the comprehensiveness or the breadth of the program. It determines how much of what it is possible to teach has been included in the program at hand. A program of limited scope may be desirable for teaching a specific skill, or as a supplement to an existing program which is weak in a particular area or variable.

(5) What is the sequencing of skills or items or units?

Sequence is the order the subject matter or elements are to be taught. Some materials are sequentially dependent so that mastery at each level is required before continuing to the next. Sequentially dependent curricula leave little room for flexible use or the pulling out of components. Other materials are "spiralled" so that the topic may be left and then returned to later. Paradoxically, spiralling may be helpful or detrimental. Sometimes leaving an area of difficulty for a while has the effect of desensitization. However, it may also be possible that mastery is never actually accounted for in a spiralled curriculum except when the particular topic disappears from "mention." Sequence may also be based upon several factors other than the sequential/spiral question. Logical organization of the subject matter may be a determiner; the curriculum may proceed from immediate to remote life experiences, or it may move from concrete to abstract symbolism.

(6) How is the curriculum paced?

Regulation of pacing is presently one of the major ways of controlling individualization of instruction. Several bits of information provide clues to intended and actual pacing of the materials or program:

(a) Are there differing starting times for various groups or individuals, and then essentially the same pacing along the way? If so, the modification is not in "pacing" but in readiness for the program.

(b) Are "mastery" suggestions made along the way for those who need more or different experiences at various points? How is it suggested that such modifications be managed if in a group situation?

(c) Do suggested instructional time lines presented elsewhere in the program mitigate against modifications in the pacing of instruction?

(7) Is there evidence of any psychological principles of instruction which are content-free?

(8) What are the specific techniques of instruction for each lesson?

The more highly structured the lessons, the less likely it is that the success of the program depends upon teacher experience and previous training. More highly structured programs also lend themselves to use by aides and volunteers under the supervision of the teacher. On the other hand, it may happen that if little teacher variation is allowed or encouraged, the lesson may not be readily modifiable.

(9) What are the specific modifications suggested for individualization?

(a) Is the individualization on a one-to-one basis, or intended for instruction within the group situation?

(b) What are the bases for the suggestions made?

(c) What is the range of suggestions or are they all pretty much alike?

(d) What range of differences is accounted for?

(e) Are the suggestions general, or are they specifically tied to potential instructional problems?

(10) Is a prerequisite skill level or information base needed to administer the program?

(a) Is there a formalized, separate "package" of instruction available?

(b) Is the training continuous as an integral part of each unit or lesson?

(c) Are there ways to determine the instructional competency of personnel who would work with the program?

(11) Are there "readiness" behaviors specified which are prerequisites for the student?

    (a) Are assessment strategies included?

    (b) How are the behaviors to be acquired or taught?

(12) How is reinforcement used in the program?

    (a) If mentioned at all, note the definition well. In the majority of non-special education programs there is a tendency to equate reinforcement with repetition.

    (b) What kinds of reinforcement are suggested, e.g., social, tangible, edible, visual ... ?

    (c) Are there suggestions for how to determine what is reinforcing to an individual child?

    (d) Are schedules of reinforcement considered?

    (e) Are there specific examples, or generalized suggestions?

    (f) Is there a procedure for fading from tangible to social reinforcement?

    (g) Is there any discrepancy between notions of reinforcement and practices such as paper-grading or marking?

(13) What is the format of the material to be presented?

    (a) Is the material in kit, book, worksheet, chart or some other form?

    (b) How are the units organized?

    (c) What kind of type is used? Size? Style? Compactness?

    (d) If pictures are included, what kinds are there, and what are their purposes?

    (e) Are the page arrangements likely to make any difference to the learners?

(14) How independently can the material be used?

    (a) If independence of use is recommended, is there a systematic program to teach the child *how* to use the materials independently?

    (b) How is progress in work habits or independence to be monitored?

(15) Has any effort been made to assess or control the complexity of the language of instruction, either receptively or expressively?

(16) What is the developmental interest level of the materials?

Materials which are obviously intended for younger children are probably inappropriate for older students. On the other hand, the teacher actually may have to develop or provide background experience, information or interests for some students. It should be noted that statements of "mental age" do not necessarily correspond to the "interest age" or to the "social age" of the child.

(17) Are there behavioral objectives for the program or for the lessons?

    (a) Is there any attempt to justify the objectives or to determine their value?

    (b) Are the objectives linked in any way to prior or to subsequent objectives?

    (c) Are the statements complete in the sense of meeting behavioral criteria?

    (d) What are the consequences of objectives assessment in terms of future instructional procedures?

    (e) Is the program built on predetermined objectives, or do the objectives follow the nature of the program?

(18) What diagnostic assessments are provided?

    (a) Type

    (b) Frequency?

    (c) Pre/post, or continuous during instructional sequences?

    (d) Feedback mechanisms to the learner and to the instructional program?

    (e) What are the consequences of assessment feedback?

(19) Is this program coordinated with any other programs?

    (a) Is the program part of a series or a unified approach by the same publisher? Can it be readily separated from other components?

    (b) Are there recommendations for companion programs, or for previous and subsequent programs?

(20) Have there been any attempts to determine readability or learner interest?

What processes have been used, and are the results available?

(21) What is the comparative cost of the program?

(22) What is the realistic availability of the instructional components?

(23) Are testimonials, research, author claims, and published claims clearly differentiated?

    (a) Evidence of formative evaluation?

    (b) Evidence of summative evaluation?

    (c) Is there congruence between the program objectives and activities?

    (d) Are the program development processes specified?

(24) What are the target populations for whom the materials were developed?

If the population characteristics are stated, it is easier to assess the potential relevance of the materials to your population of interest.

(25) Is it possible to foresee—and does the author note—any potential problems which might be encountered in using these materials?

(a) How surmountable are the problems?

(b) How readily can the materials be modified to resolve the problems?

(26) Can any of the features of this material or program be adapted or incorporated into other programs?

Features such as self-correctional procedures, reinforcement techniques, etc., may be noted for use in other instructional situations.

(27) Are any significant changes in the organization and management of the institutional situation required?

(a) Are there special space and/or equipment requirements?

(b) Will the time/event schedule of the day need to be replanned?

(c) Will present child groupings be significantly affected? How?

(d) Are the descriptions of how the program is to be organized and managed stated clearly enough so that the program may be readily implemented?

(28) Is it possible to isolate sensory channels as a major instructional variable?

Keep in mind that for this purpose not only must the material itself be examined, but also the circumstances surrounding its actual presentation in the instructional situation.

(29) How durable are the materials?

Items that undergo a great deal of handling should be made of strong materials with protected surfaces. Storage or carrying of materials in kits or package form should also be considered in terms of the convenience and sturdiness of the packaging materials.

(30) Is there any apparent or subtle bias toward or against a particular target group, e.g., women, blacks, Chicanos, or Indians?

Many states or local school districts will have guidelines available for this kind of analysis.

(31) Other significant features omitted from this list but which should be noted as relevant for user purposes.

Considerations such as potential interaction patterns, the predominance of convergent/divergent responses, or detailed linguistic analysis may be of interest to special interest users. (Brown, 1975, pp. 15–17)

Effective evaluation of instructional materials is best undertaken by the individual(s) who is contemplating or actually using them. The time required to carry out such an evaluation is sometimes formidable. Consequently, several teachers may wish to take various parts of the materials and analyze them separately. Whenever possible, it is advisable to assess two programs purporting to contain the same content simultaneously. This practice serves to highlight structural similarities and differences and to aid in determining which materials best suit the needs of the children in question. When desired, careful evaluation indicates where to modify existing materials to more closely approximate the philosophy of the teacher. In every case, the materials that are eventually chosen for use with a handicapped child must not be thought of as a substitute for the curriculum that has been devised by the teacher him/herself. Rather, materials must *supplement* the basic curricular components established by the instructional personnel. If they do not, it is untenable to employ them in educating handicapped youngsters.

Physical Arrangements of the Educational Setting

The physical arrangements within a public agency can also affect the manner in which the child is able to progress toward meeting specified goals and objectives. Obviously, if a child is physically impaired and has limited mobility skills, barriers in the overall physical plant (such as stairs or inappropriate lavatory facilities) will seriously impede his/her opportunities to participate in a variety of school experiences. While agencies receiving federal funds must modify physical arrangements to accommodate the handicapped, this does not necessarily apply to schools, state institutions, and other settings where the disabled are routinely taught. Consequently, if an IEP team is unsure of the accessibility of various aspects of the school or other facilities as they relate to children who are unable to move easily in the environment, the physical components of the setting should be evaluated and modifications made whenever indicated to ensure a child has access to all meaningful aspects of school life.

Additional concerns regarding the physical arrangements of the educational setting pertain to the manner in which self-contained classrooms and resource rooms are located in relation to the total school environment. In some instances, public agency administrators have attempted to *segregate* special education placements within a school plant. Temporary classrooms (usually located in a back lot), storerooms, and stages in auditoriums have all been employed to serve as instructional arrangements for handicapped youngsters. These settings, of course, merely indicate the true priority given to providing services to the handicapped and are seldom conducive to allowing the child to participate in regular education programs. Such attempts at covert isolation commonly result in the instructional staff and handicapped children being perceived and perceiving themselves as "different" and less important than other faculty and students. The overall atmosphere created by these types of instructional arrangements is also commonly acquired by regular education students and staff and culminates in the general impression

367

that disabled children are "crazy," "dumb," and should be avoided. All these factors make successful matriculation into the mainstream of school life extremely difficult and can be circumvented by attempting to manipulate the physical arrangements of an educational setting so that it resembles regular programming as much as possible.

A related factor to the location of physical setting within a school environment is the mode of transportation that permits some handicapped children to attend a variety of educational activities. When necessary, public agencies must provide such specialized equipment as special or adapted buses, lifts, and other devices that make education in a least-restrictive environment a definite and feasible proposition. For many handicapped youngsters, availability of these and similar techniques is required if an appropriate education is to be offered. IEP teams need to be continually aware of the services afforded by public agencies as a prelude to structuring viable educational programs. If the physical arrangements and specialized services available are not adequate to meet the needs of disabled youngsters, modifications must be made to accommodate their unique needs and to provide them appropriate instructional opportunities.

SUMMARY OF EVALUATING AND REVISING INDIVIDUALIZED EDUCATION PROGRAMS

Evaluating and revising the various components of the individualized education program, besides being a mandated aspect of the rules and regulations of PL 94–142, represent an extremely important facet of the educational provisions provided handicapped children. The well-conducted evaluation and revision indicates those goals and objectives that are adequate or in need of change and permits estimating the adequacy of educational services that are either facilitating or impeding movement toward increased self-sufficiency. In order to be most efficient in conducting evaluation and revisions, educators must be aware that it is impossible to separate these activities from ongoing instruction. Rather, evaluation and revision, particularly of short-term instructional objectives, is best viewed as a process in which each component of the IEP is judged in relation to each other component. A breakdown in any aspect of the planning or implementation of the elements of the IEP (including service delivery arrangements) significantly and pervasively affects the total efficacy of the entire program. For example, the sequence of short-term instructional objectives and their direct relationship to general objectives and annual goals is crucial to the child exhibiting increasingly sophisticated behavior patterns. The specific elements to consider in evaluating and revising the individualized education program include schedules and responsibilities, the instructional components of the IEP, and assessing the educational services provided the handicapped child.

The schedules and responsibilities in evaluation and revision are relatively straightforward. In that the IEP must be reviewed at least annually, public agencies are required to reconvene the IEP team and determine whether a child's educational progress has been adequate. In most instances, evaluating short-term instructional objectives should be continuous rather than once a year in order to make needed changes as they are indicated through ongoing teaching activities. Since they are more broad-based and subjective, assessing general objectives and annual goals can be accomplished at longer time intervals. Responsibilities for actually conducting the evaluation and revision should be divided among those instructional and related staff members who have had contact with the child.

Instructional components of the IEP include statements regarding short-term instructional objectives, general objectives, and annual goals. The differences in evaluation strategies used when assessing these components are because of the degree of specificity with which each may be stated. Short-term instructional objectives, with their accompanying criteria for mastery, may be evaluated immediately by observing the change in behavior exhibited by the youngster on a daily or weekly basis. General objectives and annual goals do not provide the specificity of short-term objectives and consequently must be assessed more subjectively and on a longer time schedule. Since goals and objectives do constitute the "specially designed instruction" provided handicapped children, their evaluation and revision must be carefully done in order to ensure that the youngster is progressing adequately in attaining desired skills and abilities.

In addition to the instructional components of the IEP, educators also need to address the educational services through which the child is being instructed. Such factors as the general adequacy of instructional opportunities, climate of the learning environment, amount of time spent in special and regular education, and the extent of special services, viability of instructional materials, and the utility of the location and physical arrangements afforded the youngster are considered under the heading of educational services. The reason for focusing upon these variables is that they may positively or negatively affect the ultimate progress made by a student. If a child is noted to be making insufficient movement toward the mastery of goals and objectives, and they themselves seem appropriate, it is likely that the problem can be located in the type and quality of educational services being provided. Educators

369

need to develop their own policies and guidelines as to how to conduct this evaluation.

References

Brown, V. A basic Q-sheet for analyzing and comparing curriculum materials and proposals. *Journal of Learning Disabilities*, 1975, 7:10–17.

Fox, R. S.; Schmuck, R.; van Egmond, E.; Ritvo, M.; and Jung, C. *Diagnosing professional climates of schools*. Fairfax, Va.: NTL Learning Resources Corporation, 1975.

Fox, R. S.; Luszki, M. B.; Schmuck, R. *Diagnosing classroom learning environments*. Chicago: Science Research Associates, 1966.

9

The IEP Meeting

Convening the IEP meeting should represent the culmination of a series of activities that have been instituted to provide the best educational services to handicapped children. Prior to the IEP meeting, the public agency must have determined that the referred child does indeed possess a handicapping condition that has been verified through a careful and exhaustive evaluation process. The parents of the disabled youngster have been contacted to approve, in writing, the evaluation procedures utilized and hopefully have had the results of the assessment process communicated to them. The public agency must have also contacted various instructional staff as well as the parents in order to establish a convenient time and place as to when and where to hold the IEP meeting. Preplanning efforts should have been initiated permitting the delineation of the child's educational needs in the areas of self-help/basic living, sociobehavioral, career/vocational, and academics. This data, when coupled with available information derived from the referral, screening, and evaluation, should allow estimation of (1) the child's present level of educational performance; (2) viable annual goals, general objectives, and short-term instructional objectives germane to the specified handicap; (3) special education and related services required to accomplish the goals and objectives; (4) extent to which the youngster is able to participate in regular education program, if at all; (5) projected dates for initiation and duration of needed services; and (6) appropriate objective criteria to evaluate whether specified short-term instructional objectives have been achieved.

The activities designed to produce a tentative and preliminary instructional plan most commonly are undertaken by the disabled child's teacher(s) and other instructional staff who have knowledge regarding

371

curriculum planning and/or information pertaining to the unique needs of the disabled youngster. This plan, which is to be generated in the elapsed time between termination of the evaluation and convening of the IEP meeting (not to exceed 30 days) must not be considered as the final IEP document. Rather, this plan serves as a starting point from which the participants in the IEP meeting may begin their deliberations. Consequently, the tentative IEP must be considered flexible so as to permit necessary input from other sources with knowledge and expertise regarding the youngster and the handicapping condition.

In order for public agencies to convene and conduct effective IEP meetings, a number of factors must be considered. Initially, the specific purposes of the IEP must be delineated and understood by all participants. The professional and lay persons who are actually to constitute the IEP team must be contacted and their responsibilities made clear. Since the IEP team is to be composed of individuals from diverse backgrounds and levels of expertise, consideration must be given to establishing an open communication system to facilitate cooperation and the sharing of information. Finally, in the rare cases where there are insurmountable disputes between the parents and public agency, due process safeguards must be initiated through a mandated hearing process that is intended to ensure that the handicapped child is receiving the most appropriate educational opportunities available. Each of these factors is addressed in the following sections. The final portion of this chapter presents a discussion of the completed IEPs on the children who have been followed throughout Chapters 3, 4, 5, and 6.

PURPOSES OF THE IEP MEETING

The primary purpose of the IEP meeting is to *devise a written statement* for a handicapped child that results in delineating the special education, related services, and educational placements necessary to ensure that the disabled youngster will receive appropriate educational opportunities. In order to be of maximum benefit to the child, the individualized education program must be composed and implemented as early as possible. The factors that influence how quickly the IEP is written depend on the availability of necessary staff and service systems. It is important to note, however, that it is required in the rules and must be held within *thirty calendar days* of a determination that the youngster needs special education and related services. That is, once the child has been evaluated formally and found handicapped, public agencies must move to formulate the individualized education program as a prelude to providing an appropriate education.

In addition to the mandates governing how quickly the IEP must be developed for a given disabled child, it is also the responsibility of the public agency to initiate and conduct meetings to review each child's individualized education program periodically. When found necessary, the IEP must be revised to accommodate the changing needs and abilities of the handicapped youngster. The meeting to review and revise the existing IEP must be held at least once a year. Some public agencies schedule those meetings on the anniversary date of the last IEP meeting. While a 12-month review of IEPs might be adequate for some children, there can be little doubt that this time period is much too long for other youngsters. It is obvious that, in cases where the special education and related services delineated for a particular child are being used on a trial basis, more frequent meetings should be scheduled to ascertain their effectiveness. The timing of the review meetings is left to the discretion of the agency and typically is specified during the initial IEP meeting. Consequently, one major outcome of the individualized education program meeting should be to determine the frequency with which follow-up sessions should be scheduled in order to ensure the effectiveness of the instructional efforts.

One of the first concerns of the public agency in attempting to convene an IEP meeting is to *select those individuals who can best plan for a given child*. Obviously, the professionals who are brought together to consider the educational needs of handicapped youngsters will vary from situation to situation. To illustrate, the instructional provisions for a deaf-blind child will differ markedly from those of a youngster who is exhibiting characteristics of a less pervasive condition with the primary manifestations of significant academic underachievement. The professionals convened to deal with these disparate disorders will, by necessity, possess decidedly different areas of expertise in educational programming. The deaf-blind child probably requires extensive assistance in self-help/basic living skills, in a special day school or self-contained classroom, while academic remediation in a resource room is often the primary focus of the mildly handicapped student. The knowledge base of the instructional staff dealing with these and other educational problems should be evaluated carefully to ensure that the most appropriately trained persons are assembled to plan for specific children.

In addition to school staff, other persons should be included on the IEP team to develop the best programs for children. The child's parents must be included in the meeting and extensive steps have been devised to ensure their participation. The child him/herself can often be a valuable member of the team and contribute to discussions pertaining to the methods of instruction considered, educational placements, reinforcement systems, and so on. At the discretion of the public agency and parents, other personnel may also be invited to the IEP meeting. If the child is or will be placed in a private facility, a representative of that agency must be involved in writing and reviewing the IEP document. Obviously, an additional purpose of the IEP meeting is to bring all concerned partners together in order to devise appropriate educational strategies for the disabled youngster in question.

Once the participants of the IEP team have been selected and are convened, it is necessary to finalize those annual goals, general objectives, short-term instructional objectives, and placements that result in appropriate educational services. At this point, the tentative IEP can be of great assistance in serving as a point of departure for discussion by the participants. Procedures as to how to determine these goals, objectives, and services have been discussed in some detail in Chapters 4, 5, 6, and 8. In that these elements of the IEP actually represent the instruction to be provided the child, they must be considered with great care. The extent to which the goals and objectives are adequately stated and serve as a basis for providing viable educational opportunities to disabled children depends to some degree on the level of cooperation elicited among the various team members. At the conclusion of the IEP meeting, all participants must indicate their approval of the stated goals, objectives, and educational placements deemed necessary to provide for the child. Facilitating the development of a feasible and appropriate individualized education program is a vital and indispensable purpose of the IEP meeting.

After the individualized education program with all its component parts has been formulated, it is advisable to *assign responsibility to various persons* to accomplish the stated annual goals, general and short-term instructional objectives. This activity must be undertaken with much thought since some youngsters require the services of many special education and related service personnel. To ensure that there is no confusion as to who is to be responsible for which goal or objective, some forethought is frequently required. The parents of the disabled child, the child him/herself, and other noninstructional individuals should not be overlooked as potentially important in the total scheme of how to deliver services. The specification of responsibilities is very helpful in follow-up sessions where the purpose is to determine how well objectives have been met. Individuals who have been particularly successful or unsuccessful in teaching the child are able to speak to the specifics of the situation that contributed to the success or failure. This information is invaluable in planning later instructional opportunities.

An additional purpose of the IEP meeting entails discussing the *duties, when to begin instruction, and projections of how long the child will be in need of the services.* Determining the initiation of service should be quite simple in that it can be begun as soon as possible after the conclusion of the IEP meeting. The length of time necessary for the child to be in special education should be a true projection since a variety of overt and covert factors can significantly influence the type and length of service required by a given youngster. The reason to consider this point initially, and on at least a yearly basis, is to ensure that a child is not kept in special education beyond the point where such services are no longer necessary. Formulating projections serves to cause the IEP team members to consider the possibility that the youngster at some point may be able to function independently of the services provided in special education.

Establishing a purposeful and active communication system among the various IEP participants is another desired outcome of the IEP meeting. At a minimum level, the IEP meeting should result in the parents and schools developing a formal mechanism by which they may consult regularly regarding the status of the child and the success of the IEP in fostering desired skills and abilities. This communication system may be formalized through a report card system or by such informal methods as weekly telephone calls. Communication between special education staff and those persons providing related services should be kept open so that responsibilities are not confused and services duplicated or inadvertently omitted from the child's program. In cases where the IEP is found inadequate in facilitating learning in the youngster, changes should be approved by all team members. By establishing a communications system and keeping it functioning, the process of gaining the necessary approval for modifications can usually be a relatively straightforward proposition. If lines of communication have not been maintained, approval can be much more difficult to acquire in that confusion as to what is actually being done with the child may be present.

Determining the *manner in which to evaluate the IEP* is a significant aspect of the IEP meeting. The evaluation or *accountability* of the public agency and parents in providing an appropriate education to handicapped children is an essential aspect of all individualized education programs. If the program is not evaluated, it is extremely difficult to ascertain whether it is resulting in needed services for the child or is in need of revision. In that the evaluation of the short-term instructional objectives is a mandated component of the IEP, it must be addressed in the IEP meeting. The evaluation can be conducted on a daily, weekly, or monthly basis and any variations in expected outcomes should be noted. If progress is particularly accelerated or depressed beyond what was originally expected in the IEP meeting, it is probable that a meeting to revise the IEP should be convened and new goals, objectives, and services devised. Chapter 7 discussed various evaluation models that may be used for this purpose.

From the above discussion it is evident that no one person is able to accomplish all the purposes of the IEP meeting. Rather, the individuals assembled to finalize the individualized education program should assume certain responsibilities pertaining to the successful conclusion of the various elements of the IEP meeting. The following section delineates the participants of the IEP team and discusses their responsibilities in developing the instructional programs.

PARTICIPANTS AND THEIR RESPONSIBILITIES

The individuals who are to participate in a given IEP meeting should be chosen carefully. Obviously, these persons should include those who are knowledgeable regarding the service delivery arrangements within the public agency, possess specific information as to the child's problem and associated behaviors, are responsible for providing the special education and related services dictated by the completed IEP, and are expert in the evaluation procedures that were employed to document the handicapping condition. The parents of the handicapped child must also be included in the meeting. Depending on the child and the nature and extent of the handicap, the number of participants in any particular IEP meeting can vary widely. The only criterion to follow in determining the number of participants is that all professionals having information that directly pertains to the instructional arrangements ultimately provided the child should be in attendance.

It is apparent that the composition of a team charged with finalizing the IEP differs markedly for children found to be suffering from various handicapping conditions. For example, the makeup of an IEP team convened to address the educational plan of a deaf-blind child undoubtedly would differ from a team charged with planning for a youngster who has been diagnosed as learning disabled. In the former instance, a detailed medical report may be required necessitating the presence of a physician and specialized teaching strategies doubtlessly should be employed requiring a teacher with particular expertise in the pervasive effects of this disabling condition. In most cases, the learning-disabled child does not need the ongoing services of a physician (that is, no more than a child without a handicap), and does require instructional staff capable of interpreting and utilizing evaluation information directed at language usage and academic achievement. Data garnered from the referral, screening, and evaluation and any follow-up diagnostic study usually provide the public agency with adequate information to bring together those individuals who can best deal with the problems exhibited by a particular handicapped youngster.

The rules and regulations governing PL 94–142 stipulate certain participants who must be included on an IEP team. These mandated participants are (1) a representative of the public agency, other than the child's teacher, who is qualified to provide or supervise the provision of special education; (2) the child's teacher; (3) one or both of the child's parents; (4) the child, where appropriate; and (5) other individuals at the discretion of the parent and public agency. For a handicapped child who has been evaluated for the first time, the public agency must also involve either a member of the evaluation team who documented a handicapping condition or someone who is knowledgeable regarding the evaluation procedures used with the child and is familiar with the results of the evaluation (see Section 121a.344 of the Implementation of Part B of the Education of the Handicapped Act). The roles and responsibilities of each participant vary as they pertain to the construction of the IEP. The following sections briefly delineate potential and mandated team members and discuss their likely contributions to the formulation of the individualized education program.

Representative of the Public Agency

The representative of the public agency must be someone other than the child's teacher and be qualified to provide or supervise the provision of special education services. In actual practice, this individual would commonly be someone who could be *actively* involved in overseeing the activities that are eventually to be provided the handicapped child. Depending on the public agency, its representative typically would be a school principal, special education supervisor, or other administrative staff responsible for supervising instruction. The responsibilities of this person in relation to the IEP meeting centers on three main factors. The first of these is that, in order for all participants to be aware of the meeting and the time and place it is to be held, someone must be responsible for such tasks as telephoning parents and contacting other staff who will be attending the conference, scheduling a meeting room, ensuring that appropriate forms are prepared and available, and so on. In other words, the representative of the public agency should serve as a facilitator of those mechanical functions that are indispensable for a coordinated and smooth-running IEP meeting.

Contacting parents is a particularly important aspect of the public agency representative in that the rules and regulations of PL 94–142 mandate certain procedures or steps that must be taken in order to facilitate the attendance of one or both of the parents at the IEP meeting. Specifically, the public agency must notify the parents of the meet-

377

ing early enough to ensure that they have the opportunity to attend and schedule the meeting at a *mutually* agreed upon time and place. The parents must also be informed as to who will be in attendance at the meeting and should be advised that they may invite other persons as they see fit. If neither parent can attend, the public agency must use other methods to ensure parent participation including individual or conference calls. An IEP meeting may be conducted without a parent in attendance if the public agency is unable to convince the parents that they should attend. In this eventuality, the public agency must have a record of its attempts to arrange a mutually agreed upon time and place such as:

1. Detailed records of telephone calls made or attempted and the results of those calls,
2. Copies of correspondence sent to the parents and any responses received, and
3. Detailed records of visits made to the parents' home or place of employment, and the results of those visits. (Implementation of Part B of the Education of the Handicapped Act, 1977, p. 42491)

In addition, the public agency must take whatever action is necessary to make certain that the parents understand the proceedings at the meeting, including arranging for an interpreter for parents who are deaf or whose native language is other than English. The parents are also entitled, upon request, to receive a copy of the completed individualized education program.

The second responsibility of the public agency representative is to be knowledgeable regarding the various service delivery arrangements available within the agency they represent. In addition, this individual must be familiar with other potential placements that may be required by the child outside the public agency. For example, if a disabled youngster needs residential care or the services provided in a special day school, the representative of the public agency should be able to communicate the particular characteristics of the placement so as to allow other team members to judge its appropriateness in relation to the problems exhibited by a particular handicapped child. Since the public agency is responsible for providing necessary transportation between the child's home and the setting where he/she is to receive needed educational services, the representative must be aware of the modes of transportation available to disabled children. This information is crucial to finalizing the most appropriate IEP for any handicapped youngster.

The third responsibility of the representative of the public agency is to serve as a facilitator in (1) preparing the tentative statements that will constitute the IEP (for example, statements of levels of educational performance, annual goals, general objectives, short-term instructional objectives, and least-restrictive environment) and (2) conducting the actual IEP meeting. As was mentioned in preceding chapters of this book, it is essential that some preliminary and tentative work be done prior to the IEP meeting in order to isolate those goals, objectives, and educational placements that are potentially germane to the youngster's specific educational needs. This information can be derived from activities that were discussed in Chapters 4, 5, 6, and 7. That is, when provided with viable referral, screening, and evaluation data and with informal diagnostic information when available, it should be possible to generate a feasible instructional plan for the disabled child. This educational plan must be very flexible and cannot be considered final until it has been approved by all participants of the IEP meeting. In ideal situations, the preliminary educational plan merely serves as a departure point from which discussion can flow. The individuals who actually devise the tentative IEP may be the public agency representative, the regular or special educator, school psychologist, educational diagnostician, or any other person(s) knowledgeable in specially designed instruction. In common school practice, the informal educational plan will, in all probability, be the product of a group effort where a number of persons contribute to its formulation. In any event, constructing this preliminary plan will not come about if someone does not take the time and effort necessary to ensure its development. The public agency representative is the most logical person to accomplish this task.

Once the IEP meeting has been convened, there are several variables to consider in order for the meeting to progress smoothly. For example, the parents must be made to feel comfortable and that their contributions are essential and relevant. Every member of the IEP team must be heard and their observations and comments regarding the child duly considered. No person should be allowed to dominate the proceedings and circumvent the best opinions, thoughts, and conclusions of the group in toto. Obviously, the finalized IEP must be written in an acceptable form and be approved (signed) by all participants. A mechanism to permit the evaluation of attaining short-term instructional objectives must also be developed and plans made to implement it. Invariably, attaining these and other activities necessary to culminate in a successful meeting occur by design and not happenstance. Careful planning and coordination are necessary to ensure the generation of an appropriate IEP for every handicapped child. Much of the responsibility for this task falls to the public agency representative.

Teacher(s)

The teacher(s) of the handicapped child in question must also be included on any team charged with the responsibility of formulating an individualized education program. In many ways, the teacher(s) (that is, the person(s) who has or will be providing direct instruction to the child) included on the IEP team is its most important member in that he/she alone is knowledgeable regarding the specific *educational* characteristics and needs of the youngster that will serve to mold and direct the goals, objectives, and services eventually delineated in the IEP. While the participants function to provide structure to the meeting and afford relevant insights into the child's skills and abilities, the teacher(s) is the person(s) who has had closest contact with the handicapped child in the school and is in the best position to estimate the potential effectiveness of the developing individualized education program. His/her knowledge regarding instructional techniques and educational placements that have and have not been proven appropriate for the youngster can do much to circumvent needless waste of both time and energy.

While it is a simple matter to state that the teacher(s) must be a participant in the IEP meeting, the arrangements necessary to permit this involvement are not always easy to implement. Since the teacher(s) to be included has instructional responsibilities throughout the school day, it is necessary to (1) exercise selectivity as to when to hold the meeting or (2) provide a substitute teacher or released time in order to allow the teacher(s) the time necessary to be a full and meaningful member of the IEP team. Of course, it is unrealistic to expect the teacher(s) to give up his/her rare "breaks" in the school day to attend the IEP meeting. This is unfair and does not provide adequate time to fulfill his/her tasks in developing the IEP. In addition, scheduling the IEP meeting after school hours frequently conflicts with school-based teacher meetings and may also be unacceptable to parents because of commitments in the home. For these reasons, making arrangements for the IEP meeting must entail strategies for releasing a teacher(s) in order to plan for and attend the meeting. Some school districts routinely budget for a specified number of days in which substitutes are employed for the purpose of permitting various instructional staff to attend IEP meetings. In other cases, using teacher aides and volunteers can be an effective way of freeing the teacher's time and permitting attendance at the meeting. Regardless of the method utilized, school systems and other public agencies should develop policies regarding this matter and ensure that teachers are afforded adequate time to meet their responsibilities in generating individualized education programs.

The teacher(s) assigned to participate in the IEP meeting has several responsibilities. The most obvious of these entails generating statements regarding an individual child's present level of educational performance, annual goals, general and short-term instructional objectives, and educational placements necessary to educate the disabled student. As was mentioned in previous chapters, delineating these statements for specific children takes careful planning and, in most instances, some informal diagnoses. It falls to the child's teacher to perform the bulk of this task. There can be little doubt that such relevant and detailed *instructional* assessment and planning can be accomplished only by the professional who is actively involved in the day-to-day process of educating the youngster. This does not mean that other team participants cannot contribute to the instructional statements set forth in the IEP. However, the teacher(s) of the child should be considered the person(s) with most direct knowledge of the instruction required by the child and the person most likely to speak realistically to the utility of suggested activities that are offered as possible approaches to circumvent or correct the handicapped condition.

In a similar vein, the teacher(s) of the disabled child, through direct instruction efforts, is best able to determine the attainment of annual goals, general and short-term instructional objectives. Evaluating goals and objectives must be formally accomplished at least once a year. While possibly appropriate for determining the feasibility of broad-based goals, this time span is unrealistically long when applied to general and short-term objectives. Obviously, instruction staff should be able to ascertain the progress a child is making virtually on a daily basis. If it is found that the objectives formulated for a student are not leading to attaining an annual goal, an alternative plan to facilitate desired outcomes must be restructured and instituted. This effort to reconstitute a child's instructional objectives when needed is the responsibility of the teacher(s) in conjunction with input from various supervisory personnel. Consequently, the onus for evaluating the IEP, from the standpoint of both daily instruction as well as attaining annual goals, is left largely to the ongoing activities of the teacher.

In that many handicapped children either have or soon will have more than one teacher, it is necessary to consider which should be included on the IEP team. From the viewpoint of maximum service to the child, it is recommended that *all* teachers currently serving, or who are likely to serve the youngster, be included since they will all play a direct role in providing educational services. More specifically, the following teachers should be routinely involved in developing the IEP: (1) all the special education and regular education teachers presently servicing the youngster; (2) any special education or regular teachers possibly being considered to service the child; and (3) any related service personnel directly or tangentially serving in the educational effort directed at the disabled child. The reason for including all staff who may come into instructional contact with disabled youngsters is to provide input from a variety of sources and, importantly, to avoid confusion as to role responsibilities. At the conclusion of IEP meetings, no doubt should be evidenced regarding which professionals are responsible for which services. If such confusion occurs, the chances for successfully implementing the IEP will be greatly diminished.

Parents

The parents of handicapped children represent an important and vital source of information within the context of the IEP meeting. The regulations governing PL 94–142 specify a series of steps that must be taken to ensure that parents are encouraged to take an active role in the educational planning of their disabled child. These steps, outlined in the section dealing with the responsibilities of the public agency representative, are quite comprehensive and usually result in the parent being in attendance at the meeting in which the individualized education program is to be formulated. The parents of the handicapped child can supply much relevant information regarding their youngster that can directly influence the development of the IEP.

In many school systems, when the parents are contacted initially and informed that their child has a handicapping condition, they are asked to begin a file that sheds light upon the youngster's behavior patterns in the home. This data can be particularly helpful as it relates to those children who exhibit problems in the sociobehavioral and basic living/self-help areas. That is, where children are thought to evidence relatively pervasive disorders, variations in severity between home and school can be revealing as to the true nature of the condition. In many cases, parents can be instructed in techniques of systematic observation that yield reliable and valid information. The prime reason for maintaining detailed records regarding home functioning is that variations on the severity of the problems exhibited in the home and school directly relate to such factors as reinforcement systems and schedules, parental attention, appropriateness of current educational placements, and the influence of siblings and peers.

Parental input can also be of value when the child demonstrates academic and career/vocational disabilities. Validation of attitudes and interests generated from inventories and other assessment devices administered to the child can be provided by parents. Information as to work habits, personal cleanliness, hobbies, acquaintances, sense of time, preferred tasks, and so on, permit a more complete picture of the youngster's abilities to function successfully in the job market or sheltered workshop setting. The child's academic levels and potential may also be elaborated upon by parents. Types of reading, mathematics, and written expression activities enjoyed in the home can supply educators with valuable insights into the child's motivation and tolerance level to academic-related tasks. In addition, the manner of instruction (such as modeling or using repetition) in which the youngster seems to learn best may also affirm or contradict observations of the child made in the school environment.

Not only can parents provide meaningful insights regarding their child's behavior, but they can also play an important role in carrying out the goals and objectives specified in the IEP. Although in the past parents have been frequently ignored as partners in educational efforts, they can be utilized very effectively to reinforce instruction presented in the school. Helping with homework assignments and ancillary teaching of concepts necessary for attaining academically related objectives can be adequately accomplished by parents if provided some training. Ensuring that appropriate behavior patterns in the schools are being rewarded in the home is also possible. For example, various school systems have established home-school communication programs that operate upon "report cards" sent home each day. The report cards are meant to relate to parents the child's progress toward attaining goals and objectives of both an academic and social nature. Based on the child's accomplishment of instructional or social tasks (previously agreed upon by the parents, teachers, and child), reinforcements may either be given or withheld in the home. That is, if the youngster is making adequate progress toward appropriate goals and objectives, he/she may be allowed to play with friends after school, stay up later, or have extra desserts. If satisfactory progress is not made, home privileges may be withheld. Since the child may alter his/her status as to home privileges by cooperating and working toward goals and objectives in school, no privileges are likely to be denied the youngster permanently. Rather, systematic manipulations of reinforcers only available at home are employed to facilitate academic and social progress in the schools. Readers wishing further information regarding the particulars of the home-school communications program should consult Dickerson, Spellman, Larsen, and Tyler (1972) and Kroth (1975).

Other Individuals

In addition to the public agency representative, teachers, and parents, other persons may also be included in the IEP meeting. One logical person who might provide viable assistance in planning the IEP is the child or adolescent for whom the individualized education program is being developed. The student may be involved if either the public agency or parents deem it advisable. School systems may find it valuable to devise their own guidelines or policies regarding student participation. As a rule of thumb, it is probably to the parent's and educational agency's advantage to include the pupil whenever he/she is capable of understanding and participating in the discussions that take place.

Because of the specifics of a given problem, the public agency may wish to involve other personnel who have knowledge or expertise regarding the child or available and potentially appropriate educational programs. In those instances where a youngster requires extensive related services to benefit from special education, the professionals who will be providing the services should be included. Physically and orthopedically impaired students may require the regular services of the physical and occupational therapist. Persons qualified in this area should, of course, play an active role in planning the IEP. Supervisory personnel, counselors, physical education teachers, recreation specialists, school nurses, etc., may, at certain times, all contribute to generalizing appropriate goals and objectives.

For a variety of reasons, the parents of the disabled youngster may also wish to involve additional individuals in the IEP team. For many reasons, parents may feel insecure when initially contacted and informed that their child is suspected of having a disabling condition. When the fact has been confirmed and the IEP scheduled, it is not unreasonable to expect that they may feel the need for support and advice. Frequently, family physicians, other family members, neighbors, or friends and advocates familiar with the process of IEP development may accompany the parents. These individuals can often be quite helpful in clarifying perceptions regarding the child as well as providing the parents the support necessary to be active and meaningful participants in the IEP meeting.

Evaluation Personnel

The IEP team must involve a member of the public agency's evaluation personnel if the child has been evaluated for the first time and may include evaluation specialists for meetings regarding youngsters currently served. The purposes for including this individual are obvious. If questions arise regarding the procedures employed in the assessment process, someone must be present who can either explain the purposes and format of the tests used or provide fuller interpretations of the results. If possible, the member of the evaluation team to be involved in the IEP meeting should be the person who actually conducted the assessment of the child. It is this individual who can relate specifics as to how the child responded to particular items on the evaluation procedures utilized. These observations, which may not be reflected in the test score itself, can commonly be of value in estimating a child's true ability in the area assessed.

As was mentioned previously, the evaluation of a handicapped child must be completely redone on at least a three-year basis. Where the child has been served previously in special education, the already developed IEP must be reviewed annually and, if necessary, revised. In these cases, an evaluation staff member should be present to answer potential questions regarding the original diagnosis and to recommend procedures that may be necessary at the present time. Obviously, when the evaluation of a handicapped child is three years old or the IEP has been in effect for one year, more current assessment procedures are needed to document progress and continued movement toward stated goals and objectives.

In the rare event that a member of the agency's evaluation personnel is not available for the IEP meeting, it is possible to conduct the meeting if the representatives of the public agency, a teacher, or other person is knowledgeable regarding assessment procedures. In the absence of an individual certified or licensed by the state agency to conduct individual evaluations of students, this person must be able to interpret the results of the testing. Most special education teachers are proficient in a variety of testing strategies and would be able to fill this role adequately. When specialized procedures have been administered (such as language samples or attitude surveys), professionals competent in these techniques should be consulted for purposes of interpretations.

Private School Representative

Prior to the public agency placing or referring a handicapped child to a private school or facility, the agency is responsible for initiating and conducting a meeting to devise an individualized education program. When the meeting is convened, a representative of the private school or facility must be in attendance. If it is not possible to secure the presence of a representative, the public agency must use other methods to ensure participation including individual or conference telephone calls.

After the disabled child enters the private school or facility, any meetings to review and revise the youngsters IEP must be conducted at the private school or facility at the discretion of the public agency. If the private facility initiates such a meeting, the public agency must ensure that the parents and an agency representative (1) are involved in any decision about the child's individualized education program and

(2) agree to any proposed changes in the programs before those changes are implemented. Even after the private school or facility implements a child's IEP, responsibility for compliance ultimately rests with the public agency and state education agency.

From the foregoing discussion it is possible to see that the participants in the IEP meeting may number from a minimum of three (that is, representative of the public agency, one or both of the parents, and the child's teacher(s)) to as many as are considered necessary to plan appropriate instructional services and placements for a disabled youngster. Since generating the IEP is to be the result of a group process, it is essential to establish an open communication system. All members of the IEP team must feel free to speak frankly and to be made to sense that their contributions are needed and worthy of consideration. This is a particularly important point in relation to the parents and other members of the team who may not have great experience in the specific purposes of the IEP meeting and how it is to be conducted. In general, there are three major elements to address when facilitating communication in a group: listening, questioning, and nonverbal interactions. The following section provides discussions of each of these elements.

TECHNIQUES TO FACILITATE COMMUNICATION

To a great extent the level and extent of communication elicited in the IEP meeting determines its ultimate success. The primary purpose of the IEP meeting is to generate the best educational program possible for a given handicapped child. This purpose requires a good deal of cooperation among participants before the plan can actually be implemented. Written approval of each team member as to the services to be provided the youngster is standard policy in most school districts and other public agencies. It is apparent that the members of any IEP team come to the meeting with various levels of expertise in relation to instructional methodology and service delivery systems. Consequently, the participants who are thoroughly familiar with the necessary *products* of the meeting commonly need to provide direction to the activities of the meeting, at least initially, in order to ensure that observable progress is maintained.

As was mentioned above, parents and other noneducational personnel may experience some basic feelings of uneasiness and uncertainty in the IEP meeting as a result of being involved in a new and potentially difficult situation. In many instances, the first few minutes of the session determine the general affective tenor that will likely be present through-

386

out the entire meeting. During this time, the parents and others new to the IEP process should be made to feel welcome and accepted. In order to circumvent problems and to put participants at ease, the representative of the public agency and teachers who have undoubtedly attended IEP meetings previously are well advised to adopt an attitude that contains the following:

1. *Acceptance of other persons and their knowledge of the child's problem.*
2. *Allowing all participants to express their own perceptions of the child and to contribute fully to amelioration of the handicapping condition.*

While it may be compelling for professionals in the group to "tell" other participants the "best" way to deal with the child and his/her disability, this frequently accomplishes little and may possibly be offensive to some members of the team. Effective communication patterns do not convey a feeling of uselessness to parents and other noninstructional persons. Rather, effective communication transmits the idea that all participants must help each other in order to manage the problems exhibited by the handicapped child. The specific techniques necessary to promote helping relationships among participants include questioning, listening, and nonverbal interactions that enhance the communication process. This section discusses these techniques in relation to the IEP meeting.

Questioning

Participants involved in the IEP meeting must focus on *data* that have been collected and organized. The focus on data tends to alleviate feelings of emotion among some team members that, if made the focal point of the meeting, makes attaining an IEP very difficult. Consequently, professionals familiar with the required outcomes of the meeting should use the available data as a major reference point to aid all participants in understanding the needs of the child. In order for the participants to achieve a realistic picture of the type and severity of the problem and to reach a decision on appropriate educational interventions, questioning techniques should be employed effectively. The purposes of questioning in the IEP meeting include:

1. Stimulating the participants to talk
2. Securing additional information
3. Broadening the discussion

4. Including additional facts
5. Challenging perceptions that are interfering with conclusions
6. Clarifying thinking
7. Developing new thoughts
8. Offering alternatives
9. Facilitating decision making and choosing between alternatives
10. Securing agreement
11. Obtaining commitments to assume responsibilities and implement the IEP

Perhaps the major power of a question lies in the fact that it calls for an answer. Asking appropriate questions can assist participants in ferreting out the roots of an issue or misunderstanding and gain information to clarify essential points. Formulating questions is simple and is accomplished by most people every day. However, to be most beneficial the questions used must be short and easily understood. Long and cumbersome questions frequently confuse matters and institute anxiety in those who are not knowledgeable regarding the technicalities of educational practices. Professionals should endeavor to omit words that may not be readily comprehended by other team members. Terminology such as "dyslexia," "scope and sequence," "audiogram," "telebinocular," "ecological mapping," when used *without proper explanation* do not convey the meanings for which they were intended. Too frequently, jargon was employed with parents and others for the purpose of intimidation and to stave off potentially embarrassing questions. Of course, this practice is untenable to competent professionals and must be avoided. To illustrate this point, Kratoville (1975) graphically describes the confusion parents frequently experience when confronted with technical language:

> The dialogue does not improve as it comes. The counselor with that battery of test results ("his performance is so much better than his verbal") seems to grow taller. The parents seem to shrink by the time they are shown the door . . . their heads are reeling under the impact of a series of unfathomable statements. What for goodness sake is an "Itpah" or a "Wisk?" What is hyperkinetic behavior? What is sibling rivalry? What is a modality? What is "ead-i-ology?" And most of all, what did she tell us to do? (p. 136)

Obviously, professional educators must talk to noninstructional persons in simple, direct language. If this practice is not employed, a coequal relationship among the team participants is exceedingly difficult to attain.

According to Acevedo, Elliot, and Valverde (1976), six basic steps are necessary to conduct an orderly and cohesive session and to assure that participants review all substantial and pertinent information and come to realize its full meaning (see Figure 9–1). *Opening dialogue* and *expanding conversation* usually take place as the IEP meeting is initiated and the evaluation data presented. *Clarifying thoughts* and *providing information* are employed to elaborate upon the thoughts and feelings of the participants and to allow inclusion of observations and other data that either contradict or validate the results of the evaluation efforts. *Narrowing future actions* and *reaching agreement* relate specifically to formulating the IEP and assigning responsibilities for attaining short-term instructional objectives.

Attaining an effective questioning cycle necessitates using two types of questions: procedural and content. Figure 9–1 indicates the types of *procedural* questions valuable in facilitating each step of the questioning cycle (*opening dialogue* is usually not accomplished by specific questions since this phase is merely intended to allow participants to state their purposes for the meeting). The particular types of procedural questions that correspond to steps in the questioning cycles are given in Table 9–1. Each type is accompanied by the purpose of the question and examples.

Concurrent with progressing through the IEP meeting from one step to another, it is also necessary to present the collected and organizational data in a coherent fashion. That is, the procedural aspects of the meeting, while very important, are secondary to the participants reach-

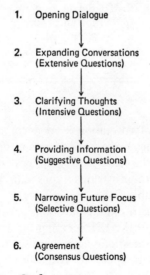

1. Opening Dialogue

2. Expanding Conversations
   (Extensive Questions)

3. Clarifying Thoughts
   (Intensive Questions)

4. Providing Information
   (Suggestive Questions)

5. Narrowing Future Focus
   (Selective Questions)

6. Agreement
   (Consensus Questions)

FIGURE 9–1 Questioning Cycle

TABLE 9–1 Procedural-Type Questions

Type	Purpose	Examples
Extending questions	1. To broaden the discussion	1. "What other factors are important?" 2. "What is the relationship of the behavior to fear of school?"
Intensive questions	1. To challenge questionable perceptions 2. To clarify thinking	1. "Why do you think so?" 2. "Why do you think this is important?" 3. "How will it affect Bob's instruction?"
Suggesting questions	1. To develop new ideas 2. To consider possible approaches	1. "What ideas have you thought about that we haven't considered before?" 2. "Suppose we did it this way—what would happen?" 3. "This works with other children—is it feasible here?"
Selecting questions	1. To make a choice between two or more alternative courses of action	1. "Which of these solutions is best for you and Maria, A or B?"
Consensus questions	1. To reach agreement 2. To define responsibilities and tasks to be accomplished	1. "Is it agreed?" 2. "Who can do this?" 3. "How long will it take?"

ing conclusions and interpretations. To accomplish this, *content* questions can be used to encourage persons attending the meeting to achieve an understanding of the data and gain realization of their meaning. Content questions in their various types can be used throughout the question cycle (see Table 9–2).

Open-ended or unstructured questions are particularly helpful during the opening stages of the IEP meeting but can be employed throughout. These types of questions are worded in a general manner to encourage participants to speak to virtually any aspect of the problem or to relate any possible perceptions or thoughts. Open-ended questions

TABLE 9–2   Content-Type Questions

Type	Purpose	Example
Open-ended: general in nature	1. To broaden view-point	1. "What else might be important?"
	2. To introduce a new phase	2. "Where could we go here?"
Direct: addressed to a specific area	1. To request specific information	1. "Precisely what would be your suggestions?"
	2. To isolate and probe in-depth	2. "Can you be more specific?"
		3. "What experiences have you had with it?"
Relay: referred back to previous dialogue or situation	1. To help avoid giving one's own opinion	1. "How does this relate to what you said earlier?"
	2. To establish continuity of thought	2. "Isn't this connected with . . . ?"
Reverse: referred back to person	1. To encourage questioner to think for him/herself	1. "First, what do you mean by . . . ?"
	2. To clarify understanding	2. "Tell me what this says to you?"
Basic: the "W" questions: who, what, when, where, why	1. To elicit fundamental information	1. "What other procedures did you use?

are stimulus free and response free and can be utilized at various points to extend the range of comment responses beyond what is given.

Direct or *relay* questions are helpful in gaining responses to specific aspects of the situations and to facilitate retrospection. Both types of questions serve to focus attention on the problem rather than on a mere description of it. In addition, using direct and relay questions can cause members of the team to reflect on previous and, perhaps, erroneous statements made and to visualize aspects of the problem more clearly. Employing these types of questions usually causes participants to develop a continuity of thought that makes conclusions easier.

Reverse and "W" questions serve two functions. The first is to assist team members in sensing their own feelings regarding particular aspects of the problem. In many instances, using reverse questions enables a person to discover, at least partially, an answer for him/herself if provided the opportunity to talk about a question. If necessary, the reverse question can be followed by a "W" question to elicit a more direct reply.

This process serves to direct respondents to focus attention on items and issues to which they may not have responded on their own initiative.

The major purpose of questioning techniques is to guide the participants through the steps necessary to reach conclusions. Questions should be asked in such a fashion that equal weight is given to both facts *and* feelings. They should never be used to imply criticism, seek to impose views, or to interrupt. To be effective, the atmosphere in which questions are asked must be supportive and nonjudgmental. Readers wishing to explore the area of questioning are encouraged to consult Brammer (1973) and Merton, Fiske, and Kendall (1956).

Listening

In the IEP meeting (as well as in any other session involving two or more people), asking questions requires effective *listening*. Listening is not the mere act of hearing what is said. Rather, this essential tool of efficient communication involves trying to understand the implicit and explicit messages being sent by another person. This is a difficult proposition that requires discipline, concentration, freedom from distraction, patience, and open-mindedness (Barbara, 1971). Most importantly, listening requires *active* participation, alertness, appropriate questions, and following main ideas. Rarely do people engage in active listening on a routine basis; however, it is necessary for participants in the IEP meeting to do this in order to develop a good individualized education plan.

Active listening is an essential tool in the IEP meeting since it assists an individual to understand what another person is thinking and feeling. The inevitable use of terms unfamiliar to some participants requires that some of them must be defined and explained or the primary purpose of communication will be defeated. Kroth (1975) lists several factors that, in many instances, may be deterrents to listening. Although these are written from the teacher-parent point of view, they can (with slight modification) be easily applied to all other members of the IEP team. It may be helpful to pursue these points with some care in that if a slowdown or stopping of the communication process is noted, it frequently can be traced back to one of these points. Kroth's deterrents to listening are given below.

1. *Fatigue.* Listening is work. If the mind or body is tired, then one will be a much poorer listener. We have all had the experience of sitting in lectures when we have been so tired that we cannot follow the speaker. If the teacher has a number of conferences in a row and she has really worked at listening, she will find her mind wandering

toward the end of the day. A break should be scheduled to walk around and perhaps have a cup of coffee.

2. *Strong Feelings*. At times a particular child will cause strong feelings of anger because of some behavior. It is usually better to have a cooling-off period before having a conference with the parents. This may be a time that the teacher will want to talk to the school counselor about her own feelings. Other strong feelings, including sadness and happiness, on the part of the teacher will make it difficult for her to be a listener during a conference. It is usually wise to take stock of oneself before entering into a conference with a parent.

3. *Words*. The children's verse that ends "But words will never hurt me" is far from true. Consider for a moment the impact of the following:

"You're fired!"
"I'm pregnant."
"Your child's retarded."
"This is the Police."
"I love you."

The very words one uses or hears can make the pulse beat more rapidly, sweat appear, and the eyes dilate. The teacher must carefully consider the words she uses in a conference and realize that certain words may deter or end listening on the part of the parent.

In discussing with parents of exceptional children the effects of the conference when a diagnostic label was applied to their child, many indicated that they heard nothing after being informed that their child was "retarded" or "emotionally disturbed." Parents apparently go through a series of psychological reactions such as shock, denial, guilt, rejection, blame, anger, embarrassment, and hostility before they accept the diagnosis and begin the productive steps of habilitation. The teacher who realizes that parents are having a difficult time in adapting to the reality of having a handicapped child will allow the parents every opportunity to talk over their feelings as these feelings relate to the child.

Realizing that parents may enter a conference with "strong feelings" (point 2), the teacher should not be surprised if certain words used during a conference may end "listening" on the part of parents. When this happens, it may be expedient to suggest that parents take some time to think about what was discussed and to set a date in the near future to continue the conference.

4. *Teacher Talk*. High percentages of teacher "talk" time in a parent/teacher conference reduces the amount of listening time. A teacher once asked to have a tape of one of her parent conferences critiqued. By using a stopwatch it was determined that the teacher had talked eighty percent of the time during the conference. If as Wendell Johnson (1956, p. 23) says ". . . we come in time to realize that every speaker is his own most captive listener," then the teacher probably learned more about how she felt about the child than the

parents learned about how they felt about the child. Basically, she spent very little time in listening to the parents and allowing them to listen to themselves discuss their child. There are times that a teacher needs to "listen" to herself by talking about a child, but it may be that this is best done by talking to a listener other than the parent. The above mentioned conference was probably more therapeutic for the teacher than for the parents.

The time, therefore, that the teacher engages in talking during a conference will reduce the time she can spend in listening. If listening is considered important, then it is wise to analyze the time spent in talking by the various participants during the conferences one holds.

5. *The Environment.* The physical surroundings can have an effect in listening. It is difficult to attend to another person if there is a great deal of distraction, either visually or auditorally. Even the physical comfort of the parent can have an effect on the interaction.

A businessman once had two chairs in his office for people who came to see him. On one chair he cut two inches off the front legs and on the other chair he cut two inches off the back legs. If he wanted the interview to be short, he put the client in the chair with the front legs shortened and if he was in no hurry, he seated the client in the chair with the short back legs. Merely controlling the seating arrangement seemed to have the desired effect.

6. *Writing.* Writing during a conference is a controversial subject. For some parents writing seems to inhibit the flow of conversation, for other parents it seems to increase the flow. Many professional people take notes during an interview—i.e., doctors, lawyers, etc. There also seems to be something about writing that helps the listener focus on the messages being relayed. Perhaps this is more true when the listener is fatigued than when she is alert. Students sometimes say that taking notes during a boring lecture is one way of keeping attention focused on the subject. (pp. 36–38)

If deterrents to listening can be avoided by carefully using questions, nonverbal behaviors, and manipulating the physical environments, it will be possible to be fully alert and listen for a variety of reactions. The person who is an effective listener typically can pinpoint inconsistencies, sarcasm, double meanings, and estimate the accuracy of information provided. At the same time, it is possible to grasp the main ideas of a verbal message and convey sincere interest and concern crucial to the cooperative relationship. Table 9–3 provides a list of listening techniques that are helpful in obtaining information that is necessary for a successful IEP meeting (Acevedo, Elliot, and Valverde, 1976). The techniques of attending, clarifying, restating, reflecting, and summarizing are listed with accompanying purposes and examples, and structures are provided whereby persons can take responsibility for altering their attitudes and behavior as well as influencing those of others.

TABLE 9–3   Listening Techniques

Type	Purpose	Examples
Attending	1. Conveys interest 2. Encourages further verbalizations	1. "I see." 2. "Uh, huh." 3. "Yes, go on." 4. Nodding head affirmatively.
Clarifying	1. Brings vague material into sharper focus 2. Examines statement(s) and pinpoints issue 3. Brings out related issues	1. "I'm not clear about how you feel." 2. "Could you state the issue again?" 3. "Are there other problems?" 4. "Is there something else?"
Restating	1. Restates important points in order to get agreement 2. Indicates that you are listening and understanding the problem	1. "This is your decision and the reasons are . . . ?" 2. "If I understand your idea, it is . . . ."
Reflecting	1. Focuses on the person's feeling—tone rather than content 2. Reflects person's own feelings and brings them into clearer awareness	1. "You feel strongly about . . ." 2. "It was a shocking thing to hear . . ." 3. "I sense that you're not satisfied."
Summarizing	1. Pulls together essential facts and ideas 2. Serves as a checkpoint for further discussion	1. "These are the key ideas you have." 2. "Can we say, then, that we have accomplished the following . . . ?"

Nonverbal Interactions

Intimately intertwined with the techniques of questioning and listening are nonverbal expressions that are an invariable component of the communication process. Nonverbal expressions include such commonplace actions as body stance, facial movements, touching, tone and voice quality, and environmental artifacts. Depending on the type and intent of the nonverbal cue, it may either support a question or statement or deny its sincerity. For example, a negative facial expression when accompanying the words, "I am happy to be here" tends to belie the speaker's honesty. However, head nodding, eye contact, and body posture can enhance a verbal message and favorably accent what is being said.

All participants of the IEP meeting, and particularly those who are given either the direct or indirect charge of managing the meeting, should be continually alert to the effects of nonverbal messages emanating from themselves or others. This is not an easy task since these messages are generally complex and interrelated with each other as well as with the verbal statements and questions that are being spoken. There are so many nonverbal cues that convey a myriad of meanings that it is impossible to describe them all. Table 9–4 provides a sample of types of nonverbal behaviors that can positively or negatively influence the process of communication that focuses upon specific effects of human behavior and physical environment upon the receiver or listener. Interested readers are encouraged to consult these texts.

The typical IEP meeting usually lasts anywhere from 45 minutes to three hours. Some situations require multiple sessions in order to generate appropriate instructional goals and objectives and to select feasible service delivery systems. The tenor of most meetings is businesslike with the majority of time devoted to pursuing the facts and establishing strategies that should result in good educational programming. Successful culmination of this task requires an open exchange of ideas and information. To facilitate this process, the meeting should be held in a place where privacy is assured and at a time that permits participants to eliminate interruptions. Essential information (such as evaluation results, observation results, and forms) should be immediately available. Environmental factors that might inhibit participants from being at ease must be considered in order to facilitate communications. Appropriate questioning and listening strategies should be utilized so that the meeting can begin, proceed, and end on as positive a note as possible. All IEP team members should review the following points as a means of conducting an effective meeting:

1. Use questioning cycle
2. Use active listening
3. Avoid argument
4. Avoid abrupt interruptions and change of subject
5. Allow short pauses in the conversation to permit reflection
6. Phrase responses clearly
7. Understand and accept the feelings and responses of others

TABLE 9–4   NonVerbal Behaviors

Type	*Example*	*Meaning(s)*
Facial expressions and eye contact	1. Smile and direct eye contact	1. Affiliation, involvement, liking.
	2. Direct eye contact	2. Seeking feedback at end of remarks; signaling that channel is open.
	3. Looking away— avoiding eye contact	3. Boredom; avoiding interaction; dislike of speaker or message.
	4. Subdued expression, lowered eyes	4. Thinking about message; sadness
	5. Tightened lips and raised brows or forehead	5. Anger; disgust.
Postural cues	1. Turning to face speaker	1. Desire to relate, interact.
	2. Turning away	2. Avoidance—"Don't intrude," "Leave me alone."
	3. Leaning forward	3. Positive attitude, accepting.
	4. Leaning away	4. Negative attitude.
Vocal cues	1. Low-pitched voice	1. Conveys security, positive manner.
	2. Loud, fast-paced, blaring voice	2. Anger or impatience.
	3. Soft, slow, low-pitched voice	3. Affection; sadness.
	4. Monotone, low-pitched, moderately slow	4. Boredom.

8. Avoid rash judgments
9. Avoid implying answers to questions
10. Summarize agreed-upon conclusions
11. Follow through—everyone should receive copies of all final documents

ADVISEMENT OF RIGHTS

In most instances, the IEP meeting progresses smoothly and results in developing a set of statements that specify the child's present level of educational performance, annual goals, general objectives, short-term instructional objectives, and the necessary special education and related services required to afford the handicapped child a free and appropriate education. In addition, the extent to which the child will participate in regular educational programs (if at all), dates for the initiation and duration of services, and evaluative criteria will also have been determined so as to permit conclusions regarding the effectiveness of the written individualized education program in providing for the needs of the disabled youngster. In order for the IEP to become final, its contents must be approved by all team participants. Once approval of the final IEP is acquired, the youngster may be placed in the designated setting that has been judged most appropriate to his/her unique educational needs and special education and related services begun.

One of the most important and vital components in the process that culminates in the finalized IEP is that both the public agency and parents *mutually agree* upon the procedures used to identify and evaluate the child as well as the educational plan and placements to be employed to educate the youngster. The concept of mutual agreement is crucial in that the mandates of PL 94–142 stipulate a series of safeguards or procedures that public agencies must carry out to ensure that the handicapped child's rights to an appropriate education are being exercised. In order to fully understand these rights, it is convenient to group them under the broad headings of (1) procedural safeguards and (2) due process. Procedural safeguards are those strategies that relate specifically to the parents rights including (1) the right to prior written notice, (2) the right to examine all pertinent records pertaining to their child before the public agency initiates identification, evaluation, or educational placement of the handicapped child, (3) the right to approve each evaluation procedure to be used with the disabled youngster, and (4) the right to participate in the decisions regarding the formulation of the individualized education program and the instructional placement deemed necessary to best educate the handicapped child. Due process refers to those procedures available for the parents and public agencies to secure a hearing when the child's right to privacy of records is violated or a disagreement arises as to the child's evaluation contents of the IEP or type of placement utilized. These two components of a child's rights to a free and appropriate education are discussed in the following section.

Procedural Safeguards

The procedural safeguards provided parents and public agencies are intended to ensure that all rights created by law are in fact made available to children who have disabilities, their families, and public agencies.

At the beginning of the IEP meeting (or before if possible), it is incumbent upon the public agency to advise the parents of the procedural safeguards available to them and this, of course, would include the parents' right to initiate a due process hearing if the child's right to privacy is not maintained or if they and the public agency are in insurmountable disagreement regarding the educational services proposed for a given youngster. The major elements of procedural safeguards involve (1) prior notice and parental consent; (2) opportunity to examine records; (3) independent educational evaluation, if desired; and (4) the individualized education program and placement of the child.

Prior notice and parental consent. One of the major safeguards provided under PL 94–142 is that written notice must be given to the parents of a handicapped child at a reasonable time before the public agency proposes to initiate or change the identification, evaluation, or educational placement of the youngster or the provision of a free appropriate public education to the child. In the instance where the parents or other individuals wish to change the youngster's status and the public agency refuses, the public agency must provide a written notice to that effect.

Parental *consent* must be obtained before a replacement evaluation is initiated or prior to the child being placed in a program providing special education and related services. Importantly, changes in the youngster's special education program after the initial placement do not require *consent* on the part of the parents. Rather, the parents must be notified to the effect that a change in services is proposed. If the parents are in disagreement as to the proposal of the public agency, they may attempt to arbitrate their differences or institute a due process hearing.

The content of the notice provided the parents by the public agency must follow certain guidelines. The content of the notice for either identification, education, and placement of the youngster must provide a description of the action proposed or refused by the agency, an explanation of why the agency proposes or refuses to take action, and description of all options considered by the agency and the reasons why the options were rejected.

In their written notice regarding the evaluation, the public agency must provide a description of each evaluation procedure, test, record, or report the agency uses as a basis for the proposal or refusal. The public agency's notice must be written in a language easily understandable by the general public and provided in the native language of the parent or mode of communication used by the parent. This is particularly important in cases where the parents are deaf (and do not read well enough to understand the written notice) and require the message to be delivered in sign or other manual means of communication. Blind parents probably need the written notice presented in braille if they are to understand what the public agency is proposing. In instances where the parents are nonreaders or cannot understand the notice written in English, it must be translated orally or by other means to the parents in their native language or other mode of communication. Public agencies must maintain records that they have complied with the mandate of prior notice to parents.

Opportunity to examine records. For many years, the policies and standards governing a child's right to privacy have been assumed and have not been protected in practice or law. PL 94–142 specifies that parents of disabled children must be afforded an opportunity to inspect, review, and possibly, amend all records pertaining to their child. Once the parent requests to secure the files that the public agency has collected, maintained, or used in relation to planning for the individualized education program or a hearing convened to determine the appropriateness of the identification, evaluation, or placement of the child, the public agency must respond with all due speed. In no case should the response by the public agency exceed 45 days from the time of the initial request.

The right to inspect and review educational records includes *responses* from the public agency to reasonable requests for explanations and interpretations of the records. The public agency must also supply copies of the records containing the required information if failure to provide the records would prevent the parents from utilizing their right. The public agency may charge the parents for the cost of copying the records. However, the cost charged by the agency cannot be such that it would prevent the parents from inspecting and reviewing the records. In addition to the parents, a representative designated by the parents (such as family physician, lawyer, or education specialist) may also receive the records for purposes of review.

PL 94–142 also provides for those instances where parents may wish to modify the records that have been generated regarding their child. If parents feel that the educational records maintained on their youngster are inaccurate or misleading or violate the privacy of the child, they may request the public agency that maintains the records to amend the available information. After the public agency receives a request to amend the educational records of a particular child, it must decide whether to do so. If the agency decides not to after receiving the information that is believed inaccurate or misleading or violates the privacy of the child, the parents must be informed of the refusal and be advised of their rights to a due process hearing.

Other federal law also addresses the issue of collecting, maintaining, and disseminating information regarding children. PL 93–380 (Family Educational Rights and Privacy Act—commonly referred to as the Buckley amendment) was enacted in 1974 and provided for the protection of privacy of all persons. Essentially, this law stipulates that any public agency that receives federal funding must give parents the opportunity to inspect, challenge, and correct their children's records. Students aged 18 or older are given the same rights in relation to their own records. The Buckley amendment also mandates that no public agency may release identifiable data without the parents' written consent.

Similarly, PL 94–142 states that a public agency must keep detailed accounts of all parties permitted access to a child's records. This accounting must include the name of the party who was given access, date that access was given, and the purpose for which the records were employed. If necessary, the agency must also provide parents a complete listing of the types and locations of the educational records collected, maintained, or used by the agency.

Independent educational evaluation. An important procedural safeguard revolves around the parents' right to obtain an independent educational evaluation of their child. When parents choose to exercise this right, it is usually to question the public agency's decision that their child is, in fact, handicapped. It is not uncommon, however, to find informed and knowledgeable parents who perceive their child as needing specially designed instruction and related services when the public agency has conducted an evaluation and has come to the conclusion that the youngster does not meet the criteria to be placed in special education within that school system. Regardless of the reasons for why parents may wish to secure the independent evaluation, if they are in disagreement with the evaluation obtained by the public agency, they have the procedural safeguard to request an evaluation conducted outside the public agency.

An independent educational evaluation means an evaluation conducted by a qualified examiner who is *not* employed by the public agency responsible for educating the child in question. In addition, the evaluation may be done at public expense if the public agency agrees. "Public expense" is defined as the public agency paying for the full cost of the evaluation or insuring that the evaluation is provided at no cost to the parent. Whenever an independent evaluation is done at public expense, the criteria under which the evaluation is obtained, including the location of the evaluation and the qualifications of the examiner, must be the same as the criteria the public agency uses when it initiates an evaluation. In the event the public agency feels the evaluation conducted within the public agency has been thorough and complete, a due process hearing may be convened to show that this, in fact, is true. If the due process hearing upholds the public agency's contention, the parents still have the right to an independent evaluation, but *not* at public expense.

If the parents exercise their right to obtain an independent evaluation (either at public expense or not), the results must be considered by the agency in all decisions made with respect to providing a free and appropriate education to the disabled child. This data will certainly be used in any due process hearings that are held to question a public agency's decision to either provide or withhold special education and related services from a child. In the event that a due process hearing is desired by the parents or public agency, specific policies and procedures must be followed. The impartial hearing officer must consider the results of the evaluation obtained by the public agency. It is important to note that the parents do have recourse to due process hearings if they are in disagreement with the public agency's findings and conclusions regarding the manner in which the child's education is to be provided.

Due Process

Throughout the discussion on procedural safeguards, it has been repeatedly stated that parents and public agencies have recourse to "due process hearings" if they are in disagreement as to the identification, evaluation, or educational placement of a particular child. In addition, parents may also legally question the manner in which the youngster's records have been handled or that they have received inadequate notice regarding when a public agency initiates or refuses to initiate a change in the child's educational program or placement. It is hoped that the actual due process proceedings will be used rarely since they are frequently expensive, time consuming, and possibly result in a delay of service being provided to the disabled youngster. Most school systems devise a series of mediation efforts before a due process hearing is actually convened. The efforts at mediation are intended to resolve differences between parents and public agencies informally. These activities may be conducted by members of the state education agency or local education agency personnel who have not previously been involved in the case. Ideally, mediation culminates in a resolution of differences without developing an adversarial relationship and with minimum stress to the parents and child. However, public agencies must be careful to ensure that the mediation process used is not done for the purpose of denying or delaying parents' rights to a due process hearing.

If mediation efforts prove unsuccessful, it may be necessary to initiate an impartial due process hearing. The specifications for this meeting are straightforward and entail appointing an impartial hearing officer, the rights available during the hearing, administrative appeal, and possible civil action. The major elements of the due process hearing are discussed below.

Due process hearing and impartial hearing officer. The due process hearing must be conducted by the state education agency or the public agency directly responsible for educating the disabled child. The policy as to which agency is to convene the meeting is determined by state statute, state regulation, or written policy of the state education agency. The agency to conduct the meeting must inform the parents of any free or low-cost legal and other relevant services available in their immediate geographical area.

The hearing must be chaired by an impartial hearing officer. Stipulating this individual to be in charge of the meeting is meant to provide a fair representation of all relevant facts and to render decisions that are not influenced by concerns other than what is in the best interests of the youngster. The impartial hearing officer may not be a person who is an employee of the public agency involved in educating the child. In addition, this person is not to have a personal or professional interest that would conflict with his/her objectivity in the hearing. The public agency or state education agency is required to maintain a list of persons who qualify to serve as hearing officers. This list must contain the qualifications of each of those persons.

The issue of impartial hearing officers has been much debated in educational circles. Some states have utilized their retired citizens as hearing officers. Other states have located personnel in local colleges and universities and civic groups who would qualify to serve in this role. Whoever is chosen to function as an impartial hearing officer should receive some basic training in the procedures to follow in the due process hearing and, if not familiar with special education, an orientation to the terminology and procedures commonly discussed in the hearing. Selecting an impartial hearing officer is crucial to the rights of both the parents and public agency and should be considered with great care.

Hearing rights. The parties involved in a due process hearing have available several basic rights that are meant to ensure that all relevant information is considered and that their interests are being duly exercised. Both the public agency and the parents have the right to be accompanied and advised by counsel and by individuals with special knowledge or training with respect to the needs of the handicapped child. These persons may present evidence and confront, cross-examine, and compel the attendance of a witness. Evidence that has not been disclosed to the parents or public agency five days before the hearing may be kept from being introduced into the hearing. A written or electronic verbatim record of the proceedings must be maintained and made available to the parents upon request. Similarly, a written statement as to the findings of fact and decisions shall also be provided the parents when they so desire. The child who is subject to the hearings may be present at the proceedings if the parents feel it is imperative to do so. The parents must also be given the right to open the hearing to the public.

The decision made as a result of the due process hearing is considered final unless an *appeal* is initiated. If the hearings were conducted by a public agency *other* than the state education agency, the state education agency must institute an impartial review of the hearing. This review includes an examination of the entire hearing record to document that the procedures employed during the hearing were consistent with the requirements of due process. If necessary, additional information germane to the particular case can be obtained and afford both the public agency and parents the opportunity for oral and written argument at the discretion of the reviewing official. The parents and public agency continue to have the right to be represented by counsel. Once an independent decision has been reached at the completion of the review, a written copy of the decision is given to the adversaries. The decision made by the reviewing official is considered final unless the parents choose to pursue civil action. In the case where the *initial* due process hearing was conducted by the state education agency, and the parents are still in disagreement, their legal recourse is to proceed with appropriate civil action.

Timelines and child's status during proceedings. Upon request for a hearing, the public agency other than the state education agency must within 45 days (1) reach a final decision through the due process hearing and (2) mail a copy of the decision to the public agency and parents. If the state education agency is to conduct the due process hearing, it must respond to the request within 30 days so as to reach a decision and inform both parties of the results of the hearing. In some instances, an impartial hearing officer or reviewing officer may grant specific extensions of timelines if desired by either the public agency or parents.

Unless the parents and public agency agree otherwise, the child's status during any administrative or judicial proceedings is to remain in his/her present educational placement. If the hearings are to admit a child to enroll in a public school for the first time, with the consent of the parents the child must be placed in the public school program until completion of the hearings.

SUMMARY OF CONDUCTING
IEP MEETINGS

The initiation, maintenance, and successful completion of the IEP meeting are of vital concern in providing a free and appropriate education to handicapped children. If the meeting is successful, its ultimate outcome entails finalization of statements pertaining to the child's present level of educational performance, annual goals, general objectives, and short-term instructional objectives. The educational placement that best fosters the youngster's progress toward attaining the stated goals and objectives will be specified and the system by which to judge the effectiveness of the instructional efforts will have been delineated. In toto, the completed IEP provides a "blueprint" for whatever educational efforts are to be instituted in order to afford the handicapped child the best instructional opportunities possible.

As a prelude to completing the IEP, several variables must be addressed. The first of these relates to the fact that all individuals to participate in the IEP meeting must be intimately familiar with the purposes for which the meeting was convened. These purposes include providing parents with information regarding procedural safeguards and due process procedures that are available to them in order to ensure that their child is receiving a free and appropriate education. Team participants must be chosen and contacted to secure their cooperation in participating in the IEP meeting. Available forms necessary to document that procedural safeguards are being maintained must be kept and efforts made to hold the meeting in a room free from outside distractions. Completing the goal and objective statements by cooperative interchange among team members must be achieved and a method devised to evaluate the degree to which they are being attained. Finally, an educational placement that is most efficient in facilitating the delivery of special education and related services to the handicapped youngster should be designed and prepared for implementation.

The individuals to participate in the IEP meeting vary from a minimum of three to as many as seven or eight. The mandated members of the IEP team include a representative of the public agency, the child's parents, and the child's teacher(s). A member of the public agency's evaluation personnel must also be involved if the child is being evaluated for the first time. Additional team members may also include the child when appropriate and other individuals at the discretion of the public agency or parents. These persons may include the family physician, lawyers, psychologists, family members, advocates for the child, and so on. When the disabled youngster is to be placed in a private facility, a member of that agency must be involved in formulating the IEP. Regardless of the team's actual composition, each participant should be aware of his/her responsibilities both in planning as well as in carrying out the designated instructional program. For example, the representative of the public agency probably should be responsible for contacting the team members and organizing the various administrative arrangements necessary to finalize the IEP document. Usually this person also takes

405

the lead in preplanning efforts (during the 30 days between the evaluation and the IEP meeting) that serves to direct the delineation of the goals and objectives necessary for the child to receive specially designed instruction. Parents are responsible for relating problem behaviors in the home and specifying the particular strong points that might shed light upon the child's most urgent educational needs. The teacher(s) frequently conducts informal diagnostic procedures to provide more precise data of an instructional nature. Teachers may also speak to the youngster's relevant characteristics that might be of assistance in selecting appropriate educational placements.

In the final analysis, the IEP meeting is a group process that necessitates attention to those elements that help in facilitating open lines of communication. At minimum, the types of questions asked, listening techniques employed, and nonverbal interactions all significantly influence the way in which the meeting proceeds. If attention is devoted to these features of the communication process, a successful conclusion of the IEP probably will be realized. On the other hand, if communication patterns are less than satisfactory, parents or the public agency may wish to exercise their right to due process.

Due process refers to the formalized procedures by which a concerned party may demand a hearing when they suspect that their procedural safeguards have been violated. Procedural safeguards are those rights granted to public agencies and parents that relate to the child's rights of privacy of records, a free and appropriate education, opportunity to inspect all documents used in making educational decisions regarding the youngster, prior written notice before any actions are taken to the evaluation or education of the child, and to question the desirability of the completed IEP or educational placement. If parents are in serious doubt as to whether their child has received his/her rights as granted under the law and are unable to come to agreement with the public agency, they may initiate a due process hearing. If the hearing is not satisfactory to the parents they may, in certain instances, request an appeal to be conducted by the state education agency. If this process is deemed nonacceptable, they may take civil action. While new in the education of the handicapped, the procedures entailing due process are reasonable and serve to provide disabled children with their guaranteed rights to a free and appropriate education.

References

Acevedo, M. A.; Elliot, C.; and Valverde, L. A. A guide for conducting an effective feedback session. Special Education Supervisor Training Project, Document No. 15, The University of Texas at Austin, 1976.

Brammer, L. M. *The helping relationship.* Englewood Cliffs, N.J.: Prentice-Hall, 1973.

Dickerson, D.; Spellman, C.; Larsen, S.; and Tyler, J. L. Home-school communication program: A contingency management system. *Teaching Exceptional Children,* 1973, 5:44–49.

Kratoville, B. L. What parents feel. In L. Buscaglia (ed.), *The disabled and their parents.* Thoroface, N.J.: Charles B. Slack, 1975.

Kroth, R. L. *Communicating with parents of exceptional children.* Denver: Love Publishing Company, 1975.

Merton, R. H.; Fiske, M.; and Kendall, P. *The focused interview.* Glencoe, Ill.: The Free Press, 1956.

CASE STUDY 1

Introduction to Jon

Case study 1 follows the development of an educational program for Jon, a seven-year-old male student entering first grade for the first time next year. He had been enrolled in a regular public school kindergarten program the past year while receiving the assistance of the physical therapist, occupational therapist, and language specialist. Although special assistance was granted during his kindergarten year, Jon had not been officially admitted as a special ed student nor had an IEP been developed for him. He was referred to the special education program in the local school district by his parents before starting kindergarten and now prior to first grade. The purpose of this second referral was to officially qualify Jon to receive special education services and to initiate IEP development. A brief overview is provided below prior to presenting the actual documents involved in referral, evaluation, and IEP development.

At the time of referral by his parents to this particular school district, Jon was age six and had already undergone extensive psychological evaluations. His parents, both professionals, had noted early, severe lags in Jon's motoric, language, and social development. Motorically, Jon did not sit alone until age 11 months and began walking at the age of 24 months. Presently, at age seven, Jon still has an unusually labored gait and trouble with most gross motor movements such as running and climbing. Fine motor problems prevent his being able to dress himself independently. In addition, Jon has considerable difficulty printing his name.

Language development was similarly delayed, particularly with regard to comprehension of language and meaningful communication of ideas. Jon spoke his first words at a normal age; however response to simple commands did not develop until the age of four. Until age six, Jon's oral expression consisted predominantly of bizarre forms of echolalia such as repetition of lines heard on TV game shows or direct quotes from printed labels or written text. Jon was, and to some degree still is, unable to express his feelings in words, particularly when he is in a state of excitement or anxiety. In addition to poor communication patterns, Jon has many difficulties differentiating socially appropriate behaviors in various situations.

Jon's behavior problems are not the traditional problems associated with disruptive or destructive behaviors. Rather his behavior seems to be more a result of not understanding that specific actions are appropriate only within certain situations. For example, calling his sister disparaging names when she does not comply with his wishes is typical of children his age. Jon also uses these same expressions when he is upset with his teachers. He also has trouble distinguishing other normal everyday home behaviors from public behaviors. The inability to communicate with others has also, to some degree, led Jon to solve problems with peers physically rather than verbally. An additional characteristic of Jon's social behavior is his tendency to isolate himself from persons the majority of the time with the exception of his immediate family and some other adults.

Jon also has several highly unusual strengths. It was not long after his parents became worried over his oral language development that they noted Jon reading children's books aloud to himself. This began at the age of three with no previous instruction. At age five, Jon not only now read adult-level books aloud but would laugh in appropriately humorous sections. This led most observers to believe Jon was not only word calling but also comprehending what was read. This unusual talent became quite reinforcing to him and was often used as a mechanism to isolate himself from groups of peers or adults. Other aspects indicating Jon's abilities include his skill in communicating to other persons with the typewriter. He also has an uncanny way of remembering persons names, important dates, and the proper spelling of most words.

As we will see throughout the development of his educational program, Jon is a good example of a handicapped child "qualified" by many labels. It is interesting to note that these labels do not serve any valuable purpose in establishing his educational program. However, the labels have allowed him to receive special education and related services.

REFERRAL

Jon's referral to special education was conducted primarily through parent initiative and correspondence with the school district special education offices. Written correspondence was necessary initially because Jon's family was in the process of moving to that particular city at the time of referral. Correspondence was initiated as Jon was reaching the age of six. Although Jon had attended two years of kindergarten and preschool, Jon's parents felt he was unready for first grade public school experience primarily because of his immature social and language development. The initial referral then was in the form of request for transfer to an elementary school in the city where there was easy access to a number of special services. The following correspondence more clearly elaborates the process of referral followed to initiate Jon's special education and related services. The final referral initiated prior to his placement in first grade is the one of concern in the subsequent screening, evaluation, and IEP development sections of the case study. This referral at the conclusion of public kindergarten was initiated by Jon's kindergarten teacher after consultation with his parents. All three persons felt it best if Jon's "paperwork" for special education preceded his first grade entry. Therefore, a screening committee meeting was initiated through the kindergarten teacher.

> Drs. Paul and Barbara Jones
> 3101 Willow Springs Rd.
> Willow Springs
> May 1, 1977

Mr. James Smith
Director, Pupil Service
Willow Independent School District
Willow Springs

Dear Mr. Smith:

I am writing to request a transfer for my son, Jon, into the regular kindergarten program at Willow School for the period commencing August, 1977. Jon has an unusual combination of developmental strengths and weaknesses. He has been extensively evaluated (psychologically, neurologically, etc.), and is currently receiving therapy at both the University Communication Disorders and Perceptual-Motor Clinics. This request is made on the recommendation of Mr. Jones, staff psychologist at the Speech Clinic and has been discussed with Mr. Hughes, Willow Principal. Our own opinion as Jon's parents and as a medical doctor and clinical psychologist is that the Willow School program represents the most appropriate school setting available in the Willow Springs area.

Thank you for your consideration. I look forward to hearing from you regarding our request at your earliest possible convenience. Should you require additional information, please don't hesitate to contact me.

Sincerely,

Paul R. Jones, M.D.
Barbara S. Jones, Ph.D.

cc: Mr. Jones
   Mr. Hughes

WILLOW INDEPENDENT SCHOOL DISTRICT

Division of Educational Development
Department of Pupil Services

May 27, 1977

Drs. Paul and Barbara Jones
3101 Willow Springs Road
Willow Springs

Dear Drs. Jones:
This acknowledges your request for a transfer for:
Student's Name

Jon Jones   To: Willow Elementary   From: Maple Elementary
Grade K
This transfer is approved on adjustment basis for the 1977–78 school year. It is granted contingent upon any changes that might occur as a result of action now pending in the courts over which we have no jurisdiction.

Sincerely,

Mr. James Smith
Director, Pupil Services

cc: Principal, Willow
   Principal, Maple

SCREENING

A screening committee met to discuss Jon's referral. The purpose of this meeting was to determine the degree to which special education services were needed and plan for any future evaluation. The committee consisted of the special education teachers in the elementary school where Jon attended kindergarten, the language therapist, occupational therapist, physical therapist, Jon's kindergarten teacher, and the school principal. Several special education support staff members from the central administrative offices were also present. Jon's parents and a private educational specialist were also present. During the meeting the parents shared all previous test data with the school representatives as well as their appreciation for efforts extended over the past year. The data were reviewed by the team and consensus was made that the accumulated evaluations certainly qualified Jon to receive special education services. It was also revealed that Jon had participated in several years of private language and motoric therapies prior to his entry into the public schools.

Members of the entire team who had some knowledge of Jon's past performance discussed general goals and concerns regarding his education. It was determined that in both school, home, and therapy sessions the same three concerns were manifested—language, socialization, and motor abilities. It was agreed that further evaluation was needed in these areas in order to document present levels of educational performance and to give some starting point for educational planning. His parents also volunteered to secure copies of Jon's vision and hearing exams obtained this past year. Committee members also unanimously supported Jon's partial placement in the regular school program in order to continue peer relationships he had built during kindergarten. It was also recommended that Jon's kindergarten teacher be instrumental in selecting his first grade classroom utilizing what she knew about Jon and other classroom teachers. Because of the positive relationships that developed between Jon and his parents and teachers, interactional observations were not conducted. In describing peer relationships between Jon and fellow classmates, the kindergarten teacher expressed the following:

> Jon's best friend is Bill, a youngster with similar motor problems and, like Jon, highly creative and bright. Several of the more popular girls in the class tend to assist Jon in many difficult activities like cutting, pasting, printing and dealing with his lunch box. Jon loves their attentions and often calls them his "girlfriends." Most of the children are quite aware that Jon is different and respect him for his ability to read stories to them. As far as his handicaps they appear to understand and often want to help him. When Jon becomes anxious or excited he has more trouble with conducting himself in a socially appropriate manner with peers and adults.

In addition to this initial data-gathering session, the committee also reviewed basic entrance procedures and advised them of their rights.

Permission forms for further educational evaluation were signed as well as a summary of the screening meeting. The final IEP meeting date was set for the following month to review further evaluations, placement, and develop program goals and objectives.

EVALUATION

For several years Jon has undergone numerous and extensive psychological and neurological examinations. These examinations have resulted in his being labeled with a multitude of handicapping conditions. Over the years the conditions exhibited by Jon have been diagnosed as aphasic, autistic-like, dull-normal to neurologically dysfunctioned, speech and language disordered, perceptually handicapped, minimal brain dysfunction, emotionally unstable, and severely learning disabled. Each of these early private evaluations was shared in full with the screening team as well as the IEP team. The following section is provided to give the reader an overview of some of the measures that have been administered to Jon and their results. In addition, excerpts regarding diagnoses made from several neurological exams are provided. These are taken directly from several written evaluative reports. Actual educational evaluation for the purpose of documenting present levels of performance in language, social skills, and motor abilities is reported in the introductory section of Jon's IEP. Subsequent school diagnosis for placement and vision and hearing results are also reported in the IEP document.

Previous Test Results

Electroencephalogram—1976
"indicated a right parieto-occipital focus with bilateral synchrony."

WPPSI—1976
Verbal IQ 73% ile
Performance IQ 6% ile
Full scale 35% ile

Illinois Test of Psycholinguistic Abilities (ITPA)—1976

CA	5-3
PLA	4-7
Mean scaled score	33.0

Subtests	Age Score	Scaled Score
Auditory Reception	4-0	30
Visual Reception	4-4	33
Auditory Association	5-3	37
Visual Association	3-2	22

Subtests	Age Score	Scaled Score
Verbal Expression	4-3	32
Manual Expression	3-2	27
Grammatic Closure	6-2	47
Visual Closure	3-6	25
Auditory Memory	6-6	42
Visual Memory	5-10	40

Ayres Figure Ground—1976 $s = -2.4$

Leiter International Performance Scale—1977
$CA = 5\text{-}9$ $MA = 7\text{-}3$

Reitan-Indiana Neuropsychological Test Battery—R—1977
Results suggested right hemisphere, parietal lobe dysfunction.

Ayres Perceptual Motor Test Battery—1977
Crossing the Midline $s = 0.2$
Right-Left Discrimination $s = 0.8$
Bilateral Motor Coordination $s = 0.7$
Initiation of Posture $s = -2.6$

Frostig Developmental Test of Visual Perception—1977

Eye Motor Coordination	average
Figure Ground 3	average
Form Constancy	average
Position in Space	average
Spatial Relations	below average
Perceptual Quotient	98

Previous Diagnoses

Results of the Neuropsychological Examination suggest a right hemisphere, parietal lobe dysfunction. The dysfunction does not appear to be generalized across the entire parietal area, but possibly of a multifocal origin. There may also be some mild dysfunction of the left parietal region. Accordingly, tasks that involve integrity of parietal lobes (i.e. spatial orientation tasks) may be impaired particularly when performed with only the left hand. The impairment that Jon exhibits, however, is task specific as Jon can readily perform some spatial orientation tasks quite effectively and efficiently. Thus, Jon's deficit cannot be considered a generalized one. When Jon is required to make a motor response based on limited tactile input alone, errors inevitably occur, particularly if the response is limited to the left hand. The spatial orientation tasks that he can do most effectively are those tasks that are based on multiple cues and the use of several sensory modalities.

However, if Jon is required to perform simultaneous motor responses with both his right and left hands, even with multi-modal sensory input, he will tend to make errors with the left hand as the complexity of the task increases. The lower Performance IQ as compared with Verbal IQ on WISC-R testing also supports the above interpretations and findings.

The other aspects of the examination were well within normal limits, and on some items Jon performed exceptionally well. On some tests (i.e. Category Test) Jon exhibited excellent cognitive skills in terms of abstraction and problem solving insight. Jon's emotional immaturity and lability also interfere with his performance. Just as a matter of maturation there should be some significant gains in terms of some of the problems outlined above. (1978)

Jon is an anxious child with a realistic concept of his adequacies and inadequacies. He does appear to feel an unusual amount of pressure. However, he is not an "emotionally sick" child at this time but rather his emotionality appears to be a component of motor problems, auditory perceptual problems, and difficulty in getting across what he wants to say. Primary problem is believed to be language disorder, probably based on neurological dysfunction with secondary problem being an emotional reaction to his perceived actual inadequacies. Jon is a very intelligent child.

Concentrated language and perceptual motor therapy is a must. In addition, this creative child must find other outlets than speech and reading for his creativity.

School placement will be difficult. He needs to learn social skills, communication skills, improve motor development (all primarily kindergarten level) yet continue in his advanced reading and typing abilities.

Clinical Impression: Representational level disability. (1978)

The Leiter shows Jon to have superior nonverbal intelligence. At age 5–9, he attained a mental age of 7–3. He talked his way through the items as well as encouraging himself with statements such as, "This is real easy. It's got to be easy. I've got to remember. That's very important for me. I think this is very important." He appeared to be under a great deal of pressure, to be critical of self, and tense. Visual perception, discrimination, and association are above average. (1977)

Jon was a very pleasant and cooperative boy. He worked very hard and concentrated on each task. He conversed in a mature manner and seemed to possess advanced ability in reading. Jon was not discouraged or negative about any of the tasks he attempted. In general, Jon showed developmental lags in gross motor control, fine motor control, basic visual perception capacities and body awareness concepts. (1977)

1. Developmental lags in gross motor control.
2. Developmental lags in fine motor control.

3. Developmental lags in visual perception capacities.
4. Developmental lags in body awareness concepts.
5. Difficulty in obtaining meaning from what he sees and hears.
6. Bizarre verbal output—generative speech lag. (1977)

Present results of the Wechsler Preschool and Primary Scale of Intelligence and the Stanford-Binet Scale of Intelligence show this child to be functioning in the range of average intelligence. On the Wechsler Preschool and Primary Scale of Intelligence his Verbal Score was twenty-nine points higher than his Performance Score. On the Stanford-Binet Intelligence Scale he had much scatter. The test results show him to have difficulty with fine and gross motor coordination and to have an eye-hand integration problem as reflected in his drawings and on the Performance Scale of the WPPSI. On the other hand, this child reads words up through a seventh-grade level but has difficulty in comprehending what he reads, especially in the presence of a strange person. He likes a routine and does not like changes in his environment. In a testing situation, he is very apprehensive. Jon also responds to verbal questions with inappropriate answers and tells stories which are not coherent. This child also seems to be somewhat ambidextrous and appears unable to decide which hand he wants to use. In addition to the neurological diagnosis, it is felt that Jon has some emotional difficulties. He needs a school situation in which he can feel secure, have a routine, and learn to interact with his peer group. It is felt that he will need to have the teacher assist him in learning appropriate interaction. He is somewhat immature and dependent upon his family at this time. Jon also needs to have some help in the area of visual-motor integration. It is felt that help in this area should be in the form of games and should be pleasurable to him. Because of his stressful reactions to a change in routine, it is felt that he should stay in one school for as long as possible and not change rapidly from one school to another. In spite of his above average reading ability, on entering first grade Jon is likely to need help from a Special Education teacher. (1976)

Jon appears to be a child with significant difficulty getting meaning from what he hears and sees. This, combined with his strengths in automatic tasks such as memory and closure, appear sufficient to account for his expressive difficulties. It is recommended that he begin language therapy as soon as possible and that Mrs. Jones be involved in carry-over of therapy procedures in the home. Because of Jon's good memory skills, care should be taken to avoid his memorization of particular responses; generalization of understanding to novel situations should be stressed. Jon may be referred to the University Speech and Hearing Clinic or the Willowdale Speech, Language and Hearing Center for therapy. (1976)

As one can see from the above excerpts, no educationally relevant data is available. Though diagnoses appear to be quite specific, not only are they instructionally irrelevant, but they also contain many contradictions. The evaluation team, composed of many of the members of the screening committee, proceeded to conduct an educational evaluation. As recommended in Chapters 3 and 4 this evaluation should be written into the introduction to Jon's individual education program. In this manner, relevant present levels of performance, as well as evaluation for placement, preface actual goals and objectives. Including evaluation data serves to consolidate Jon's program and decreases unnecessary duplication of special education documents.

INDIVIDUALIZED EDUCATION PROGRAM

Name:	Jon Jones	Parents:	Dr. Paul Jones, M.D.
Birthdate:	6–31–71		Dr. Barbara Jones,
Age:	Six		Ph.D.
School:	Willow Elementary		
Teacher:	Kindergarten—Mrs. Roberts	Address:	3101 Willow Springs Road
Date of		Phone:	HE7–2242
Examinations:	April–May 1978	Examiners:	Mr. Jones, Language
			Ms. Phillips, Social Worker
			Mr. Cox, Physical Therapist
			Ms. Fuller, Occupational Therapist
			Ms. Simmons, Academics

Introduction

Referral. Jon was referred to the screening committee at Willow by his kindergarten teacher and parents who both stressed the importance of planning a program for Jon prior to the beginning of his first grade year. His parents shared previous diagnostic reports with the screening committee. It was decided at that time that attention should be directed to:

1. officially qualifying Jon for special and related services
2. conducting educational evaluations of present performance levels in language

3. collecting data regarding fine and gross motor skills and including writing

4. collecting data regarding Jon's social skills

These evaluations as conducted are reported below.

Background. Jon is a delightful and extremely bright six year old (soon to be seven) who has attended kindergarten at Willow for one year. Prior to this year, Jon attended a private kindergarten for two years. During this time, Jon has also received speech-language, physical, and occupational therapies. He seemed eager to work with adults during examinations and appears to accept special one-on-one educational situations as a part of the normal routine. He has attended various private clinics since the age of four. There is some indication from private reports shared by his parents that Jon has been diagnosed as having some neurological problems and was born with a slight heart malformation. This medical problem has not, however, had any effect upon his level of activity.

Evaluation for Placement

Although Jon has had several diagnostic labels applied to him by various psychologists and therapists in the past, for our purposes Jon qualifies as a child experiencing specific learning disabilities. The data below qualify him on the basis of oral expression delay and normal intelligence. In addition to the language problem, Jon experiences motor and socialization difficulties. Results of vision and hearing screening by private physicians indicate that with correction Jon's vision is normal and his hearing is also well within normal ranges.

WISC-R

Full scale	87	Performance	77
Verbal	100	Picture completion	6
Information	11	Picture arrangement	7
Similarities	11	Block design	10
Arithmetic	11	Object assembly	0
Vocabulary	9	Coding	10
Comprehension	8		

Cashin's Gross Motor Control Test Battery		*Williams' Process Checklist*
Static balance	below average	Overall immaturity noted in
Dynamic balance	0	hopping, galloping, running,

Body agility   below average   catching, and throwing. Left-
Twenty-yard dash   below average   leg tasks especially immature.
50 hool hop   0
Standing broad jump below average
Ball bounce   below average

	Test of Oral Language Development	
	(mean)	
Picture vocabulary	10	
Oral expression (bl. av.)	6	
Grammatic understanding	10	
Sentence imitation	10	
Grammatic completion	10	

Peabody Individual Achievement

Test	Grade Levels
Math	3-8
Reading recognition	8-2
Reading comprehension	5-6
Spelling	7-3
General information	6-4

Vineland Social Maturity Scale

Total score	60.5
Age equivalent	5.8
Social quotient	85

Writing Sample
(see attachment)

Behavior Rating Profile (Scaled Score Mean $= 10$ SD $= 3$)
Self-rating scale
    Home 9   Parent rating home   8
    School 6   Teacher rating school 6
    Social 9   Sociogram   7

On the basis of these results, the evaluation team recommends Jon be classified as learning disabled and that an educational program be developed to emphasize:

1. Oral expression
2. Fine motor skills in the self-help and penmanship areas
3. Gross motor skills with particular emphasis in self-help and PE-related skills
4. Social and behavioral skills integrated throughout all curriculum areas

The following sections define more clearly goals and objectives developed for Jon's program in each of these four areas. These recommendations are based on informal evaluations and observations as well as the general evaluation data presented above.

tHe QUICKGrAYFox

JUMPeD OVer tHe IAZy

BrOWN DOG

Handwriting Sample—Jon Jones—age 7—June/1978

Goals and Objectives

Special Education Area: Academics
  Performance Area: Oral language
  Annual Goal I: To increase Jon's receptive language by responding to various forms of spoken questions and commands.

  General Objective A Wh-questions.
  Short-term Instructional Objectives. Criteria: 100% accuracy with language therapist and two other individuals.
  1. Jon will answer appropriately to questions concerning time or parts of a day. (2, 3)**
  2. Jon will answer appropriately to how + verb questions. *(2, 3)
  3. Jon will answer appropriately to why, what if, and how come questions. *(2, 3)
  4. Jon will answer by description (other than "that one") to questions using the word "which." *(2, 3)

Note: Appropriate an echolalic or bizarre response

  General Objective B Response to commands.
  Short-term Instructional Objectives. Criteria: 100% accuracy with language therapist, regular teacher, and one other person.

* See also sociobehavioral skills to incorporate here.
** Parentheses designate persons primarily responsible for short-term objective instruction and continuous evaluation, thereof.
1 = Regular Teacher 2 = Resource Teacher 3 = Language Therapist
4 = Occupational Therapist 5 = Physical Therapist

1. Jon will follow a series of three commands given at one time. (2, 3)
2. Jon will respond to a series of four commands given at one time. (2, 3)

Annual Goal II: To increase Jon's oral language expression with regard to expression of feelings, logical explanations, and elaborate verbal descriptions.

General Objective A Discuss feelings of self and others.

Short-term Instructional Objectives. Criteria: without assistance in structured situation.

1. Jon will describe a character's feelings after listening to a story or film. (2)
2. Jon will describe how he might feel given various situations. (2)
3. Jon will describe his feelings immediately following classroom incidents. (2)
4. Jon will participate in small groups and discuss his feelings expressed by others. (2)

General Objective B Make logical explanations.

Short-term Instructional Objectives. Criteria: without assistance but in structured situation.

1. Jon will be able to choose the most logical statement between two explanations for action. (2)
2. Jon will be able to explain why people perform certain activities when viewing a film or listening to a story. (2)

General Objective C Use elaborate verbal descriptions.

Short-term Instructional Objectives. Criteria: without assistance or unusual verbalisms.

1. Jon will describe nouns with aid of pictorial representations. (3)
2. Jon will extensively describe scenes shown in pictures. (3)
3. Jon will describe scenes around him and actions as they occur. (3)

Special Education Area: Self-Help/Basic Living
Performance Area: Motor control
Annual Goal I: Increase proficiency in fine motor skills.

General Objective A: Dressing—fasteners.

Short-term Instructional Objectives (additive)

1. Jon will be able to put a button shirt on and prepare to button. (5)
2. Jon will be able to button his shirt. (4)
3. Jon will be able to put on coat and hat. (5)
4. Jon will be able to unfasten trousers and take off trousers. (5)

421

5. Jon will be able to pull trousers up. (5)
6. Jon will be able to tuck shirt into pants. (5)
7. Jon will be able to button or snap trouser top. (4)
8. Jon will be able to zip trouser front. (4)
9. Jon will be able to put on socks. (4)
10. Jon will be able to put on shoes. (4)

General Objective B: Penmanship.
Short-term Instructional Objectives

1. Jon will trace 3-in. words of his choice (five per day). (2)
2. Jon will write needed spelling words on 3-in. tagboard. (1)
3. Jon will trace writing exercises in regular class. (1)
4. Jon will type when extensive expression is needed. (1, 2)

General Objective C: Cutting.
Short-term Instructional Objectives

1. Jon will cut textured materials with assistance and four-finger scissors. (2)
2. Jon will cut textured materials without assistance. (1)
3. Jon will cut straight lines on paper without assistance. (1)
4. Jon will cut 5-in. circles without assistance. (1)

Annual Goal II: Increase proficiency in gross motor skills.

General Objective A: Walking and running.
Short-term Instructional Objectives

1. Jon will be able to walk with class on trips without tiring. (5)
2. Jon will be able to carry 10 lbs. for 20 yds. (5)
3. Jon will be able to walk for 20 minutes. (5)

Special Education Area: Sociobehavioral
Performance Area: Social Skills—Adults
Annual Goal I: Jon will decrease inappropriate behavior toward adults.

General Objective A: Negative remarks, name calling.
Short-term Instructional Objectives

1. Jon will not call his regular or special teachers names (big face, etc.) by end of semester. (1, 2)
2. Jon will not say "I can't" and other negative remarks more than once per day.

Performance Area: Social Skills—Peers
Annual Goal I: Jon will increase positive interactions with peers.

General Objective A: Play behavior.
Short-term Instructional Objectives

1. Jon will play with two other peers on one game for 10 minutes at a time increasing to 30 minutes. (1)
2. Jon will participate in group activities during recess once a week increasing to five times per week. (1)

General Objective B: Feelings.

Short-term Instructional Objectives

1. Jon will discuss his feelings with adults immediately following episodes. (2)
2. Jon will discuss feelings in front of small groups of peers. (1, 2)
3. Jon will repeat others' feelings after listening to discussions. (1, 2)

Performance Area: Behavioral—Crying, Hitting
Annual Goal I: Jon will learn to express anxiety in positive manner.

General Objective A: Removes self from situation.

Short-term Instructional Objectives

1. Jon will remove himself from situations when he becomes upset before hitting peer or crying. (1)

General Objective B: Seeks help when anxious.

1. Jon will go to counselor or resource teacher to discuss interaction. (2)

Services

Times	Regular	Special	Related
8:00– 8:30	(M-F Opening)		
8:30– 9:00	Reading Skills	(Resource Rm. MWF)	(TTH Language)
9:00– 9:30	(M-F Reading Aloud)		
9:30–10:00	(M-F Math)		
10:30–11:00	Writing	(Resource Rm.)	(MF Physical Therapy)
11:00–11:45	(M-F Lunch)		
11:45–12:00	(M-F Language Arts)		
12:00–12:30	(M-F Storytime)		
12:30– 1:00	Art, Music	(Resource Rm.)	(W Occupational Therapy)
1:00– 1:15	Recess	(Resource Rm.)	(TH Occupational Therapy)
1:15– 1:45	(Science, Social Studies)		
1:45– 2:15	(M-F Closing)		

( ) = Jon's schedule

The above schedule of services appears at this time to be the most efficient with regard to implementing instructional objectives and general concern that, at this time, Jon be integrated with peers. Any changes in this schedule, other than unforeseen daily scheduling conflicts, must be reviewed and agreed upon prior to change.

Evaluation

Annual goals. The following formal tests should be readministered at the conclusion of the year to provide some measure of Jon's progress toward annual goals:

- Test of Oral Language Development (Resource Teacher)
- Peabody Individual Achievement Test (Resource Teacher)
- Cashin's Gross Motor Control Test (Physical Therapist)
- Behavior Rating Profile (Teacher, Parent, Student)

Short-term instructional objectives. Short-term instructional objectives are to be reviewed by Jon's special and regular teacher each Friday. Once mastered, items are to be checked and strategies discussed for mastering others. In addition, each of the checked short-term instructional objectives is to be assessed through formal behavioral observation by Jon's teachers in December. All short-term objectives are to be reevaluated through extensive behavior data collection in April prior to the follow-up IEP meeting in May. In the event continuous assessment reveals difficulties in meeting short-term objectives (or new objectives are needed), the team can be reassembled to discuss additional strategies by contacting Mr. White, principal of Willow Elementary.

General objectives. General objectives are to be reestablished if any of the short-term objectives under them have not been met or need to be reestablished. Otherwise completion of all short-term objectives will suffice as accomplishment of general objective. However, many of the general objectives established for Jon will need extension of short-term objectives in order to meet mastery.

＊＊＊＊＊＊＊＊＊＊＊＊＊

In order to plan the most appropriate and successful educational experience for Jon Jones during the upcoming school year, the following persons met and participated in the development of an Individualized Education Program. The document, itself, completed on June 1, 1978, was agreed to be the most appropriate program for Jon for the next school year. The IEP team understands that no changes in services, evaluations, or objectives will be made without reconvening the team for the purpose of revision. Each member also understands his or her role in the program implementation.

_____June 1, 1978_____   _____H L Hughe_____
Date   Principal

                        _____MARCAret Simmons_____
                        Special Education Teacher

                        _____Mrs. Roberts-K_____
                        Regular Education Teacher

                        _____E Q mes B Jones_____
                        Parent(s)

                        _____Samuel James_____
                        Language Therapist

                        _____J. L. Cox_____
                        Physical Therapist

                        _____Diana Fuller_____
                        Occupational Therapist

CASE STUDY 2

Introduction to Juanita

Case study 2 follows the development of an individualized education program for 11-year-old Juanita, a deaf child, who had previously not received any school services. Juanita was referred originally in June 1978 through an anonymous call received in the child count offices of Harrison Independent School District. Harrison is the headquarters for a four-county rural special education cooperative. The call was presumably prompted through a public service advertisement shown on a local TV station that advised the public on new federal laws dealing with handicapped children's rights to free public education. The caller merely told the school that Juanita lived in a certain neighborhood in a rural area and that there was something obviously wrong with her. Juanita had apparently never attended school. The school staff investigated the situation through a home visit. It was found that the family had no telephone.

Juanita was found to be living with her widowed grandmother and had developed only a few crude signs for her repertoire of language behaviors. In addition to severe language delay, Juanita exhibited significant behavior problems. Unlike Jon, it will be discovered that Juanita cannot be integrated into any regular classroom situation and needs intensive one-to-one special educational instruction. Skills in attending to task and amelioration of destructive behaviors will dominate Juanita's first educational program.

REFERRAL

Following an anonymous call regarding a child residing at a specific address who had never been in school, a home visiting team from the

426

Harrison schools located Juanita, an 11-year-old deaf child. Upon investigation the school staff discovered that Juanita lived alone with her grandmother, Mrs. Valdez. Juanita appeared animal-like in her behavior and was controlled only through physical force. Her grandmother, somewhat leery of the school staff, discussed a little of Juanita's background. It appeared she had been the sole support for Juanita since age two when her mother left Juanita at the grandmother's home and was never heard from again. Mrs. Valdez indicated that Juanita's mother did not want her when she discovered Juanita was deaf. The diagnosis of deafness was made by a pediatrician who had advised special placement to help Juanita develop language skills. Juanita had developed a few gross hand signals indicating physical needs. Her behavior of running from one thing to the next was quieted when Mrs. Valdez walked over and sat in a rocker. This was apparently an indicator to Juanita that grandmother was ready to hold her. The child was obviously fond of being rocked. While observing in the home, Juanita was locked in her room for several minutes while Mrs. Valdez went about questioning the school staff regarding the reason for their appearance.

During the initial visit, the school staff discussed arrangements whereby Juanita would be seen by medical doctors and language specialists. Mrs. Valdez agreed to go with Juanita and the staff when appointments were secured.

SCREENING

A screening meeting was held the following week with the home visitation team, regional director for deaf education programs, school psychologists, and special education director and support staff from Harrison ISD. Mrs. Valdez declined to join the meeting but offered her support. Results of the meeting were shared with her in her home following the screening meeting. Mrs. Valdez reconfirmed her interest in pursuing assistance.

Recommendations made by the screening committee included:

1. Transporting Juanita and her grandmother to a nearby metropolitan area medical center for a thorough medical, visual, and audiological evaluation (transportation and expenses for the two-day stay to be paid by Harrison ISD)
2. Evaluating intelligence factors
3. Detailed observation of Juanita's home behavior for clues to reinforcement and self-help and other skills not detected on measures of intelligence

4. Assisting Mrs. Valdez in securing financial assistance through various community and welfare agencies

5. A follow-up meeting to plan an appropriate program for Juanita, approximately August 1, when all evaluations would be complete

6. Assigning two staff members as primary contacts with Mrs. Valdez based on personal relations developed during the initial interview. These staff members will accompany Mrs. Valdez during the two-day medical center evaluation.

EVALUATION

Juanita's evaluation was coordinated by Ms. Britton, home-bound teacher (regional program for the deaf), and Mrs. Sparks, psychologist, both from the special education support staff.

Medical Evaluation

Juanita and her grandmother were taken to a medical center of a large university for a complete medical examination that included a thorough audiological and visual evaluation. The center was located 150 miles from their town, necessitating at least one overnight stay. Mrs. Sparks and Ms. Britton accompanied Juanita and Mrs. Valdez in order to facilitate the examination process and to observe Juanita in a setting different from her home. The following sections are the summaries obtained from the evaluation.

General physical condition. The findings from the physical examination showed Juanita, while somewhat undernourished, to be in adequate physical condition. Other than a relatively severe case of mumps at two and a half years of age, she seemed to be free of common childhood illnesses. Since Juanita had seen a doctor only once (as a consequence of the mumps), she did not have inoculations for polio, measles, and so on. These were provided while she was at the medical center. Reflex testing and fine motor functioning were judged to be well within normal limits. Since Juanita was obviously hearing impaired, the pediatrician conducting the medical evaluation recommended that she be seen by specialists in hearing and vision. The evaluation of her visual functioning was recommended because the pediatrician felt that Juanita would need to rely heavily upon the visual modality in order to profit from educational opportunities.

428

Audiological evaluation. The audiological evaluation was conducted by Dr. Jerome, an otolaryngologist. Examination of the peripheral hearing mechanism indicated that Juanita had suffered repeated middle-ear infections as exhibited by scarring of both ear drums. While the tonsils and adenoids were slightly enlarged, they posed no threat at the present time. Mrs. Valdez stated that Juanita frequently had a "runny nose" and sneezed "at least 10 times a day." Dr. Jerome recommended allergy tests, the results of which showed no allergies to commonly encountered substances. Decongestants and antihistamines were prescribed to help control the runny nose and sneezing as well as to lessen the possibility of middle-ear infections.

Testing and hearing acuity was undertaken by a staff audiologist. After an initial period of questioning Mrs. Valdez regarding Juanita's medical and social history pertaining to potential deleterious conditions to auditory functioning, the testing was begun. Mrs. Valdez and Juanita were seated in a soundproof booth while being presented various environmental sounds at successively higher decibel (db) levels. The sound was presented in free field. It was observed that Juanita consistently responded (by quizzical facial expressions) at 95 db. The response was noted at frequency levels between 500 and 2000 hertz with every environmental sound attempted. It was concluded that Juanita's hearing loss was probably the result of middle- and inner-ear damage and not due to deficits at the level of the central nervous system. The diagnosis of deafness or hard of hearing was not applied since it was impossible to determine whether the use of a hearing aid would permit processing linguistic information. It was recommended that a hearing aid be obtained for Juanita and that intensive language development activities be initiated. Careful recording of progress in therapy would allow the determination of whether she would ever be able to utilize residual hearing for purposes of facilitating communication.

Visual evaluation. The evaluation of visual acuity was undertaken by an ophthalmologist. Inspection of the visual mechanism indicated no damage or dysfunction of any type. Based upon observations of Juanita's behavior during the examination and comments made by her grandmother, it was judged that Juanita possessed normal visual acuity. However, it was recommended that her responses to visual stimuli be monitored consistently to note any aberrations in visual acuity.

Observations

Assessment through observation probably provided the most educationally meaningful data regarding Juanita. Extensive observation was conducted during the two-day visit to the medical center. Specifically, the two staff members had an opportunity to observe self-help skills, communication skills, reinforcement patterns, and behavior patterns. Unique insights were made that were helpful in planning an appropriate educational program for Juanita.

Self-help skills. Several important variables were noted in Juanita's ability to maintain herself. First of all, twice during the first day and once during the second day Juanita soiled herself. Mrs. Valdez said that at home Juanita usually soiled herself a couple of times per week. With regard to dressing skills she appeared able to put on clothes (skirts, pants, and blouse), but in no instance did she attempt any fasteners. Juanita made no attempts at grooming until her grandmother took a brush at which time Juanita made a slight attempt to run the brush through (over) her hair. Mrs. Valdez reports that she bathes Juanita herself but that "she could if she wanted to." Mrs. Valdez also explained that Juanita enjoyed imitating some household chores and was quite proficient in washing dishes, cabinets, her dolls, and dusting. Motor skills seemed to be unhampered.

Communication. Interestingly, it was noted that Mrs. Valdez and Juanita had a quite extensive communication system between them. The system appeared to consist mainly of signals for nouns and verbs, particularly things Juanita wanted; warnings for poor behavior; desire to be rocked; offers to rock; the expression of pleasure and displeasure with each other; and the expression of needs, such as toilet needs, food, and drink. Very little combination of manual symbols was observed. Each of these signs was noted and coded for future use. In addition, Mrs. Valdez was observed to actually prime Juanita's responses to tasks at the medical center. The girl seemed quite proficient in modeling her grandmother after being primed for a response only once.

Reinforcement patterns. In addition to being rocked by her grandmother, Juanita allowed a nurse to rock her with slight encouragement from Mrs. Valdez who placed Juanita in her lap. Other reinforcers observed were: pats on the head or face, smiles, candy and fast-moving segments of television. These were all noted for future use.

Behavior patterns. Several important observations were made regarding specific problem behaviors exhibited by Juanita. When shown or demonstrated a task that seemed to confuse her, Juanita became almost violent in pushing away any materials or avoiding persons attempting to get her to perform. When scolded by sign or physically punished, she responded by screaming, biting, scratching, and kicking. Her grandmother indicated that during these periods Juanita would be locked in her room for an undeterminable amount of time. It was also observed that when screaming Juanita carefully watched the faces of the other individuals present. Responses to the sound elicited during audiological testing were in the form of stillness, silence, and visual search. At one point in the testing she screamed as if in answer to a sound. Unknowingly, Mrs. Valdez physically punished her for eliciting the sound.

Each of these observations led the school staff to suspect that Juanita was not as intellectually retarded as first imagined. Upon return to Harrison, Juanita was administered an intelligence scale appropriate for children who are deaf.

Intelligence

The intelligence assessment was conducted in the Valdez home on four separate occasions. During the first session two examiners and Mrs. Valdez worked on getting Juanita to respond to the examiner's modeling cues. The task of locating a piece of candy under the appropriate cup was used first. Modeling training was successful. The Nebraska Test of Learning Aptitude (NTLA) (Hiskey, 1966) was administered in three sessions in the home. Although Juanita's overall learning age was calculated on this measure to be approximately six years, the validity of the results with a child of this little experience was questioned. Tasks on the NTLA which were simplest for Juanita to model, although she did not perform at norm for any eleven-year-old deaf youngster, included: Bead Patterns, Memory for Colors, Picture Identification, Paper Folding, and Block Patterns. The most difficult subtests included Picture Association, Visual Attention Span, and Completion of Drawings.

Welfare Assistance

Upon their return from the medical center, Mrs. Valdez was taken to the community welfare offices and assisted in filing preliminary documents. It appears Mrs. Valdez has been doing some housework during the days to support herself and Juanita; however, Juanita was locked in her room during these hours. A social/case worker was secured and promised to continue support to Mrs. Valdez in securing hardship funds and other assistance through social service agencies. It was recommended that the evaluation team follow up on this item to assure that Juanita would receive proper medical care and nutrition. Mrs. Valdez expressed her appreciation for the support. Apparently, she had never

431

understood that she might qualify for aid of this kind prior to this point. Although not directly associated with school-related tasks, this activity was viewed by the evaluation team as essential to Juanita's ability to benefit from special education (that is, a related service).

With this initial phase of evaluation completed, Juanita was qualified for special services as deaf/hard of hearing. The IEP team and Mrs. Valdez met on August 1 to develop Juanita's educational program formally.

INDIVIDUALIZED EDUCATION PROGRAM

Name: Juanita Valdez
Birthdate: May 13, 1967
Age: 11–3
Date: 8–1–78
Address: Route 1, Box 254
Phone: na
School: Harrison Special Services

Special Education Teacher: M. Harper
Home-bound Teacher: Ms. Britton
Regional Director (Deaf Program): J. L. Stokes
Psychologist: Mrs. Sparks
Principal: J. L. Stokes, Director
Language Therapist: H. Mays

Introduction

Eleven-year-old Juanita was referred through the child count office of Harrison ISD in June. Since that time evaluations conducted reveal that Juanita is a deaf child of no school experience who exhibits severe communication deficits and behavioral disorders. She resides with her widowed grandmother and has since she was abandoned at the age of two. Juanita is an attractive Mexican-American child who is rather small and thin for her age.

Test Results

Formal test results, though listed below, are considered inadequate to define Juanita's present level of performance at this time. Reevaluation

** Code in parentheses indicates persons responsible for instruction in this objective. (1 = Homebound Teacher with Grandmother, 2 = Special Ed Teacher, 3 = Language Therapist)

will be recommended following the establishment of more substantive relationships with Juanita and the facilitation of more complex communication patterns.

Nebraska Test of Learning Aptitudes

- Learning age—6 (due to poor response patterns validity of these results questioned).
- Audiological—Juanita exhibited consistent response to sound in free field at 90–95 db. She was fitted with amplification devices.
- Visual screening—appears to be normal, no test was administered.
- Medical—generally fair health; medication given for nasal congestion; slightly malnourished.

General directions. From the formal data gathered and general observations made, there are three major areas that should be of concern in educational programming for Juanita. These areas include:

1. Primarily, establishing a beginning language system;
2. Establishing certain self-help skills; and
3. Behavioral and socialization skills.

The following sections delineate goals and objectives for each of these areas.

Goals and Objectives

Special Education Area: Academics
  Performance Area: Language
  Annual Goal I: To establish a beginning repertoire of signs and speech using the total communication approach. (Note: These skills may also be classified under Self-Help Sensorial, Training)

  General Objective A Auditory training (1, 2, 3)**.
  Short-term Instructional Objectives
  1. Juanita will at all times when awake wear appropriately calibrated amplification devices.
  2. Juanita will stop tasks to attend to sound.
  3. Juanita will watch teacher place familiar objects (candy, beads, etc.) in containers, listen to their sound next to her ear, and select on the basis of sound which one she wishes to have.
  4. Juanita will, with continuous reinforcement, respond vocally at the completion of a given sound segment.

433

General Objective B Vocalization and lip reading (3, 2, 1).

Short-term Instructional Objectives. Criteria: gross approximations

1. Juanita will elicit sounds on cue with 100% consistency.
2. Juanita will, when directed, visually attend to the movement of the teacher's lips for up to 30 seconds.
3. Juanita will elicit sounds in unstructured situations and be reinforced immediately for doing so.

General Objective C Simple nouns and verbs (standard signs) (1, 2, 3).

Short-term Instructional Objectives. Criteria: Juanita uses new signs spontaneously, self-directed.

1. Juanita will utilize the standard form for signs; she now has a nonstandard form.
2. Juanita will respond to certain response cue signs (for modeling, for repetition, etc.).
3. Juanita will utilize basic signs needed in her new school environment.
4. Juanita will utilize signs and gross approximations of vocalizations to indicate her desires and needs (toilet needs, food, drink, play, watch TV, etc.).

Special Education Area: Self-Help/Basic Living
Performance Area: Personal skills
Annual Goal I: Health and hygiene.

General Objective A Toilet skills (1, 2).

Short-term Instructional Objectives

1. Juanita will use a standard sign when using the restroom.
2. Juanita will indicate yes or no when shown the sign for using the restroom at frequent intervals.
3. Juanita will indicate on her own need to use restroom by using the appropriate sign with 100% accuracy at home and school.

General Objective B Washing (1).

Short-term Instructional Objectives

1. Juanita will wash hands and face by modeling teacher.
2. Juanita will stand under shower.
3. Juanita will use wash cloths and soap in shower.
4. Juanita will prepare the shower water and use soap.
5. Juanita will, in addition to the above, wash her hair.

Annual Goal II: Grooming (1, 2).

General Objective A Hair care.

Short-term Instructional Objectives

1. Juanita will brush hair using down strokes while looking in mirror and modeling teacher.
2. Juanita will brush hair into place while looking in a mirror.
3. Juanita will comb out hair when wet.

Annual Goal III: Dressing.

General Objective A Fasteners (1).
Short-term Instructional Objectives. Criteria: independent performance with immediate reinforcement.

1. Juanita will unbutton/button, snap/unsnap, zip/unzip on dressing board or doll.
2. Juanita will button and unbutton her own blouse.
3. Juanita will button or snap and zip her pants following toileting (1, 2).
4. Juanita will tuck blouse into pants and button, snap and zip pants following toileting (1, 2).
5. Juanita will button or hook and zip skirt when put on.

Special Education Area: Sociobehavioral
Performance Area: Socialization
Annual Goal I: Social interactions—adults.

General Objective A Play (1, 2, 3).
Short-term Instructional Objectives. Criteria: without prompting.

1. Juanita will participate with teachers in unstructured physical exercise such as running, taking a walk, and jumping.
2. Juanita will participate in desk-top hand games with teachers.
3. Juanita will play simple structured games on desk top with teachers.
4. Juanita will, using new standard signs, direct teacher to perform certain tasks.

Annual Goal II: Social interactions—peers (2).

General Objective A Observation.
Short-term Instructional Objectives

1. Juanita will remain in classroom with teacher and two other deaf peers.
2. Juanita will watch peers interact with classroom teacher.
   Note: Teacher will socially reinforce Juanita when looking at group and reinforce immediately with primary reinforcer offered for any physical approach to group.
3. Juanita will observe at increasingly closer proximities. Criteria—is within reach of teacher to hand reinforcers.

General Objective B Modeling (2).

Short-term Instructional Objectives

1. Juanita will spontaneously attempt to respond like a peer (reinforced immediately).
2. Juanita will model peer-teacher interaction to a task presented to her following observation of same task with another child.

General Objective C Play (2).

Short-term Instructional Objective. Criteria: spontaneous.

1. Juanita will attempt some interaction during free play with a peer.

Performance Area: Task-related behaviors
Annual Goal I: Increase attention in language and desk tasks with teacher.

General Objective A Eye contact (1, 3).

Short-term Instructional Objectives

1. Juanita will maintain eye contact with teachers during extensive language therapy (or other one-on-one work) for a total of two minutes out of every five minutes of therapy.

General Objective B Object manipulation (1, 2, 3).

1. Juanita will manipulate object from gamelike activities with teacher for a continuous period of five minutes.

Performance Area: Undesirable behaviors
Annual Goal I: Decrease tantrum behavior (1, 2, 3).

General Objective A Reduce tantrums to hitting objects alone.

Short-term Instructional Objectives

1. Juanita, when frustrated, will utilize punching bag when placed in the timeout area with teachers.
2. Juanita, when frustrated and tantruming, will stay in timeout area after being placed there.
3. Juanita will make some attempt to go to timeout area on her own. Criteria: Tantrums should be event recorded the first two weeks of school and lowered by 50%.

Services

Due to the severity of Juanita's handicapping condition exacerbated by limited experiences, Juanita's special education and related services will be delivered in both home and school settings. The following schedule of special ed related services has been selected to be initiated immediately (Monday through Friday).

Special Education Services

	9:00–11:00	Homebound teacher
		Valdez home
		To work with Juanita and grandmother on establishing and using standard signs, self-help skills, and basic behavioral management programs.
MWF	1:00– 2:30	Special education teacher
		Harrison special service building
		Juanita will be involved in free play situations with two other deaf youngsters who are attending a self-contained class for deaf youngsters, age 10–13.
TTH	1:00– 2:30	Language specialist
		Harrison special service building
		Juanita will receive intensive one-on-one auditory and speech training.

Additional Related Services

1. Provision and use of appropriately calibrated amplification device.
2. Continued assistance in obtaining welfare.
3. Training provided to Mrs. Valdez in signing and behavior management techniques.

Regular Education Services

No regular education services are appropriate at this time.

Evaluation

Because of the unusual nature of Juanita's case, the IEP team recommends complete evaluation by the end of October. The IEP team is to meet to review and discuss progress and update Juanita's IEP on November 3. Evaluations are to consist of continuous, event, duration, and interval recording (whichever is most appropriate) of behavioral criteria set forth in each preceding short-term instructional objective. These objectives are to be measured through observational recording conducted by the staff psychologist, Ms. Britton, in conjunction with specific teachers in each service situation. In addition, Mrs. Valdez is to be asked to do some simple event recording in the home. Review of the IEP in November is to consider extension of or exclusion of stated objectives as well as review of service delivery systems. Reevaluation with formal measures is to be conducted in January 1979.

Mrs. Valdez will provide the staff with input as to the success or failure of welfare attempts as well as show some proficiency in utilizing appropriate signs, techniques in language development, and behavior-management procedure.

`❊ ❊ ❊ ❊ ❊ ❊ ❊ ❊ ❊ ❊ ❊ ❊`

Members of the central IEP team of Harrison School District met on August 1 to review the educational program for Juanita. It was decided that contents of this program were the most appropriate directions to follow for the next two months at which time the meeting will be reconvened following an evaluation of progress. Each member below has signed to indicate his/her understanding of the continued goals, objectives and services and his/her responsibilities in each area. No changes wil be made in this document prior to October without reconvening the team for discussion and consent.

_____
Principal and Director of Special Services

_____
Homebound Teacher

_____
Special Education Teacher

_____
Language Therapist

_____
Psychologist

_____
Parent

Index